Guide to Graphics Software Tools

Jim X. Chen

With contributions by Chunyang Chen, Nanyang Yu, Yanlin Luo,
Yanling Liu and Zhigeng Pan

Guide to Graphics Software Tools

Second edition

 Springer

Jim X. Chen
Computer Graphics Laboratory
George Mason University
Mailstop 4A5
Fairfax, VA 22030
USA
jimxchen@gmail.com

ISBN: 978-1-84996-800-3   e-ISBN: 978-1-84800-901-1
DOI 10.1007/978-1-84800-901-1

British Library Cataloguing in Publication Data
A catalogue record for this book is available from the British Library

Library of Congress Control Number: 2008937209

Printed on acid-free paper

Springer Science+Business Media
springer.com

Preface

Many scientists in different disciplines realize the power of graphics, but are also bewildered by the complex implementations of a graphics system and numerous graphics tools. More often than not, they choose the wrong software tools and end up with unsatisfactory results. Hopefully, if we know how a graphics system works and what basic functions many graphics tools provide, we can understand and employ some graphics tools without spending much precious time on learning all the details that may not be applicable, and we can become graphics experts through such a shortcut.

Overview

This book aims to be a shortcut to graphics theory, programming, tools, and applications. It covers all graphics basics and several advanced topics without including some unnecessary implementation details in graphics applications. It categorizes current graphics tools according to their applications and provides many weblinks to important resources on the Internet. The purpose is to provide an exhaustive list of graphics tools with their major applications and functions. The reference list may contain some inaccuracies, since new tools are constantly emerging and old tools become obsolete. By explaining and categorizing these graphics tools and their primary applications, we hope to provide learners and researchers with different means and application areas in computer graphics, and help them understand and use visualization, modeling, animation, simulation, virtual reality, and many online resources.

Organization and Features

First, the book concisely introduces graphics theory and programming. It serves as a basis for better understanding the components in the later chapters of the book which categorizes popular 3D graphics tools and explains their applications and functions. We have compiled a list of 293 different 3D graphics tools.

Both graphics theory and programming are covered succinctly. A top-down approach is used to lead the audience into programming and applications up front. The theory provides a high-level understanding of all basic graphics principles without some detailed low-level implementations. The emphasis is on understanding graphics and using OpenGL or Direct3D instead of implementing a graphics system. The contents of the book are integrated with the sample programs, which are specifically designed for learning.

Chapter 1 introduces OpenGL and basic graphics concepts including object, model, image, framebuffer, scan-conversion, clipping, and anti-aliasing. Chapter 2 discusses transformation theory, viewing theory, and OpenGL programming in detail. 3D models, hidden-surface removal, and collision detection are also covered. Chapter 3 overviews color in hardware, eye characteristics, gamma correction, interpolation, OpenGL lighting, and surface shading models. The emphasis is on OpenGL lighting. Chapter 4 surveys OpenGL blending, image rendering, and texture mapping, including advanced texture image applications such as bump mapping, and light mapping.

Chapter 5 is the first of the chapters which can be used independently. It introduces OpenGL programming in Java: JOGL, and provides a basis for advanced graphics programming on the Java platform. Chapter 6 discusses existing 3D model functions in GLUT and GLU libraries. It also covers theories and programming of basic cubic curves and bi-cubic curved surfaces. Chapter 7 introduces GPUs and their parallel programming with vertex and pixel (fragment) shaders. It features Cg programming with JOGL on the Java platform. Chapter 8 introduces scene graph structure and Java3D programming basics. Chapter 9 introduces the OpenGL Shading Language (GLSL), and discusses vertex and pixel programming on the C/C++ platform in OpenGL using GLSL. Some innovative shader-based applications such as depth buffer, post-image processing, and fog are discussed here. Chapter 10 introduces basic Direct3D 10 graphics principles and shader programming with examples. Chapters 7, 9, and 10 more or less cover vertex and pixel programming, but with three different shading languages: Cg in JOGL on the Java platform, GLSL in OpenGL on the C/C++ platform, and HLSL on Microsoft's Direct3D platform. Chapter 11 wraps up basic computer graphics principles and programming with some advanced concepts and methods for advanced courses.

In Part II, 293 different graphics tools are listed in Appendix B with Chapters 12 to 18 introducing the basic concepts and categories of the tools. Low-level graphics libraries, visualization, modeling and rendering, animation and simulation, virtual reality, Web3D tools and networked environments, and finally 3D file format converters are covered in their respective chapters. For each tool listed in Appendix B, we include information on its platforms, prices, vendor or supplier, applications, and Web resources. The list of tools is a reference for scientific researchers as well as advanced computer graphics learners and programmers. The tools are indexed according to their alphabetic order in the Table of Contents and their application categories in Appendix B. Appendix A includes some basic mathematics for the 3D graphics used in this book.

The following Web address contains all the updates and additional information, including how to set up the programming environment, sample program sources, and accompanying Microsoft PowerPoint course notes for learners and instructors as well:

```
http://www.cs.gmu.edu/~jchen/graphics/
```

Audience

The book is intended for a very wide range of readers, including scientists in different disciplines, undergraduates in Computer Science, and Ph.D. students and advanced researchers who are interested in learning and using computer graphics.

Chapters 1 through 4 are suitable for a one-semester graphics course or self-learning. These chapters should be covered in order. Prerequisites for this part are good C programming skills and basic knowledge of linear algebra and trigonometry. Chapters 5 to 11 are independent introductions suitable for additional advanced graphics courses.

The end section of the book, especially the list of tools in the Appendix B, is mainly a reference or informational toolkit for computational engineers, computer programmers, and graphics researchers. No prerequisite knowledge is needed for this.

Acknowledgments

Dr. Chunyang Chen and Nanyang Yu provided support and guidance for the book. Dr. Yanlin Luo edited Appendix B on software tools. Dr. Tianshu Zhou authored Chapter 9 on OpenGL Shading Language (GLSL). Dr. Yanling Liu wrote Chapter 10 about Direct3D programming and High Level Shading Language (HLSL). Dr. Zhigeng Pan provided support. My friend Denise O'Toole helped with editing and proofreading the book. Without her support, this book would not be possible to be finished on schedule and with quality. Some of my former students in CS 451, CS 652, CS 752, and INFT 852 at George Mason University contributed to the graphics software reviews.

I acknowledge the anonymous reviewers and the whole production team at Springer Verlag. Their precious comments, editings, and help have significantly improved the quality and value of the book.

Jim Xiong Chen
With contributions by
Chunyang Chen, Nanyang Yu, Yanlin Luo, Yanling Liu, and Zhigeng Pan
August 2008

Contents

Chapter 2

Transformation and Viewing

Chapter 3

Color and Lighting

Chapter 5

OpenGL Programming in Java: JOGL

Chapter 6

Curved Models

Chapter 7

Vertex Shading, Pixel Shading, and Parallel Processing

Chapter 10

Direct3D Shader Programming

Chapter 11

Advanced Topics

Chapter 12

Low-Level Graphics Libraries

Chapter 13

Visualization

Chapter 18

3D File Formats

Appendix A

Basic Mathematics for 3D Computer Graphics 377

Appendix B

Graphics Software Tools 387

1
Objects and Models

Chapter Objectives:

- Introduce basic graphics concepts — object, model, image, graphics library, frame buffer, scan-conversion, clipping, and anti-aliasing

- Set up an OpenGL programming environment

- Understand simple OpenGL programs

1.1 Graphics Models and Libraries

A graphics *display* is a drawing area comprised of an array of fine points called pixels. At the heart of a graphics system there is a magic pen, which can move at lightning speed to a specific pixel and draw the pixel with a specific color — a red, green, and blue (RGB) vector value. This pen can be controlled directly by hand through an input device (mouse or keyboard) like a simple paintbrush. In this case, we can draw whatever we imagine, but it takes a real artist to come up with a good painting. Computer graphics, however, is about using this pen automatically through programming.

A real or imaginary *object* is represented in a computer as a model, and is displayed as an image. A *model* is an abstract description of the object's shape (vertices) and attributes (colors), which can be used to find all the points and colors on the object corresponding to the pixels in the drawing area. Given a model, the application program will control the pen through a graphics library to generate the corresponding image. An *image* is simply a 2D array of pixels.

A *graphics library* provides a set of graphics commands or functions. These commands can be bound in *C*, *C++*, *Java*, or other programming languages on different platforms. Graphics commands can specify primitive 2D and 3D geometric

J.X. Chen, *Guide to Graphics Software Tools*, doi: 10.1007/978-1-84800-901-1_1,
© Springer-Verlag London Limited 2008

models to be digitized and displayed. Here *primitive* means that only certain simple shapes (such as points, lines, and polygons) can be accepted by a graphics library. To draw a complex shape, we need an application program to dissect it into pieces of simple shapes (primitives). We have the magic pen that draws a pixel. If we can draw a pixel, we can draw a line, a polygon, a curve, a block, a building, an airplane, and so forth. A general application program can be included into a graphics library as a command to draw a complex shape. Since our pen is magically fast, we can draw a complex object, clear the drawing area, draw the object at a slightly different location, and repeat the above processes — the object is now *animated*.

OpenGL is a graphics library, which we will integrate with the *C programming language* to introduce graphics theory, programming, and applications.

1.2 OpenGL Programming

OpenGL is the most widely used graphics library (GL) or application programming interface (API), which is supported across all popular desktop and workstation platforms, ensuring wide application deployment. First, let's spend some time to set up our working environment, compile Example 1.1.point.c, and run the program. The following file contains links to all the example programs in this book, and detailed information for setting up working environments on different platforms:

```
http://www.cs.gmu.edu/~jchen/graphics/setup.html
```

/* Example 1.1.point.c: draw randomly generated points */

```
#include <stdlib.h>
#include <GL/glut.h>

#define Height 400
#define Width 400


void display(void)
{
    int x, y;

    //a. generate a random point
    x = rand() % Width;
    y = rand() % Height;
```

```
    //b. specify a drawing color: red
    glColor3f(1, 0, 0);

    //c. specify to draw a point
    glBegin(GL_POINTS);
        glVertex2i (x,y);
    glEnd();

    //d. start drawing
    glFlush();
}


static void reshape(int w, int h)
{
    //e. specify the window's coordinates
    glMatrixMode (GL_PROJECTION);
    glLoadIdentity ();
    glOrtho(0, Width, 0, Height, -1.0, 1.0);
}


int main(int argc, char **argv)
{
    //f. initialize a drawing area
    glutInit(&argc, argv);
    glutInitDisplayMode(GLUT_SINGLE);
    glutInitWindowSize(Width, Height);
    glutCreateWindow("Example 1.1.point.c");

    //g. specify event callback functions
    glutReshapeFunc(reshape);
    glutDisplayFunc(display);
    glutIdleFunc(display);
    glutMainLoop();
}
```

1.2.1 Understanding Example 1.1

Example 1.1 is complex to us at this point of time. We only need to understand the following:

1. The OpenGL Utility Toolkit (GLUT) helps set up a drawing area and handle user interactions for OpenGL. Since it is intended to be system independent, our program can be compiled and run on a PC, SGI workstation, or other platforms. All GLUT commands have the prefix "glut":

```
//f. initialize a drawing area
glutInit(&argc, argv);
glutInitDisplayMode(GLUT_SINGLE);
glutInitWindowSize(Width, Height);
glutCreateWindow("Example 1.1.point.c");
```

The above functions set up a single drawing area of *Width × Height* pixels. A corresponding window titled *Example 1.1.point.c* will appear after *glutMainLoop()* is called.

2. An *event* is often a user input (or a system state change), which is queued with other earlier events. GLUT will check out each event from the queue and take actions until the queue is empty. Our program is event-driven: GLUT waits for an event to appear in the event queue and then calls the appropriate function to handle the event. We can set up the event handling functions (namely *callback* functions) through GLUT so that when GLUT detects a specific event, it can call its corresponding callback function.

```
//g. event callback functions
glutReshapeFunc(reshape);
glutDisplayFunc(display);
glutIdleFunc(display);
glutMainLoop();
```

The above commands set up three callback functions each corresponding to a different event: Reshape, Display, and Idle. The last command puts our program into an infinite loop: checking out an event and calling its callback function. The Reshape and Display events are generated when the display area appears on the screen the first time. In other words, *reshape()* and *display()* will be called once early in the event loop, and the system passes the width (*w*) and height (*h*) of the current display area to the Reshape callback function. When the event queue is empty, GLUT will detect an Idle event, and call its corresponding callback function, which is *display()* here. Therefore, *display()* will be called many times whenever there are no other events in the event queue.

3. If we move or stretch the window display area using the mouse, a Reshape event is generated. Soon GLUT will check out this event and call its callback function *reshape()*.

```
//e. specify the window coordinates
glMatrixMode (GL_PROJECTION);
glLoadIdentity ();
glOrtho(0, Width, 0, Height, -1.0, 1.0);
```

The above lines set up the window coordinates, which are specified as $0 \leq x \leq$ *Width* from the left to the right side of the window, $0 \leq y \leq$ *Height* from the bottom to the top side of the window, and $-1 \leq z \leq 1$ in the direction perpendicular to the window. The z direction is ignored in 2D applications.

4. All OpenGL commands are prefixed with "gl".

5. *glFlush()* tells the graphics system to execute the drawing.

In summary, *main()* creates a window of drawing area, sets up callback functions, and waits for events in the *glutMainLoop()*. It calls *reshape()* and *display()* once to set up the coordinates of the window and draw a randomly generated pixel. After that, whenever the event loop is idle, it calls *display()* again. In *display()*, a random point in the window is generated and a red pixel is drawn.

1.3 Frame Buffer, Scan-conversion, and Clipping

The graphics system digitizes a specific model into a frame of discrete color points saved in a piece of memory called a *frame buffer*. This digitization process is called *scan-conversion*. Sometimes *drawing* or *rendering* is used to mean scan-conversion. However, drawing and rendering are more general terms that do not focus on the digitization process. The color points in the frame buffer will be sent to the corresponding pixels in the display device by a piece of hardware called the *video controller*. Therefore, whatever is in the frame buffer corresponds to the image on the screen. The application program accepts user input, manipulates the models (creates, stores, retrieves, and modifies the descriptions), and produces an image through the graphics system. The display is also a window for us to manipulate the model behind the image through the application program. A change on the display corresponds to a change in the model. A programmer's tasks concern mostly creating the model, changing the model, and handling user interaction. OpenGL, GLUT and C functions are the interfaces between the application program and the graphics hardware (Fig. 1.1).

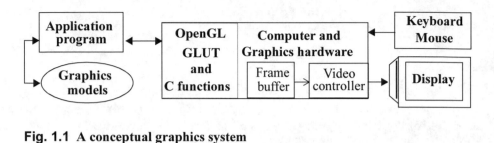

Fig. 1.1 A conceptual graphics system

Before using OpenGL primitive drawing functions directly, let's look at how these functions are implemented. Graphics libraries may be implemented quite differently, and many functions can be implemented in both software and hardware.

1.3.1 Scan-converting Lines

A line object is described as an abstract model with two end points (x_0, y_0) and (x_n, y_n). It is scan-converted into the frame buffer by a graphics library function. The line equation is $y = mx + B$, where the slope $m = (y_n-y_0)/(x_n-x_0)$ and B is a constant. Let's assume $-1 \leq m \leq 1$. For the pixels on the line, $x_{i+1} = x_i + 1$ and $y_{i+1} = mx_{i+1} + B = m(x_i + 1) + B = (mx_i + B) + m = y_i + m$. To scan-convert the line, we need only to draw all the pixels at $(x_i, \text{Round}(y_i))$ for $i=0$ to n.

/* Example 1.2.line.c: draw random generated lines */

```
void line(int x0,int y0,int xn,int yn)
{
    int x; float m, y;

  m = (float) (yn-y0)/(xn-x0);
  x=x0; y=y0;

  while (x<xn+1) {
      // write a pixel into the framebuffer
      glBegin(GL_POINTS);
          glVertex2i (x, (int) (y+0.5));
      glEnd();

      x++; y+=m;/* next pixel's position */
  }
}
```

Bresenham[1] developed a line scan-conversion algorithm using only integer operations, which can be implemented very efficiently in hardware. Let's assume pixel (x_p, y_p) is on the line and $0 \leq m \leq 1$ (Fig. 1.2). Which pixel should we choose next: E or NE? The line equation is $y = mx + B$, i.e. $F(x, y) = ax + by + c = 0$, where $a = dy = (y_n - y_0)$, $b = -dx = -(x_n - x_0) < 0$, and $c = B*dx$.

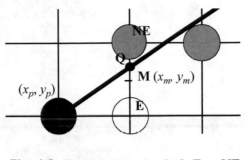

Fig. 1.2 Finding the next pixel: E or NE

Because $b < 0$, if y increases, $F(x, y)$ decreases, and vice versa. Therefore, if the midpoint $M(x_m, y_m)$ between pixels NE and E is on the line, $F(x_m, y_m) = 0$; if $M(x_m, y_m)$ is below the line, $F(x_m, y_m) > 0$; and if $M(x_m, y_m)$ is above the line, $F(x_m, y_m) < 0$.

If $F(x_m, y_m) > 0$, Q is above $M(x_m, y_m)$, we choose NE; otherwise we choose E. Therefore, $F(x_m, y_m)$ is a *decision factor: d_{old}*. From d_{old}, we can derive the decision factor d_{new} for the next pixel. We can see that $x_m = x_p + 1$ and $y_m = y_p + 1/2$. Therefore we have:

$$d_{old} = F(x_m, y_m) = F(x_p+1, y_p+1/2) = F(x_p, y_p) + a + b/2 = a + b/2. \qquad \text{(EQ 1)}$$

If $d_{old} \leq 0$, E is chosen, the next middle point is at $(x_p+2, y_p+1/2)$:

$$d_{new} = F(x_p+2, y_p+1/2) = d_{old} + a. \qquad \text{(EQ 2)}$$

If $d_{old} > 0$, NE is chosen, the next middle point is at $(x_p+2, y_p+3/2)$:

$$d_{new} = F(x_p+2, y_p+3/2) = d_{old} + a + b. \qquad \text{(EQ 3)}$$

We can see that only the initial d_{old} is not an integer. If we multiply by 2 on both sides of Equation 1, 2, and 3, all decision factors are integers. Note that if a decision factor is greater/smaller than zero, multiplying it by 2 does not change the fact that it is still

1. Bresenham, J.E., "Algorithm for Computer Control of Digital Plotter," *IBM Systems Journal*, 4 (1), 1965, 25–30.

greater/smaller than zero. So the decision remains the same. Let $dE = 2dy$, $dNE = 2(dy - dx)$, and $d_{old} = 2dy - dx$:

$$\text{If } E \text{ is chosen, } d_{new} = d_{old} + dE; \qquad \textbf{(EQ 4)}$$

$$\text{If } NE \text{ is chosen, } d_{new} = d_{old} + dNE. \qquad \textbf{(EQ 5)}$$

Therefore, in the line scan-conversion algorithm, the arithmetic needed to evaluate d_{new} for any step is a simple integer addition.

```
//Bresenham's Middle point Line algorithm (for 0≤m≤1)

void line(int x0, int y0, int xn, int yn)
{
    int dx, dy, incrE, incrNE, d, x, y;

    dy=yn-y0; dx=xn-x0; x=x0; y=y0;
    d=2*dy-dx; incrE=2*dy; incrNE=2*(dy-dx);

    while (x<xn+1) {
        writepixel(x,y); /* write framebuffer */
        x++; /* consider next pixel */
        if (d<=0) d+=incrE;
        else { y++; d+=incrNE; };
    }
}
```

We need to consider the cases in which the line's slope is in an arbitrary orientation. Fortunately, an arbitrary line can be mapped into the case above through a mirror around x axis, y axis, or the diagonal line ($m=1$). The following is an implementation of Bresenham's algorithm that handles all these cases. In this program, we can reshape the display window (i.e., the viewport) by dragging the window's corner. Function *main()* is omitted because it is the same as the one in Example 1.1. In the rest of this book, most of the examples are only segments. The complete source code can be downloaded online or from the provided CD.

/* Example 1.3.line.c: draw random lines (Bresenham's Alg.)*/

```
#include <stdlib.h>
#include <math.h>
```

```
#include <GL/glut.h>
int Height=400, Width=400;


void swapd(int *a, int *b)
{// swap the numbers
   int tmp;

   tmp=*a; *a=*b; *b=tmp;
}


void writepixel(int x, int y, int flag)
{ // write the pixel into the framebuffer

   glBegin(GL_POINTS); // flag for different slope cases
      if (flag==0) glVertex2i (x,y);
      else if (flag==1) glVertex2i (y,x);
      else if (flag==10) glVertex2i (x,-y);
      else if (flag==11) glVertex2i (y,-x);
   glEnd();
}


void line(int x0,int y0,int xn,int yn)
{ // Bresenham's midpoint line algorithm
   int dx, dy, incrE, incrNE, d, x, y, flag = 0;

   if (xn<x0) { swapd(&x0,&xn); swapd(&y0,&yn); }
   if (yn<y0) { y0 = -y0; yn = -yn; flag=10; }

   dy=yn-y0; dx=xn-x0;

   if (dx<dy) {
      swapd(&x0,&y0);swapd(&xn,&yn); swapd(&dy,&dx);
      flag++;
   }

   x=x0; y=y0; d=2*dy-dx;
   incrE=2*dy; incrNE=2*(dy-dx);

   while (x<xn+1) {
      writepixel(x,y,flag);

      x++; // next pixel
      if (d<=0) d+=incrE;
      else { y++; d+=incrNE; };
   }
}
```

```
void display(void)
{ // generate a random line
    int x0, y0, xn, yn;

    x0 = (rand() % Width) - Width/2;
    y0 = (rand() % Height) - Height/2;
    xn = (rand() % Width) - Width/2;
    yn = (rand() % Height) - Height/2;

    glColor3f(1, 1, 1); // white color

    // draw the generated line
    line(x0, y0, xn, yn);

    glFlush();
}


static void Reshape(int w, int h)
{
    // clear the framebuffer to black color (background color)
    glClearColor (0.0, 0.0, 0.0, 1.0);
    glClear(GL_COLOR_BUFFER_BIT);

    //Reshape() receives adjusted window size (w, h) from GLUT
    Width = w; Height = h;

    //adjust the size of the drawing area
    glViewport (0, 0, w, h);

    glMatrixMode (GL_PROJECTION);
    glLoadIdentity ();

    //adjust the coordinates accordingly
    glOrtho(-w/2, w/2, -h/2, h/2, -1.0, 1.0);
}
```

Of course, OpenGL has a line scan-conversion function. To draw a line, we can simply call

```
glBegin(GL_LINES);

    glVertex2i(x0,y0);
    glVertex2i(xn,yn);

glEnd();
```

1.3.2 Scan-converting Circles and Other Curves

Although the above example (Example 1.3) is really a simulation, because the program does not directly manipulate the frame buffer, it does help us understand the scan-conversion process. Given a line equation, we can scan-convert the line by calculating and drawing all the pixels corresponding to the equation in the frame buffer. Similarly, given a circle equation, we can calculate and draw all the pixels of the circle into the frame buffer. This applies to all different types of curves. To speed up the scan-conversion process, we often use short lines to approximate short curve segments. Therefore, a curve can be approximated by a sequence of short lines. As line scan-conversion, there are many different ways of scan-conversion for curves and other primitives.

As an example, a simple 2D circle equation with radius (r) and centered at (cx, cy) can be expressed in parametric function as:

$$x = r*cos(\theta)+cx;$$ **(EQ 6)**

$$y = r*sin(\theta)+cy;$$ **(EQ 7)**

For θ changes from 0 to 2π, we can draw line segments to approximate a circle. If we draw a complete circle with pixels only, which will be accurate but slower, we need to find how many pixels we need to draw. Given a radius (r) in device coordinates, the perimeter is $2\pi r$ in pixels. Therefore, we need a delta angle of $1/r$ to calculate new pixel locations:

```
theta = theta + 1/r;
```

1.3.3 Scan-converting Triangles and Polygons

A wireframe object is an object composed of only lines and curves without filled surfaces. Because a wireframe polygon is composed of line segments, we extend to discuss scan-converting filled triangles and polygons. Given three vertices corresponding to a triangle, we have three lines (edges). Because we can find all the pixels on the lines, we can scan-convert the triangle by drawing all pixels between the pixel pairs on different edges that have the same y coordinates. In other words, we can find the intersections of each horizontal line (called a scan-line) on the edges of the triangle and fill the pixels between the intersections that lie in the interior of the triangle.

The following is an implementation example of scan-converting a triangle. For scan-line y_i, the next scan-line will be $y_{i+1} = y_i + 1$. That is, the next horizontal scan-line will increase by one pixel from previous scan-line. We can derive how to calculate the corresponding x on an edge of the triangle. According to a line equation $y = mx + b$ where m is the slope of the line and b is a constant, we have:

$$y_i = mx_i + b \qquad\qquad \text{(EQ 8)}$$

$$y_{i+1} = mx_{i+1} + b \qquad\qquad \text{(EQ 9)}$$

We know that

$$y_{i+1} = y_i + 1 \qquad\qquad \text{(EQ 10)}$$

Putting Equation 8 and Equation 9 into Equation 10, we can arrive at:

$$x_{i+1} = x_i + 1/m \qquad\qquad \text{(EQ 11)}$$

That is, we can iteratively find end points of the horizontal scan-lines on the edges of the triangle along y to fill the triangle.

If we can scan-convert a triangle, we can scan-convert a polygon because a polygon can be divided into triangles. Also, we can develop a general polygon scan-conversion algorithm extending the triangle algorithm as follows. For each y from the bottom to the top of the display window, we can find all the points on the polygon edges that have the same y coordinates. Then we order the edge points from left to right according to their current x coordinates. If we draw a horizontal scan-line, the first (third, fifth, etc.) edge point is where we enter the polygon, the second (fourth, sixth, etc.) edge point is where we leave the polygon, and so on. We can scan-convert the polygon by drawing all pixels between the odd-even point pairs on different edges that have the same y coordinates. In other words, we can find the intersections of each scan-line with the edges of the polygon and fill the pixels between the intersections that lie in the interior of the polygon.

The following is an algorithm example for general polygon scan-conversion. Given a list of vertices, we can build a data structure called an Edge Table as shown in Fig. 1.3. An Edge Table has entries corresponding to each possible horizontal scan-line, but only some entries are stored with edge items. For a pair of vertices (x, ymin) and (x', ymax), where ymin<ymax, the corresponding edge item is saved in the Edge Table as follows:

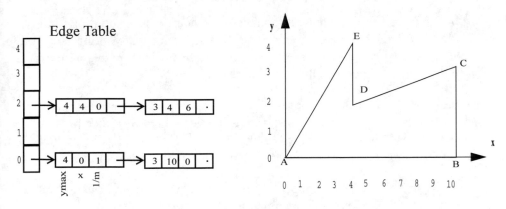

Fig. 1.3 General polygon scan-conversion algorithm: Edge Table

1. ymin is the index to the edge item structure in the edge table. In other words, if we search the Edge Table by going from $y=0$ and $y = y+1$ until the end, the current item we encounter in the Edge Table is always the lower end starting point of an edge in the polygon. Multiple edges with the same ymin are linked together in the same index slot.

2. For each edge item in the data structure, the first slot is ymax, which is checked to decide the end of the edge or the end of scan-converting the edge if our current scan-line is ymax.

3. The next two slots are the x coordinate of vertex (x, ymin) and the inverse of the edge's slope. The information is used to find the next point on the edge for the next scan-line (Equation 11 on page 12).

After constructing the Edge Table, we can start scan-conversion by going through each scan-line from $y=0$ until the end of Edge Table:

1. For the current y, if there are items in the Edge Table, move them into a linked list called Active Edge Table. Sort the Active Edge Table on slot x, and fill in the spans between pairs of x coordinates at the current y.

2. $y = y+1$. Remove those items in the Active Edge Table that ymax $= y$, and update x by $x = x + 1/m$. As we know, *1/m* is just next to x in the edge item.

3. Repeat Step 1 and 2 until there is no item in the Edge Table and Active Edge Table.

Fig. 1.4 is an example of polygon scan-conversion process steps according to Fig. 1.3. You may have noticed that when y=ymax and there is no entry at y in the Edge Table, we reach the end of the primitive. we need to draw an extra pixel or line before removing the pair of edges from the Active Edge Table.

The general concept of polygon scan-conversion is important because many other functions are related to its operations. For example, when we talk about hidden-surface removal or lighting later in the book, we need to calculate each pixel's depth or color information during scan-converting a pixel into the frame buffer.

A graphics library provides basic primitive functions. For example, OpenGL draws a convex polygon with the following commands:

```
gl.glBegin(GL.GL_POLYGON);
    // a list of vertices
    ...
gl.glEnd();
```

A *convex* polygon means that all the angles inside the polygon formed by the edges are smaller than 180 degrees. If a polygon is not convex, it is *concave*. Convex polygons can be scan-converted faster than concave polygons.

In summary, different scan-conversion algorithms for a graphics primitive (line, polygon, etc.) have their own merits. If a primitive scan-conversion function is not provided in a graphics library, we know now that we can create one or implement an existing one.

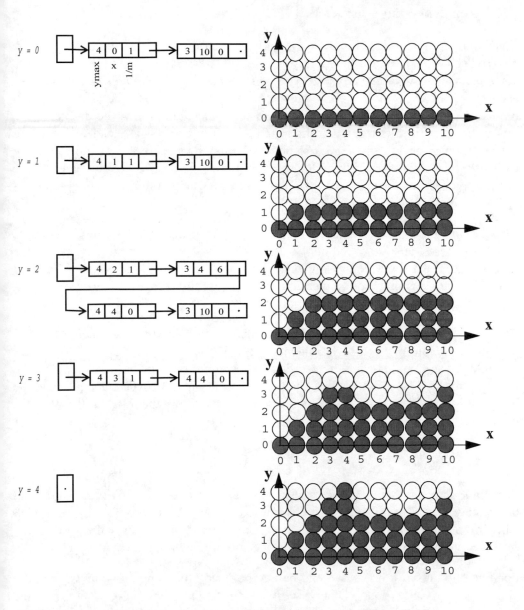

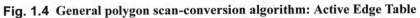

Fig. 1.4 General polygon scan-conversion algorithm: Active Edge Table

1.3.4 Scan-converting Characters

Characters are polygons. However, they are used so often that we prefer saving the polygon shapes in a library called the *font library*. The polygons in the font library are not represented by vertices. Instead, they are represented by *bitmap font* images — each character is saved in a rectangular binary array of pixels. The shape of small bitmaps do not scale well. Therefore, more than one bitmap must be defined for a given character for different sizes and type faces. Bitmap fonts are loaded into a font cache (fast memory) to allow quick retrieval. Displaying a character is simply copying its image from the font cache into the frame buffer at the desired position. During the copying process, colors may be used to draw into the frame buffer replacing the 1s and 0s in the bitmap font images.

Another method of describing character shapes is using straight lines and curve sections. These fonts are called *outline font*s. Outline fonts require less storage since each variation does not require a distinct font cache. However, the scaled shapes for different font sizes may not be pleasing to our eyes, and it takes more time to scan-convert the characters into the frame buffer.

Although the idea is simple, accessing fonts is often platform-dependent. GLUT provides a simple platform-independent subset of font functions. If you need more flexibility, you may look into a specific platform/environment in the future. On the Unix platform, GLX provides font functions and interfaces between OpenGL and the X window system. WGL is the equivalent of GLX on the Microsoft Windows platform.

1.3.5 Clipping

When a graphics system scan-converts a model, the model may be much larger than the display area. The display is a window used to look at a portion of a large model. Clipping algorithms are necessary to clip the model and display only the portion that fits the window. For a point, it is simple to decide if it is within a rectangular area.

For line clipping, if a line's two end points are inside the clipping window, then the clipping is trivially done. Otherwise, we can cut the line into sections at the boundaries of the clipping window, and keep only the section that lies inside the window.

For polygon clipping, we can walk around the vertices of the polygon. If a polygon's edge lies inside the clipping window, the vertices are accepted for the new polygon. Otherwise, we can throw out all vertices outside a window boundary, cut the two edges that go out of and into a window boundary, and generate two new vertices along a window boundary between the two edges to replace the vertices that are outside a window boundary. The clipped polygon has all vertices in the window after the four boundaries are processed.

In OpenGL, we only need clipping against primitives (points, lines, and polygons), because all other objects are really reduced into the primitives before scan-conversion. There are clipping algorithms for the primitives against other shapes than a window area. In addition to primitive 2D rectangular clipping, clipping algorithms have also been developed to cut models in 3D volumes.

1.4 Attributes and Antialiasing

In general, any parameter that affects the way a primitive is to be displayed is referred to as an attribute parameter. For example, a line's attributes include color, intensity (or brightness), type (solid, dashed, dotted), width, cap (shape of the end points: butt, round, etc.), join (miter, round, etc.), and so forth.

The display and the corresponding frame buffer are discrete. Therefore, a line, curve, or an edge of a polygon is often like a zigzag staircase. This is called *aliasing*. We can display the pixels at different intensities to relieve the aliasing problem. Methods to relieve aliasing are called *antialiasing* methods, and we introduce several below. In order to simplify the discussion, we only consider line antialiasing.

1.4.1 Area Sampling

A displayed line has a width. Here we simply consider a line as a rectangular area overlapping with the pixels (Fig. 1.5(a)). We may display the pixels with different intensities or colors to achieve the effect of antialiasing. For example, if we display those pixels that are partially inside the rectangular line area with colors between the line color and the background color, the line looks less jaggy. Fig. 1.5(b) shows parallel lines that are drawn with or without antialiasing. Area sampling determines a pixel intensity by calculating the overlap area of the pixel with the line.

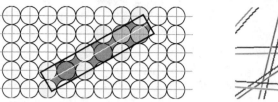
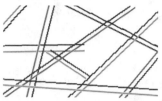

a) A line is a rectangular area   *b) Parallel lines with or without antialiasing*

Fig. 1.5 Antialiasing: area sampling

Unweighted area sampling determines the pixel intensity by the overlap area only. For unweighted area sampling, if a pixel is not completely inside or outside the line, it is cut into two or more areas by the boundaries of the rectangular line area. The portion inside the line determines the pixel intensity.

Weighted area sampling allows equal areas within a pixel to contribute unequally: an area closer to the pixel's center has greater influence on the pixel's intensity than an equal area further away from the pixel's center. For weighted area sampling, we assume each pixel is occupied by a 3D solid cone (called a *cone filter*) or a bun-shaped volume (*Gaussian filter*) with the flat bottom sitting on the pixel. The bottom of the cone may even be bigger than the pixel itself. The boundaries of the rectangular line area cut through the cone in the direction perpendicular to the display, and the portion (volume) of the cone inside the line area determines the corresponding pixel's intensity. The center area in the pixel is thicker (higher) than the boundary area of the pixel, and thus has more influence on the pixel's intensity. Also, you can see that if the bottom of the cone is bigger than the pixel, the pixel's intensity is affected even though the line only passes by without touching the pixel.

1.4.2 Antialiasing a Line with Weighted Area Sampling

For weighted area sampling, calculating a pixel's intensity according to the cone filter or Gaussian filter takes time. Instead, we can build up an intensity table, and use the distance from the center of the pixel to the center of the line as an index to find the intensity for the pixel directly from the table. The intensities in the table are precalculated according to the filter we use and the width of the line. The following is an implementation of scan-converting an antialiased line.

If we assume the distance from the current pixel to the line is D, then the distances from the E, S, N, and NE pixels can be calculated, respectively. The distances are shown in Fig. 1.6. (The distances from the pixels above the line are negatively labeled, which are useful for polygon edge antialiasing.) We can modify Bresenham's algorithm to scan-convert an antialiased line. The distances from the pixels closest to the line are calculated iteratively.

Given a point (x, y), the function *IntensifyPixel(x, y, D)* will look up the intensity level of the point according to the index D and draw the pixel (x, y) at its intensity into the frame buffer. In our example, instead of building up a filter table, we use a simple equation to calculate the intensity. Here we implement a three-pixel wide antialiased line algorithm as an example.

In Bresenham's algorithm, the distance from the center of the pixel to the center of the line is $|D| \leq 0.5$. Therefore, the distance from N (the pixel above the current pixel) is $|D - \cos\alpha| \leq 1.5$, and the distance from S is $|D + \cos\alpha| \leq 1.5$. Given the current pixel's color *(r, g, b)*, we can modify the intensity by: *(r, g, b)*(1-D/1.5)*. When a pixel is exactly on the line *(D=0)*, the pixel's intensity is not changed. When a pixel is far away from the center of the line *(D=1.5)*, the pixel's intensity is modified to *(0, 0, 0)*. Therefore, the pixels have different intensity levels depending on their distances from the center of the line. The following example (Example 1.4) is simplified without considering all different slopes, which we discussed in Example 1.3.

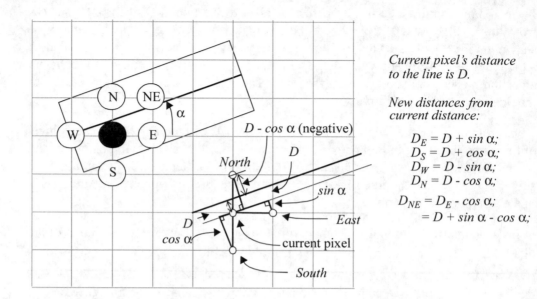

Current pixel's distance to the line is D.

New distances from current distance:

$$D_E = D + sin\ \alpha;$$
$$D_S = D + cos\ \alpha;$$
$$D_W = D - sin\ \alpha;$$
$$D_N = D - cos\ \alpha;$$
$$D_{NE} = D_E - cos\ \alpha;$$
$$= D + sin\ \alpha - cos\ \alpha;$$

Fig. 1.6 **Iteratively calculating the distances from the pixels to the line**

/* Example 1.4.line.c: scan-convert 3 pixel wide lines with antialiasing */

```
void IntensifyPixel(int x,int y, double D)
{
    float d, r1, g1, b1;

    if (D<0) d = -D;
    else d = D;

    r1=r*(1-d/1.5); g1=g*(1-d/1.5); b1=b*(1-d/1.5);
    glColor3f(r1, g1, b1);
    writepixel(x,y);
}
void antialiasedLine(int x0,int y0,int xn,int yn)
{
    int dx, dy, incrE, incrNE, d, x, y;
    float D=0, sin_a, cos_a, smc_a, Denom;

    dy=yn-y0; dx=xn-x0; x=x0; y=y0; d=2*dy-dx;
    incrE=2*dy; incrNE=2*(dy-dx);

    Denom = sqrt(dx*dx + dy*dy);
```

```
sin_a = dy / Denom; cos_a = dx / Denom;
smc_a = sin_a - cos_a;

while (x<xn+1) {
    IntensifyPixel(x,y,D); // current pixel
    IntensifyPixel(x,y+1,D-cos_a); // North
    IntensifyPixel(x,y-1,D+cos_a); // South

    x++;
    if (d<=0) { D+=sin_a; d+=incrE; }
    else { D+=smc_a; y++; d+=incrNE; };
    }
} /* AntiAliased Midpoint Algorithm */
```

1.5 Double-buffering for Animation

A motion picture effect can be achieved by projecting images at 24 frames per second on a screen. Animation on a computer can be achieved by drawing or refreshing frames of different images. Here, the display *refresh rate* is the speed of reading from the frame buffer and sending the pixels to the display by the video controller. A refresh rate at 60 (frames per second) is smoother than one at 30, and 120 is marginally better than 60. Refresh rates faster than 120 frames per second are not necessary, since the human eye cannot tell the difference. Let's assume that the refresh rate is 60 frames per second. We can then build an animation program as follows:

```
open_window_with_single_buffer_mode();

for (i = 0; i < 100; i++) {
    clear_buffer();
    draw_frame(i);
    wait_until_1/60_of_a_second_is_over();
}
```

Items drawn first are visible for the full 1/60 second; items drawn toward the end are instantly cleared as the program starts on the next frame. This causes the display to present a blurred or jittered animation.

To solve this problem, we can have two frame buffers instead of one, which is known as double-buffering. One frame buffer named the *front buffer* is being displayed while the other, named the *back buffer,* is being drawn for scan-converting models. When the drawing of a frame is complete, the two buffers are swapped. That is, the back buffer becomes the front buffer for display, and the front buffer becomes the back buffer for scan-conversion. The animation program looks as follows:

```
open_window_with_double_buffer_mode();

for (i = 0; i < 100; i++) {
    clear_back_buffer();
    draw_frame_into_back_buffer(i);
    wait_until_1/60_of_a_second_is_over();
    swap_buffers();
}
```

What often happens is that a frame is too complicated to draw in 1/60 second. If this happens, each frame in the front buffer is displayed more than once and the display refresh rate is still 1/60. However, the image frame rate is much lower, and the animation could be jittering. The image frame rate depends on how fast frames of images are scan-converted, which corresponds to the rate of swapping the buffers. To achieve smooth animation, we need high performance algorithms as well as graphics hardware to carry out many graphics functions efficiently.

Example 1.5 demonstrates animation: drawing a circle with a radius that is changing every frame. It also helps us review vector operations. The circle is approximated by a set of triangles, as shown in Fig. 1.7. At the beginning, *v1, v2, v3, v4,* and the center of the coordinate *v0* are provided. When the variable *depth=0,* we draw four triangles, and the circle is approximated by a square. When

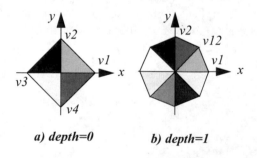

a) depth=0   *b) depth=1*

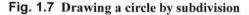

Fig. 1.7 Drawing a circle by subdivision

depth=1, each triangle is subdivided into two and we draw eight triangles. Given *v1* and *v2,* how do we find *v12*? Let's consider *v1, v2,* and *v12* as vectors. Then, *v12* is in the direction of $(v1 + v2) = (v1_x + v2_x, v1_y + v2_y, v1_z + v2_z)$ and the lengths of the vectors are equal: $|v1| = |v2| = |v12|$. If the radius of the circle is one, then *v12 = normalize(v1 + v2).* Normalizing a vector is equivalent to scaling the vector to a unit vector. In general, *v12* = *circleRadius**normalize(*v1* + *v2*), and for every frame the program changes the value of *circleRadius* to achieve animation. We can find all other unknown vertices in Fig. 1.7(b) similarly through vector additions and normalizations. This subdivision process goes on depending on the value of the *depth*. Given a triangle with two vertices and the coordinate center, *subdivideCircle()* recursively subdivides the triangle *depth* times and draws 2^{depth} triangles.

/* **Example 1.5.circle.c: animation and cycle by subdivision** */

```
#include <stdio.h>
#include <stdlib.h>
#include <math.h>
#include <GL/glut.h>

int Height=400, Width=400;
int depth=0, circleRadius=2, cnt=1;


static float vdata[4][3] = {
// four vertices on the circle

   {1.0, 0.0, 0.0}, {0.0, 1.0, 0.0},
   {-1.0, 0.0, 0.0}, {0.0, -1.0, 0.0}
};


void normalize(float v[3]) {
// normalize vector v, so |v|=1

   float d = sqrt(v[0]*v[0]+v[1]*v[1]+v[2]*v[2]);

   if (d == 0) {
      printf("zero length vector");
      return;
   }

   v[0] /= d;
   v[1] /= d;
   v[2] /= d;
}
void drawtriangle(float *v1, float *v2, float *v3)
{
   glBegin(GL_TRIANGLES);
      glVertex3fv(v1);
      glVertex3fv(v2);
      glVertex3fv(v3);
```

```
      glEnd();
}


void subdivideCircle(int radius,
               float *v1, float *v2, int depth)
{// subdivide the circle according to the depth

    float v11[3], v22[3], v00[3] = {0, 0, 0}, v12[3];
    int i;

    if (depth == 0) {

        // the triangle color depends on its vertices:
        // different triangles have different colors
        glColor3f(v1[0]*v1[0], v1[1]*v1[1], v1[2]*v1[2]);

        for (i=0; i<3; i++) {
            v11[i] = v1[i]*radius;
            v22[i] = v2[i]*radius;
        }

        drawtriangle(v11, v22, v00);
        return;
    }

    v12[0] = v1[0]+v2[0];
    v12[1] = v1[1]+v2[1];
    v12[2] = v1[2]+v2[2];

    normalize(v12);
    subdivideCircle(radius, v1, v12, depth - 1);
    subdivideCircle(radius, v12, v2, depth - 1);
}


void drawcircle(int circleRadius)
{
    subdivideCircle(circleRadius, vdata[0], vdata[1], depth);
    subdivideCircle(circleRadius, vdata[1], vdata[2], depth);
    subdivideCircle(circleRadius, vdata[2], vdata[3], depth);
    subdivideCircle(circleRadius, vdata[3], vdata[0], depth);
}
void display(void)
{
    if (circleRadius>Width/2 || circleRadius<2) {
        cnt=-cnt; depth++;
        depth = depth % 5;
    }
```

```
    // the radius of the circle changes every frame
    circleRadius+=cnt;

    glClear(GL_COLOR_BUFFER_BIT);
    drawcircle(circleRadius);

    // for double-buffering:swap back and front buffers;
    // It replaces glFlush() to tell the system start drawing.
    glutSwapBuffers();
}


static void Reshape(int w, int h)
{
    glClearColor (0.0, 0.0, 0.0, 1.0);
    glClear(GL_COLOR_BUFFER_BIT);

    Width = w; Height = h;
    glViewport (0, 0, Width, Height);

    glMatrixMode (GL_PROJECTION);
    glLoadIdentity ();
    glOrtho(-Width/2, Width/2, -Height/2, Height/2, -1.0, 1.0);
}


int main(int argc, char **argv)
{
    glutInit(&argc, argv);

    // here we specify double-buffering for the display window
    glutInitDisplayMode(GLUT_DOUBLE);

    glutInitWindowSize(Width, Height);
    glutCreateWindow("Example 1.5. circle.c");

    glutReshapeFunc(Reshape);
    glutDisplayFunc(display);
    glutIdleFunc(display);

    glutMainLoop();
}
```

1.6 Review Questions

1. $A(a_1,a_2,a_3)$ **and** $B(b_1,b_2,b_3)$ **are two vectors; please calculate the following:**

    a. $|A|$ b. $A - B$ c. $A \bullet B$ d. $A \times B$ e. θ between A and B

2. Please fill in the blanks between the two sides to connect the closest relations:

a. frame buffer	(_)	1. animation
b. double-buffering	(_)	2. pixmap for display
c. event	(_)	3. user input
d. graphics library	(_)	4. distance between pixels
e. scan-conversion	(_)	5. description of an object
f. resolution	(_)	6. basic graphics functions
g. 3D model	(_)	7. drawing

3. Which of the following is a graphics model?

    a. a picture on the paper   b. a pixmap in the frame buffer
    c. a data structure in the memory   d. an image on the display

4. What's the difference between bitmap fonts and outline fonts?

    a. Outline fonts are represented as 3D models   b. They have different sizes
    c. Bitmap fonts are represented as 3D models   d. They have different colors

5. The Cohen-Sutherland line-clipping algorithm works as follows: (a) At a clipping edge, if both end points are on the clipping window side, they are accepted. If both end points are not, they are rejected; (b) if not accepted or rejected, the line is divided into two segments at the clipping edge; (c) repeat (a) and (b) for the segment that is not rejected on the other three clipping edges. For an arbitrary line, what is the maximum number of comparisons and intersection calculations?

    Comparisons_____; Intersections _____.

6. The Sutherland-Hodgman's polygon-clipping algorithm works as follows: we walk around the polygon boundary to generated a new clipped polygon represented by a list of vertices. For each boundary edge, (a) At a clipping edge, if both end points are on the clipping window side, they are accepted. If both end points are not, they are rejected. If accepted, the vertices are in the new polygon. If rejected, they are discarded; (b) if non-trivial, the intersection on the clipping edge is a generated vertex in the new polygon replacing the vertex outside; (c) repeat (a) and (b) until all of the polygon's edges are considered; (d) repeat (a), (b), and (c) for the other three clipping edges to have a final clipped polygon. For a triangle, what is the maximum number of comparisons and intersection calculations?

    Comparisons_____; Intersections _____.

7. *Supersampling* is to achieve antialiasing by

    a. increasing sampling rate   b. decreasing the sampling rate
    c. using OpenGL antialiasing function   d. calculating the areas of overlap

8. In the antialiased line algorithm, D is the distance from the center of the current pixel to the center of the line. Given D, please calculate the distances from NE and X pixels (D_X and D_{NE}).

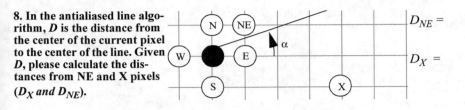

$D_{NE} =$

$D_X =$

9. In the antialiased line algorithm, d is the decision factor for choosing East or Northeast, and D is the distance from the center of the current pixel to the center of the line. Given the line starting $(0,0)$ as in the figure, please calculate d and D for the dark pixel.

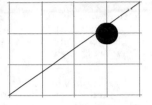

$d =$ _____ $D =$ _____

10. In drawing a filled circle in the book, we start with 4 triangles. Please calculate if we subdivide n times, how many triangles we will have in the final circle.

1.7 Programming Assignments

1. Draw a point that moves slowly along a circle. You may want to draw a circle first, and a point that moves on the circle with a different color.

2. Draw a point that bounces slowly in a square or circle.

3. Draw a star in a circle that rotates, as shown on the right. You can only use glBegin(GL_POINTS) to draw the star.

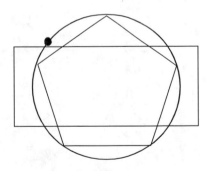

4. Write down "Bitmap" using Glut bitmap font function and "Stroke" using Glut stroke font function in the center of the display.

5. With the star rotating in the circle, implement the clipping of a window as shown on the right.

6. Implement an antialiasing line algorithm that works with the background that has a texture. The method is to blend the background color with the foreground color. You can get the current pixel color in the frame buffer using glGet() with GL_CURRENT_RASTER_COLOR.

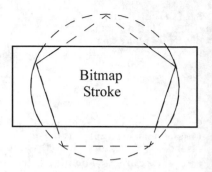

7. Implement a triangle filling algorithm for J1_3_Triangle class that draws a randomly generated triangle. Here you can only use glBegin(GL_POINTS) to draw the triangle.

8. Draw (and animate) the star with antialiasing and clipping. Add a filled circle inside the star using the subdivision method discussed in this chapter. You should use your own triangle filling algorithm. Also, clipping can be trickily done by checking the point to be drawn against the clipping window.

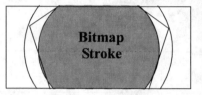

2
Transformation and Viewing

Chapter objectives:

- Understand basic transformation and viewing methods

- Understand 3D hidden-surface removal and collision detection

- Design and implement 3D models (cone, cylinder, and sphere) and their animations in OpenGL

2.1 Geometric Transformation

In Chapter 1, we discussed creating and scan-converting primitive models. After a computer-based model is generated, it can be moved around or even transformed into a completely different shape. To do this, we need to specify the rotation axis and angle, translation vector, scaling vector, or other manipulations to the model. The ordinary *geometric transformation* is a process of mathematical manipulations of all the vertices of the model through matrix multiplications, where the graphics system then displays the final transformed model. The transformation can be predefined, such as moving along a planned trajectory; or interactive, depending on the user input. The transformation can be permanent — the coordinates of the vertices are changed and we have a new model replacing the original one; or just temporary — the vertices return to their original coordinates. In many cases a model is transformed in order to be displayed at a different position or orientation, and the graphics system discards the transformed model after scan-conversion. Sometimes all the vertices of a model go through the same transformation and the shape of the model is preserved; sometimes different vertices go through different transformations, and the shape is dynamic.

A model can be displayed repetitively with each frame going through a small transformation step. This causes the model to be animated on display.

J.X. Chen, *Guide to Graphics Software Tools*, doi: 10.1007/978-1-84800-901-1_2,
© Springer-Verlag London Limited 2008

2.2 2D Transformation

Translation, *rotation*, and *scaling* are the basic and essential transformations. They can be combined to achieve most transformations in many applications. To simplify the discussion, we will first introduce 2D transformation, and then generalize it into 3D.

2.2.1 2D Translation

A point (x, y) is translated to (x', y') by a distance vector (d_x, d_y):

$$x' = x + d_x,$$

(EQ 12)

$$y' = y + d_y.$$

(EQ 13)

In the homogeneous coordinates, we represent a point (x, y) by a column vector $P = \begin{bmatrix} x \\ y \\ 1 \end{bmatrix}$. Similarly, $P' = \begin{bmatrix} x' \\ y' \\ 1 \end{bmatrix}$. Then, translation can be achieved by matrix multiplication:

$$\begin{bmatrix} x' \\ y' \\ 1 \end{bmatrix} = \begin{bmatrix} 1 & 0 & d_x \\ 0 & 1 & d_y \\ 0 & 0 & 1 \end{bmatrix} \begin{bmatrix} x \\ y \\ 1 \end{bmatrix}.$$

(EQ 14)

Let's assume $T(d_x, d_y) = \begin{bmatrix} 1 & 0 & d_x \\ 0 & 1 & d_y \\ 0 & 0 & 1 \end{bmatrix}$. We can denote the translation matrix equation as:

$$P' = T(d_x, d_y)P.$$

(EQ 15)

If a model is a set of vertices, all vertices of the model can be translated as points by the same translation vector (Fig. 2.1). Note that translation moves a model through a distance without changing its orientation.

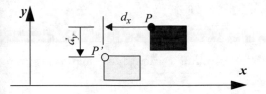

Fig. 2.1 Basic transformation: translation

2.2.2 2D Rotation

A point $P(x, y)$ is rotated counter-clockwise to $P'(x', y')$ by an angle θ around the origin $(0,0)$. If the rotation is clockwise, the rotation angle θ is then negative. The rotation axis is perpendicular to the 2D plane at the origin:

$$x' = x\cos\theta - y\sin\theta, \qquad \text{(EQ 16)}$$

$$y' = x\sin\theta + y\cos\theta. \qquad \text{(EQ 17)}$$

In the homogeneous coordinates, rotation can be achieved by matrix multiplication:

$$\begin{bmatrix} x' \\ y' \\ 1 \end{bmatrix} = \begin{bmatrix} \cos\theta & -\sin\theta & 0 \\ \sin\theta & \cos\theta & 0 \\ 0 & 0 & 1 \end{bmatrix} \begin{bmatrix} x \\ y \\ 1 \end{bmatrix}. \qquad \text{(EQ 18)}$$

Let's assume $R(\theta) = \begin{bmatrix} \cos\theta & -\sin\theta & 0 \\ \sin\theta & \cos\theta & 0 \\ 0 & 0 & 1 \end{bmatrix}$. The simplified rotation matrix equation is:

$$P' = R(\theta)P. \qquad \text{(EQ 19)}$$

If a model is a set of vertices, all vertices of the model can be rotated as points by the same angle around the same rotation axis (Fig. 2.2). Rotation moves a model around the origin of the coordinates. The distance of each vertex to the origin is not changed during rotation.

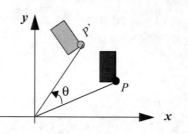

Fig. 2.2 Basic transformation: rotatio

2.2.3 2D Scaling

A point $P(x, y)$ is scaled to $P'(x', y')$ by a scaling vector (s_x, s_y) :

$$x' = s_x x,$$ (EQ 20)

$$y' = s_y y.$$ (EQ 21)

In the homogeneous coordinates, again, scaling can be achieved by matrix multiplication:

$$\begin{bmatrix} x' \\ y' \\ 1 \end{bmatrix} = \begin{bmatrix} s_x & 0 & 0 \\ 0 & s_y & 0 \\ 0 & 0 & 1 \end{bmatrix} \begin{bmatrix} x \\ y \\ 1 \end{bmatrix}.$$ (EQ 22)

Let's assume $S(s_x, s_y) = \begin{bmatrix} s_x & 0 & 0 \\ 0 & s_y & 0 \\ 0 & 0 & 1 \end{bmatrix}$. We can denote the scaling matrix equation as:

$$P' = S(s_x, s_y)P.$$ (EQ 23)

If a model is a set of vertices, all vertices of the model can be scaled as points by the same scaling vector (Fig. 2.3). Scaling amplifies or shrinks a model around the origin of the coordinates. Note that a scaled vertex will move unless it is at the origin.

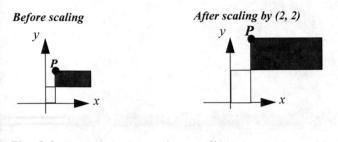

Before scaling   *After scaling by (2, 2)*

Fig. 2.3 Basic transformation: scaling

2.2.4 Composition of 2D Transformations

A complex transformation is often achieved by a series of simple transformation steps. The result is a composition of translations, rotations, and scalings. We will study this through the following three examples.

Example 2.1: finding the coordinates of a moving clock hand in 2D

Consider a single clock hand. The center of rotation is given at $c(x_0, y_0)$, and the end rotation point is at $h(x_1, y_1)$. If we know the rotation angle is θ, can we find the new end point h' after the rotation? As shown in Fig. 2.4, we can achieve this by a series of transformations.

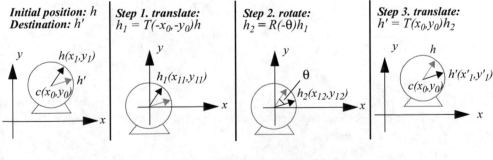

Initial position: h | *Step 1. translate:* | *Step 2. rotate:* | *Step 3. translate:*
Destination: h' | $h_1 = T(-x_0,-y_0)h$ | $h_2 = R(-\theta)h_1$ | $h' = T(x_0,y_0)h_2$

Fig. 2.4 Moving the clock hand by matrix multiplications

1. Translate the hand so that the center of rotation is at the origin. Note that we only need to find the new coordinates of the end point h:

$$\begin{bmatrix} x_{11} \\ y_{11} \\ 1 \end{bmatrix} = \begin{bmatrix} 1 & 0 & -x_0 \\ 0 & 1 & -y_0 \\ 0 & 0 & 1 \end{bmatrix} \begin{bmatrix} x_1 \\ y_1 \\ 1 \end{bmatrix}.$$

(EQ 24)

That is, $h_1 = T(-x_0, -y_0)h$.

(EQ 25)

2. Rotate θ degrees around the origin. Note that the positive direction of rotation is counter-clockwise:

$$h_2 = R(-\theta)h_1.$$

(EQ 26)

3. After the rotation. We translate again to move the clock back to its original position:

$$h' = T(x_0, y_0)h_2.$$

(EQ 27)

Therefore, putting Equations 19 to 21 together, the combination of transformations to achieve the clock hand movement is:

$$h' = T(x_0, y_0)R(-\theta)T(-x_0, -y_0)h.$$

(EQ 28)

That is:
$$\begin{bmatrix} x'_1 \\ y'_1 \\ 1 \end{bmatrix} = \begin{bmatrix} 1 & 0 & x_0 \\ 0 & 1 & y_0 \\ 0 & 0 & 1 \end{bmatrix} \begin{bmatrix} \cos\theta & \sin\theta & 0 \\ -\sin\theta & \cos\theta & 0 \\ 0 & 0 & 1 \end{bmatrix} \begin{bmatrix} 1 & 0 & -x_0 \\ 0 & 1 & -y_0 \\ 0 & 0 & 1 \end{bmatrix} \begin{bmatrix} x_1 \\ y_1 \\ 1 \end{bmatrix}.$$

(EQ 29)

In the future, we will write matrix equations concisely using only symbol notations instead of full matrix expressions. However, we should always remember that the symbols represent the corresponding matrices.

Let's assume $M=T(x_0, y_0)R(-\theta)T(-x_0, -y_0)$. We can further simplify the equation:

$$h' = Mh.$$

(EQ 30)

The order of the matrices in a matrix expression matters. The sequence represents the order of the transformations. For example, although matrix M in Equation 30 can be calculated by multiplying the first two matrices first $[T(x_0,y_0)R(-\theta)]T(-x_0,-y_0)$ or by multiplying the last two matrices first $T(x_0,y_0)[R(-\theta)T(-x_0,-y_0)]$, the order of the matrices cannot be changed.

When we analyze a model's transformations, we should remember that, logically speaking, the order of transformation steps are from right to left in the matrix expression. In this example, the first logical step is: $T(-x_0,-y_0)h$; the second step is: $R(-\theta)[T(-x_0,-y_0)h]$; and the last step is: $T(x_0,y_0)[R(-\theta)[T(-x_0,-y_0)]]$.

Example 2.2: reshaping a rectangular area

In OpenGL, we can use the mouse to reshape the display area. In the Reshape callback function, we can use *glViewport()* to adjust the size of the drawing area accordingly. The system makes corresponding adjustments to the models through the same transformation matrix. Viewport transformation will be discussed later in Viewing.

Here, we discuss a similar problem: a transformation that allows reshaping a rectangular area directly. Let's assume the coordinate system of the screen is as in Fig. 2.5. After reshaping, the rectangular area (and all the vertices of the models) go through the following transformations: translate so that the lower-left corner of the area is at the origin, scale to the size of the new area, and then translate to the scaled area location. The corresponding matrix expression is:

$$T(P_2)S(s_x,s_y)T(-P_1).\qquad\qquad\text{(EQ 31)}$$

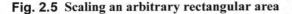

Fig. 2.5 Scaling an arbitrary rectangular area

Example 2.3: drawing a 2D robot arm with three moving segments

A 2D robot arm has 3 segments rotating at the joints in a 2D plane (Fig. 2.6). Given an arbitrary initial posture (A, B, C), let's find the transformation matrix expressions for another posture (A_f, B_f, C_f) with respective rotations (α, β, γ) around the joints. Here we specify (A, B, C) on the x axis, which is used to simplify the visualization. (A, B, C) can be initialized arbitrarily. There are many different methods to achieve the same goal. Here, we elaborate three methods to achieve the same goal.

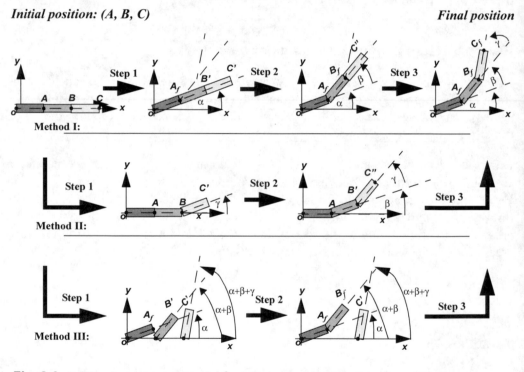

Fig. 2.6 A 2D robot arm rotates (α, β, γ) degrees at the 3 joints, respectively

Method I.

1. Rotate $oABC$ around the origin by α degrees:

$$A_f = R(\alpha)A; \ B' = R(\alpha)B; \ C' = R(\alpha)C.$$ **(EQ 32)**

2. Consider $A_f B'C'$ to be a clock hand like the example in Fig. 2.4. Rotate $A_f B'C'$ around A_f by β degrees. This is achieved by first translating the hand to the origin, rotating, then translating back:

$$B_f = T(A_f)R(\beta)T(-A_f)B'; \; C'' = T(A_f)R(\beta)T(-A_f)C'. \hspace{1cm} \textbf{(EQ 33)}$$

3. Again, consider $B_f C''$ to be a clock hand. Rotate $B_f C''$ around B_f by γ degrees:

$$C_f = T(B_f)R(\gamma)T(-B_f)C''. \hspace{1cm} \textbf{(EQ 34)}$$

Method II.

1. Consider BC to be a clock hand. Rotate BC around B by γ degrees:

$$C' = T(B)R(\gamma)T(-B)C. \hspace{1cm} \textbf{(EQ 35)}$$

2. Consider ABC' to be a clock hand. Rotate ABC' around A by β degrees:

$$B' = T(A)R(\beta)T(-A)B; \; C'' = T(A)R(\beta)T(-A)C'. \hspace{1cm} \textbf{(EQ 36)}$$

3. Again, consider $oAB'C''$ to be a clock hand. Rotate $oAB'C''$ around the origin by α degrees:

$$A_f = R(\alpha)A; \hspace{1cm} \textbf{(EQ 37)}$$

$$B_f = R(\alpha)B' = R(\alpha)T(A)R(\beta)T(-A)B; \hspace{1cm} \textbf{(EQ 38)}$$

$$C_f = R(\alpha)C'' = R(\alpha)T(A)R(\beta)T(-A)T(B)R(\gamma)T(-B)C. \hspace{1cm} \textbf{(EQ 39)}$$

Method III.

1. Consider oA, AB, and BC as clock hands with the rotation axes at o, A, and B, respectively. Rotate oA by α degrees, AB by $(\alpha+\beta)$ degrees, and BC by $(\alpha+\beta+\gamma)$ degrees:

$$A_f = R(\alpha)A; \; B' = T(A)R(\alpha+\beta)T(-A)B; \; C' = T(B)R(\alpha+\beta+\gamma)T(-B)C. \hspace{0.5cm} \textbf{(EQ 40)}$$

2. Translate AB' to A_fB_f:

$$B_f = T(A_f)T(-A)B' = T(A_f)R(\alpha+\beta)T(-A)B.$$

(EQ 41)

Note that $T(-A)T(A) = I$, which is the identity matrix: $I = \begin{bmatrix} 1 & 0 & 0 \\ 0 & 1 & 0 \\ 0 & 0 & 1 \end{bmatrix}$. Any matrix

multiplied by the identity matrix does not change. The vertex is translated by vector A, and then reversed back to its original position by translation vector $-A$.

3. Translate BC' to B_fC_f:

$$C_f = T(B_f)T(-B)C' = T(B_f)R(\alpha+\beta+\gamma)T(-B)C.$$

(EQ 42)

2.3 3D Transformation and Hidden-surface Removal

2D transformation is a special case of 3D transformation where $z=0$. For example, a 2D point (x, y) is $(x, y, 0)$ in 3D, and a 2D rotation around the origin $R(\theta)$ is a 3D rotation around the z axis $R_z(\theta)$ (Fig. 2.7). The z axis is perpendicular to the display with the arrow pointing towards the viewer. We can assume the display to be a view of a 3D drawing box, which is projected along the z axis direction onto the 2D drawing area at $z=0$.

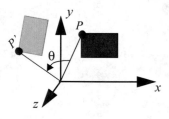

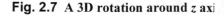

Fig. 2.7 A 3D rotation around z axi

2.3.1 3D Translation, Rotation, and Scaling

In 3D, for translation and scaling, we can translate or scale not only along the x and the y axis, but also along the z axis. For rotation, in addition to rotating around the z axis, we can also rotate around the x axis and the y axis. In the homogeneous coordinates, the 3D transformation matrices for translation, rotation, and scaling are as follows:

$$\text{Translation: } T(d_x, d_y, d_z) = \begin{bmatrix} 1 & 0 & 0 & d_x \\ 0 & 1 & 0 & d_y \\ 0 & 0 & 1 & d_z \\ 0 & 0 & 0 & 1 \end{bmatrix}; \qquad \text{(EQ 43)}$$

$$\text{Scaling: } S(s_x, s_y, s_z) = \begin{bmatrix} s_x & 0 & 0 & 0 \\ 0 & s_y & 0 & 0 \\ 0 & 0 & s_z & 0 \\ 0 & 0 & 0 & 1 \end{bmatrix}; \qquad \text{(EQ 44)}$$

$$\text{Rotation around } x \text{ axis: } R_x(\theta) = \begin{bmatrix} 1 & 0 & 0 & 0 \\ 0 & \cos\theta & -\sin\theta & 0 \\ 0 & \sin\theta & \cos\theta & 0 \\ 0 & 0 & 0 & 1 \end{bmatrix}; \qquad \text{(EQ 45)}$$

$$\text{Rotation around } y \text{ axis: } R_y(\theta) = \begin{bmatrix} \cos\theta & 0 & \sin\theta & 0 \\ 0 & 1 & 0 & 0 \\ -\sin\theta & 0 & \cos\theta & 0 \\ 0 & 0 & 0 & 1 \end{bmatrix}; \qquad \text{(EQ 46)}$$

$$\text{Rotation around } z \text{ axis: } R_z(\theta) = \begin{bmatrix} \cos\theta & -\sin\theta & 0 & 0 \\ \sin\theta & \cos\theta & 0 & 0 \\ 0 & 0 & 1 & 0 \\ 0 & 0 & 0 & 1 \end{bmatrix}. \qquad \text{(EQ 47)}$$

For example, the 2D transformation Equation 37 can be replaced by the corresponding 3D matrices:

$$A_f = R_z(\alpha)A, \qquad \text{(EQ 48)}$$

where $A = \begin{bmatrix} A_x \\ A_y \\ A_z \\ 1 \end{bmatrix}$, $A_f = \begin{bmatrix} A_{fx} \\ A_{fy} \\ A_{fz} \\ 1 \end{bmatrix}$, and $A_z=0$. We can show that $A_{fz}=0$ as well.

2.3.2 Transformation in OpenGL

As an example, we will implement in OpenGL the robot arm transformation *Method II* in Fig. 2.6. We consider the transformation to be a special case of 3D at $z=0$.

In OpenGL, all the vertices of a model are multiplied by the matrix on the top of the MODELVIEW matrix stack and then by the matrix on the top of the PROJECTION matrix stack before the model is scan-converted. Matrix multiplications are carried out on the top of the matrix stack automatically in the graphics system. The MODELVIEW matrix stack is used for geometric transformation. The PROJECTION matrix stack is used for viewing, which will be discussed later. Here, we explain how OpenGL handles the geometric transformations in the following example (Example 2.4, which implements *Method II* in Fig. 2.6.)

1. Specify that current matrix multiplications are carried out on the top of the MOD-ELVIEW matrix stack:

   ```
   glMatrixMode (GL_MODELVIEW);
   ```

2. Load the current matrix on the matrix stack with the identity matrix:

   ```
   glLoadIdentity ();
   ```

   The identity matrix for 3D homogeneous coordinates is: $I = \begin{bmatrix} 1 & 0 & 0 & 0 \\ 0 & 1 & 0 & 0 \\ 0 & 0 & 1 & 0 \\ 0 & 0 & 0 & 1 \end{bmatrix}$.

3. Specify the rotation matrix $R_z(\alpha)$, which will be multiplied by whatever matrix is on the current matrix stack already. The result of the multiplication replaces the matrix currently on the top of the stack. If the identity matrix is on the stack, then $IR_z(\alpha)=R_z(\alpha)$:

```
glRotatef (alpha, 0.0, 0.0, 1.0);
```

4. Draw a robot arm — a line segment between point O and A. Before the model is scan-converted into the frame buffer, O and A will first be transformed by the matrix on the top of the MODELVIEW matrix stack, which is $R_z(\alpha)$. That is, $R_z(\alpha)O$ and $R_z(\alpha)A$ will be used to scan-convert the line (Equation 37):

```
drawArm (O, A);
```

5. In the following code section, we specify a series of transformation matrices, which in turn will be multiplied by whatever is already on the current matrix stack: I, $[I]R(\alpha)$, $[[I]R(\alpha)]T(A)$, $[[[I]R(\alpha)]T(A)]R(\beta)$, $[[[[I]R(\alpha)]T(A)]R(\beta)]T(-A)$. Before *drawArm (A, B)*, we have $M = R(\alpha)T(A)R(\beta)T(-A)$ on the matrix stack, which corresponds to Equation 38:

```
glPushMatrix();
    glLoadIdentity ();
    glRotatef (alpha, 0.0, 0.0, 1.0);
    drawArm (O, A);

    glTranslatef (A[0], A[1], 0.0);
    glRotatef (beta, 0.0, 0.0, 1.0);
    glTranslatef (-A[0], -A[1], 0.0);
    drawArm (A, B);
glPopMatrix();
```

The matrix multiplication is always carried out on the top of the matrix stack. *glPushMatrix()* will move the stack pointer up one slot, and duplicate the previous matrix so that the current matrix on the top of the stack is the same as the matrix immediately below it. *glPopMatrix()* will move the stack pointer down one slot. The obvious advantage of this mechanism is to separate the transformations of the current model between *glPushMatrix()* and *glPopMatrix()* from the transformations of models later.

Let's look at the function *drawRobot()* in Example 2.4 below. Fig. 2.8 shows what is on the top of the matrix stack, when *drawRobot()* is called once and then again. At *drawArm(B, C)* right before *glPopMatrix()*, the matrix on top of the stack is $M = R(\alpha)T(A)R(\beta)T(-A)T(B)R(\gamma)T(-B)$, which corresponds to Equation 39.

Status of the OpenGL MODELVIEW matrix stack

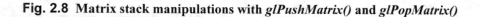

a) Before   b) After   c) Before   d) After
  glPushMatrix()   glPushMatrix()   glPopMatrix()   glPopMatrix()

Fig. 2.8 Matrix stack manipulations with *glPushMatrix()* and *glPopMatrix()*

6. Suppose we remove *glPushMatrix()* and *glPopMatrix()* from *drawRobot()*, if we call *drawRobot()* once, it appears fine. If we call it again, you will see that the matrix on the matrix stack is not an identity matrix. It is the previous matrix on the stack already (Fig. 2.9).

Status of the OpenGL MODELVIEW matrix stack

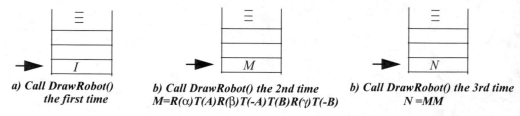

a) Call DrawRobot()   b) Call DrawRobot() the 2nd time   b) Call DrawRobot() the 3rd time
  the first time   M=R(α)T(A)R(β)T(-A)T(B)R(γ)T(-B)   N =MM

Fig. 2.9 Matrix stack manipulations without using *glPushMatrix()* and *glPopMatrix()*

For beginners, it is a good idea to draw the state of the current matrix stack while you are reading the sample programs or writing your own programs. This will help you clearly understand what the transformation matrices are at different stages.

Methods I and III (Fig. 2.6) cannot be achieved using OpenGL transformations directly, since OpenGL provides matrix multiplications, but not the vertex coordinates after a vertex is transformed by the matrix. This means that all vertices are always fixed at their original locations. This method avoids floating point accumulation errors. We can use *glGetDoublev(GL_MODELVIEW_MATRIX, M[])* to get the current 16 values of the matrix on the top of the MODELVIEW stack, and multiply the coordinates by the matrix to achieve the transformations for Methods I and III. Of course, you may implement your own matrix multiplications to achieve all the different transformation methods.

/* Example 2.4.robot2d.c: 2D three segments arm transformation */

```
float O[3] = {0.0, 0.0, 0.0}, A[3] = {0.0, 0.0, 0.0},
      B[3] = {0.0, 0.0, 0.0}, C[3] = {0.0, 0.0, 0.0};

float alpha, beta, gama, aalpha=.1, abeta=.3, agama=0.7;


void drawArm(float *End1, float *End2)
{
   glBegin(GL_LINES);
      glVertex3fv(End1);
      glVertex3fv(End2);
   glEnd();
}


 void drawRobot(float *A, float *B, float*C,
               float alpha, float beta, float gama)
{
   glPushMatrix();

      glColor3f(1, 0, 0);
      glRotatef (alpha, 0.0, 0.0, 1.0);

      // R_z(alpha) is on top of the matrix stack
      drawArm (O, A);

      glColor3f(0, 1, 0);
      glTranslatef (A[0], A[1], 0.0);
      glRotatef (beta, 0.0, 0.0, 1.0);
      glTranslatef (-A[0], -A[1], 0.0);

      // R_z(alpha)T(A)R_z(beta)T(-A) is on top of the stack
      drawArm (A, B);
```

```
        glColor3f(0, 0, 1);
        glTranslatef (B[0], B[1], 0.0);
        glRotatef (gama, 0.0, 0.0, 1.0);
        glTranslatef (-B[0], -B[1], 0.0);

        // R_z(alpha)T(A)R_z(beta)T(-A)T(B)R_z(gama)T(-B)
        drawArm (B, C);

    glPopMatrix();
}


void display(void)
{
    if (rand() % 10000 == 0) aalpha = -aalpha;

    // arm rotation angles
    alpha+= aalpha; beta+= abeta; gama+= agama;

    glClear(GL_COLOR_BUFFER_BIT);
    drawRobot(A, B, C, alpha, beta, gama);

    glutSwapBuffers();
}


void Reshape(int w, int h)
{
    glClearColor (0.0, 0.0, 0.0, 1.0);

    //initialize robot arm end positions
    A[0] = (float) w/7;
    B[0] = (float) w/5;
    C[0] = (float) w/4;

    Width = w; Height = h;
    glViewport (0, 0, Width, Height);

    // hardware set to use PROJECTION matrix stack
    glMatrixMode (GL_PROJECTION);
    // initialize the current top of matrix stack to identity
    glLoadIdentity ();
    glOrtho(-Width/2, Width/2, -Height/2, Height/2, -1.0, 1.0);

    // hardware set to use model transformation matrix stack
    glMatrixMode (GL_MODELVIEW);
    // initialize the current top of matrix stack to identity
    glLoadIdentity ();
}
```

2.3.3 Hidden-surface Removal

Bounding volumes. We first introduce a simple method, called *bounding volume* or *minmax testing*, to determine visible 3D models without using a time-consuming hidden-surface removal algorithm. Here we assume that the viewpoint of our eye is at the origin and the models are in the negative z axis. If we render the models in the order of their distances to the viewpoint of the eye along z axis from the farthest to the closest, we will have correct overlapping of the models. We can build up a rectangular box (bounding volume) with the faces perpendicular to the *x*, *y*, or *z* axis to bound a 3D model, and compare the minimum and maximum bounds in the *z* direction between boxes to decide which model should be rendered first. Using bounding volumes to decide the priority of rendering is also known as *minmax testing*.

The z-buffer (depth-buffer) algorithm. In OpenGL, to enable the hidden-surface removal (or visible-surface determination) mechanism, we need to enable the depth test once and then clear the depth buffer whenever we redraw a frame:

```
// enable zbuffer (depthbuffer) once
glEnable(GL_DEPTH_TEST);

// clear both framebuffer and zbuffer
glClear(GL_COLOR_BUFFER_BIT | GL_DEPTH_BUFFER_BIT);
```

Corresponding to a frame buffer, the graphics system also has a z-buffer, or depth buffer, with the same number of entries. After *glClear()*, the z-buffer is initialized to the *z* value farthest from the view point of our eye, and the frame buffer is initialized to the background color. When scan-converting a model (such as a polygon), before writing a pixel color into the frame buffer, the graphics system (the z-buffer algorithm) compares the pixel's *z* value to the corresponding *xy* coordinates' *z* value in the z-buffer. If the pixel is closer to the view point, its *z* value is written into the z-buffer and its color is written into the frame buffer. Otherwise, the system moves on to considering the next pixel without writing into the buffers. The result is that, no matter what order the models are scan-converted, the image in the frame buffer only shows the pixels on the models that are not blocked by other pixels. In other words, the visible surfaces are saved in the frame buffer, and all the hidden surfaces are removed.

A pixel's *z* value is provided by the model at the corresponding *xy* coordinates. For example, given a polygon and the *xy* coordinates, we can calculate the *z* value according to the polygon's plane equation *z=f(x,y)*. Therefore, although scan-conversion is drawing in 2D, 3D calculations are needed to decide hidden-surface removal and others (as we will discuss in the future: lighting, texture mapping, etc.).

A plane equation in its general form is $ax + by + cz + 1 = 0$, where (a, b, c) corresponds to a vector perpendicular to the plane. A polygon is usually specified by a list of vertices. Given three vertices on the polygon, they all satisfy the plane equation and therefore we can find (a, b, c) and $z=-(ax + by + 1)/c$. By the way, because the cross-product of two edges of the polygon is perpendicular to the plane, it is proportional to (a, b, c) as well.

2.3.4 Collision Detection

In addition to visible-model determination, bounding volumes are also used for *collision detection*. To avoid two models in an animation penetrating each other, we can use their bounding volumes to decide their physical distances and collision. Of course, the bounding volume can be in a different shape other than a box, such as a sphere. If the distance between the centers of the two spheres is bigger than the summation of the two radii of the spheres, we know that the two models do not collide with each other. We may use multiple spheres with different radii to more accurately bound a model, but the collision detection would be more complex. Of course, we may also detect collisions directly without using bounding volumes, which is likely much more complex and time consuming.

2.3.5 3D Models: Cone, Cylinder, and Sphere

Approximating a cone. In Example 1.5, we approximated a circle with subdividing triangles. If we raise the center of the circle along the z axis, we approximate a cone, as shown in Fig. 2.10. We need to make sure that our model is contained within the defined coordinates (i.e., the viewing volume):

```
glOrtho(-Width/2, Width/2, -Height/2,
          Height/2, -Width/2, Width/2);
```

Fig. 2.10 A cone

/* **Example 2.5.cone: draw a cone by subdivision** */
```
int depth=5, circleRadius=200, cnt=1;
```

```
static float vdata[4][3] = {
    {1.0, 0.0, 0.0}, {0.0, 1.0, 0.0},
    {-1.0, 0.0, 0.0}, {0.0, -1.0, 0.0}
};


void subdivideCone(float *v1, float *v2, int depth)
{
    float v0[3] = {0, 0, 0}, v12[3];
    int i;

    if (depth == 0) {
        glColor3f(v1[0]*v1[0], v1[1]*v1[1], v1[2]*v1[2]);

        drawtriangle(v1, v2, v0); // bottom cover of the cone
        v0[2] = 1; // height of the cone, the tip on z axis
        drawtriangle(v1, v2, v0); // side cover of the cone
        return;
    }

    for (i=0; i<3; i++) v12[i] = v1[i]+v2[i];
    normalize(v12);
    subdivideCone(v1, v12, depth - 1);
    subdivideCone(v12, v2, depth - 1);
}


void drawCone(void)
// draw a unit cone: center at origin and bottom in xy plane
{
    subdivideCone(vdata[0], vdata[1], depth);
    subdivideCone(vdata[1], vdata[2], depth);
    subdivideCone(vdata[2], vdata[3], depth);
    subdivideCone(vdata[3], vdata[0], depth);
}


void display(void)
{
    // clear both framebuffer and zbuffer
    glClear(GL_COLOR_BUFFER_BIT | GL_DEPTH_BUFFER_BIT);

    glRotatef(1.1, 1., 0., 0.); // rotate 1.1 deg. alone x axis
    glPushMatrix();
        glScaled(circleRadius, circleRadius, circleRadius);
        drawCone();
    glPopMatrix();
    glutSwapBuffers();
}
```

```
static void Reshape(int w, int h)
{
    glClearColor (0.0, 0.0, 0.0, 1.0);

    // enable zbuffer (depthbuffer) for hidden-surface removal
    glEnable(GL_DEPTH_TEST);

    Width = w; Height = h;
    glViewport (0, 0, Width, Height);

    glMatrixMode (GL_PROJECTION);
    glLoadIdentity ();

    // make sure the cone is within the viewing volume
    glOrtho(-Width/2, Width/2 -Height/2,
            Height/2, -Width/2, Width/2);

    glMatrixMode (GL_MODELVIEW);
    glLoadIdentity ();
}
```

Approximating a cylinder. If we can draw a circle at $z=0$, then we can draw another circle at $z=1$. If we connect the rectangles of the same vertices on the edges of the two circles, we have a cylinder, as shown in Fig. 2.11.

Fig. 2.11 A cylinder

/* Example 2.6.cylinder.c: draw a cylinder by subdivision */

```
void subdivideCylinder(float *v1, float *v2, int depth)
{
    float v11[3], v22[3], v00[3] = {0, 0, 0}, v12[3];
    float v01[3], v02[3];
    int i;

    if (depth == 0) {
        glColor3f(v1[0]*v1[0], v1[1]*v1[1], v1[2]*v1[2]);

        for (i=0; i<3; i++) {
            v01[i] = v11[i] = v1[i];
            v02[i] = v22[i] = v2[i];
        }

        // the height of the cone along z axis
        v01[2] = v02[2] = 1;
```

```
// draw the side rectangles of the cylinder
glBegin(GL_POLYGON);
     glVertex3fv(v11);
     glVertex3fv(v22);
     glVertex3fv(v02);
     glVertex3fv(v01);
glEnd();

     return;
}

for (i=0; i<3; i++)
          v12[i] = v1[i]+v2[i];
normalize(v12);

subdivideCylinder(v1, v12, depth - 1);
subdivideCylinder(v12, v2, depth - 1);
}
```

Approximating a sphere. Let's assume that we have an equilateral triangle with its three vertices (v_1, v_2, v_3) on a sphere and $|v_1|=|v_2|=|v_3|=1$. That is, the three vertices are unit vectors from the origin. We can see that $v_{12} = normalize(v_1+v_2)$ is also on the sphere. We can further subdivide the triangle into four equilateral triangles, as shown in Fig. 2.12(a). Example 2.7 uses this method to subdivide an octahedron (Fig. 2.12(b)) into a sphere.

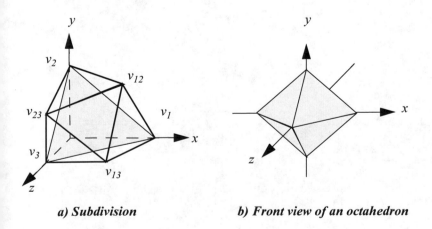

a) Subdivision   b) Front view of an octahedron

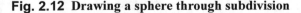

Fig. 2.12 Drawing a sphere through subdivision

/* Example 2.7.sphere.c: draw a sphere by subdivision */

```c
static float vdata[6][3] = {
    {1.0, 0.0, 0.0}, {0.0, 1.0, 0.0}, {0.0, 0.0, 1.0},
    {-1.0, 0.0, 0.0}, {0.0, -1.0, 0.0}, {0.0, 0.0, -1.0}
};


void subdivideSphere(float *v1,
                float *v2, float *v3, long depth)
{
    float v12[3], v23[3], v31[3];
    int i;

    if (depth == 0) {
        glColor3f(v1[0]*v1[0], v2[1]*v2[1], v3[2]*v3[2]);
        drawtriangle(v1, v2, v3);
        return;
    }

    for (i = 0; i < 3; i++) {
        v12[i] = v1[i]+v2[i];
        v23[i] = v2[i]+v3[i];
        v31[i] = v3[i]+v1[i];
    }

    normalize(v12);
    normalize(v23);
    normalize(v31);
    subdivideSphere(v1, v12, v31, depth - 1);
    subdivideSphere(v2, v23, v12, depth - 1);
    subdivideSphere(v3, v31, v23, depth - 1);
    subdivideSphere(v12, v23, v31, depth - 1);
}


void drawSphere(void)
{
    // draw eight triangles to cover the octahedron
    subdivideSphere(vdata[0], vdata[1], vdata[2], depth);
    subdivideSphere(vdata[0], vdata[2], vdata[4], depth);
    subdivideSphere(vdata[0], vdata[4], vdata[5], depth);
    subdivideSphere(vdata[0], vdata[5], vdata[1], depth);

    subdivideSphere(vdata[3], vdata[1], vdata[5], depth);
    subdivideSphere(vdata[3], vdata[5], vdata[4], depth);
    subdivideSphere(vdata[3], vdata[4], vdata[2], depth);
    subdivideSphere(vdata[3], vdata[2], vdata[1], depth);
}
```

2.3.6 Composition of 3D Transformations

Example 2.8 implements the robot arm in Example 2.4 with 3D cylinders, as shown in Fig. 2.13. We also add one rotation around the y axis, so the robot arm moves in 3D.

Fig. 2.13 A 3-segment robot arm

/* Example 2.8.robot3d.c: 3D 3-segment arm transformation */

```
drawArm(float End1, float End2) {

    float scale;

    scale = End2-End1;

    glPushMatrix();

        // the cylinder lies in the z axis;
        // rotate it to lie in the x axis
        glRotatef(90.0, 0.0, 1.0, 0.0);
        glScalef(scale/5.0, scale/5.0, scale);

        drawCylinder();
    glPopMatrix();
}


static void drawRobot(float alpha, float beta, float gama)
{
    ...
    // the robot arm is rotating around the y axis
    glRotatef (1.0, 0.0, 1.0, 0.0);
    ...
}
```

Example 2.9 is a simplified solar system. The earth rotates around the sun and the moon rotates around the earth in the *xz* plane. Given the center of the earth at $E(x_e, y_e, z_e)$ and the center of the moon at $M(x_m, y_m, z_m)$, let's find the new centers after the earth rotates around the sun *e* degrees, and the moon rotates around the earth *m* degrees. The moon also revolves around the sun with the earth (Fig. 2.14).

This problem is exactly like the clock problem in Fig. 2.4, except that the center of the clock is revolving around *y* axis as well. We can consider the moon rotating around the earth first, and then the moon and the earth as one object rotating around the sun.

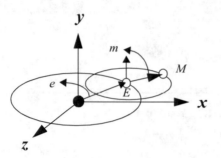

The moon rotates first:

$M' = T(E) R_y(m) T(-E) M;$

$E_f = R_y(e) E;$

$M_f = R_y(e) M';$

The earth-moon rotates first:

$E_f = R_y(e) E;$

$M' = R_y(e) M;$

$M_f = T(E_f) R_y(m) T(-E_f) M'$

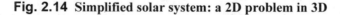

Fig. 2.14 Simplified solar system: a 2D problem in 3D

In OpenGL, since we can draw a sphere at the center of the coordinates, the transformation would be simpler.

/* Example 2.9.solar.c: draw a simplified solar system */

```
void drawSolar(float E, float e, float M, float m)
{
  glPushMatrix();
      glRotatef(e, 0.0, 1.0, 0.0); // rotate around the "sun"
      glTranslatef(E, 0.0, 0.0);
      drawSphere(); // Ry(e)Tx(E)

      glRotatef(m, 0.0, 1.0,0.0); // rotate around the "earth"
      glTranslatef(M, 0.0, 0.0);
      drawSphere(); // Ry(e)Tx(E)R(m)Tx(M)
  glPopMatrix();
}
```

Next, we change the above solar system into a more complex system, which we call the generalized solar system. Now the earth is elevated along the y axis, and the moon is elevated along the axis from the origin towards the center of the earth, and the moon rotates around this axis as in Fig. 2.15. In other words, the moon rotates around the vector E. Given E and M and their rotation angles e and m respectively, can we find the new coordinates of E_f and M_f?

$r = sqrt(x^2+y^2+z^2);$
$\alpha = arc\ cos\ (y/r);\ \ \beta = arc\ tg\ (z/x);$

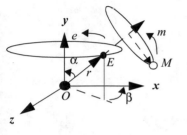

$E_f = R_y(e)\ E;$ // the earth rotate around the y axis

$M_1 = R_y(\beta)\ M;$ // the center of rotation OE is in the xy plane
$M_2 = R_z(\alpha)\ M_1$ // OE is along the y axis
$M_3 = R_y(m)\ M_2;$ // the moon rotates along the y axis
$M_4 = R_z(-\alpha)\ M_3;$ //OE returns to the xy plane
$M_5 = R_y(-\beta)\ M_4;$ // OE returns to its original orientation
$M_f = R_y(e)\ M_5;$ // the moon proceeds with the earth

$M_f = R_y(e)R_y(-\beta)\ R_z(-\alpha)\ R_y(m)\ R_z(\alpha)\ R_y(\beta)\ M;$

Fig. 2.15 Generalized solar system: a 3D problem

We cannot come up with the rotation matrix for the moon, $M,$ immediately. However, we can consider E and M as one object and create the rotation matrix by several steps. Note that for M's rotation around E, we do not really need to rotate E, but we use it as a reference to explain the rotation.

1. As shown in Fig. 2.15, the angle between the y axis and E is $\alpha = arc\ cos\ (y/r);$ the angle between the projection of E on the xz plane and the x axis is $\beta = arc\ tg\ (z/x);$ $r = sqrt(x^2+y^2+z^2).$

2. Rotate M around the y axis by β degrees so that the new center of rotation E_1 is in the xy plane:

$$M_1 = R_y(\beta)M;\ E_1 = R_y(\beta)E. \qquad\qquad \textbf{(EQ 49)}$$

3. Rotate M_1 around the z axis by α degrees so that the new center of rotation E_2 is coincident with the y axis:

$$M_2 = R_z(\alpha)M_1; \ E_2 = R_z(\alpha)E_1.$$

(EQ 50)

4. Rotate M_2 around the y axis by m degree:

$$M_3 = R_y(m)M_2.$$

(EQ 51)

5. Rotate M_3 around the z axis by $-\alpha$ degree so that the center of rotation returns to the xz plane:

$$M_4 = R_z(-\alpha)M_3; \ E_1 = R_z(-\alpha)E_2.$$

(EQ 52)

6. Rotate M_4 around y axis by $-\beta$ degree so that the center of rotation returns to its original orientation:

$$M_5 = R_y(-\beta)M_4; \ E = R_y(-\beta)E_1.$$

(EQ 53)

7. Rotate M_5 around y axis e degree so that the moon proceeds with the earth around the y axis:

$$M_f = R_y(e)M_5; \ E_f = R_y(e)E.$$

(EQ 54)

8. Putting the transformation matrices together, we have:

$$M_f = R_y(e)R_y(-\beta) \ R_z(-\alpha) \ R_y(m) \ R_z(\alpha) \ R_y(\beta) \ M$$

(EQ 55)

Again, in OpenGL, we start with the sphere at the origin. The transformation is simpler. The following code demonstrates the generalized solar system. The result is as shown in Fig. 2.16. Incidentally, *glRotatef(m, x, y, z)* specifies a single matrix that rotates a point along the vector *(x, y, z)* by *m* degrees. Now, we know that the matrix is equal to $R_y(-\beta)$ $R_z(-\alpha) \ R_y(m) \ R_z(\alpha) \ R_y(\beta)$.

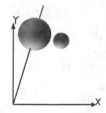

Fig. 2.16 Generalized solar system

/* Example 2.10.gensolar.c: draw a generalized solar system */

```
void drawSolar(float E, float e, float M, float m)
{
    float alpha=30;

  glPushMatrix();
      glRotatef(e, 0.0, 1.0, 0.0); // rotate around the "sun"
      glRotatef(alpha, 0.0, 0.0, 1.0); // tilt angle
      glTranslatef(0., E, 0.0);
      drawSphere(); // the earth

      glRotatef(m, 0.0, 1.0, 0.); // rotate around the "earth"
      glTranslatef(M, 0., 0.);
      drawSphere(); // the moon
  glPopMatrix();
}
```

The generalized solar system corresponds to a top that rotates and proceeds as shown in Fig. 2.17(b). The rotating angle is *m* and the proceeding angle is *e*. The earth *E* is a point along the center of the top and the moon *M* can be a point on the edge of the top. We learned to draw a cone in OpenGL. We can transform the cone to achieve the motion of a top. In the following example (Example 2.11), we have a top that rotates and proceeds, and a sphere that rotates around the top (Fig. 2.17(c)).

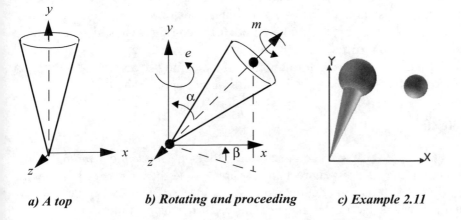

  a) A top   *b) Rotating and proceeding*   *c) Example 2.11*

Fig. 2.17 **Generalized solar system: a top rotates and proceeds**

/* Example 2.11.conesolar.c: draw a cone solar system */

```
void drawSolar(float E, float e, float M, float m)
{
    float alpha=30;

    glPushMatrix();
        // rotating around the "sun"; proceed angle
        glRotatef(e, 0.0, 1.0, 0.0);
        glRotatef(alpha, 0.0, 0.0, 1.0); // tilt angle
        glTranslatef(0., E, 0.0);
        glPushMatrix();
            glScalef(E/8,E,E/8);
            glRotatef(90, 1.0, 0.0, 0.0); // orient the cone
            drawCone();
        glPopMatrix();

        glRotatef(m, 0.0, 1.0, 0.); // rotate around the "earth"
        glTranslatef(M, 0., 0.);
        glScalef(E/8,E/8,E/8);
        drawSphere();
    glPopMatrix();
}
```

2.4 Viewing

The display has its device coordinate system in pixels, and our model has its (virtual) modeling coordinate system in which we specify and transform our model. We need to consider the relationship between the modeling coordinates and the device coordinates so that our virtual model will appear as an image on the display. Therefore, we need a *viewing* transformation — the mapping of an area or volume in the modeling coordinates to an area in the display device coordinates.

2.4.1 2D Viewing

In 2D viewing, we specify a rectangular area called the *modeling window* in the modeling coordinates and a display rectangular area called the *viewport* in the device coordinates (Fig. 2.18). The modeling window defines what is to be viewed; the viewport defines where the image appears. Instead of transforming a model in the modeling window to a model in the display viewport directly, we can first transform the modeling window into a square with the lower left corner at (-1,-1) and the upper right corner at (1,1). The coordinates of the square are called the *normalized* coordinates. Clipping of the model is then calculated in the normalized coordinates against the square. After that, the normalized coordinates are scaled and translated to the device coordinates. We should understand that the matrix that transforms the modeling window to the square will also transform the models in the modeling coordinates to the corresponding models in the normalized coordinates. Similarly, the matrix that transforms the square to the viewport will also transform the models accordingly. The process (or pipeline) in 2D viewing is shown in Fig. 2.18. Through normalization, the clipping algorithm avoid dealing with the changing sizes of the modeling window and the device view port.

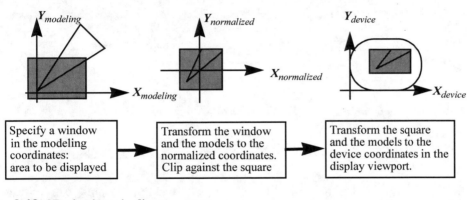

Fig. 2.18 2D viewing pipeline

2.4.2 3D Viewing

The display is a 2D viewport, and our model can be in 3D. In 3D viewing, we need to specify a viewing volume, which determines a projection method (*parallel* or *perspective*) — for how 3D models are projected into 2D. The projection lines go from the vertices in the 3D models to the projected vertices in the projection plane — a 2D *view plane* that corresponds to the viewport. A parallel projection has all the projection lines parallel. A perspective projection has all the projection lines converging to a point named the *center of projection*. The center of projection is also called the *view point*. You may consider that your eye is at the view point looking into the viewing volume. Viewing is analogous to taking a photograph with a camera. The object in the outside world has its own 3D coordinate system, the film in the camera has its own 2D coordinate system. We specify a viewing volume and a projection method by pointing and adjusting the zoom.

As shown in Fig. 2.19, the viewing volume for the parallel projection is like a box. The result of the parallel projection is a less realistic view, but can be used for exact measurements. The viewing volume for the perspective projection is like a truncated pyramid, and the result looks more realistic in many cases, but does not preserve sizes in the display — objects further away are smaller.

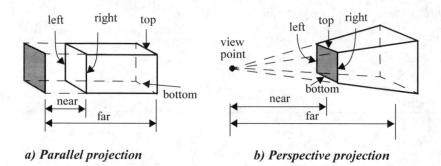

  a) Parallel projection   *b) Perspective projection*

Fig. 2.19 **View volumes and projection methods**

In the following, we use the OpenGL system as an example to demonstrate how 3D viewing is achieved. The OpenGL viewing pipeline includes normalization, clipping, perspective division, and viewport transformation (Fig. 2.20). Except for clipping, all other transformation steps can be achieved by matrix multiplications. Therefore, viewing is mostly achieved by geometric transformation. In the OpenGL system, these transformations are achieved by matrix multiplications on the PROJECTION matrix stack.

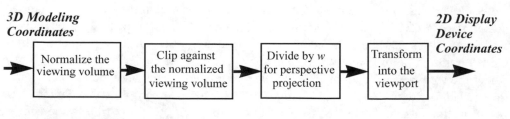

Fig. 2.20 **3D viewing pipeline**

Specifying a viewing volume. A parallel projection is called an *orthographic projection* if the projection lines are all perpendicular to the view plane. *glOrtho*(left, right, bottom, top, near, far) specifies an orthographic projection as shown in Fig. 2.19(a). *glOrtho()* also defines six plane equations that cover the orthographic viewing volume: *x*=left, *x*=right, *y*=bottom, *y*=top, *z*=-near, and *z*=-far. We can see that (left, bottom, -near) and (right, top, -near) specify the (*x, y, z*) coordinates of the lower-left and upper-right corners of the near clipping plane. Similarly, (left, bottom, -far) and (right, top, -far) specify the (*x, y, z*) coordinates of the lower-left and upper-right corners of the far clipping plane.

glFrustum(left, right, bottom, top, near, far) specifies a perspective projection as shown in Fig. 2.19(b). *glFrustum()* also defines six planes that cover the perspective viewing volume. We can see that (left, bottom, -near) and (right, top, -near) specify the (*x, y, z*) coordinates of the lower-left and upper-right corners of the near clipping plane. The far clipping plane is a cross section at *z*=-far with the projection lines converging to the view point, which is fixed at the origin looking down the negative *z* axis.

Normalization. Normalization transformation is achieved by matrix multiplication on the PROJECTION matrix stack. In the following code section, we first load the identity matrix onto the top of the matrix stack. Then, we multiply the identity matrix by a matrix specified by *glOrtho()*.

```
// hardware set to use projection matrix stack
glMatrixMode (GL_PROJECTION);
glLoadIdentity ();
glOrtho(-Width/2, Width/2, -Height/2, Height/2,-1.0, 1.0);
```

In OpenGL, *glOrtho()* actually specifies a matrix that transforms the specified viewing volume into a *normalized* viewing volume, which is a cube with six clipping planes as shown in Fig. 2.21 (*x*=1, *x*=-1, *y*=1, *y*=-1, *z*=1, and *z*=-1). Therefore, instead of calculating the clipping and projection directly, the normalization transformation is carried out first to simplify the clipping and the projection.

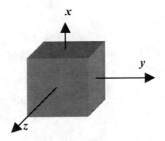

Fig. 2.21 Normalized viewing volume — a cube with (-*1* to *1*) along each axis

Similarly, *glFrustum()* also specifies a matrix that transforms the perspective viewing volume into a normalized viewing volume as in Fig. 2.21. Here a division is needed to map the homogeneous coordinates into 3D coordinates. In OpenGL, a 3D vertex is represented by (x, y, z, w) and transformation matrices are 4×4 matrices. When $w=1$, (x, y, z) represents the 3D coordinates of the vertex. If $w=0$, (x, y, z) represents a direction. Otherwise, $(x/w, y/w, z/w)$ represents the 3D coordinates. A perspective division is needed simply because after the *glFrustum()* matrix transformation, $w \neq 1$. In OpenGL, the perspective division is carried out after clipping.

Clipping. Since *glOrtho()* and *glFrustum()* both transform their viewing volumes into a normalized viewing volume, we only need to develop one clipping algorithm. Clipping is carried out in homogeneous coordinates to accomodate certain curves. Therefore, all vertices of the models are first transformed into the normalized viewing coordinates, clipped against the planes of the normalized viewing volume ($x=-w$, $x=w$, $y=-w$, $y=w$, $z=-w$, $z=w$), and then transformed and projected into the 2D viewport.

Perspective Division. The perspective normalization transformation *glFrustum()* results in homogenous coordinates with $w \neq 1$. Clipping is carried out in homogeneous coordinates. However, a division for all the coordinates of the model (x/w, y/w, z/w) is needed to transform homogeneous coordinates into 3D coordinates.

Viewport transformation. All vertices are kept in 3D. We need the z values to calculate hidden-surface removal. From the normalized viewing volume after dividing by w, the viewport transformation calculates each vertex's (x, y, z) corresponding to the pixels in the viewport, and invokes scan-conversion algorithms to draw the model into the viewport. Projecting into 2D is nothing more than ignoring the z values when scan-converting the model's pixels into the frame buffer. It is not necessary but we may consider that the projection plane is at $z=0$. In Fig. 2.19, the shaded projection planes are arbitrarily specified.

Summary of the viewing pipeline. Before scan-conversion, an OpenGL model will go through the following transformation and viewing processing steps:

- *Modeling*: each vertex of the model will be transformed by the current matrix on the top of the MODELVIEW matrix stack

- *Normalization*: after the MODELVIEW transformation, each vertex will be transformed by the current matrix on the top of the PROJECTION matrix stack

- *Clipping*: each primitive (point, line, polygon, etc.) is clipped against the clipping planes in homogeneous coordinates

- *Perspective division*: all primitives are transformed from homogeneous coordinates into cartesian coordinates

- *Viewport transformation*: the model is scaled and translated into the viewport for scan-conversion

2.4.3 3D Clipping Against a Cube

Clipping a 3D point against a cube can be done in six comparisons. If we represent a point by its six comparisons in six bits, we can easily decide a 3D line clipping.

```
Bit 6 = 1 if x<left;
Bit 5 = 1 if x>right;
Bit 4 = 1 if y<bottom;
Bit 3 = 1 if y>top;
Bit 2 = 1 if z<near;
Bit 1 = 1 if z>far;
```

If the two end points of a line's 6 bits are 000000 (the logic OR is equal to zero), then the end points of the line are inside the cube. If there is a same bit in the two end points is not equal to zero (the logic AND is not equal to zero), then the two end points are outside the viewing volume. Otherwise, we can find the lines intersections with the cube. Given two end points (x_0, y_0, z_0) and (x_1, y_1, z_1), the parametric line equation can be represented as:

$$x = x_0 + t(x_1 - x_0)$$ (EQ 56)

$$y = y_0 + t(y_1 - y_0)$$ (EQ 57)

$$z = z_0 + t(z_1 - z_0)$$ (EQ 58)

Now if any bit is not equal to zero, say Bit 2 = 1, then z=near, and we can find t in Equation 58. and therefore find the intersection point (x, y, z) according to Equation 56 and Equation 57.

For a polygon in 3D, we can extend the above line clipping algorithm to walk around the edges of the polygon against the cube. If a polygon's edge lies inside the clipping volume, the vertices are accepted for the new polygon. Otherwise, we can throw out all vertices outside a volume boundary plane, cut the two edges that go out of and into a boundary plane, and generate new vertices along a boundary plane between the two edges to replace the vertices that are outside a boundary plane. The clipped polygon has all vertices in the viewing volume after the six boundary planes are processed.

Clipping against the viewing volume is part of OpenGL view pipeline discussed earlier. Actually, clipping against an arbitrary plane can be calculated similarly as discussed below.

2.4.4 Clipping Against an Arbitrary Plane

A plane equation in general form can be expressed as follows:

$$ax + by + cz + d = 0. \qquad \text{(EQ 59)}$$

We can clip a point against the plane equation. Given a point (x_0, y_0, z_0), if $ax_0 + by_0 + cz_0 + d \geq 0$, then the point is accepted. Otherwise it is clipped. For an edge, if the two end points are not accepted or clipped, we can find the intersection of the edge with the plane by putting Equation 56, Equation 57, and Equation 58 into Equation 59. Again, we can walk around the vertices of a polygon to clip against the plane.

OpenGL has a function *glClipPlane()* that allows specifying and clipping plane. You can enable the corresponding clipping plane so that objects below the clipping plane will be clipped.

2.4.5 An Example of Viewing in OpenGL

Viewing transformation is carried out by the OpenGL system automatically. For programmers, it is more practical to understand how to specify a viewing volume through *glOrtho()* or *glFrustum()* and to make sure that your models are in the viewing volume after being transformed by the MODELVIEW matrix. The following descriptions explain Example 2.12.

1. *glutInitWindowSize()* in *main()* specifies the display window on the screen in pixels.

2. *glViewport()* in *Reshape()* specifies the rendering area within the display window. The viewing volume will be projected into the viewport area. When we reshape the drawing area, the viewport aspect ratio (*w/h*) changes accordingly.

3. *glOrtho()* or *glFrustum()* specify the viewing volume. The models in the viewing volume will appear in the viewport area on the display.

4. The first matrix we multiply on the MODELVIEW matrix stack, after loading the identity matrix, is a translation along the *z* axis. This translation can be viewed as the last transformation in modeling coordinates. That is, after finishing all modeling and transformation, we move the origin of the modeling coordinates (and all the models after being transformed in the modeling coordinates) along *z* axis into the center of the viewing volume.

5. When we analyze a model's transformations, logically speaking, the order of transformation steps are bottom-up from the closest transformation above the drawing command to where we specify the viewing volume.

6. In *display()*, you may think that a robot arm is calculated at the origin of the modeling coordinates. Actually, the robot arm is translated along *z* axis *-(zNear+zFar)/2* in order to put the arm in the middle of the viewing volume.

7. Another way of looking at the MODELVIEW matrix is that the matrix transforms the viewing method instead of the model. Translating a model along the negative *z* axis is like moving the viewing volume along the positive *z* axis. Similarly, rotating a model along an axis by a positive angle is like rotating the viewing volume along the axis by a negative angle.

8. When we analyze a model's transformation by thinking about transforming its viewing, the order of transformation steps are topdown from where we specify the viewing volume to where we specify the drawing command. We should remember that the signs of the transformation are logically negated in this perspective.

/* **Example 2.12.robotSolar.c: 3D transformation/viewing** */

```
void display(void)
{
```

```
    glClear(GL_COLOR_BUFFER_BIT | GL_DEPTH_BUFFER_BIT);

    // draw a robot arm from the origin
    drawRobot(A, B, C, alpha, beta, gama);

    glutSwapBuffers();
}

static void Reshape(int w, int h)
{
    float zNear=w, zFar=3*w;

    glClearColor (0.0, 0.0, 0.0, 1.0);
     glEnable(GL_DEPTH_TEST);

    // viewport lower left corner (0,0), aspect ratio w/h
    glViewport (0, 0, w, h);

    // hardware set to use projection matrix stack
    glMatrixMode (GL_PROJECTION);
    glLoadIdentity ();
    //glOrtho(-w/2, w/2, -h/2, h/2, zNear, zFar);
    glFrustum(-w/2, w/2, -h/2, h/2, zNear, zFar);

    // hardware set to use model transformation matrix stack
    glMatrixMode (GL_MODELVIEW);
    glLoadIdentity ();
    // the origin is at the center between znear and zfar
    glTranslatef (0., 0., -(zNear+zFar)/2);
}
```

2.5 Review Questions

1. An octahedron has v1=(1,0,0), v2=(0,1,0), v3=(0,0,1), v4=(−1,0,0), v5=(0,−1,0), v6=(0,0,−1). Please choose the triangles that face the outside of the octahedron.

   a. (v1v2v3, v1v3v5, v1v5v6,v1v2v6)   b. (v2v3v1, v2v1v6, v2v6v4, v2v4v3)

   c. (v3v2v1, v3v5v1, v3v4v2, v3v4v5)   d. (v4v2v1, v4v5v1, v3v4v2, v3v4v5)

2. If we subdivide the above octahedron 8 times (depth=8), how many triangles we will have in the final sphere.

   No. of triangles:

3. Choose the *matrix expression* that would transform square ABCD into square A'B'C'D' in 3D as shown in the figure below.

   a. $T(−1,−1, 0)R_y(−90)$
   b. $R_y(−90) T(−1,−1, 0)$
   c. $T(−2,−2, 0)R_z(−90)R_y(90)$
   d. $R_y(90)R_z(−90)T(−2,−2, 0)$

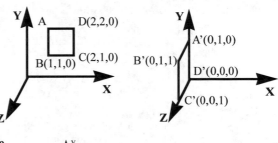

4. *myDrawTop()* will draw a top below on the left. Write a section of OpenGL code so that the top will appear as specified on the right with tip at A(x1, y1, z1), tilted α, and proceeded θ around an axis parallel to *y* axis.

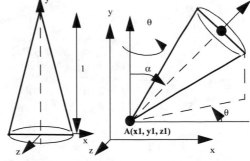

5. *myDrawTop()* will draw an object in oblique projection as in the question above with height equals 1 and radius equals 0.5. Please draw two displays in orthographic **projection according to the program on the right (as they will appear on the screen where the *z* axis is perpendicular to the plane).**

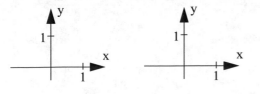

```
glLoadIdentity();
glRotatef (-90, 0.0, 1.0, 0.0);
myDrawTop(); // left
glRotatef (-90, 0.0, 0.0, 1.0);

glPushMatrix();
glTranslatef (0.0, 0.0, 1.0);
myDrawTop(); //right
glPopMatrix();
```

6. In the scan-line algorithm for filling polygons, if z-buffer is used, when should the program call the z-buffer algorithm function?

    a. at the beginning of the program   b. at the beginning of each scan-line
    c. at the beginning of each pixel   d. at the beginning of each polygon

7. *Collision detection* avoids two models in an animation penetrating each other; which of the following is FALSE:

    a. bounding boxes are used for efficiency purposes in collision detection
    b. both animated and stationary objects are covered by the bounding boxes
    c. animated objects can move whatever distance between frames of calculations
    d. collision detection can be calculated in many different ways

8. After following transformations, what is on top of the matrix stack at `drawObject2()`?

    glLoadIdentity(); glPushMatrix(); glMultMatrixf(S); glRotatef(a,1,0,0); glTranslatef(t,0,0); *drawObject1();* glGetFloatv(GL_MODELVIEW_MATRIX, &tmp); glPopMatrix(); glPushMatrix(); glMultMatrixf(S); glMultMatrixf(&tmp);*drawObject2();* glPopMatrix();

    a. $SSR_x(a)T_x(t)$ b. $ST_x(t)R_x(a)S$ c. $T_x(t)R_x(a)SS$
    d. $R_x(a)SST_x(t)$ e. $SR_x(a)T_x(t)$

9. Given glViewport (u, v, w, h) and gluOrtho2D(xmin, xmax, ymin, ymax), choose the 2D transformation `matrix expression` that maps a point in the modeling (modelview) coordinates to the device (viewport) coordinates.

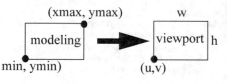

    a. $S(1/(xmax - xmin), 1/(ymax - ymin))$
              $T(-xmin,-ymin)T(u,v)S(w,h)$
    b. $S(1/(xmax - xmin), 1/(ymax - ymin))S(w,h)T(-xmin,-ymin)T(u,v)$
    c. $T(u,v)S(w,h)S(1/(xmax - xmin), 1/(ymax - ymin))T(-xmin,-ymin)$
    d. $T(-xmin,-ymin)T(u,v)S(1/(xmax - xmin), 1/(ymax - ymin))S(w,h)$

10. Given a 2D model and a modeling window, please draw the object in normalized coordinates after `clipping` and in the device as it appears on a display.

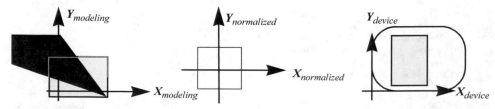

11. In the OpenGL graphics pipeline, please order the following according to their order of operations:

    (__) clipping   (__) viewport transformation
    (__) modelview transformation   (__) normalization

(__) perspective division   (__) scan conversion

12. Please implement the following viewing command: gmuPerspective(fx, fy, d, s),
where the viewing direction is from the origin looking down the negative z **axis. fx is the field of**
view angle in the x **direction; fy is the field of view angle in the** y **direction; d is the distance from the**
viewpoint to the center of the viewing volume, which is a point on the negative z **axis; s is the dis-**
tance from d to the near or far clipping planes.

gmuPerspective(fx, fy, d, s) {

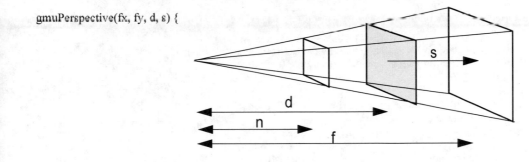

       glFrustum(l, r, b, t, n, f);
}

2.6 Programming Assignments

1. Implement myLoadIdentity, myRotatef, myTranslatef, myScalef, myPushMatrix, and myPop-
Matrix just like their corresponding OpenGL commands. Then, in the rest of the programming
assignments, you can interchange them with OpenGL commands.

2. Check out online what is polarview transformation; implement your own polarview with a dem-
onstration of the function.

3. As shown in the figure on the right, use 2D transforma-
tion to rotate the stroke font and the star.

4. The above problem can be extended into 3D: the outer
circle rotates along y **axis, the inner circle rotates around** x
axis, and the star rotates around z **axis.**

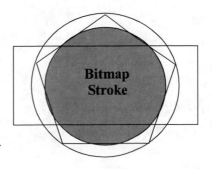

5. Draw a cone, a cylinder, and a sphere that bounce back
and forth along a circle, as shown in the figure. When the
objects meet, they change their directions of movement.
The program must be in double-buffer mode and have hid-
den surface removal.

6. Draw two circles with the same animation as above. At the same time, one circle rotates around x axis, and the other rotates around y axis.

7. Implement a 3D robot arm animation as in the book, and put the above animation system on the palm of the robot arm. The system on the palm can change its size periodically, which is achieved through scaling.

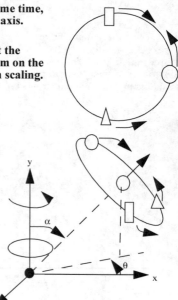

8. Draw a cone, a cylinder, and a sphere that move and collide in the moon's trajectory in the generalized solar system. When the objects meet, they change their directions of movement.

9. Put the above system on the palm of the robot arm.

10. Implement myPerspective and myLookAt just like gluPerspective and gluLookAt. Then, use them to look from the cone to the earth or cylinder in the system above.

11. Display different perspectives or direction of viewing in multiple viewports.

3
Color and Lighting

Chapter objectives:

- Introduce RGB color in the hardware, eye characteristics, and gamma correction

- Understand color interpolation and smooth shading in OpenGL

- Set up OpenGL lighting: ambient, diffuse, specular, and multiple light sources

- Understand back-face culling and surface shading models

3.1 Color

In a display, a pixel color is specified as a red, green, and blue (RGB) vector. The RGB colors are also called the *primaries*, because our eye sees a different color in a vector of different primary values. The RGB colors are additive primaries — we construct a color on the black background by adding the primaries together. For example, with equal amounts of R, G, and B: $G+B \Rightarrow$ cyan, $R+B \Rightarrow$ magenta, $R+G \Rightarrow$ yellow, and $R+G+B \Rightarrow$ white. RGB colors are used in the graphics hardware, which we will discuss in more detail.

Cyan, magenta, and yellow (CMY) colors are the complements of RGB colors, respectively. The CMY colors are subtractive primaries — we construct a color on a white background by removing the corresponding RGB primaries. Similarly, with equal amounts of R, G, and B: $C = RGB - R$, $M = RGB - G$, and $Y = RGB - B$.

The CMY colors are used in color printers. Adding certain amounts of CMY inks to a point on a white paper is like removing certain amounts of RGB from the white color at that point. The resulting color at the point on the paper depends on the portions of individual inks. Black ink is used to generate different levels of greys replacing using equal amounts of CMY inks.

J.X. Chen, *Guide to Graphics Software Tools*, doi: 10.1007/978-1-84800-901-1_3,
© Springer-Verlag London Limited 2008

3.1.1 RGB Mode and Index Mode

If each pixel value in the frame buffer is an RGB vector, the display is in *RGB mode*. Each pixel value can also be an index into a color look-up table called a *colormap*, as shown in Fig. 3.1. Then, the display is in *index mode*. The pixel color is specified in the colormap instead of the frame buffer.

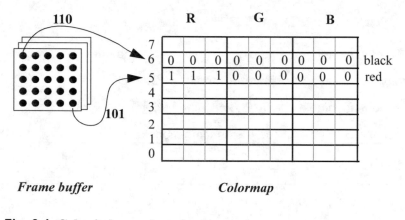

Fig. 3.1 Color-index mode and colormap

Let's assume that we have 3 bits per entry in the frame buffer. That is, the frame buffer has 3 *bitplanes*. In RGB mode, we have access to 8 different colors: black, red, green, blue, cyan, magenta, yellow, and white. In index mode, we still have access to only 8 different colors, but the colors can vary depending on how we load the colormap. If the graphics hardware has a limited number of bitplanes for the frame buffer, index mode allows more color choices, even though the number of colors is the same as that of RGB mode at the same time. For example, in the above example, if we have 12 bitplanes per entry in the colormap, we can choose 8 colors from $2^{12} = 4096$ different colors. The colormap does not take much space in memory, which had been a significant advantage when fast memory chips were very expensive. In GLUT, we use *glutInitDisplayMode(GLUT_INDEX)* to choose the index mode. RGB mode is the default. Index mode can also be useful for doing various animation tricks. However, in general, since memory is no longer a limitation and RGB mode is easier and more flexible, we use it in the examples. Also, in OpenGL programming, each color component (R, G, or B) value is in the range of 0 to 1. The system will scale the value to the corresponding hardware bits during compilation transparent to the users.

3.1.2 Eye Characteristics and Gamma Correction

A pixel color on a display is the emission of light that reaches our eye. An RGB vector is a representation of the *brightness* level that our eye perceives. The *intensity* is the amount of physical energy used to generate the brightness. Our eye sees a different color for a different RGB vector. We may not have noticed, but certain colors cannot be produced by RGB mixes, and hence cannot be shown on an RGB display device.

The eye is more sensitive to yellow-green light. In general, the eye's sensitivities to different colors generated by a constant intensity level are different. Also, for the same color, the eye's perceived brightness levels are not linearly proportional to the intensity levels. To generate evenly spaced brightness levels, we need to use logarithmically-spaced intensity levels. For example, to generate n evenly-spaced brightness levels for a color component λ (which represents R, G, or B), we need corresponding intensity levels at:

$$I_{i\lambda} = r^i I_{0\lambda} \text{ for } i=0, 1, ..., n-1, \hspace{2cm} \text{(EQ 60)}$$

where $I_{0\lambda}$ is the lowest intensity available in the display hardware and $r=(1/I_{0\lambda})^{1/(n-1)}$.

For a CRT display monitor, $I_{i\lambda}$ depends on the energy in voltage that is applied to generate the electrons lighting the corresponding screen pixels (phosphor dots):

$$I_{i\lambda} = KV^{\gamma}. \hspace{2cm} \text{(EQ 61)}$$

The value of γ is about 2.2 to 2.5 for most CRTs. Therefore, given an intensity $I_{i\lambda}$, we can find the corresponding voltage needed in the hardware:

$$V = (I_{i\lambda}/K)^{1/\gamma}. \hspace{2cm} \text{(EQ 62)}$$

This is called *gamma correction*, since γ is used in the equation to find the voltage to generate the correct intensity. Without gamma correction, the brightness levels are not even, and high brightness pixels appear to be darker. Different CRTs have different K's and γ's. Instead of calculating the voltages, CRT manufactures can build up a look-up table for a CRT (in the CRT monitor or in the corresponding graphics card that refreshes the CRT) by measuring the corresponding brightness levels and voltages. In the look-up table, the indices are the brightness levels and the values are the corresponding voltages.

Usually, the hardware gamma correction allows software modifications. That is, we can change the contents of the look-up table. Today, most color monitors have hardware gamma corrections. Due to different material properties (phosphor composites) and gamma corrections, the same RGB vector appears in different colors and brightness on individual monitors. Effort is needed to make two CRT monitors appear exactly the same.

To simplify the matter, since the difference between the intensity and the brightness is solved in the hardware, we use the intensity to mean the brightness or the RGB value directly. Also, we use I_λ to represent the brightness level i of an RGB component directly. That is, I_λ represents a perceived brightness level instead of an energy level.

3.2 Color Interpolation

In OpenGL, we use *glShadeModel(GL_FLAT)* or *glShadeModel(GL_SMOOTH)* to choose between two different models (flat shading and smooth shading) of using colors for a primitive. With *GL_FLAT*, we use one color that is specified by *glColor3f()* for all the pixels in the primitive. For example, in Example 3.1, if we call *glShadeModel(GL_FLAT)*, only one color will be used in *drawtriangle()*, even though we have specified different colors for different vertices. Depending on the OpenGL systems, the color may be the color specified for the last vertex in a primitive.

For a line, with *GL_SMOOTH*, the vertex colors are linearly interpolated along the pixels between the two end vertices. For example, if a line has 5 pixels, and the end point colors are (0,0,0) and (0,0,1), then, after the interpolation, the 5 pixel colors will be (0,0,0), (0,0,1/4), (0,0,2/4), (0,0,3/4), and (0,0,1), respectively. The intensity of each RGB component is interpolated separately. In general, given the end point intensities ($I_{\lambda 1}$ and $I_{\lambda 2}$) and the number of pixels along the line (N), the intensity increment of the linear interpolation is:

$$\Delta I_\lambda = \frac{I_{\lambda 2} - I_{\lambda 1}}{N - 1}.$$

(EQ 63)

That is, for each pixel from the starting pixel to the end pixel, the color component changes ΔI_λ.

For a polygon, OpenGL first interpolates along the edges, and then along the horizontal scan-lines during scan-conversion. All we need to do to carry out interpolation in OpenGL is to call *glShadeModel(GL_SMOOTH)* and set up different vertex colors.

/* **Example 3.1.shading.c: OpenGL flat or smooth shading** */

```
void drawtriangle(float *v1, float *v2, float *v3)
{
    glBegin(GL_TRIANGLES);

        glColor3f(1,0,0); glVertex3fv(v1);
        glColor3f(0,1,0); glVertex3fv(v2);
        glColor3f(0,0,1); glVertex3fv(v3);

    glEnd();
}


void drawColorCoord(float zlen)
{
    glBegin(GL_LINES);
        glColor3f(1,1,1); glVertex3f(0,0,0);
        glColor3f(0,0,1); glVertex3f(0,0,zlen);
    glEnd();
}


void display(void)
{
    cnt++;
    glClear(GL_COLOR_BUFFER_BIT | GL_DEPTH_BUFFER_BIT);

// alternating between flat & smooth
    if (cnt % 50 == 0) glShadeModel(GL_SMOOTH);
    if (cnt%100 == 0) glShadeModel(GL_FLAT);

    drawColorCoord(1.);
    drawtriangle(vdata[0], vdata[1], vdata[2]);

    glutSwapBuffers();
}
```

3.3 Lighting

A pixel color is a reflection or emission of light from a point on a model to our eye. Therefore, instead of specifying a color for a point directly, we can specify light sources and material properties for the graphics system to calculate the color of the point according to a lighting model. The real world lighting is very complex. In graphics, we adopt simplified methods (i.e., lighting or illumination models) that work relatively fast and well.

We use the OpenGL lighting system as an example to explain lighting. The OpenGL lighting model includes four major components: ambient, diffuse, specular, and emission. The final color is the summation of these components. The lighting model is developed to calculate the color of each individual pixel that corresponds to a point on a primitive. The method of calculating the lighting for all pixels in a primitive is called the *shading model*. As introduced in Section 3.2, OpenGL calculates vertex pixel colors and uses interpolation to find the colors of all pixels in a primitive when we call *glShadeModel(GL_SMOOTH)*. If we use *glShadeModel(GL_FLAT)*, only one vertex color is used for the primitive. However, the vertex colors are calculated by the lighting model instead of being specified by *glColor()*.

3.3.1 Lighting Components

Emissive Component. The emission intensity of a vertex pixel with an emissive material is calculated as follows:

$$I_{\lambda e} = M_{\lambda emission}, \qquad \text{(EQ 64)}$$

where λ is an RGB component or A (alpha), and $M_{\lambda emission}$ is the material's emission property. Each color component is calculated independently. Since the *alpha* value will be discussed in the next chapter, we can ignore it in our current examples. In OpenGL, *emission* is a material property that is neither dependent on any light source nor considered a light source. Emissive material does not emit light, it displays its own color. The vertex's corresponding surface has two sides, the front and the back, which can be specified with different material properties.

In Example 3.2, the material is emitting a white color and all objects will be white until we change the emission material component to something else. Here according to Equation 64, the calculated RGB color is *(1., 1., 1.)*. If we only specify the emission component, the effect is the same as specifying *glColor3f(1., 1., 1.)*.

/* Example 3.2.emission.c: emissive material component */

```
init() {
    float white[] = {1., 1., 1., 1.}; // RGBA

    glEnable(GL_LIGHTING);
    glMaterialfv(GL_FRONT, GL_EMISSION, white);
}
```

When lighting is enabled, *glColor3f()* is turned off. In other words, even though we may have *glColor3f()*s in the program, they are not used. Instead, the OpenGL system uses the current lighting model to calculate the vertex color automatically. We may use *glColorMaterial()* with *glEnable(GL_COLOR_MATERIAL)* to tie the color specified by *glColor3f()* to a material property.

Ambient Component. The ambient intensity of a vertex pixel is calculated as follows:

$$I_{\lambda a} = L_{\lambda a}M_{\lambda a},$$ **(EQ 65)**

where $L_{\lambda a}$ represents the light source's ambient intensity and $M_{\lambda a}$ is the material's ambient property. Ambient color is the overall intensity of multiple reflections generated from a light source in an environment. We do not even care where the light source is as long as it exists. In Example 3.3, according to Equation 65, the calculated RGB color is *(1., 1., 0.)*.

/* Example 3.3.ambient.c: ambient color */

```
init() {
    float white[] = {1., 1., 1., 1.}; // RGBA
    float yellow[] = {1., 1., 0., 1.};

    glEnable(GL_LIGHTING);
    glEnable(GL_LIGHT0); // enable light source zero
    glLightfv(GL_LIGHT0, GL_AMBIENT, white);
    glMaterialfv(GL_FRONT, GL_AMBIENT, yellow);
}
```

Diffuse Component. The diffuse intensity of a vertex pixel is calculated as follows:

$$I_{\lambda d} = L_{\lambda d}M_{\lambda d}(\boldsymbol{n} \bullet \boldsymbol{L}),$$ (EQ 66)

where $L_{\lambda d}$ is the light source's diffuse intensity, $M_{\lambda d}$ is the material's diffuse property, $\boldsymbol{L}$ is the light source direction, and $\boldsymbol{n}$ is the surface normal direction from the pixel, which is a vector perpendicular to the surface. Here the light source is a point generating equal intensity in all directions. Diffuse color is the reflection from a dull surface material that appears equally bright from all viewing directions.

In OpenGL, $\boldsymbol{L}$ is a unit vector (or normalized vector) pointing from the current vertex to the light source position. The normal is specified by *glNormal*() right before we specify the vertex. As shown in Fig. 3.2, $\cos\theta = \dfrac{\boldsymbol{n} \bullet \boldsymbol{L}}{|\boldsymbol{n}|}$, which is between *0* and *1* when θ is between *0°* and *90°*. When θ is greater than *90°*, the diffuse intensity is set to zero.

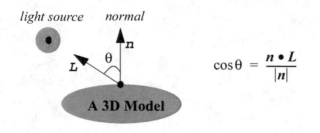

$$\cos\theta = \frac{\boldsymbol{n} \bullet \boldsymbol{L}}{|\boldsymbol{n}|}$$

Fig. 3.2 The angle between L and n at the vertex

The length of the normal is a factor in Equation 66. We can initially specify the normal to be a unit vector. However, normals are transformed similar to vertices so that the lengths of the normals may be scaled. (Actually, normals are transformed by the inverse transpose of the current matrix on the matrix stack.) If we are not sure about the length of the normals, we can call *glEnable(GL_NORMALIZE)*, which enables the OpenGL system to normalize each normal before calculating the lighting. This, however, incurs the extra normalization calculations. Also, the light source position has four parameters: (x, y, z, w) as in homogeneous coordinates. If w is *1*, (x, y, z) is the light source position. If w is *0*, (x, y, z) represents the light source direction at infinity, in which case the light source is in the same direction for all pixels at different locations. If a point light source is far away from the object, it has essentially the same angle with all surfaces that have the same surface normal direction. Example 3.4 shows how to specify the diffuse parameters in OpenGL.

/* Example 3.4.diffuse.c: diffuse light & material components */

```
init()
{
    //xyzw, light source at infinity
    float position[] = {0., 0., 1., 0.};
    float white[] = {1., 1., 1., 1.}; // RGBA

    glEnable(GL_LIGHTING);
    glEnable(GL_NORMALIZE);

    glEnable(GL_LIGHT0);
    glLightfv(GL_LIGHT0, GL_POSITION, position);
    glLightfv(GL_LIGHT0, GL_DIFFUSE, white);

    glMaterialfv(GL_FRONT, GL_DIFFUSE, white);
}


void drawConeSide(float *v1, float *v2, float *v3)
{
    float v11[3], v22[3], v33[3];
    int i;

    for (i=0; i<3; i++) {
        v11[i] = v1[i] + v3[i]; // normal for cone vertex 1
        v22[i] = v2[i] + v3[i]; // normal for cone vertex 2
        v33[i] = v11[i] + v22[i]; // normal for cone vertex 3
    }

    glBegin(GL_TRIANGLES);

        glNormal3fv(v11);
        glVertex3fv(v1);
        glNormal3fv(v22);
        glVertex3fv(v2);
        glNormal3fv(v33);
        glVertex3fv(v3);

    glEnd();
}
```

Object shading depends on how we specify
the normals as well. For example (Fig. 3.3),
if we want to display a pyramid, the
normals for the triangle vertices v1, v2, and
v3 should be the same and perpendicular to
the triangle. If we want to approximate a
cone, the normals should be perpendicular
to the cone's surface. If we assume that the
radius of the cone's base and the height of
the cone have the same length, then the
normals are *n1*=v1+v3, *n2*=v2+v3, and
n3=*n1*+*n2*. Here, the additions are vector

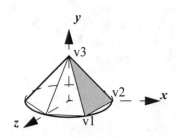

**Fig. 3.3 The radius and the height
of the cone are the same (unit length)**

additions, as in the function *drawConeSide()* in Example 3.4 above. The OpenGL
system interpolates the pixel colors in the triangle. We can set all the vertex normals to
n3 to display a pyramid.

Specular Component. The specular intensity of a vertex pixel is calculated as follows:

$$I_{\lambda s} = L_{\lambda s} M_{\lambda s} \left(\frac{n \bullet (L + V)}{|L + V|} \right)^{shininess}$$

(EQ 67)

where $L_{\lambda s}$ is the light source's specular intensity, $M_{\lambda s}$ is the material's specular
property, V is the view point direction from the pixel, and *shininess* is the material's
shininess property. Specular color is the highlight reflection from a smooth-surface
material that depends on the reflection direction R (which is L reflected along the

normal) and the viewing direction V. As shown in Fig. 3.4, $\cos\alpha = \dfrac{n \bullet (L + V)}{|n||L + V|}$,

which is between 0 and 1 when α is between $0°$ and $90°$. When θ or α is greater than
$90°$, the specular intensity is set to zero. The viewer can see specularly reflected light
from a mirror only when the angle α is close to zero. When the *shininess* is a very

large number, $(\cos\alpha)^{shininess}$ is attenuated towards zero unless $(\cos\alpha)$ equals one.

The view point, as we discussed in the viewing transformation, is at the origin (facing
the negative z axis). We use *glLightModeli(GL_LIGHT_MODEL_LOCAL_VIEWER,
GL_TRUE)* to specify the view point at *(0, 0, 0)*. However, to simplify the lighting
calculation, OpenGL allows us to specify the view point at infinity in the *(0, 0, 1)*

direction. This is the default in the same direction for all vertex pixels. Since this assumption is only used to simplify lighting calculations, the view point is not changed for other graphics calculations, such as projection. Example 3.5 shows how to specify the specular parameters in OpenGL.

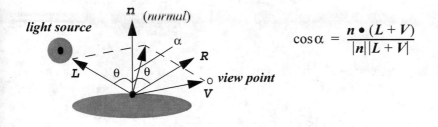

$$\cos\alpha = \frac{n \bullet (L + V)}{|n||L + V|}$$

Fig. 3.4 The angle between n and ($L+V$) at the vertex

/* Example 3.5.specular.c: specular light & material components */

```
init() {
    float position[] = {0., 0., 1., 0.};
    float white[] = {1., 1., 1., 1.}; // RGBA

    glEnable(GL_LIGHTING);
    glEnable(GL_NORMALIZE);

    glEnable(GL_LIGHT0);
    glLightfv(GL_LIGHT0, GL_POSITION, position);
    glLightfv(GL_LIGHT0, GL_SPECULAR, white);

    glMaterialfv(GL_FRONT, GL_SPECULAR, white);
    glMaterialf(GL_FRONT, GL_SHININESS, 50.0);
}
```

3.3.2 OpenGL Lighting Model

Both the light source and the material have multiple components: ambient, diffuse, and specular. The final vertex color is an integration of all these components:

$$I_\lambda = I_{\lambda e} + I_{\lambda a} + I_{\lambda d} + I_{\lambda s}.$$ **(EQ 68)**

We can simplify Equation 68 as:

$$I_\lambda = I_{\lambda e} + I_{\lambda L},$$

(EQ 69)

where $I_{\lambda L} = I_{\lambda a} + I_{\lambda d} + I_{\lambda s}$. While ambient, diffuse, and specular intensities depend on the light source, emissive intensity does not. OpenGL scales and normalizes the final intensity to a value between 0 and 1.

In previous examples, even though we didn't specify all the components, OpenGL used the default values that are predefined. If necessary, we can specify all different lighting components (Example 3.6). Fig. 3.5 is a comparison among the different lighting component effects from the examples we have discussed.

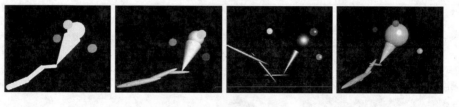

Example 3.3:	*Example 3.4:*	*Example 3.5:*	*Example 3.6:*
Ambient/Emissive	**Diffuse**	**Specular**	**Multiple components**

Fig. 3.5 The OpenGL lighting components and integration

/* **Example 3.6.materials.c: multiple light and material components** */

```
init() {

    float position[] = {0., 0., 1., 0.};
    float white[] = {1., 1., 1., 1.};
    float whitish[] = {.7, .7, .7, 1.};
    float black[] = {0., 0., 0., 1.};
    float blackish[] = {.2, .2, .2, 1.};

    glEnable(GL_LIGHTING);
    glEnable(GL_NORMALIZE);
    glEnable(GL_LIGHT0);
```

```
glLightfv(GL_LIGHT0, GL_POSITION, position);
glLightfv(GL_LIGHT0, GL_AMBIENT, whitish);
glLightfv(GL_LIGHT0, GL_DIFFUSE, white);
glLightfv(GL_LIGHT0, GL_SPECULAR, white);

glMaterialfv(GL_FRONT, GL_AMBIENT, blackish);
glMaterialfv(GL_FRONT, GL_DIFFUSE, whitish);
glMaterialfv(GL_FRONT, GL_SPECULAR, white);
glMaterialf(GL_FRONT, GL_SHININESS, 100.0);

}
```

Movable Light Source. In OpenGL, a light source is invisible. If the light source is directional at infinity with $w=0$, it is always fixed. Otherwise, the light source position is transformed as a geometric object by the current matrix when it is specified. In other words, if the matrix is modified at run time, the light source can be moved around like an object. Lighting is calculated according to the transformed position. To simulate a visible light source, we can specify the light source and draw an object at the same position. As in Example 3.7, the light source and the sphere are transformed by the same matrix. We may specify the sphere's emission property to correspond to the light source's parameters, so that the sphere looks like the light source.

/* Example 3.7.movelight.c: movable light source */

```
void drawSolar(float M, float m)
{
    float position[] = {0., 0., 0., 1.};

    glPushMatrix();

        // the moon rotates around the earth
        glRotatef(m, 0., 1., 0.);

        glTranslatef(M, 0., 0.);

        glLightfv(GL_LIGHT0, GL_POSITION, position);

        // the center of the sphere is at the origin
        drawSphere();

    glPopMatrix();

}
```

Spotlight Effect. A real light source may not generate equal intensity in all directions:

$$I_\lambda = I_{\lambda e} + f_{spot} I_{\lambda L} \qquad \text{(EQ 70)}$$

where f_{spot} is called the *spotlight effect factor*. In OpenGL, it is calculated as follows:

$$f_{spot} = (-L \bullet D_{spot})^{spotExp} \qquad \text{(EQ 71)}$$

where (**-L**) is a unit vector pointing from the light source to the vertex pixel, D_{spot} is the direction of the light source, and *spotExp* is a specified constant. As shown in Fig. 3.6, $\cos\gamma = \dfrac{(-L) \bullet D_{spot}}{|D_{spot}|}$. When the *spotExp* is a large number, $(\cos\gamma)^{spotExp}$ is attenuated towards zero and the light is concentrated along the D_{spot} direction.

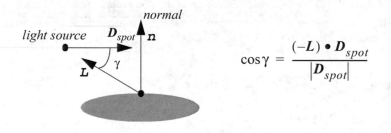

$$\cos\gamma = \frac{(-L) \bullet D_{spot}}{|D_{spot}|}$$

Fig. 3.6 The angle between (**-L**) and D_{spot}

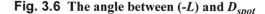

The light source may have a *cutoff angle* as shown in Fig. 3.7, so that only the vertex pixels inside the cone area are lit. There is no light outside the cone area. To be exact, the cone area is infinite in the D_{spot} direction without a bottom.

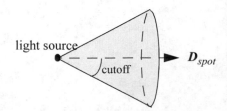

Example 3.8 shows how to specify spotlight parameters. The D_{spot} direction vector is **Fig. 3.7 The light source cutoff angl**
also transformed by the current modelview matrix, as the vertex normals.

/* **Example 3.8.spotlight.c: spotlight effect** */

```
void drawSolar(float M, float m)
{
    float position[] = {0., 0., 0., 1.};
    float spot_direction[] = {-1., 0., 0., 1.};

    glPushMatrix();
        // "Moon" rotating around the "Earth"
        glRotatef(m, 0.0, 1.0, 0.);
        glTranslatef(M, 0., 0.);

        glLightf(GL_LIGHT0,GL_SPOT_CUTOFF,30.0);
        glLightfv(GL_LIGHT0,GL_SPOT_DIRECTION,spot_direction);
        glLightf(GL_LIGHT0,GL_SPOT_EXPONENT,2.0);
        glLightfv(GL_LIGHT0, GL_POSITION, position);

        drawSphere();
    glPopMatrix();
}
```

Light Source Attenuation. The intensity from a point light source to a vertex pixel can be attenuated by the distance the light travels:

$$I_\lambda = I_{\lambda e} + f_{att}f_{spot}I_{\lambda L},$$ (EQ 72)

where f_{att} is called the *light source attenuation factor*. In OpenGL, f_{att} is calculated as follows:

$$f_{att} = \frac{1}{A_c + A_l d_L + A_q d_L^2},$$ (EQ 73)

where d_L is the distance from the point light source to the lit vertex pixel, A_c, A_l, and A_q are constant, linear, and quadratic attenuation factors. Example 3.9 shows how to specify these factors.

/* **Example 3.9.attlight.c: light source attenuation effect** */

```
void drawSolar(float M, float m)
{
    float position[] = {0., 0., 0., 1.};

    glPushMatrix();
        // moon rotate around the "earth"
        glRotatef(m, 0.0, 1.0, 0.);
        glTranslatef(M, 0., 0.);
        glLightf(GL_LIGHT0,GL_CONSTANT_ATTENUATION, 1.0);
        glLightf(GL_LIGHT0,GL_LINEAR_ATTENUATION,0.0002);
        glLightf(GL_LIGHT0,GL_QUADRATIC_ATTENUATION,0.0001);
        glLightfv(GL_LIGHT0, GL_POSITION, position);
        drawSphere(position);
    glPopMatrix();
}
```

Multiple Light Sources. We can also specify multiple light sources:

$$I_\lambda = I_{\lambda e} + \sum_{i=0}^{k-1} f_{atti} f_{spoti} I_{\lambda Li}, \qquad \text{(EQ 74)}$$

where k is the number of different light sources. Each light source's parameters and position can be specified differently. There may be fixed as well as moving light sources with different properties. The emission component, which is a material property, does not depend on any light source. We can also use *glLightModel()* to specify a global ambient light that does not depend on any light source. Fig. 3.8 is a comparison among the different lighting component effects from the examples we have discussed.

/* Example 3.10.lights.c: fixed and multiple moving light sources */

```
init() {
    float position[] = {0., 0., 1., 0.};

    glEnable(GL_LIGHTING);
    glEnable(GL_NORMALIZE);
    glEnable(GL_CULL_FACE);
    glEnable(GL_LIGHT0);
    glEnable(GL_LIGHT1);
    glEnable(GL_LIGHT2);
```

```
glEnable(GL_LIGHT3);
...
// fixed light source
glLightfv(GL_LIGHT0, GL_POSITION, position);

// lights 1, 2, and 3 are specified as local
//      and movable positions
}
```

| *Example 3.7:* **Moving light source** | *Example 3.8:* **Spotlight effect** | *Example 3.9:* **Light source attenuation** | *Example 3.10:* **Multiple light sources** |

Fig. 3.8 The OpenGL light sources: moving, spotlight, and attenuation

3.4 Visible-Surface Shading

Shading models are methods for calculating the lighting of a surface instead of just one vertex or point pixel. As we discussed, OpenGL provides flat shading and smooth shading for polygonal surfaces. A polygon on a surface is also called a *face*. We will discuss some issues related to improving the efficiency and quality of face shading.

3.4.1 Back-Face Culling

We can speed up drawing by eliminating some of the hidden surfaces before rendering. Given a solid object such as a polygonal sphere, we can see only half of the faces. The visible faces are called *front-facing* polygons or *front faces*, and the invisible faces are called *back-facing* polygons or *back faces*. The invisible back faces should be eliminated from processing as early as possible, even before the z-buffer algorithm is called. The z-buffer algorithm, as discussed in Section 2.3.3 on page 45, needs significant hardware calculations. Eliminating back-facing polygons before rendering is called *back-face culling*.

In OpenGL, if the order of the polygon vertices is counter-clockwise from the view point, the polygon is front-facing (Fig. 3.9). Otherwise, it is back-facing. We use *glEnable(GL_CULL_FACE)* to turn on culling and call *glCullFace(GL_BACK)* to achieve back-face culling. Therefore, if we use back-face culling, we should make sure that the order of the vertices are correct when we specify a face by a list of vertices. Otherwise, we will see some holes (missing faces) on the surface displayed. Also, as in

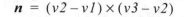

$$n = (v2 - v1) \times (v3 - v2)$$

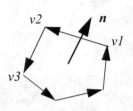

Fig. 3.9 A front face and its norma

the following function (Example 3.10), we often use the cross product of two edge vectors of a face to find its normal **n**. An edge vector is calculated by the difference of two neighbor vertices. The correctness of the surface normal depends on the correct order and direction of the edge vectors in the cross product, which in turn depend on the correct order of the vertices as well. The faces that have normals facing the wrong direction will not be shaded correctly.

```
void drawBottom(float *v1, float *v2, float *v3){
    // normal to the cone or cylinder bottom
    float v12[3], v23[3], vb[3];
    int i;

    for (i=0; i<3; i++) { // two edge vectors
        v12[i] = v2[i] - v1[i];
        v23[i] = v3[i] - v2[i];
    }

    // vb = normalized cross prod. of v12 X v23
    ncrossprod(v12, v23, vb);
    glBegin(GL_TRIANGLES);
        glNormal3fv(vb);
        glVertex3fv(v1); glVertex3fv(v2); glVertex3fv(v3);
    glEnd();
}
```

Given a hollow box or cylinder without a cover, we will see both front and back faces. In this case, we cannot use back-face culling. We may turn on lighting for both front and back faces: *glLightModeli(GL_LIGHT_MODEL_TWO_SIDE, TRUE)*. If we turn on two-side lighting, each polygon has two sides with opposite normals and OpenGL will decide to shade the side that the normal is facing the view point. We may also supply different material properties for both the front-facing polygons and the back-facing polygons: *glMaterialfv(GL_FRONT, GL_AMBIENT, red); glMaterialfv(GL_BACK, GL_AMBIENT, green)* .

3.4.2 Polygon Shading Models

The appearances of a surface under different shading models differ greatly. Flat shading, which is the simplest and fastest, is used to display a flat-face object instead of a curved-face object. In approximating a curved surface, using flat shading with a finer polygon mesh turns out to be ineffective and slow. Smooth shading (also called Gouraud shading), which calculates the colors of the vertex pixels and interpolates the colors of every other pixel in a polygon, is often used to approximate the shading of a curved face. In OpenGL, we can use *glShadeModel(GL_FLAT)* or *glShadeModel(GL_SMOOTH)* to choose between the two different shading models (flat shading and smooth shading), and the shadings are calculated by the OpenGL system. In OpenGL, the vertex normals are specified at the programmer's discernment. To eliminate intensity discontinuities, the normal of a vertex is often calculated by averaging the normals of the faces sharing the vertex on the surface. In general, we try to specify a vertex normal that is perpendicular to the curved surface instead of the polygon. Also, we may specify normals in the directions we prefer in order to achieve special effects.

Here we present an example to demonstrate how Gouraud shading is achieved. As shown in Fig. 3.10, the light source and the viewpoint are both at P, the normal N_A is parallel to CP that is perpendicular to AE, N_E is pointing toward P, ABCDEP is in a plane, and AP=EP=2CP. We can calculate the colors at A and E using a given lighting model, such as Equation 74 on page 84. Then, we can interpolate and find the colors for all pixels on

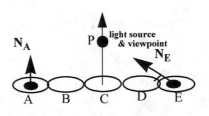

Fig. 3.10 Shading calculations

the line. For example, let's calculate an intensity according to the following lighting model (which includes only diffuse and specular components):

$$I = \frac{n \bullet L + \left(\dfrac{n \bullet (L + V)}{|L + V|}\right)^2}{2}.$$

(EQ 75)

Then,

$$I_A = \frac{N_A \bullet \overrightarrow{AP} + \left(\dfrac{N_A \bullet (\overrightarrow{AP} + \overrightarrow{AP})}{|\overrightarrow{AP} + \overrightarrow{AP}|}\right)^2}{2} = \frac{\cos 60^o + (\cos 60^o)^2}{2} = \frac{3}{8},$$

(EQ 76)

$$I_E = \frac{N_E \bullet \overrightarrow{EP} + \left(\dfrac{N_E \bullet (\overrightarrow{EP} + \overrightarrow{EP})}{|\overrightarrow{EP} + \overrightarrow{EP}|}\right)^2}{2} = \frac{\cos 0^o + (\cos 0^o)^2}{2} = 1,$$

(EQ 77)

and

$$\Delta I = \frac{I_E - I_A}{N - 1} = \frac{1 - \dfrac{3}{8}}{5 - 1} = \frac{5}{32}.$$

(EQ 78)

According to the Gouraud shading method, with the intensities at A and B, the intensities at B, C, and D can be calculated, respectively:

$$I_B = I_A + \Delta I = \frac{3}{8} + \frac{5}{32} = \frac{17}{32},$$

(EQ 79)

$$I_C = I_B + \Delta I = \frac{17}{32} + \frac{5}{32} = \frac{11}{16},$$

(EQ 80)

$$I_D = I_C + \Delta I = \frac{11}{16} + \frac{5}{32} = \frac{27}{32}. \qquad \text{(EQ 81)}$$

Another popular shading model, the normal-vector interpolation shading (called Phong shading), calculates the normals of the vertex pixels and interpolates the normals of all other pixels in a polygon. Then, the color of every pixel is calculated using a lighting model and the interpolated normals. Phong shading is much slower than Gouraud shading and therefore is not implemented in the OpenGL system.

For example, we use the same example and lighting model as shown in Fig. 3.10 to demonstrate Phong shading. First we calculate the normals through interpolations:

$$\Delta N = \frac{N_E - N_A}{N - 1} = \frac{0 - 60^o}{5 - 1} = 15^o \qquad \text{(EQ 82)}$$

Therefore,

$$N_B = N_A + \Delta N = 60^o - 15^o = 45^o, \qquad \text{(EQ 83)}$$

$$N_C = N_B + \Delta N = 45^o - 15^o = 30^o, \qquad \text{(EQ 84)}$$

$$N_D = N_C + \Delta N = 30^o - 15^o = 15^o. \qquad \text{(EQ 85)}$$

Then, all the pixel intensities are calculated by the lighting model:

$$I_B = \frac{N_B \bullet \overrightarrow{BP} + \left(\frac{N_B \bullet (\overrightarrow{BP} + \overrightarrow{BP})}{|\overrightarrow{BP} + \overrightarrow{BP}|} \right)^2}{2} = \frac{\cos 45^o + (\cos 45^o)^2}{2} = 0.604 \qquad \text{(EQ 86)}$$

$$I_C = \frac{N_C \bullet \overrightarrow{CP} + \left(\dfrac{N_B \bullet (\overrightarrow{CP} + \overrightarrow{CP})}{|\overrightarrow{CP} + \overrightarrow{CP}|}\right)^2}{2} = \frac{\cos 30^o + (\cos 30^o)^2}{2} = 0.808 \quad \textbf{(EQ 87)}$$

$$I_D = \frac{N_D \bullet \overrightarrow{DP} + \left(\dfrac{N_B \bullet (\overrightarrow{DP} + \overrightarrow{DP})}{|\overrightarrow{DP} + \overrightarrow{DP}|}\right)^2}{2} = \frac{\cos 15^o + (\cos 15^o)^2}{2} = 0.949 \quad \textbf{(EQ 88)}$$

Phong shading allows specular highlights to be located in a polygon, whereas Gouraud shading does not. In contrast, if a highlight is within a polygon, smooth shading will fail to show it, because the intensity interpolation makes it such that the highest intensity is only possible at a vertex. Also, if we have a spotlight source and the vertices fall outside the cutoff angle, smooth shading will not calculate the vertex colors and thus the polygon will not be shaded. You may have noticed that when the sphere subdivisions are not enough, lighting toward the sphere with a small cutoff angle may not show up.

All of the above shading models are approximations. Using polygons to approximate curved faces is much faster than handling curved surfaces directly. The efficiency of polygon rendering is still the benchmark of graphics systems. In order to achieve better realism, we may calculate each surface pixel's color directly without using interpolations. However, calculating the lighting of every pixel on a surface is in general very time consuming.

3.4.3 Ray Tracing and Radiosity

Ray tracing and *radiosity* are advanced global lighting and rendering models that achieve better realism, which are not provided in OpenGL. They are time-consuming methods so that no practical real-time animation is possible with the current graphics hardware. Here we only introduce the general concepts.

Ray tracing is an extension to the lighting model we learned. The light rays travel from the light sources to the viewpoint. The simplest ray tracing method is to follow the rays in reverse from the viewpoint to the light sources. A ray is sent from the viewpoint through a pixel on the projection plane to the scene to calculate the lighting of that pixel. If we simply use the lighting model (Equation 74) once, we would produce a similar image as if we use the OpenGL lighting directly without ray tracing. Instead, ray tracing accounts for the global specular reflections among objects and calculates the ray's recursive intersections that include reflective bounces and refractive transmissions. Lighting is calculated at each point of intersection. The final pixel color is an accumulation of all fractions of intensity values from the bottom up. At any point of intersection, three lighting components are calculated and added together: current intensity, reflection, and transmission.

The current intensity of a point is calculated using the lighting method we learned already, except that we may take shadows into consideration. Rays (named feeler rays or shadow rays) are fired from the point under consideration to the light sources to decide the point's current intensity using Equation 74. If an object is between the point and a light source, the point under consideration will not be affected by the blocked light source directly, so the corresponding shadows will be generated.

The reflection and transmission components at the point are calculated by recursive calls following the reflected ray and transmitted ray (Fig. 3.11). For example, we can modify Equation 74:

$$I_\lambda = I_{\lambda e} + \sum_{i=0}^{k-1} f_{atti} f_{spoti} I_{\lambda Li} + I_{\lambda r} + I_{\lambda t}, \qquad \text{(EQ 89)}$$

where $I_{\lambda r}$ accounts for the reflected light component, and $I_{\lambda t}$ accounts for the transmitted light component, as shown in Fig. 3.11.

The reflection component $I_{\lambda r}$ is a specular component, which is calculated recursively by applying Equation 89. Here, we assume that the "viewpoint" is the starting point of the reflected ray R and the point under consideration is the end point of R:

$$I_{\lambda r} = M_{\lambda s} I_\lambda, \qquad \text{(EQ 90)}$$

where $M_{\lambda s}$ is the "viewpoint" material's specular property. The transmission component $I_{\lambda t}$ is calculated similarly:

$$I_{\lambda t} = M_{\lambda t} I_\lambda,$$

(EQ 91)

where $M_{\lambda t}$ is the "viewpoint" material's transmission coefficient.

The recursion terminates when a user-defined depth is achieved where further reflections and transmissions are omitted, or when the reflected and transmitted rays don't hit objects. Computing the intersections of the ray with the objects and the normals at the intersections is the major part of a ray tracing program, which may take hidden-surface removal, refractive transparency, and shadows into its implementation considerations.

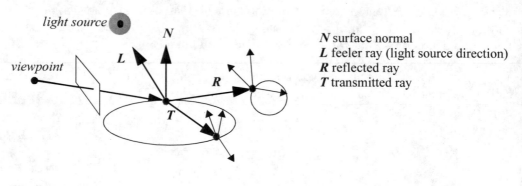

N surface normal
L feeler ray (light source direction)
R reflected ray
T transmitted ray

Fig. 3.11 Recursive ray tracing

As an example, we discuss details of implementing a recursive raytracing, which is the simplest case.

1. First we initial light sources, spheres, and two planes;

2. We specify a view point on *z* axis: viewpt(0, 0, z0);

3. For each pixel on the screen raypt(x, y, 0), we fire a ray from viewpt to raypt, which is a vector in the direction from viewpt to raypt;

4. rayTracing(color, viewpt, raypt, depth) is a recursive function that bounces "depth" times along viewpt to raypt, returning a final color, which is the result of the ray tracing;

5. intersect(vpt, rpt, p, n) will find the closest intersection of the ray (vpt, rpt) with an object. If there is no intersection, a null normal will return. Otherwise, the intersection point p and the normal will return, so that the point and normal are used to calculate lighting according to a lighting model. We can calculate the intersection of the ray with the spheres and the planes as follows. Given the parametric line equation represented as:

$$y = vpt_y + t(rpt_y - vpt_y) \qquad \text{(EQ 92)}$$

and plane equation as:

$$y = yPlane \qquad \text{(EQ 93)}$$

We can solve Equation 92 and Equation 93 to find the parameter t at which the ray intersects with the plane. When $t=0$, the ray starts at vpt. When $t>0$, the ray fires from vpt in the direction of rpt. Therefore, $t>0$ if there is an intersection.

Similarly, for a sphere as follows:

$$(x - x_0)^2 + (y - y_0)^2 + (z - z_0)^2 = r^2 \qquad \text{(EQ 94)}$$

We can put Equation 92 (with x and z similar equations) into Equation 94 to find t at which the ray intersects with the sphere. In this case, Quadratic Formula will be used to find the roots. For a quarterback equation:

$$at^2 + bt + c = 0, \qquad \text{(EQ 95)}$$

if ($b^2 - 4ac \geq 0$), there are likely two roots in the solutions:

$$t = \frac{-b \pm \sqrt{b^2 - 4ac}}{2a}. \qquad \text{(EQ 96)}$$

We should use the smaller $t>0$, which is the closer intersection with the ray.

6. After finding the intersection point, the point and the normal of the point's corresponding object at the point are returned. We then use phong(color, p, vD, n) to find the lighting of the point according to the light sources and the point normal using the shading model as we discussed earlier in Equation 74.

7. The reflected ray is used as one step further recursive ray tracing. The process is the same as from Step 2 to Step 6, except that vpt is now the current intersection point, rpt is now a reflection point from the vpt along the normal. Given a ray *A* and a normalized normal *n*, the reflected ray *B = 2n(n•A) - A*. The final color is the current color added with the accumulated reflected color.

A snapshot of rendering results is shown in Fig. 3.12. Here only reflected ray and feeler ray are considered. There is no transmitted ray calculation.

As we can see, the edges of the spheres are not smooth because the intersections are based on discrete pixel locations. The aliasing artifacts in ray tracing can be alleviated by tracing multiple rays around the center of a pixel, which is known as supersampling. Here we generate random rays around the center of a pixel, which is called stochastic sampling. The final pixel color is the average of the results of supersampling. A snapshot of rendering results is shown in Fig. 3.13.

Fig. 3.12 **Recursive ray tracing with aliasing problems**

Fig. 3.13 Ray tracing with stochastic sampling

Adaptive sampling is one of the supersampling methods. For example, we can trace four rays from the pixel square corners. If the intensity of one of the rays is significantly different from the other three, then the pixel is split into four rectangular portions for further sampling. This process repeats until a threshold is satisfied. Stochastic sampling is another antialiasing method used in ray tracing. Instead of firing rays with regular patterns, a stochastic distribution of rays within a pixel are fired to generate multiple samples, which are then put together to generate the final pixel color. In general, supersampling is a time consuming approximate method, but the method alleviates aliasing problems.

Radiosity assumes that each small area or patch is an emissive as well as reflective light source. The method is based on thermal energy radiosity. We need to break up the environment into small discrete patches that emit and reflect light uniformly in the entire area. Also, we need to calculate the fraction of the energy that leaves from a patch and arrives at another, taking into account the shape and orientation of both patches. The shading of a patch is a summation of its own emission and all the emissions from other patches that reach the patch. The finer the patches, the better the results are at the expense of longer calculations.

Although both ray tracing and radiosity can be designed to account for all lighting components, ray tracing is viewpoint dependent, which is better for specular appearance, and radiosity is viewpoint independent, which is better for diffuse appearance. Currently, raytracing and radiosity are mostly used to achieve stunning visual appearance for entertainment.

3.5 Review Questions

1. Which of the following statements is correct:

a. RGB are subtractive primaries.

c. CMY are the complements of RGB.

b. CMY are additive primaries.

d. RGB are color inks in printers.

2. An RGB mode 512*512 frame buffer has 24 bits per pixel.

What is the total memory size needed in bits?   (   )

How many distinct color choices are available?   (   )

How many different colors can be displayed in a frame? (   )

3. An index mode 1280*1024 frame buffer has 8 bits per entry. The color look-up table (CLT) has 24 bits per entry.

What is the total memory size (frame buffer+CLT) in bits? (   )

How many distinct color choices are available?   (   )

How many different colors can be displayed in a frame? (   )

4. An index display has 2 bits per pixel and a look-up table with 6 bits per entry (2 bits for R, G, and B, respectively). We scan-converted an object as shown in the frame buffer: a 5-pixel blue horizontal line, a 3-pixel green vertical line, and two red pixels. The rest are black. Please provide the pixel values in the frame buffer.

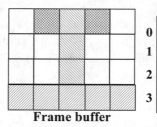

Frame buffer

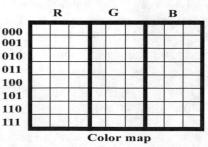

Color look-up table

5. An index raster display has 3 bits per pixel and a color look-up table (color map) with 9 bits per entry (3 bits each for R, G, and B, respectively). We want to load the color map for scan-converting a grayscale object. Assuming the index in the frame buffer corresponds to the intensity, please load the complete color map.

000
001
010
011
100
101
110
111

Color map

6. Which of the following statements is WRONG?

a. Our eyes are sensitive to ratios of intensity.

b. Our eyes average fine detail of the overall intensity.

c. Our eyes have constant sensitivity to all colors.

d. Some colors cannot be generated on an RGB display device.

7. Given the vertex (pixel) colors of the triangle as specified, please use interpolation to find the pixel color in the middle (specified as bold).

Color = (_____ , _____ , _____)

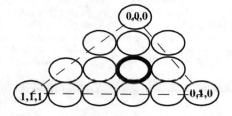

8. About a movable light source, which of the following is correct about its location?

    a. It should be specified at its physical location.
    b. It should be visible once it is specified.
    c. It should be specified at infinity in the direction of its physical location.
    d. It is used for lighting calculation at its specified location.

9. The vertex normals ($N = N_A = N_B = N_C$) are perpendicular to the triangle. The light source L is making $30°$ angle with N_A, N_B, and N_C. The viewpoint V is at infinite in the direction of N, the normal of the triangle. Please use Gouraud shading and Phong shading to find the pixel color in the middle (specified as bold).
Reminder: $I_\lambda = [1 + (N \cdot L) + (R \cdot V)^3]/3$, where λ is R, G, or B; N, L, R, and V are all normalized.

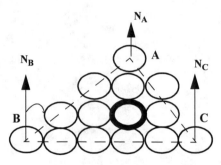

Gouraud shading = (_____ , _____ , _____)

Phong shading = (_____ , _____ , _____)

10. The light source (P) & the viewpoint (V) are at the same position as in the figure, which is right in the normal of vertex C. The vertex normals of triangle ABC are in the same direction perpendicular to the triangle. Angle VAC = 30 degree. Angle VBC = 45 degree. Please use the following equation to calculate the intensities of the vertices, and use interpolation to find the pixel intensity in the middle (specified as bold).

Reminder: $I = [1 + (N \cdot L) + (R \cdot V)^2]/3$, where N is the normal direction, L is the light source direction, R is the reflection direction, and V is the viewpoint direction from the vertex in consideration. All vectors are normalized vectors.

a. $N_A \cdot L_A =$ _____ ; $R_A \cdot V_A =$ _____ ;

b. Intensity A = _____ ; B = _____ ; C = _____

c. Intensity at the bold pixel = _____

11. In an OpenGL program, we have a local light source with a small cutoff angle facing the center of a triangle. However, we cannot see any light on the triangle. Which of the following is least likely the problem?

    a. The light source is too close to the triangle.   b. The cutoff angle is too small.
    c. The triangle is too small.   d. The normals of the vertices are facing the wrong direction.

12. *Light source attenuation* is calculated according to the distance?

    a. from the viewpoint to the pixel   b. from the pixel to the light source
    c. from the light to the origin   d. from the origin to the viewpoint
    e. from the pixel to the origin   f. from the origin to the pixel

---

13. drawtriangle() on the right draws a piece on the side of the cone. The normals are specified wrong. If the radius equals the height of the cone, which of the following is correct for the normal of v1?

    a. glNormal3fv(normalize(v1+v2));
    b. glNormal3fv(normalize(v1+v3));
    c. glNormal3fv(normalize(v2+v3));
    d. glNormal3fv(normalize(v1));
    (here "+" is a vector operator)

```
void drawtriangle(float *v1, float *v2, float *v3)
{
    glBegin(GL_TRIANGLES);
    glNormal3fv(v1);
    glVertex3fv(v1);
    glNormal3fv(v2);
    glVertex3fv(v2);
    glNormal3fv(v3);
    glVertex3fv(v3);
    glEnd();
}
```

14. **Given a triangle as shown below. Please find the normal that is perpendicular to the cone's surface at v1.**

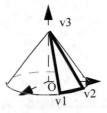

a) $(v2 - v1) \times (v3 - v1)$

b) $v2 \times v1$

c) $(v3 \times v1) \times (v3 - v1)$

d) $(v2 \times v1) \times (v3 - v1)$

e) $(v2 \times v1) \times (v2 - v1)$

15. **In OpenGL, normals are transformed with the associated vertices. Prove that normals are transformed by the inverse transpose of the matrix that transforms the corresponding vertices.**

16. **The light source(P) is at the position as in the figure, which is right in the normal of vertex C. The view point is at infinity in the direction of the normal C. The vertex normals of triangle ABC are in the same direction. Angle PAC = 45 degree. Angle PBC = 45 degree. Please use the following equation to calculate the intensities of the pixel intensity in the middle using Gouraud shading and Phong shading (specified as bold).** `Reminder:` $I = [1 + max(N \cdot L, 0) + (max(R \cdot V, 0))^2]/3$, **where N is the normal direction, L is the light source direction, R is the reflection direction, and V is the viewpoint direction from the vertex in consideration. All vectors are normalized vectors.**

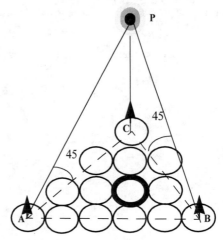

a) Gouraud shading at the bold pixel =

_____

b) Phong shading at the bold pixel = _____

17. **In the recursive ray tracing, please associate the following:**

feeler ray (__)   1. refraction
reflected ray (__)   2. shadow
transmitted ray (__)   3. final result
color   (__)   4. $B = 2n(n \cdot A) - A$

3.6 Programming Assignments

1. Make the cone, cylinder, and sphere three different movable light sources pointing toward the center of the earth in the previous problem in the past chapter. The light sources are bouncing back and forth with collision detection. Design your own light source and material properties.

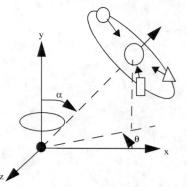

2. Modify the above program with multiple viewports. Each viewport demonstrates one lighting property of your choice. For example, we can demonstrate light source attenuation interactively as follows: turn on just one light source and gradually move it away from the earth. When the lighting is dim, move it toward the earth.

3. Implement a OpenGL smooth-shading environment that has a sphere, box, and cone on a plane. You can specify the light source and materials of your own.

4. Implement a Phong-shading and a corresponding ray-tracing environment that has a sphere, box, cylinder, and cone on a plane with adaptive sampling. You can specify the light source and materials of your own.

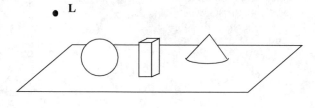

4
Blending and Texture Mapping

Chapter objectives:

- Understand OpenGL blending to achieve transparency, antialiasing, and fog
- Use images for rendering directly or for texture mapping
- Understand OpenGL texture mapping programs

4.1 Blending

Given two color components $I_{\lambda1}$ and $I_{\lambda2}$, the blending of the two values is an interpolation between the two:

$$I_\lambda = \alpha I_{\lambda1} + (1 - \alpha)I_{\lambda2} \qquad \text{(EQ 97)}$$

where α is called the alpha blending factor, and λ is R, G, B, or A. Transparency is achieved by blending. Given two transparent polygons, every pixel color is a blending of the corresponding points on the two polygons along the projection line.

In OpenGL, without blending, each pixel will overwrite the corresponding value in the frame buffer during scan-conversion. In contrast, when blending is enabled, the current pixel color component (namely the source $I_{\lambda1}$) is blended with the corresponding pixel color component already in the frame buffer (namely the destination $I_{\lambda2}$). The blending function is an extension of Equation 97:

$$I_\lambda = B_1 I_{\lambda1} + B_2 I_{\lambda2} \qquad \text{(EQ 98)}$$

J.X. Chen, *Guide to Graphics Software Tools*, doi: 10.1007/978-1-84800-901-1_4,
© Springer-Verlag London Limited 2008

where B_1 and B_2 are the source and destination blending factors, respectively.

The blending factors are decided by the function: *glBlendFunc(B1, B2)* where *B1* and *B2* are predefined constants to indicate how to compute B_1 and B_2, respectively. As in Example 4.1 (Fig. 4.1), *B1* = *GL_SRC_ALPHA* indicates that the source blending factor is the source color's alpha value, which is the A in the source pixel's RGBA. That is, B_1 = A, and *B2* = *GL_ONE_MINUS_SRC_ALPHA* indicates that B_2 = 1-A. When we specify a color directly, or specify a material property in lighting, we now specify and use the alpha value as well. In Example

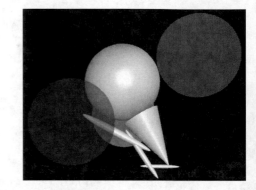

Fig. 4.1 Transparent spheres

4.1, when we specify the material properties, we choose A=0.3 to represent the material's transparency property. Here, if we choose A=0.0, the material is completely transparent. If A=1.0, the material is opaque.

/* Example 4.1.blending.c: transparent spheres */

```
void drawSolar(float E, float e, float M, float m)
{
    float red[] = {1., 0., 0., .3};

    drawSphere(); // opaque sphere
    glEnable (GL_BLEND);
    glBlendFunc (GL_SRC_ALPHA, GL_ONE_MINUS_SRC_ALPHA);
    glMaterialfv(GL_FRONT, GL_AMBIENT, red);
    drawSphere(); // transparent sphere
    glDisable (GL_BLEND);
}
```

4.1.1 OpenGL Blending Factors

Example 4.1 chooses the alpha blending factor as in Equation 97, which is a special case. OpenGL provides more constants to indicate how to compute the source or destination blending factors through *glBlendFunc()*.

If the source and destination colors are (R_s, G_s, B_s, A_s) and (R_d, G_d, B_d, A_d) and the source (src) and destination (dst) blending factors are (S_r, S_g, S_b, S_a) and (D_r, D_g, D_b, D_a), then the final RGBA value in the frame buffer is $(R_sS_r+R_dD_r, G_sS_g+G_dD_g, B_sS_b+B_dD_b, A_sS_a+A_dD_a)$. Each component is eventually clamped to $[0,1]$. The predefined constants to indicate how to compute (S_r, S_g, S_b, S_a) and (D_r, D_g, D_b, D_a) are as follows:

Constant	Relevant Factor	Computed Blend Factor
GL_ZERO	src or dst	$(0, 0, 0, 0)$
GL_ONE	src or dst	$(1, 1, 1, 1)$
GL_DST_COLOR	src	(R_d, G_d, B_d, A_d)
GL_SRC_COLOR	dst	(R_s, G_s, B_s, A_s)
GL_ONE_MINUS_DST_COLOR	src	$(1,1,1,1) - (R_d, G_d, B_d, A_d)$
GL_ONE_MINUS_SRC_COLOR	dst	$(1,1,1,1) - (R_s, G_s, B_s, A_s)$
GL_SRC_ALPHA	src or dst	(A_s, A_s, A_s, A_s)
GL_ONE_MINUS_SRC_ALPHA	src or dst	$(1,1,1,1) - (A_s, A_s, A_s, A_s)$
GL_DST_ALPHA	src or dst	(A_d, A_d, A_d, A_d)
GL_ONE_MINUS_DST_ALPHA	src or dst	$(1,1,1,1) - (A_d, A_d, A_d, A_d)$
GL_SRC_ALPHA_SATURATE	src	$(f,f,f,1)$; $f=\min(A_s, 1-A_d)$

Depending on how we choose the blending factors and other parameters, we can achieve different effects of transparency, antialiasing, and fog, which will be discussed later.

OpenGL blending achieves nonrefractive transparency. The blended points are along the projection line. In other words, the light ray passing through the transparent surfaces is not bent. Refractive transparency, which needs to take the geometrical and optical properties into consideration, is significantly more time consuming. Refractive transparency is often integrated with ray tracing.

4.1.2 Transparency and Hidden-Surface Removal

It is fairly complex to achieve the correct transparency through blending if we have multiple transparent layers, since the order of blending of these layers matters. As in Equation 98, the source and the destination parameters are changed if we switch the order of drawing two polygons. We would like to blend the corresponding transparent points on the surfaces in the order of their distances to the view point. However, this requires keeping track of the distances for all points on the different surfaces, which we avoid doing because of time and memory requirements.

If we enabled the depth-buffer (z-buffer) in OpenGL, obscured polygons may not be used for blending. To avoid this problem, while drawing transparent polygons, we may make the depth buffer read-only. Also, we should draw opaque objects first, and then enable blending to draw transparent objects. This causes the transparent polygons' depth values to be compared to the values established by the opaque polygons, and blending factors to be specified by the transparent polygons. As in Example 4.2, *glDepthMask(GL_FALSE)* makes the depth-buffer become read-only, whereas *glDepthMask(GL_TRUE)* restores the normal depth-buffer operation (Fig. 4.2).

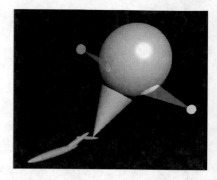

Fig. 4.2 Depth-buffer read only

/* **Example 4.2.opaque.c: transparency / hidden-surface removal** */

```
void drawSolar(float E, float e, float M, float m)
{
    ...
        drawCone(); // draw opaque object first
        glEnable (GL_BLEND);
        glDepthMask (GL_FALSE); // make depth-buffer read-only
        glBlendFunc (GL_SRC_ALPHA, GL_ONE_MINUS_SRC_ALPHA);
        drawCone();
        glDepthMask (GL_TRUE);
        glDisable (GL_BLEND);
    ...
}
```

Example 4.3 uses transparent cones to simulate the lighting volumes of the moving and rotating spotlight sources.

/* **Example 4.3.translight.c: cones to simulate moving spotlights** */

```
void drawSolar(float E, float e, float M, float m)
{
    ...
        glRotatef(e+m, 0, 1, 0); // the light source is rotating
```

```
        glLightfv(GL_LIGHT1, GL_POSITION, position);
        glLightfv(GL_LIGHT1,GL_SPOT_DIRECTION,spot_direction);
        glLightf(GL_LIGHT1,GL_SPOT_CUTOFF,10.0);

        glEnable (GL_BLEND);
        glDepthMask (GL_FALSE);

        // cone tip 10 degree
        glScalef(1,tan(PI*10/180),tan(PI*10/180));
        drawCone();

        glDepthMask (GL_TRUE);
        glDisable (GL_BLEND);
     ...
}
```

4.1.3 Antialiasing

In OpenGL, antialiasing can be achieved by blending. If you call *glEnable()* with *GL_POINT_SMOOTH*, *GL_LINE_SMOOTH*, or *GL_POLYGON_SMOOTH*, OpenGL will calculate a coverage value based on the fraction of the pixel square that covers the point, line, or polygon edge with specified point size or line width, and multiply the pixel's alpha value by the calculated coverage value. You can achieve antialiasing by using the resulting alpha value to blend the pixel color with the corresponding pixel color already in the frame buffer. The method is the same as the unweighted area sampling method discussed in Section 1.4.1 on page 17. You can even use *glHint()* to choose a faster or slower but better quality sampling algorithm in the system.

4.1.4 Fog

Fog is the effect of the atmosphere between the rendered pixel and the eye, which is called the depth cuing or atmosphere attenuation effect. Fog is also achieved by blending:

$$I_\lambda = fI_{\lambda 1} + (1 - f)I_{\lambda f} \qquad \text{(EQ 99)}$$

where f is the fog factor, $I_{\lambda 1}$ is the incoming pixel component, and $I_{\lambda f}$ is the fog color. In OpenGL, as in Example 4.4 (Fig. 4.3), the fog factor and the fog color are specified by *glFog*()*. The fog color can be the same as, or different from, the background color. The fog factor *f* depends on the distance (*z*) from the view point to the pixel on the object. We can choose different equations if we specify the fog mode to *GL_EXP* (Equation 100), *GL_EXP2* (Equation 101), or *GL_LINEAR* (Equation 102):

$$f = e^{-(density \cdot z)}$$ (EQ 100)

$$f = e^{-(density \cdot z)^2}$$ (EQ 101)

$$f = \frac{end - z}{end - start}$$ (EQ 102)

In Equation 102, when *z* changes from *start* to *end*, *f* changes from 1 to 0. According to Equation 99, the final pixel color will change from the incoming object pixel color to the fog color. We may supply *GL_FOG_HINT* with *glHint()* to specify whether fog calculations are per pixel (*GL_NICEST*) or per vertex (*GL_FASTEST*) or whatever the system has (*GL_DONT_CARE*).

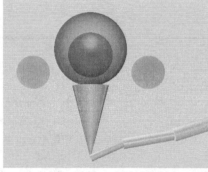

Fig. 4.3 Fog in OpenGL

/* Example 4.4.fog.c: fog and background colors */

```
init() {
    float fogColor[4] = {0.8, 0.8, 0.7, 1.0};

    glClearColor (0.8, 0.8, 0.7, 1.0);

    glEnable(GL_FOG);

    glHint (GL_FOG_HINT, GL_DONT_CARE);
    glFogi (GL_FOG_MODE, GL_LINEAR);
    glFogfv (GL_FOG_COLOR, fogColor);
    glFogf (GL_FOG_START, 1.5*Width);
    glFogf (GL_FOG_END, 3.8*Width);
}
```

4.2 Images

We have discussed rendering and scan-converting 3D models. The result is an image, or an array of RGBAs stored in the frame buffer. Instead of going through transformation, viewing, hidden-surface removal, lighting, and other graphics manipulations, OpenGL provides some basic functions that manipulate image data in the frame buffer directly: *glReadPixels()* reads a rectangular array of pixels from the frame buffer into the (computer main) memory, *glDrawPixels()* writes a rectangular array of pixels into the frame buffer from the memory, *glBitmap()* writes a single bitmap (a binary image) into the frame buffer from the main memory, etc. The function *glRasterPos*()* specifies the current raster position (x, y, z, w) where the system starts reading or writing. The position (x, y, z, w), however, goes through the transformation pipeline as a vertex in a 3D model.

The image data stored in the memory might consist of just the overall intensity of each pixel (R+G+B), or the RGBA components, respectively. As image data is transferred from memory into the frame buffer, or from the frame buffer into memory, OpenGL can perform several operations on it. Also, there are certain formats for storing data in the memory that are required or are more efficient on certain kinds of hardware. We use *glPixelStore*()* to set the pixel-storage mode of how data is unpacked from the memory into the frame buffer or from the frame buffer to the memory. Example 4.5 (Fig. 4.4) reads an image from a file, and draws the image into the frame buffer directly as the background of the 3D rendering.

Fig. 4.4 Image background

/* Example 4.5.image.c: write an image into the framebuffer */

```
void initImage(void) // called once at initialization
{
    read_stars_image();
    // inform the system about image storage format in memory
    glPixelStorei(GL_UNPACK_ALIGNMENT, 1);
}
```

```
void drawImage(float x, float y, float z)
{
  glRasterPos3f(x, y, z);

  glDrawPixels(stars_pixels, stars_pixels,
               GL_LUMINANCE, GL_UNSIGNED_BYTE, stars_image);
}


void display(void)
{
   glClear(GL_COLOR_BUFFER_BIT | GL_DEPTH_BUFFER_BIT);

   drawImage(-2.4*Width, -2.4*Height, -1.9*Width);
   drawRobot(A, B, C, alpha, beta, gama);

   glutSwapBuffers();
}
```

4.3 Texture Mapping

In graphics rendering, an image can be mapped onto the surface of a model. That is, when writing the color of a pixel into the frame buffer, the graphics system can use a color retrieved from an image. To do this we need to provide a piece of image called *texture*. *Texture mapping* is a process of using the texture pixels (namely *texels*) to modify or replace the model's corresponding pixels during scan-conversion. Texture mapping allows many choices and is fairly complex. Here we only introduce some basics.

4.3.1 Pixel and Texel Relations

Let's consider mapping a square texture onto a rectangular polygon (Example 4.6).

First, we need to specify the corresponding vertices of the texture and the polygon. In OpenGL, this is done by associating each vertex in the texture with a vertex in the polygon, which is similar to the way of specifying each vertex normal. Given a point (s, t) in the 2D texture, the s and t are in the range of $[0, 1]$. *glTexCoord2f(s, t)* corresponds to a point in the texture. In our example, the points are the vertices of the texture, and the OpenGL system stretches or shrinks the texture to map exactly onto the polygon.

Second, in OpenGL, when the texture is smaller than the polygon, the system stretches the texture to match the polygon (magnification). Otherwise, the system shrinks the texture (minification). Either way the pixels corresponding to the texels after stretching or shrinking need to be calculated. The algorithms to calculate the mapping are called the magnification filter or minification filter (*GL_TEXTURE_MAG_FILTER* or *GL_TEXTURE_MIN_FILTER*), which are discussed below.

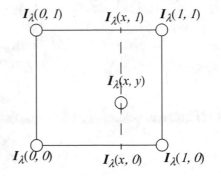

Fig. 4.5 Interpolation (GL_LINEAR)

Given a pixel location in the polygon, we can find its corresponding point in the texture. This point may be on a texel, on the line between two texels, or in the square with four texels at the corners as shown in Fig. 4.5. The resulting color of the point needs to be calculated. The simplest method OpenGL uses is to choose the texel that is nearest to the point as the mapping of the pixel (*GL_NEAREST*, as in *gl.glTexParameteri(GL.GL_TEXTURE_2D, GL.GL_TEXTURE_MIN_FILTER, GL.GL_NEAREST)*), which in this case is $I_\lambda(x,y) = I_\lambda(1,0)$. We can also bi-linearly interpolate the four texels according to their distances to the point to find the mapping of the pixel (*GL_LINEAR*), which is smoother but slower than *GL_NEAREST* method. That is, first-pass linear interpolations are along x axis direction for two intermediate values:

$$I_\lambda(x, 0) = xI_\lambda(1, 0) + (1 - x)I_\lambda(0, 0) \qquad \text{(EQ 103)}$$

$$I_\lambda(x, 1) = xI_\lambda(1, 1) + (1 - x)I_\lambda(0, 1) \qquad \text{(EQ 104)}$$

and second-pass linear interpolation is along y axis direction for the final result:

$$I_\lambda(x, y) = yI_\lambda(x, 1) + (1 - y)I_\lambda(x, 0) \qquad \text{(EQ 105)}$$

Third, at each pixel, the calculated texel color components (texel RGBA represented by C_t and A_t) can be used to either replace or change (modulate, decal, or blend) incoming pixel color components (which is also called a fragment and is represented by C_f and A_f). A texture environment color (C_c), which is specified by *gl.glTexEnvf(GL.GL_TEXTURE_ENV, GL.GL_TEXTURE_ENV_COLOR, parameter)*, can also be used to modify the final color components (represented as C_v and A_v).

A texel can have up to four components. L_t indicates a one-component texture. A two-component texture has L_t and A_t. A three-component texture has C_t. A four-component texture has both C_t and A_t.

If the texels replace the pixels, lighting will not affect the appearance of the polygon (*gl.glTexEnvf(GL.GL_TEXTURE_ENV, GL.GL_TEXTURE_ENV_MODE, GL.GL_REPLACE)*). If the texel components are used to modulate the pixel components, each texture color component is multiplied by the corresponding pixel color component, and the original color and shading of the polygon are partially preserved. The following table lists all the corresponding functions for different mode:

glTexEnvf(GL_TEXTURE_ENV, GL_TEXTURE_VNV_MODE, *Parameter*).

Internal Formats	GL_ MODULATE	GL_ DECAL	GL_ BLEND	GL_ REPLACE	GL_ ADD
1 or GL_ LUMINANCE	$C_v=L_tC_f$ $A_v=A_f$	*Undefined*	$C_v=(1-L_t)C_f$ $+L_tC_c; A_v=A_f$	$C_v=L_t$ $A_v=A_f$	$C_v=C_f+L_t$ $A_v=A_f$
2 or GL_ LUMINANCE _ALPHA	$C_v=L_tC_f$ $A_v=A_tA_f$	*Undefined*	$C_v=(1-L_t)C_f$ $+L_tC_c; A_v=A_tA_f$	$C_v=L_t$ $A_v=A_t$	$C_v=C_f+L_t$ $A_v=A_fA_t$
3 or GL_ RGB	$C_v=C_tC_f$ $A_v=A_f$	$C_v=C_t$ $A_v=A_f$	$C_v=(1-C_t)C_f$ $+C_tC_c; A_v=A_f$	$C_v=C_t$ $A_v=A_f$	$C_v=C_f$ $+C_t A_v=A_f$
4 or GL_ RGBA	$C_v=C_tC_f$ $A_v=A_tA_f$	$C_v=(1-A_t)C_f$ $+A_tC_t; A_v=A_f$	$C_v=(1-C_t)C_f$ $+C_tC_c; A_v=A_tA_f$	$C_v=C_t$ $A_v=A_t$	$C_v=C_f+C_t$ $A_v=A_fA_t$

Example 4.6 maps an image to a polygon. Although Example 4.5 and Example 4.6 look the same, the approaches are totally different.

/* Example 4.6.texture.c: simple texture mapping */

```
void initTexture(void)
{
    read_stars_image();
    glPixelStorei(GL_UNPACK_ALIGNMENT, 1);

    // specify the mapping between pixel & corresponding texels
    glTexParameteri(GL_TEXTURE_2D,
                GL_TEXTURE_MAG_FILTER, GL_NEAREST);
    glTexParameteri(GL_TEXTURE_2D,
                GL_TEXTURE_MIN_FILTER, GL_NEAREST);

    // specify the texture
    glTexImage2D(GL_TEXTURE_2D, 0, GL_LUMINANCE,
        stars_pixels, stars_pixels, 0,
            GL_LUMINANCE, GL_UNSIGNED_BYTE, stars_image);
}
void drawTexture(float x, float y, float z)
// the back ground stars
{
    // specify that the texels replace the pixels
    glTexEnvf(GL_TEXTURE_ENV,
                GL_TEXTURE_ENV_MODE, GL_REPLACE);

    glEnable(GL_TEXTURE_2D);

    glBegin(GL_QUADS);

        glTexCoord2f(0.0, 0.0); glVertex3f(x, y, z);
        glTexCoord2f(0.0, 1.0); glVertex3f(-x, y, z);
        glTexCoord2f(1.0, 1.0); glVertex3f(-x, -y, z);
        glTexCoord2f(1.0, 0.0); glVertex3f(x, -y, z);

    glEnd();

    glDisable(GL_TEXTURE_2D);
}


void display(void)
{
    glClear(GL_COLOR_BUFFER_BIT | GL_DEPTH_BUFFER_BIT);

    drawTexture(-2.4*Width, -2.4*Height, -1.9*Width);

    drawRobot(A, B, C, alpha, beta, gama);
```

```
    glutSwapBuffers();
}
```

4.3.2 Texture Objects

If we use several textures in the same
program (Fig. 4.6), we may load them into
texture memory and associate individual
texture parameters with their texture names
before rendering. This way we do not need to
load textures and their parameters from the
disk files during rendering, which would
otherwise be very slow. In OpenGL, this is
done by calling *glGenTextures()* and
glBindTexture().   When   we   call

Fig. 4.6 **Multiple texture objects**

glGenTextures(), we can generate the texture names or texture objects. When we call
glBindTexture() with a texture name, all subsequent *glTex*()* commands that specify
the texture and its associated parameters are saved in the memory corresponding to the
named texture. The following program segment is part of Example 4.7.

```
static GLuint iris_tex, stars_tex, earth_tex;

static GLubyte iris_image[iris_pixels][iris_pixels][3];
static GLubyte stars_image[stars_pixels][stars_pixels];
static GLubyte earth_image[earth_pixelx][earth_pixely][3];


void initTexture(void)
{
    read_stars_image();

    read_earth_image();

    glPixelStorei(GL_UNPACK_ALIGNMENT, 1);

    glGenTextures(1, &earth_tex);
    glBindTexture(GL_TEXTURE_2D, earth_tex);

    glTexParameteri(GL_TEXTURE_2D,
              GL_TEXTURE_MAG_FILTER, GL_LINEAR);
```

```
glTexParameteri(GL_TEXTURE_2D,
          GL_TEXTURE_MIN_FILTER, GL_LINEAR);

glTexImage2D(GL_TEXTURE_2D, 0, 3,
          earth_pixelx, earth_pixely,
        0, GL_RGB, GL_UNSIGNED_BYTE, earth_image);

glGenTextures(1, &stars_tex);
glBindTexture(GL_TEXTURE_2D, stars_tex);

glTexParameteri(GL_TEXTURE_2D,
          GL_TEXTURE_MAG_FILTER, GL_LINEAR);
glTexParameteri(GL_TEXTURE_2D,
          GL_TEXTURE_MIN_FILTER, GL_LINEAR);

glTexImage2D(GL_TEXTURE_2D, 0, GL_LUMINANCE,
          stars_pixels, stars_pixels,
        0, GL_LUMINANCE, GL_UNSIGNED_BYTE, stars_image);

}
```

4.3.3 Texture Coordinates

In OpenGL, *glTexCoord2f(s, t)* corresponds to a point in the texture, and *s* and *t* are in the range of [0, 1]. If the points are on the boundaries of the texture, then we stretch or shrink the entire texture to fit exactly onto the polygon. Otherwise, only a portion of the texture is used to map onto the polygon. For example, if we have a polygonal cylinder with four polygons and we want to wrap the texture around the cylinder (Example 4.7), we can divide the texture into four pieces with *s* in the range of [0, 0.25], [0.25, 0.5], [0.5, 0.75], and [0.75, 1.0]. When mapping a rectangular texture onto a sphere around the axis, texture geodesic distortion happens — especially towards the poles.

If we specify *glTexCoord2f(2, t)*, we mean to repeat the texture twice in the *s* direction. That is, we will squeeze two pieces of the texture in *s* direction into the polygon. If we specify *glTexCoord2f(1.5, t)*, we mean to repeat the texture 1.5 times in the *s* direction. In order to achieve texture repeating in *s* direction, we need to specify the following: *glTexParameteri(GL_TEXTURE_2D, GL_TEXTURE_WRAP_S, GL_REPEAT)*. In OpenGL, the texture should have width and height in the form of 2^m number of pixels, where the width and height can be different.

/* Example 4.7.texobjects.c: texture objects and coordinates */

```c
void textureCoord(float *v, float *s, float *t)
{ // given the vertex on a sphere, find its texture (s,t)

    float x, y, z, PI=3.14159, PI2=6.283;

    x = v[0]; y = v[1]; z = v[2];

    if (x>0) {
        if (z>0) *s = atan(z/x)/PI2;
        else *s = 1 + atan(z/x)/PI2;
    }
    else if (x<0)
        *s = 0.5 + atan(z/x)/PI2;
    else {
        if (z>0) *s = 0.25;
        if (z<0) *s = 0.75;
        if (z==0) *s = -1.0;
    }

    *t = acos(y)/PI;
}
void drawSphereTriangle(float *v1, float *v2, float *v3)
{
    float s1, t1, s2, t2, s3, t3;

    textureCoord(v1, &s1, &t1);
    textureCoord(v2, &s2, &t2);
    textureCoord(v3, &s3, &t3);

    // for coord at z=0, distortion happens more
    if (s1 == -1.0) s1 = (s2+s3)/2;
    else if (s2 == -1.0) s2 = (s1+s3)/2;
    else if (s3 == -1.0) s3 = (s2+s1)/2;

    glBindTexture(GL_TEXTURE_2D, earth_tex);
    glTexEnvf(GL_TEXTURE_ENV,
              GL_TEXTURE_ENV_MODE, GL_MODULATE);

    glBegin(GL_POLYGON);
        glTexCoord2f(s1, t1);
        glNormal3fv(v1);
        glVertex3fv(v1);
        glTexCoord2f(s2, t2);
        glNormal3fv(v2);
        glVertex3fv(v2);
        glTexCoord2f(s3, t3);
        glNormal3fv(v3);
```

```
        glVertex3fv(v3);
    glEnd();
}


void subdivideCylinder(float *v1,
              float *v2, int depth, float t1, float t2)
{
    float v11[3], v22[3], v00[3] = {0, 0, 0}, v12[3];
    int i;

    if (depth == 0) {
        glColor3f(v1[0]*v1[0], v1[1]*v1[1], v1[2]*v1[2]);
        drawBottom(v2, v1, v00); // draw the cylinder bottom

        for (i=0; i<3; i++) { v11[i] = v1[i]; v22[i] = v2[i];
        }
        // the height of the cone along z axis
        v11[2] = v22[2] = 1;

        glBindTexture(GL_TEXTURE_2D, iris_tex);
        glTexEnvf(GL_TEXTURE_ENV,
            GL_TEXTURE_ENV_MODE, GL_REPLACE);
        // draw the side rectangles of the cylinder
        glBegin(GL_POLYGON);
            glNormal3fv(v2);
            glTexCoord2f(t1, 0.0); glVertex3fv(v1);
            glTexCoord2f(t2, 0.0); glVertex3fv(v2);
            glNormal3fv(v1);
            glTexCoord2f(t2, 1.0); glVertex3fv(v22);
            glTexCoord2f(t1, 1.0); glVertex3fv(v11);
        glEnd();

        v00[2] = 1;
        drawBottom(v00, v11, v22); // draw the other bottom

        return;
    }
    v12[0]  = v1[0]+v2[0];
    v12[1]  = v1[1]+v2[1];
    v12[2]  = v1[2]+v2[2];
    normalize(v12);
    subdivideCylinder(v1, v12, depth - 1, t1, (t2+t1)/2);
    subdivideCylinder(v12, v2, depth - 1, (t2+t1)/2, t2);
}


void drawCylinder(void)
```

```
// draw a unit cylinder with bottom in xy plane
{
    subdivideCylinder(vdata[0], vdata[1], depth, 0, 0.25);
    subdivideCylinder(vdata[1], vdata[2], depth, 0.25, 0.5);
    subdivideCylinder(vdata[2], vdata[3], depth, 0.5, 0.75);
    subdivideCylinder(vdata[3], vdata[0], depth, 0.75, 1.0);
}


drawArm(float End1, float End2) {
    float scale;
    scale = End2-End1;

    glPushMatrix();
        glRotatef(90.0, 0.0, 1.0, 0.0);
        glScalef(scale/5.0, scale/5.0, scale);

        // roate the texture image IRIS
        glRotatef(cnt, 0.0, 0.0, 1.0);
        drawCylinder();
    glPopMatrix();
}
```

4.3.4 Levels of Detail in Texture Mapping

In perspective projection, models further away from the viewpoint will appear smaller, and we cannot see that much detail. At the same time, for texture mapping, a large texture will need to be filtered by the minification filter to a much smaller size of the projected primitive (image). If the texture is significantly smaller than the original image, the filtering process takes time and the result may appear flashing or shimmering.

OpenGL allows specifying multiple levels of detail (LOD) images at different resolutions for texture mapping. OpenGL will choose the appropriate texture image(s) according to the corresponding projected image size automatically. The different LOD images are called *mipmaps*, which must be at the dimension of power of 2. If you use LOD in OpenGL, you have to specify all mipmaps from the largest image down to the size of 1×1. For example, for a size 512×512 size image, you have to specify 512×512, 256×256, 128×128, 64×64, 32×32, 16×16, 8×8, 4×4, 2×2, and 1×1 texture images. The second parameter in *glTexImage2D()* when specifying a texture image is the *level* (of detail) of the current image, from 0 the largest image up to the 1×1 image. Also, the minification filter has to be specified to choose the nearest mipmap image for texture   mapping   (*glTexParameteri(GL_TEXTURE_2D, GL_TEXTURE_MIN_FILTER, GL_NEAREST_MIPMAP_NEAREST)*)) or linear for interpolation between the two closest textures in size to the projected primitive: (*glTexParameteri(GL_TEXTURE_2D, GL_TEXTURE_MIN_FILTER, GL_NEAREST_MIPMAP_LINEAR)*)).

4.4 Advanced Texture Mapping

Using texture to tape on 3D objects is the original texture mapping idea. The texture memory and the OpenGL mechanism are also used for some other ways beyond the conventional way of texture mapping. In the following sections we introduce some advanced methods in using textures. The methods are studied over the years by very few researchers, but they become very popular due to the advancement on pixel (fragment) shading operations. We will revisit some of these methods when we discuss GPU, vertex shader, and pixel shader.

4.4.1 Bump Mapping

Bump mapping was originally designed to display a flat surface with vertex or pixel normals perturbed or modified to simulate a bumped surface. It depends on the perturbation method to decide the surface bumps and appearances.

Today, the common method is to save the surface's bumps (height field) in a texture as a height map or save the surface bump's normals in a texture as a normal map. The surface heights or normals are precalculated and provided as an array of data stored in a texture memory. They are called bump maps as part of the texture mapping.

Bump mapping doesn't necessarily map to a flat surface. We can consider it is a layer of bump normals added on top of the current surface to modify or replace the current vertex or pixel normals. The bump mapping's surface geometry stays the same in general. There are many different ways to design bump map and to achieve the mapping for a final result. As an example, let's consider using a predefined texture as a normal map for bump mapping. Because texture only saves positive RGB values from zero to one, we have to shift the normals from negative to positive values, and restore them while calculate lighting. For a normalized normal n, its x, y, z values are negative one to positive one. So we can add one and then divide the result by two to store the values (RGB = $(n+1)/2$) in a normal map and multiply by two and subtract one when we retrieve it ($n = RGB*2 -1$).

As shown in Fig. 4.7, when we consider a vertex or pixel with normal N, the light source direction L and N are all represented in the global coordinates x, y, z. However, the bump map normal n is in its local coordinates, which is called *tangent space* or *texture space*, because we are attaching the texture tangent to the surface at the point of lighting calculation.

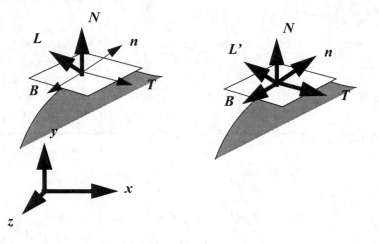

Fig. 4.7 Global space and tangent space

The tangent space coordinates can be aligned with the texture mapping or any orientation at user's preference as long as they are perpendicular to the vertex or pixel normal N, and they do not rotate around N from point to point. This can be done by specifying a T that is perpendicular to N, and use the cross product to find B:

$$B = T \times N$$

(EQ 106)

If necessary, T can be calculated by a cross product of N and S, where S is a texture direction not parallel or perpendicular to N. The bump map normals are represented in the TNB coordinates in tangent space. Now we can either transform the light source direction into tangent space or transform n into global space for final lighting calculation. Transforming n into global space involves more calculations.

Transforming the light source direction into tangent space can be done by the following coordinates transformation:

$$L' = (T \bullet L, N \bullet L, B \bullet L).$$

(EQ 107)

Bump mapping requires fine meshes or pixel operations, which used to be a slow process without real-time possibilities. The recent advancement in GPU has made bump mapping a very powerful tool in achieving surface effect in real time. We will talk more about this later in Cg programming.

4.4.2 Light Mapping

As we know, high resolution lighting calculations such as ray tracing or radiosity are very time-consuming, which therefore hinder achieving real-time calculation in interactive applications. If we have fix light sources shining on a flat surface, a simple light mapping is to precalculate or generate lighting as an intensity field for each light source saved in a texture called *light map*, and blend or modulate the rendered image texture with the light maps at runtime. This will allow us to turn on and off lights with different combinations quite efficiently without runtime lighting calculations. If there is no interaction on lighting, light map can be integrated with texture map before runtime, therefore there is only a texture map at runtime that includes lighting information.

If we consider moving objects, light sources, or viewpoint, then light mapping is fairly complex. In general, light mapping is efficient for static environment without considering moving objects or viewpoint. Most of the time, light sources are at infinity. For viewpoint independent lighting with static objects, light mapping is just align the light map with the texture. For polygonal objects, we may use polygon orientations to decide which light map to apply. Therefore, a light map can include patches for different lighting.

Light maps usually can be at a lower resolution than the texture map because lighting changes over neighboring pixels less than surface texture. Light mapping is a technique for improving efficiency. With the recent advancement on GPU parallel processing, lighting and texture mapping can be integrated more efficiently, therefore reducing the importance of light mapping in practical applications.

4.4.3 Environment Mapping

When we put a reflective object in an environment, the image of the environment, which may be distorted, appears on the object as a reflection. Environment mapping is a simplified raytracing technique. In a raytracing algorithm, we trace the ray from viewpoint into bounces among objects. In the environment mapping, we trace the ray into a texture, called an environment map as shown in Fig. 4.8. Here, the purpose of raytracing is to find the corresponding environment map's texel instead of lighting. Most environment mapping algorithms are ray casting algorithms, which means that we trace the ray once without calculate bounces. Also, the starting point of the ray and the ending point of the ray in the environment map can be designed quite differently.

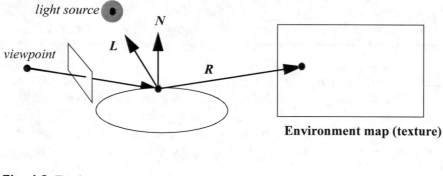

Fig. 4.8 Environment mapping

There are several different environment mapping methods. One of them is named cubic mapping, which employs a box with six faces covering the object model. The first problem is how do we construct the environment map. One simple solution is to take six pictures in six directions surrounding the object (left, right, bottom, top, front, back) and tape them onto six walls to form a unit cube ($x=-1$, $x=1$, $y=-1$, $y=1$, $z=-1$, $z=1$), as shown in Fig. 4.9. Cubic mapping is then an index scheme to find the corresponding texels in the cube maps. If we store the six cube maps separately, then the index from the intersection of the ray with the cube to a cube map's texel coordinates is a simple linear transformation. For example, if we intersect with $y=1$, then we have (x, z) as the intersection point for indexing into the texture coordinates:

$$u = x + 0.5$$

(EQ 108)

$$v = z + 0.5 \qquad\qquad \text{(EQ 109)}$$

The other cube map coordinates can be indexed similarly, as shown in Fig. 4.9.b as long the cube maps are saved accordingly.

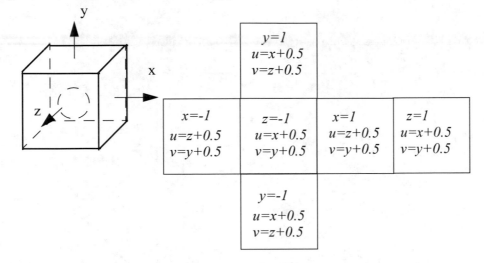

a) Cube for ray intersection   b) Cube maps

Fig. 4.9 Cubic mapping: how to save and index the cube maps

The second problem is how to find the reflection rays that intersect with the cube maps. Obviously, we can use a ray tracing method to find the intersection of rays from viewpoint to the object in the cube, and then find the reflection rays from the object in the cube to the cube faces. As we have discussed when we introduced ray tracing, given a ray A and a normalized normal n, the reflected ray $B = 2n(n{\bullet}A) - A$. For example, if we have a sphere at the center, then the reflection is calculated by the ray from the viewpoint intersecting the sphere, as shown in Fig. 4.10. This method has two severe flaws. First, it takes time to calculate ray tracing. Second, if the normal is getting perpendicular to the viewpoint ray, the reflection samples a large area, which creates an uneven sampling (aliasing) problem. We may generate a different environment map by taking a picture from a reflecting sphere, which is called a sphere map. The result will be better for a sphere, but the method is quite rigid. Sphere mapping of this kind only works for a specific viewpoint, sphere size, and sphere location.

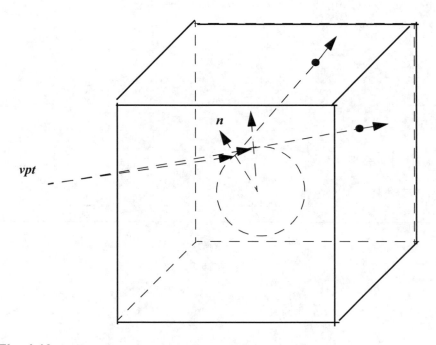

Fig. 4.10 Sphere mapping: how to generate and index the maps

4.4.4 Automatic Texture Coordinates

Environment mapping can be integrated with ray tracing to have reflections and transparencies. However, for texture mapping purposes, we may not consider viewpoint dependent ray tracing. Instead, a simplified method is to use the surface normal as an index or ray for the corresponding texel on the cube surface, as shown in Fig. 4.11, which will map textures onto a complex object accordingly.

This method can be further simplified by firing a ray from the center of the sphere through the point under consideration, and the resulting texel is the intersection on a cube surface. In other words, the texture coordinates are generated automatically in 3D space instead of an exact tapping in 2D space. In addition to cube boxes, a cylinder texture coordinates around a cylindrical object would work well for wrapping the texture around the object, as shown in Fig. 4.11b. The problem with cylindrical texture coordinates generation is that the top and bottom of the objects are omitted. It is better for generating contours or bands around the objects.

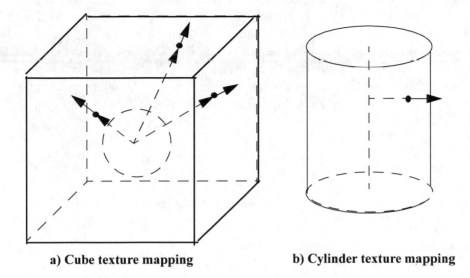

| a) Cube texture mapping | b) Cylinder texture mapping |

Fig. 4.11 **Automatic texture coordinates: texture mapping on to a complex object**

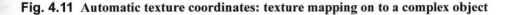

4.4.5 Displacement Mapping

In bump mapping, a height field may be used as distortion to the surface normals. We still render the surface as a flat surface. One modification to bump mapping is called parallax mapping (also named offset mapping or virtual displacement mapping). In parallax mapping, texture coordinates are shifted according to the height field and view direction. In other words, when we find the intersection of the view direction ray with the polygon, the intersection point is shifted according to the height field. The resulting point is then used as an index to the texture map. This method only shifts texture coordinates. The polygon surface remains flat. An alternative of the parallax mapping is called relief mapping, which calculates surface detail, self-occlusion, self-shadow, and other effects without actually changing the pixel's physical coordinates. The polygon surface remains flat. These methods are developed on today's GPU pixel shader. The surface detail is like a relief map on top of a flat surface in lighting environment. As we will see, the pixel shader receives a pixel location for lighting and other calculations in eye space, but not for pixel rendering in clip space or device coordinates.

In displacement mapping, the surface is raised according to the height field. In recent years, due to the advancement of graphics hardware, some GPUs allow vertex shaders to have access to textures. We can send a height map to a Vertex Shader and change the vertex position by the height map. We can consider that the surface is changed according to the height field (bump map). Therefore, an object's surface is represented in two different representations. First, it is specified as a 3D objects with vertices and polygons. Then, the surface detail is specified as height field in a bump map.

4.5 Review Questions

1. Alpha blending is used for transparency, antialiasing, and so on. Please list all the applications we have learned in this chapter.

2. Please list the order of operation for the following:

(_). drawTransparentObject();   (_). glDepthMask(GL_FALSE)
(_). drawOpaqueObject();   (_). glDepthMask(GL_TRUE)

3. *Fog* is calculated according to which of the following distances?

  a. from the light source to the viewpoint   b. from the viewpoint to the pixel
  c. from the pixel to the light source   d. from the light source to the origin
  e. from the origin to the viewpoint   f. from the pixel to the origin

4. glutBitmapString() will draw a string of bitmap characters at the current raster position. glutStrokeString() will draw a string of stroke characters at the current raster position. Please explain the differences between glutBitmapString() and glutStrokeString() in detail.

5. We have a rectangular image, and we'll wrap it around a cylinder, a sphere, and a cone as described earlier in the book. Please develop your methods of calculating your texture coordinates, and explain the distortions if any.

6. In OpenGL *texture mapping*, what is a `texture object`?

  a. A 3D model on display   b. A name with associated data saved in the memory
  c. A texture file   d. A blending of texture and material

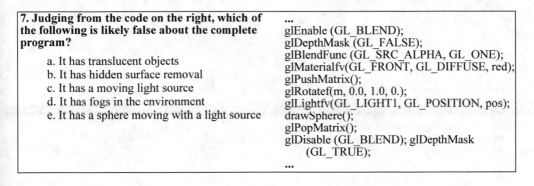

7. Judging from the code on the right, which of the following is likely false about the complete program?

   a. It has translucent objects
   b. It has hidden surface removal
   c. It has a moving light source
   d. It has fogs in the environment
   e. It has a sphere moving with a light source

```
...
glEnable (GL_BLEND);
glDepthMask (GL_FALSE);
glBlendFunc (GL_SRC_ALPHA, GL_ONE);
glMaterialfv(GL_FRONT, GL_DIFFUSE, red);
glPushMatrix();
glRotatef(m, 0.0, 1.0, 0.);
glLightfv(GL_LIGHT1, GL_POSITION, pos);
drawSphere();
glPopMatrix();
glDisable (GL_BLEND); glDepthMask
        (GL_TRUE);
...
```

8. Please use bilinear interpolation to find the corresponding pixel color's red component:

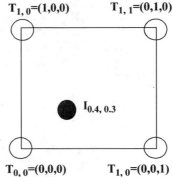

$T_{1,0}=(1,0,0)$ $T_{1,1}=(0,1,0)$

$I_{0.4, 0.3}$

$T_{0,0}=(0,0,0)$ $T_{1,0}=(0,0,1)$

$I_{0.4,0.3}$ = (_____ , __x__ , __x__)

9. Given a 3D cube with end points values A(0, 0, 0) = a, B(0, 0, 1) = b, C(1, 0, 1) = c, D(1, 0, 0) = d, E(0, 1, 0) = e, F(0, 1, 1) = f, G(1, 1, 1) = g, and H(1, 1, 0) = h, please use tri-linear interpolation to calculate a point's value inside the cube at an arbitrary position P(x,y,z).

10. Calculate the intersection of an arbitrary line from the center of a cube and the cube's face.

4.6 Programming Assignments

1. Draw randomly generated lines with antialiasing at changeable width using OpenGL functions.

2. Please implement two functions myBitmapString() and myStrokeString() that simulate their glut counterparts. Here you cannot call any font drawing functions to achieve the goal.

3. Draw a generalized solar system on a robot arm with the earth transparent and the moons opaque. The center of the earth is a light source.

4. Extend J4_8_MipMap.java so that the cones are covered by an image of your choice. The image on the cone should be distorted.

5. Take 6 pictures in an environment so that you can form a cube with the 6 pictures. Then, consider our earth is a silver sphere in the center of the cube. Each sphere triangle's vertex is a ray penetrating the cube. In other words, each triangle has three intersections on the cube. Now, if we consider the 6 pictures as 6 texture objects, we can use the intersection to set up corresponding texture mapping. For a triangle penetrating more than one texture object, you can choose just one texture object and do something at your preference. Please implement such a texture mapping, and display a solid sphere in a transparent cube with texture mapping.

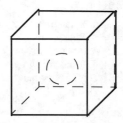

6. Draw multiple spheres bouncing in a cube or sphere. Take six pictures as cube maps. Achieve texture mapping and cubic mapping on the spheres.

5

OpenGL Programming in Java: JOGL

Chapter Objectives:

- Set up Java, JOGL programming environments
- Understand simple JOGL programs

5.1 Introduction

JOGL implements Java bindings for OpenGL. It provides hardware-supported 3D graphics to applications written in Java. It is part of a suite of open-source technologies initiated by the Game Technology Group at Sun Microsystems. JOGL provides full access to OpenGL functions and integrates with the AWT and Swing widget sets.

First, let's spend some time to set up our working environment, compile J1_0_Point.java, and run the program. The following file contains links to all the example programs in this book and detailed information for setting up working environments on different platforms for the most recent version:

```
http://cs.gmu.edu/~jchen/graphics/setup.html
```

Since JOGL has been changed significantly over time, it is better to download and update the sample programs from the web instead of typing in examples from the book.

J.X. Chen, *Guide to Graphics Software Tools*, doi: 10.1007/978-1-84800-901-1_5,
© Springer-Verlag London Limited 2008

5.2 Setting Up Working Environment

JOGL provides full access to the APIs in the OpenGL specification as well as nearly all vendor extensions. To install and run JOGL, we need to install Java Development Kit. In addition, a Java IDE is also preferred to help coding. The following steps will guide you through installing Java, JOGL, and Eclipse or JBuilder IDE.

1. Installing Java Development Kit

   Java Development Kit (JDK) contains a compiler, interpreter, and debugger. If you have not installed JDK, it is freely available from Sun Microsystems. You can download the latest version from the download section at `http://java.sun.com`. Make sure you download the JDK Java SE (Standard Edition) not the JRE (runtime environment) that matches the platform you use. After downloading the JDK, you can run the installation executable file. During the installation, you will be asked the directory "Install to:". You need to know where it is installed. For example, you can put it under: "C:\myJDK\". In default, it is put under "C:\Program Files\Java\jdkxxxx\".

2. Installing JOGL

   We need to obtain the JOGL binaries in order to compile and run applications from: `https://jogl.dev.java.net/`. Download the current release build binaries that match the platform you use. After that, you can extract and put all these files (jar and dll files) in the same directory with the Java (JOGL) examples and compile all them on the command line in the current directory with:

   ```
   "C:\myJDK\bin\javac" -classpath jogl.jar *.java
   ```

   After that, you can run the sample program with (the command in one line):

   ```
   "C:\myJDK\bin\java" -classpath .;jogl.jar;gluegen-rt.jar;
   -Djava.library.path=. J1_0_Point
   ```

   That is, you need to place the "*.jar" files in the CLASSPATH of your build environment in order to be able to compile an application with JOGL and run, and place "*.dll" files in the directory listed in the "java.library.path" environment variable during execution. Java loads the native libraries (such as the dll files for Windows) from the directories listed in the "java.library.path" environment variable. For Windows, placing the dll files under "C:\WINDOWS\system32\" directory works. This approach gets you up running quickly without worrying about the "java.library.path" setting.

3. Installing a Java IDE (Eclipse, jGRASP, or JBuilder)

Installing a Java IDE (Integrated Development Environment) is strongly recommended. Without an IDE, you can edit Java program files using any text editor, compile and run Java programs using the commands we introduced above after downloading JOGL, but that would be very difficult and slow. Java IDEs such as JBuilder, Eclipes, and jGRASP are development environments that make Java programming much faster and easier.

If you like to use jGRASP, you can download it from `http://www.jgrasp.org/`. In the project under "Settings->PATH/CLASSPATH->Workspace", you can add the directory of the *.dll files to the system PATH window, and add "*.jar" files with full path to the CLASSPATH window.

If you like to use Eclipse, you can download from `http://eclipse.org` the latest version of Eclipse that matches the platform you use. Expand it into the folder where you would like Eclipse to run from, (e.g., "C:\eclipse\"). There is no installation to run. You can put "*.jar" files under "Project->Properties->Libraries". To remove Eclipse you simply delete the directory, because Eclipse does not alter the system registry.

As another alternative, you can download a free version of JBuilder from `http://www.borland.com/jbuilder/`. JBuilder comes with its own JDK. If you use JBuilder as the IDE and want to use your downloaded JDK, you need to start JBuilder, go to "Tools->Configue JDKs", and click "Change" to change the "JDK home path:" to where you install your JDK. For example, "C:\myJDK\". Also, under "Tools->Configue JDKs", you can click "Add" to add "*.jar" files from wherever you save it to the JBuilder environment.

4. Creating a Sample Program in Eclipse

As an example, here we introduce using Eclipse. After downloading it, you can run it to start programming. Now in Eclipse you click on "File->New->Project" to create a new *Java Project* at a name you prefer. Then, you click on "File->New->Class" to create a new class with name: "J1_0_Point". After that, you can copy the following code into the space, and click on "Run->Run As->Java Application" to start compiling and running. You should see a window with a very tiny red pixel at the center. In the future, you can continue creating new classes, as we introduce each example as a new class. Alternatively, you can download all the examples from the web.

/* draw a point */

```
/* Java's supplied classes are "imported". Here the awt
(Abstract Windowing Toolkit) is imported to provide "Frame"
class, which includes windowing functions */
import java.awt.*;

// JOGL: OpenGL functions
import javax.media.opengl.*;

/* Java class definition: "extends" means "inherits". So
J1_0_Point is a subclass of Frame, and it inherits Frame's
variables and methods. "implements" means GLEventListener is
an interface, which only defines methods (init(), reshape(),
display(), and displaychanged()) without implementation.These
methods are actually callback functions handling events.
J1_0_Point will implement GLEventListener's methods and use
them for different events. */


public class J1_0_Point extends Frame implements
  GLEventListener {

 static int HEIGHT = 600, WIDTH = 600;
 static GL gl; //interface to OpenGL
 static GLCanvas canvas; // drawable in a frame
 static GLCapabilities capabilities;

 public J1_0_Point() {

  //1. specify a drawable: canvas
  capabilities = new GLCapabilities();
  canvas = new GLCanvas();

  //2. listen to the events related to canvas: reshape
  canvas.addGLEventListener(this);

  //3. add the canvas to fill the Frame container
  add(canvas, BorderLayout.CENTER);
      /* In Java, a method belongs to a class object.
      Here the method "add" belongs to J1_0_Point's
      instantiation, which is frame in "main" function.
      It is equivalent to use "this.add(canvas, ...)" */

  //4. interface to OpenGL functions
  gl = canvas.getGL();
 }


 public static void main(String[] args) {
```

```java
J1_0_Point frame = new J1_0_Point();

//5. set the size of the frame and make it visible
frame.setSize(WIDTH, HEIGHT);
frame.setVisible(true);
}


// called once for OpenGL initialization
public void init(GLAutoDrawable drawable) {

//6. specify a drawing color: red
gl.glColor3f(1.0f, 0.0f, 0.0f);
}


// called for handling reshaped drawing area
public void reshape(
  GLAutoDrawable drawable,
  int x,
  int y,
  int width,
  int height) {

  WIDTH = width; // new width and height saved
  HEIGHT = height;

//7. specify the drawing area (frame) coordinates
gl.glMatrixMode(GL.GL_PROJECTION);
gl.glLoadIdentity();
gl.glOrtho(0, width, 0, height, -1.0, 1.0);
}


// called for OpenGL rendering every reshape
public void display(GLAutoDrawable drawable) {

//8. specify to draw a point
//gl.glPointSize(10);
gl.glBegin(GL.GL_POINTS);
gl.glVertex2i(WIDTH/2, HEIGHT/2);
gl.glEnd();
}


// called if display mode or device are changed
public void displayChanged(
  GLAutoDrawable drawable,
  boolean modeChanged,
```

```
        boolean deviceChanged) {
    }
}
```

5.3 Drawing a Point

The above *J1_0_Point.java* is a Java application that draws a red point using JOGL. If you are a C/C++ programmer, you should read all the comments in the sample program carefully, because they include explanations about Java-specific terminologies and coding. Our future examples are built on top of this one. Here we explain in detail. The program is complex to us at this point of time. We only need to understand the following:

1. Class GLCanvas is an Abstract Window Toolkit (AWT) component that provides OpenGL rendering support. Therefore, the GLCanvas object, `canvas`, corresponds to the drawing area that will appear in the Frame object `frame`, which corresponds to the display window. Here *object* means an instance of a class in object-oriented programming, not a 3D object. In the future, we omit using a class name and underline its object name in our discussion. In many cases, object names are lowercases of the corresponding class names to facilitate understanding.

2. An *event* is a user input or a system state change, which is queued with other events to be handled. Event handling is to register an object to act as a listener for a particular type of event on a particular component. Here `frame` is a listener for the GL events on `canvas`. When a specific event happens, it sends `canvas` to the corresponding event handling method and invokes the method. GLEventListener has four event-handling methods:

   • *init()* is called immediately after the OpenGL context is initialized for the first time, which is a system event. It can be used to perform one-time OpenGL initialization;

   • *reshape()* is called if `canvas` has been resized, which happens when the user changes the size of the window. The listener also passes the drawable `canvas` and the display area's lower-left corner (*x*, *y*) and size (*width*, *height*) to the method. At this time, (*x*, *y*) is always (*0, 0*), and the `canvas`' size is the same as the display window's `frame`. The client can update the coordinates of the display corresponding to the resized window appropriately. *reshape()* is called at least once when program starts. Whenever *reshape()* is called, *display()* is called as well;

- *display()* is called to initiate OpenGL rendering when program starts. It is called afterwards when reshape event happens;

- *displayChanged()* is called when the display mode or the display device has been changed. Currently we do not use this event handler.

3. `canvas` is added to `frame` to cover the whole display area. `canvas` will reshape with `frame`.

4. `gl` is an interface handle to OpenGL methods. All OpenGL commands are prefixed with "gl" as well, so you will see OpenGL method like ***gl.glColor()***. When we explain the OpenGL command, we often omit the interface handle.

5. Here we set the physical size of `frame` and make its contents visible. Here the physical size corresponds to the number of pixels in x and y direction. The actual physical size also depends on the *resolution* of the display, which is measured in number of pixels per inch. At this point, the window frame appears. Depending on the JOGL version, the physical size may include the boarders, which is a little larger than the visible area that is returned as w and h in *reshape()*.

6. The foreground drawing color is specified as a vector (red, green, blue). Here (1, 0, 0) represents a red color.

7. These methods specify the logical coordinates. For example, if we use the command *glOrtho(0, width, 0, height, −1.0, 1.0)*, then the coordinates in `frame` (or `canvas`) will be $0 \leq x \leq width$ from the left side to the right side of the window, $0 \leq y \leq height$ from the bottom side to the top side of the window, and $-1 \leq z \leq 1$ in the direction perpendicular to the window. The z direction is ignored in 2D applications. It is a coincidence that the logical coordinates correspond to the physical (pixel) coordinates, because *width* and *height* are initially from `frame`'s WIDTH and HEIGHT. We can specify *glOrtho(0, 100*WIDTH, 0, 100*HEIGHT, −1.0, 1.0)* as well, then point (*WIDTH/2, HEIGHT/2*) will appear at the lower-left corner of the `frame` instead of the center of the `frame`.

8. These methods draw a point at (*WIDTH/2, HEIGHT/2*). The coordinates are logical coordinates not directly related to the canvas' size. The *width* and *height* in *glOrtho()* are actual window size. It is the same as WIDTH and HEIGHT at the beginning, but if you reshape the window, they will be different, respectively. Therefore, if we reshape the window, the red point moves.

In summary, when Frame is instantiated, constructor *J1_0_Point()* will create a drawable canvas, add event listener to it, attach the display to it, and get a handle to `gl` methods from it. *reshape()* will set up the display's logical coordinates in the window frame. *display()* will draw a point in the logical coordinates. When program starts, *main()* will be called, then `frame` instantiation, *J1_0_Point(), setSize(), setVisible(), init(), reshape(), and dsplay(). reshape()* and *dsplay()* will be called again and again if the user changes the display area. You may not find it, but a red point appears in the window.

5.4 Drawing Randomly Generated Points

J1_1_Point extends *J1_0_Point*, so it inherits all the methods from *J1_0_Point* that are not private. We can reuse the constructor and some of the methods.

/* draw randomly generated points */

```
import javax.media.opengl.*;
import com.sun.opengl.util.Animator;
import java.awt.event.*;


//built on J1_0_Point class
public class J1_1_Point extends J1_0_Point {
  static Animator animator; // drive display() in a loop


  public J1_1_Point() {

    // use super's constructor to initialize drawing

    //1. specify using only a single buffer
    capabilities.setDoubleBuffered(false);

    //2. add a listener for window closing
```

```java
  addWindowListener(new WindowAdapter() {
   public void windowClosing(WindowEvent e) {
     animator.stop(); // stop animation
     System.exit(0);
    }
  });
}


// called one-time for OpenGL initialization
public void init(GLAutoDrawable drawable) {

 // specify a drawing color: red
 gl.glColor3f(1.0f, 0.0f, 0.0f);

 //3. clear the background to black
 gl.glClearColor(0.0f, 0.0f, 0.0f, 0.0f);
 gl.glClear(GL.GL_COLOR_BUFFER_BIT);

 //4. drive the display() in a loop
 animator = new Animator(canvas);
 animator.start(); // start animator thread
}


// called for OpenGL rendering every reshape
public void display(GLAutoDrawable drawable) {
 //5. generate a random point
 double x = Math.random()*WIDTH;
 double y = Math.random()*HEIGHT;

 // specify to draw a point
 gl.glBegin(GL.GL_POINTS);
 gl.glVertex2d(x, y);
 gl.glEnd();
}


public static void main(String[] args) {
 J1_1_Point f = new J1_1_Point();

 //6. add a title on the frame
 f.setTitle("JOGL J1_1_Point");

 f.setSize(WIDTH, HEIGHT);
 f.setVisible(true);
}
}
```

1. *J1_1_Point* is built on (extends) the super (previous) class, so we can reuse its methods. The super class's constructor is automatically called to initialize drawing and event handling. Here we specify using a single frame buffer. Frame buffer corresponds to the display, which will be discussed in the next section.

2. The drawing area corresponding to the display is the frame buffer. JOGL in default is using double-buffering for animation. Here we just need a single buffer that corresponds to the frame buffer.

3. In order to avoid window hanging, we add a listener for window closing and stop animation before exit. Animation (`animator`) will be discussed later.

4. *glClearColor()* specifies the background color. OpenGL is a state machine, which means that if we specify the color, unless we change it, it will always be the same. Therefore, whenever we call *glClear()*, the background will be black unless we call *glCearClor()* to set it differently.

5. Object `animator` is attached to `canvas` to drive its *display()* method in a loop. When `animator` is started, it will generate a thread to call display repetitively. A thread is a process or task that runs with current program concurrently. Java is a multi-threaded programming language that allows starting multiple threads. `animator` is stopped before window closing.

6. A random point is generated. Because `animator` will run *display()* again and again in its thread, randomly generated points are displayed.

In summary, the super class' constructor, which is called implicitly, will create a drawable `canvas`, add event listener to it, and attach the display to it. *reshape()* will set up the display's logical coordinates in the window frame. *animator.start()* will call *display()* multiple times in a thread. *display()* will draw a point in logical coordinates. When program starts, *main()* will be called, then red points appear in the window.

5.5 Building an Executable JAR File

To facilitate sharing and deployment, we can generate an executable jar file for use with our JOGL applications as follows.

1. Set up a working directory to build your jar file.

2. Move all the necessary java class files into this directory, including all inheritance class files. For example, if you are to run program J1_1_Point, you should have your directory as follows:

```
2008-01-07  08:31   <DIR>         .
2008-01-07  08:31   <DIR>         ..
2008-01-07  09:19          1,766 J1_1_Point.class
2008 01 06  18:10          2,190 J1_0_Point.class
2008-01-07  09:19            736 J1_1_Point$1.class
              3 File(s)     4,692 bytes
```

3. Create a text file "manifest-info.txt" in the same directory that contains the following information with a carriage return at the last line:

```
Class-Path: gluegen-rt.jar jogl.jar
Main-Class: J1_1_Point
```

The Class-Path entry should include any jar files needed to run this program (jogl.jar and gluegen-rt.jar). When you run your program, you must make sure that these jar files are in the same directory. The Main-Class entry tells Java system which file contains your main method.

4. Execute the following in the same directory from the command line:

```
> "C:\myJDK\bin\jar" -cfm myexe.jar manifest-info.txt *.class
```

This will create your jar file with the specified manifest information and all of the *.class files in this directory.

5. Run your executable jar file:

You should now have your executable jar file in this directory (myexe.jar). To run the file, you need to put the library jar files (jogl.jar and gluegen-rt.jar) in the same directory. You may want to put all the dll files in the same directory as well if they are not installed in the system. Your directory will contain the following files as in our example:

```
2008-01-07  08:31   <DIR>         ..
2008-01-07  09:19          1,766 J1_1_Point.class
2008-01-06  18:10          2,190 J1_0_Point.class
2008-01-07  09:19            736 J1_1_Point$1.class
2008-01-07  09:46             61 manifest-info.txt
2008-01-07  09:46          3,419 myexe.jar
2007-04-22  02:00      1,065,888 jogl.jar
```

```
2007-04-22 02:00        17,829 gluegen-rt.jar
2007-04-22 02:00        20,480 gluegen-rt.dll
2007-04-22 02:00       315,392 jogl.dll
2007-04-22 02:00        20,480 jogl_awt.dll
          10 File(s)   1,448,241 bytes
```

Now you can either double-click on the jar file in Windows interface environment or execute it on a command line with:

```
> "C:\myJDK\bin\java" -jar myexe.jar
```

To get additional help or learn more on this topic you may visit the following place:

```
http://java.sun.com/docs/books/tutorial/deployment/jar/
index.html
```

5.6 Review Questions

1. What is provided by the Animator class in JOGL?

    a. calling reshape()

    c. calling display() repetitively

    b. implementing interface functions

    d. transforming the objects

2. What are provided by the JOGL's GLUT class?

    a. bitmap and stroke font methods

    c. calling reshape() or display()

    b. antialiasing

    d. handling display area

5.7 Programming Assignments

1. Draw a point that moves slowly along a circle. You may want to draw a circle first, and a point that moves on the circle with a different color.

2. Draw a point that bounces slowly in a square or circle.

3. Draw a star in a circle that rotates, as shown on the right. You can only use glBegin(GL_POINTS) to draw the star.

4. Write down "Bitmap" using Glut bitmap font function and "Stroke" using Glut stroke font function in the center of the display.

5. With the star rotating in the circle, implement the clipping of a window as shown on the right.

6. Implement an antialiasing line algorithm that works with the background that has a texture. The method is to blend the background color with the foreground color. You can get the current pixel color in the frame buffer using glGet() with **GL_CURRENT_RASTER_COLOR.**

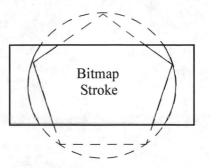

7. Implement a triangle filling algorithm for J1_3_Triangle class that draws a randomly generated triangle. Here you can only use glBegin(GL_POINTS) to draw the triangle.

8. Draw (and animate) the star with antialiasing and clipping. Add a filled circle inside the star using the subdivision method discussed in this chapter. You should use your own triangle filling algorithm. Also, clipping can be trickily done by checking the point to be drawn against the clipping window.

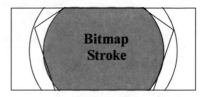

6
Curved Models

Chapter Objectives:

- Introduce existing 3D model functions in GLUT and GLU libraries
- Introduce theories and programming of basic cubic curves and bi-cubic curved surfaces

6.1 Introduction

Just as that there are numerous scan-conversion methods for a primitive, there exists different ways to create a 3D model as well. For example, we can create a sphere model through subdivision as discussed in Chapter 2. We can also use a sphere equation to find all the points on the sphere and render it accordingly. Further, we can find a set of points on a circle in the xy plane and rotate the points along x or y axis to find all the points on the corresponding sphere. Although generating 3D models is not exactly basic graphics drawing capabilities, it is part of the graphics theory. In this chapter, we introduce some existing 3D models and the corresponding function calls in GLUT and GLU libraries. Also, we provide the math foundations for some curved 3D models, including quadratic surfaces, cubic curves, and bi-cubic surfaces.

The degree of an equation with one variable in each term is the exponent of the highest power to which that variable is raised in the equation. For example, $(ax^2 + bx + c = 0)$ is a second-degree equation, as x is raised to the power of 2. When more than one variable appears in a term, as in $(axy^2 + bx + cy + d = 0)$, it is necessary to add the exponents of the variables within a term to get the degree of the equation, which is 3 in this example. Quadratic curves and surfaces are represented by second-degree equations. Cubic curves are third-degree equations.

J.X. Chen, Guide to Graphics Software Tools, doi: 10.1007/978-1-84800-901-1_6,

6.2 Quadratic Surfaces

Quadratic surfaces, or simply quadrics, are defined by the following general form second-degree (quadratic) equation:

$$ax^2 + by^2 + cz^2 + dxy + exz + fyz + gx + hy + iz + j = 0. \qquad \text{(EQ 110)}$$

There are numerous models that can be generated by the above equation, including spheres, ellipsoids, cones, and cylinders.

6.2.1 Sphere

In Cartesian coordinates, a sphere at the origin with radius r is

$$x^2 + y^2 + z^2 = r^2. \qquad \text{(EQ 111)}$$

In parametric equation form, a sphere is

$$x = r\cos\phi\cos\theta, \ 0 \le \phi \le \pi, \qquad \text{(EQ 112)}$$

$$y = r\cos\phi\sin\theta, \ 0 \le \theta \le 2\pi, \qquad \text{(EQ 113)}$$

$$\text{and } z = r\sin\phi. \qquad \text{(EQ 114)}$$

So we can find all the points on a sphere through a double for-loop:

```
for (int i=0; i<nLongitudes; i++)
for (j=0; j<nLatitudes; i++)
   drawSherePoint (
       r*cos(i*PI/nLongitudes)*cos(j*2*PI/nLatitudes),
       r*cos(i*PI/nLongitudes)*sin(j*2*PI/nLatitudes),
       r*sin(i*PI/nLongitudes));
```

Both GLUT and GLU provide wireframe or solid sphere drawing functions, which are demonstrated in Example *J5_1_Quadrics.java*. In C binding:

```
// Using GLUT to draw a sphere
glutWireSphere(r, nLongitudes, nLatitudes);
glutSolidSphere(r, nLongitudes, nLatitudes);
```

```
// USING GLU to draw a sphere
GLUquadric *sphere = gluNewQuadric();
gluQuadricDrawStyle(shpere, GLU_LINE); //GLU_FILL
glusphere(sphere, r, nLongitudes, nLatitudes);
```

6.2.2 Ellipsoid

In Cartesian coordinates, an ellipsoid at the origin is

$$\left(\frac{x}{r_x}\right)^2 + \left(\frac{y}{r_y}\right)^2 + \left(\frac{z}{r_z}\right)^2 = 1. \qquad \textbf{(EQ 115)}$$

In parametric equation form:

$$x = r_x\cos\phi\cos\theta, \ 0 \le \phi \le \pi, \qquad \textbf{(EQ 116)}$$

$$y = r_y\cos\phi\sin\theta, \ 0 \le \theta \le 2\pi, \qquad \textbf{(EQ 117)}$$

$$\text{and } z = r_z\sin\phi. \qquad \textbf{(EQ 118)}$$

Similarly, we can find all points on an ellipsoid through a double for-loop. Because ellipsoids can be achieved by scaling a sphere in graphics programming, neither GLUT nor GLU provides drawing them.

6.2.3 Cone

A cone with its height h on the z axis, bottom radius r in xy plane and tip at the origin is

$$z^2 = (x^2 + y^2)\left(\frac{h}{r}\right)^2.$$

(EQ 119)

In parametric equation form:

$$x = r\left(\frac{h-u}{h}\right)\cos\theta, \quad 0 \le u \le h,$$

(EQ 120)

$$y = r\left(\frac{h-u}{h}\right)\sin\theta, \quad 0 \le \theta \le 2\pi,$$

(EQ 121)

$$\text{and } z = u.$$

(EQ 122)

GLUT provides wireframe or solid cone drawing functions, which are demonstrated in Example *J5_1_Quadrics.java*. The function call is as follows:

```
// USING GLUT to draw a cone
glut.glutSolidCone(glu, r, h, nLongitudes, nLatitudes);
```

6.2.4 Cylinder

In parametric equation form, a cylinder is

$$x = r\cos\theta,$$

(EQ 123)

$$y = r\sin\theta, \quad 0 \le \theta \le 2\pi,$$

(EQ 124)

$$\text{and } z = z.$$

(EQ 125)

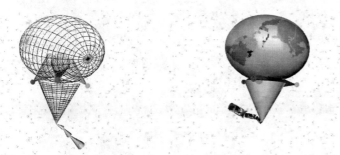

Fig. 6.1 GLUT and GLU models: wireframe or filled surfaces

Both GLUT and GLU provide wireframe or solid cylinder drawing functions, which are demonstrated in Example *J5_1_Quadrics.java*.

6.2.5 Texture Mapping on GLU Models

GLU provides automatic specifying texture coordinates in rendering its models, which is specified by *gluQuadricTexture()*. Therefore, texture mapping is made simple. We can just specify texture parameters and data as before, and we do not worry how the texture coordinates are specified on the primitives. GLUT only provides automatic texture coordinates specifications in rendering its teapot, which will be discussed later.

Fig. 6.1 is a snapshot demonstrating GLUT and GLU library functions that are employed to draw spheres, cones, and cylinders in *J5_1_Quadrics.java*. The ellipsoid is achieved through scaling a sphere instead of direct rendering from ellipsoid parametric equations.

/* GLUT and GLU quadrics */

```
import net.java.games.jogl.GLU;
import net.java.games.jogl.*;


public class J5_1_Quadrics extends J4_8_Mipmap {
```

```
GLU glu = canvas.getGLU(); // glut int. is inherited
GLUquadric cylinder = glu.gluNewQuadric();
GLUquadric sphere = glu.gluNewQuadric();

public void drawSphere() {
 double r = 1;

 // number of points along longitudes and latitudes
 int nLongitudes = 20, nLatitudes = 20;

 // switch between two textures -- effect
 if ((cnt%1000)<500) {
  gl.glBindTexture(GL.GL_TEXTURE_2D, EARTH_TEX[0]);
 } else {
  gl.glBindTexture(GL.GL_TEXTURE_2D, IRIS_TEX[0]);
 }

 gl.glTexEnvf(GL.GL_TEXTURE_ENV,
        GL.GL_TEXTURE_ENV_MODE, GL.GL_MODULATE);

 if (cnt%950<400) { // draw solid sphere with GLU

  // automatic generate texture coords
  glu.gluQuadricTexture(sphere, true);
  gl.glEnable(GL.GL_TEXTURE_2D);

  // draw a filled sphere with GLU
  glu.gluQuadricDrawStyle(sphere, GLU.GLU_FILL);
  glu.gluSphere(sphere, r, nLongitudes, nLatitudes);
 } else {

  // draw wireframe sphere with GLUT.
  glut.glutWireSphere(glu, r, nLongitudes, nLatitudes);
 }

 gl.glDisable(GL.GL_TEXTURE_2D);

 if (cnt%800<400) { // for the background texture
  gl.glBindTexture(GL.GL_TEXTURE_2D, STARS_TEX[0]);
 } else {
  gl.glBindTexture(GL.GL_TEXTURE_2D, IRIS_TEX[0]);
 }
}


public void drawCone() {
 double r = 1, h = 1;
 int nLongitudes = 20, nLatitudes = 20;
```

```
    if (cnt%950>400) { // draw wireframe cone with GLUT
      glut.glutWireCone(glu, r, h, nLongitudes, nLatitudes);
    } else { //draw solid cone with GLUT
      glut.glutSolidCone(glu, r, h, nLongitudes, nLatitudes);
    }
  }


  public void drawCylinder() {
    double r = 1, h = 1;
    int nLongitudes = 20, nLatitudes = 20;

    // switching between two texture images
    if ((cnt%1000)<5000) {
      gl.glBindTexture(GL.GL_TEXTURE_2D, IRIS_TEX[0]);
    } else {
      gl.glBindTexture(GL.GL_TEXTURE_2D, EARTH_TEX[0]);
    }

    // automatic generate texture coords
    glu.gluQuadricTexture(cylinder, true);
    gl.glEnable(GL.GL_TEXTURE_2D);

    if (cnt%950<400) { // draw solid cylinder with GLU
      glu.gluQuadricDrawStyle(cylinder, GLU.GLU_FILL);
    } else { // draw point cylinder with GLU.
      glu.gluQuadricDrawStyle(cylinder, GLU.GLU_POINT);
    }

    // actually draw the cylinder
    glu.gluCylinder(cylinder, r, r, h, nLongitudes,
            nLatitudes);

    gl.glDisable(GL.GL_TEXTURE_2D);
  }


  public static void main(String[] args) {

    J5_1_Quadrics f = new J5_1_Quadrics();

    f.setTitle("JOGL J5_1_Quadrics");
    f.setSize(WIDTH, HEIGHT);
    f.setVisible(true);
  }
}
```

6.3 Tori, Polyhedra, and Teapots in GLUT

In addition to drawing cone and sphere, GLUT provides a set of functions for rendering 3D models, including a torus, cube, tetrahedron, octahedron, dodecahedron, icosahedron, and teapot, in both solid shapes and wireframes. They are easy to use for applications, as demonstrated in *J5_2_Solids.java*, where we replace drawing sphere in our previous program (*J5_1_Quadrics.java*) with different 3D models in GLUT.

6.3.1 Tori

A torus looks the same as a doughnut, as shown in Fig. 6.2. It can be generated by rotating a circle around a line outside the circle. Therefore, a torus has two radii: r_{in} of the inner circle which is a cross section inside the doughnut, and r_{out} of the outer circle which is the doughnut as a circle. Then, the equation in Cartesian coordinates for a torus azimuthally symmetric about the *z*-axis is

$$\left(r_{in} - \sqrt{x^2 + y^2}\right)^2 + z^2 = r_{out}^2, \qquad \text{(EQ 126)}$$

and the parametric equations are

$$x = (r_{in} + r_{out}\cos\phi)\cos\theta, \quad 0 \le \phi \le 2\pi, \qquad \text{(EQ 127)}$$

$$y = (r_{in} + r_{out}\cos\phi)\sin\theta, \quad 0 \le \theta \le 2\pi, \qquad \text{(EQ 128)}$$

$$z = r_{out}\sin\phi. \qquad \text{(EQ 129)}$$

6.3.2 Polyhedra

A *polyhedron* is an arbitrary 3D shape whose surface is a collection of flat polygons. A *regular* polyhedron is one whose faces and vertices all look the same. There are only five regular polyhedra: the *tetrahedron* — 4 faces with three equilateral triangles at a vertex; the *cube* — 6 faces with three squares at a vertex; the *octahedron* — 8 faces with four equilateral triangles at a vertex; the *dodecahedron* — 12 faces with three pentagons at a vertex; and the *icosahedron* — 20 faces with five equilateral triangles at a vertex. The regular polyhedron models can be found in many books and graphics packages. However, the complex polyhedron model requires effort to be constructed.

GLUT provides functions to draw the regular polyhedra, as shown in Fig. 6.2. Polyhedra are flat-surface models, therefore they are not really curved surface models. Their counterpart is a sphere. The difference between the sphere and the polyhedra is really how the normals are specified.

6.3.3 Teapots

glutSolidTeapot() and *glutWireTeapot()* render a solid and wireframe teapot, respectively. Both surface normals and texture coordinates for the teapot are generated by the program, so texture mapping is available, as shown in Fig. 6.2 Actually, the teapot is the only model in GLUT that comes with texture coordinates. The teapot is generated with OpenGL evaluators, which will be discussed later.

The teapot's surface primitives are all back-facing. That is, the polygon vertices are all ordered clockwise. For the back-face culling purpose, we need to specify the front face as *glFrontFace(GL_CW)* before drawing the teapot to conform to the back-face culling employed in the programs, and return to normal situation using *glFrontFace(GL_CCW)* after drawing it. The teapot is very finely tessellated, so it is very slow to be rendered.

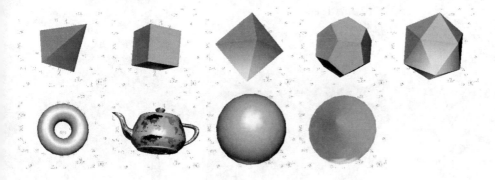

Fig. 6.2 3D models that GLUT renders

/* display GLUT solids: tori, polyhedra, and teapots */

```java
import net.java.games.jogl.GL;


public class J5_2_Solids extends J5_1_Quadrics {

    // replace the spheres with GLUT solids
  public void drawSphere() {

    gl.glPushMatrix();
    gl.glScaled(0.5, 0.5, 0.5);

    if (cnt%2000<100) {
      glut.glutSolidCone(glu, 1, 1, 20, 20);
    } else
    if (cnt%2000<200) {
      glut.glutWireCone(glu, 1, 1, 20, 20);
    } else
    if (cnt%2000<300) {
      glut.glutSolidCube(gl, 1);
    } else
    if (cnt%2000<400) {
      glut.glutWireCube(gl, 1);
    } else
    if (cnt%2000<500) {
      glut.glutSolidDodecahedron(gl);
    } else
    if (cnt%2000<600) {
      glut.glutWireDodecahedron(gl);
    } else
    if (cnt%2000<700) {
      glut.glutSolidIcosahedron(gl);
    } else
    if (cnt%2000<800) {
      glut.glutWireIcosahedron(gl);
    } else
    if (cnt%2000<900) {
      glut.glutSolidOctahedron(gl);
    } else
    if (cnt%2000<1000) {
      glut.glutWireOctahedron(gl);
    } else
    if (cnt%2000<1100) {
      glut.glutSolidSphere(glu, 1, 20, 20);
    } else
    if (cnt%2000<1200) {
      glut.glutWireSphere(glu, 1, 20, 20);
    } else
```

```
if (cnt%2000<1300) {
 gl.glBindTexture(GL.GL_TEXTURE_2D, EARTH_TEX[0]);
 gl.glTexEnvf(GL.GL_TEXTURE_ENV,
        GL.GL_TEXTURE_ENV_MODE, GL.GL_MODULATE);
 gl.glEnable(GL.GL_TEXTURE_2D);

 gl.glFrontFace(GL.GL_CW);
 // the faces are clockwise
 glut.glutSolidTeapot(gl, 1);

 gl.glFrontFace(GL.GL_CCW);
 // return to normal

 gl.glDisable(GL.GL_TEXTURE_2D);
} else
if (cnt%2000<1400) {
 glut.glutWireTeapot(gl, 1);
} else
if (cnt%2000<1500) {
 glut.glutSolidTetrahedron(gl);
} else
if (cnt%2000<1600) {
 glut.glutWireTetrahedron(gl);
} else
if (cnt%2000<1700) {
 glut.glutSolidTorus(gl, 0.5, 1, 20, 20);
} else if (cnt%2000<1800) {
 glut.glutWireTorus(gl, 0.5, 1, 20, 20);
}
gl.glPopMatrix();

// for the background texture
gl.glBindTexture(GL.GL_TEXTURE_2D, STARS_TEX[0]);
}


public static void main(String[] args) {

 J5_2_Solids f = new J5_2_Solids();

 f.setTitle("JOGL J5_2_Solids");
 f.setSize(WIDTH, HEIGHT);
 f.setVisible(true);
}
}
```

6.4 Cubic Curves

Conic sections are quadratic curves, which includes circle, ellipse, parabola, and hyperbola. Their equations are in second-degree and they represent 2D curves that always fit into planes. Cubic curves, or simply cubics, are the lowest-degree curves that are non-planar in 3D. If we consider a curve like a worm wiggles in 2D changing direction along the curve, quadratic curves have at most one wiggle, and cubic curves have at most two wiggles. As you can see, higher degree curves will have more wiggles, but they are complex and time consuming. Instead, we can connect multiple cubic curves (segments) to form a curve with the number of wiggles and shape we want.

We study curves in parametric polynomial form. In general, a parametric polynomial is expressed as:

$$f(t) = a_0 + a_1 t + a_2 t^2 + \ldots + a_n t^n, \tag{EQ 130}$$

and a curve in 3D is

$$Q(t) = (x(t), y(t), z(t)), \tag{EQ 131}$$

where for a cubic curve segment,

$$0 \le t \le 1 \tag{EQ 132}$$

and:

$$x(t) = a_{0x} + a_{1x} t + a_{2x} t^2 + a_{3x} t^3, \tag{EQ 133}$$

$$y(t) = a_{0y} + a_{1y} t + a_{2y} t^2 + a_{3y} t^3, \tag{EQ 134}$$

$$z(t) = a_{0z} + a_{1z} t + a_{2z} t^2 + a_{3z} t^3. \tag{EQ 135}$$

Because $x(t)$, $y(t)$, and $z(t)$ are in the same form but independent of each other except at drawing, where they are used together to specify a point, we discuss $p(t)$ in place of $x(t)$, $y(t)$, or $z(t)$. Therefore, we simplify the cubic parametric equations above into a representative equation as follows:

$$p(t) = at^3 + bt^2 + ct + d, \text{ where } 0 \le t \le 1.$$ **(EQ 136)**

In matrix form, we have

$$p(t) = \begin{bmatrix} t^3 & t^2 & t & 1 \end{bmatrix} \begin{bmatrix} a \\ b \\ c \\ d \end{bmatrix}$$ **(EQ 137)**

6.4.1 Continuity Conditions

The first derivative at a point on a curve, $\dfrac{d(Q(t))}{dt} = Q'(t) = (x'(t), y'(t), z'(t))$, is the tangent vector at a specific t. For easier understanding, we may assume that t is the time, then from time $t = 0$ to $t = 1$ a point moves from $Q(0)$ to $Q(1)$ and the tangent vector is the velocity (direction and speed) of the point tracing out the curve.

As we discussed, a cubic curve is a segment where $0 \le t \le 1$ (Equation 131, Equation 132 on page 152). We can connect multiple cubic curves to form a longer curve. The smoothness condition of the connection is determined by the continuity conditions as discussed below for two curves.

Parametric continuity. Zero-order parametric continuity, C^0, means that the ending-point of the first curve meets the starting-point of the second curve:

$$Q_1(1) = Q_2(0).$$ **(EQ 138)**

First-order parametric continuity, C^1, means that the first derivatives of the two successive curves are equal at their connection:

$$Q'_1(1) = Q'_2(0).$$
(EQ 139)

Second-order parametric continuity, C^2, means that both the first and second parametric derivatives of the two curves are the same at the intersection:

$$Q'_1(1) = Q'_2(0), \text{ and } Q''_1(1) = Q''_2(0).$$
(EQ 140)

Higher-order continuity conditions are defined similarly, which are meaningful for higher degree curves.

Geometric continuity. Zero-order geometric continuity, G^0, means that the end point of the first curve meets the starting-point of the second curve:

$$Q_1(1) = Q_2(0).$$
(EQ 141)

First-order geometric continuity, G^1, means that the first derivatives of the two successive curves are proportional at their connection:

$$Q'_1(1) = kQ'_2(0).$$
(EQ 142)

where k is a constant. In other words, the two tangent vector's directions are still the same, but their lengths may not be the same.

Similarly, second-order geometric continuity, G^2, means that both the first and second parametric derivatives of the two curves are proportional at the intersection:

$$Q'_1(1) = k_1Q'_2(0), \text{ and } Q''_1(1) = k_2Q''_2(0).$$
(EQ 143)

Compared to parametric continuity conditions, geometric continuity conditions are more flexible.

6.4.2 Hermite Curves

Hermite curves are specified by two end points $p(0)$ and $p(1)$ and two tangent vectors at the two ends $p'(0)$ and $p'(1)$. The end points and tangent vectors are called the *boundary constraints* of a Hermite curve. According to Equation 136 on page 153:

$$p(0) = d, \qquad \text{(EQ 144)}$$

$$p(1) = a + b + c + d, \qquad \text{(EQ 145)}$$

$$p'(0) = c, \text{ and} \qquad \text{(EQ 146)}$$

$$p'(1) = 3a + 2b + c. \qquad \text{(EQ 147)}$$

Therefore, from Equation 144 to Equation 147, we have:

$$a = 2p(0) - 2p(1) + p'(0) + p'(1), \qquad \text{(EQ 148)}$$

$$b = -3p(0) + 3p(1) - 2p'(0) - p'(1), \qquad \text{(EQ 149)}$$

$$c = p'(0), \qquad \text{(EQ 150)}$$

$$\text{and } d = p(0). \qquad \text{(EQ 151)}$$

Then, the equation for a Hermite curve is

$$p(t) = (2t^3 - 3t^2 + 1)p(0) + (-2t^3 + 3t^2)p(1) + \qquad \text{(EQ 152)}$$
$$(t^3 - 2t^2 + t)p'(0) + (t^3 - t^2)p'(1)$$

That is,

$$p(t) = H_0(t)p(0) + H_1(t)p(1) + H_2(t)p'(0) + H_3(t)p'(1), \qquad \text{(EQ 153)}$$

where $H_0(t)$, $H_1(t)$, $H_2(t)$, and $H_3(t)$ are called the *blending functions* of a Hermite curve, because they blend the four boundary constraint values to obtain each position along the curve at a specific t.

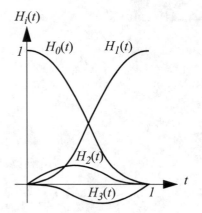

As shown in Fig. 6.3, when $t = 0$, only $H_0(0)$ is nonzero, and therefore only $P(0)$ has an influence on the curve. When $t=1$, only $H_1(1)$ is nonzero, and therefore only $P(1)$ has an influence on the curve. For all $0 < t < 1$, all boundary constraints have influences on the curve. Because the tangent vectors at the end points are specified as constants, if we connect multiple Hermite curves, we can specify C^1 or

Fig. 6.3 Hermite blending functions

G^1 continuity conditions, but we cannot specify C^2 or G^2 because the second derivatives do not exist.

We often express Hermite equation in matrix form as follows:

$$p(t) = \begin{bmatrix} t^3 & t^2 & t & 1 \end{bmatrix} \begin{bmatrix} 2 & -2 & 1 & 1 \\ -3 & 3 & -2 & -1 \\ 0 & 0 & 1 & 0 \\ 1 & 0 & 0 & 0 \end{bmatrix} \begin{bmatrix} p(0) \\ P(1) \\ p'(0) \\ p'(1) \end{bmatrix}$$

(EQ 154)

That is,

$$p(t) = TM_hP$$

(EQ 155)

where M_h is called the Hermite matrix, and P includes, as we said earlier, the boundary constraints. The following program draws Hermite curves in place of spheres in the previous example:

/* draw a hermite curve */

```java
import net.java.games.jogl.GL;
import net.java.games.jogl.GLU;
import net.java.games.jogl.GLDrawable; /**

public class J5_3_Hermite extends J5_2_Solids {

 double ctrlp[][] = { {-0.5, -0.5, -0.5}, {-1.0, 1.0, 1.0},
          {1.0, -1.0, 1.0}, {0.5, 0.5, 1.0}
 }; // control points: two end points, two tangent vectors

 public void myEvalCoordHermite(double t) {
  // evaluate the coordinates and specify the points
  double x, y, z, t_1, t2, t_2, t3, t_3;

  t_1 = 1-t;
  t2 = t*t;
  t_2 = t_1*t_1;
  t3 = t2*t;
  t_3 = t_2*t_1;

  x = t_3*ctrlp[0][0]+3*t*t_2*ctrlp[1][0]
    +3*t2*t_1*ctrlp[2][0]+t3*ctrlp[3][0];

  y = t_3*ctrlp[0][1]+3*t*t_2*ctrlp[1][1]
    +3*t2*t_1*ctrlp[2][1]+t3*ctrlp[3][1];

  z = t_3*ctrlp[0][2]+3*t*t_2*ctrlp[1][2]
    +3*t2*t_1*ctrlp[2][2]+t3*ctrlp[3][2];

  gl.glVertex3d(x, y, z);
 }



 public void drawSphere() {
  int i;

  myCameraView = true;

  gl.glLineWidth(4);
  gl.glBegin(GL.GL_LINE_STRIP);
  for (i = 0; i<=30; i++) {
   myEvalCoordHermite(i/30.0);
  }
  gl.glEnd();
  /* The following code displays the control points
```

```
 as dots. */
gl.glPointSize(6.0f);
gl.glBegin(GL.GL_POINTS);
gl.glVertex3dv(ctrlp[0]);
gl.glVertex3dv(ctrlp[3]);
gl.glEnd();

// for the background texture
gl.glBindTexture(GL.GL_TEXTURE_2D, STARS_TEX[0]);
}


public void drawCone() {
}


public static void main(String[] args) {
 J5_3_Hermite f = new J5_3_Hermite();

 f.setTitle("JOGL J5_3_Hermite");
 f.setSize(WIDTH, HEIGHT);
 f.setVisible(true);
 }
}
```

6.4.3 Bezier Curves

Bezier curves are specified by two end points: $p(0)$ and $p(1)$ and two control points C_1 and C_2 such that the tangent vectors at the two ends are $p'(0) = 3(C_1 - p(0))$ and $p'(1) = 3(p(1) - C_2)$. Similar to Hermite curve equation, according to Equation 136 on page 153 we have:

$$p(0) = d, \qquad \text{(EQ 156)}$$

$$p(1) = a + b + c + d, \qquad \text{(EQ 157)}$$

$$p'(0) = 3(C_1 - p(0)) = c, \text{ and} \qquad \text{(EQ 158)}$$

$$p'(1) = 3(p(1) - C_2) = 3a + 2b + c. \qquad \text{(EQ 159)}$$

Therefore, from Equation 156 to Equation 159, we have:

$$a = -p(0) + 3C_1 - 3C_2 + p(1),$$

(EQ 160)

$$b = 3p(0) - 6C_1 + 3C_2,$$

(EQ 161)

$$c = -3p(0) + 3C_1,$$

(EQ 162)

$$\text{and } d = p(0).$$

(EQ 163)

Then, the equation for Hermite curves is

$$p(t) = (1-t)^3 p(0) + 3t(1-t)^2 C_1 + 3t^2(1-t)C_2 + t^3 p(1).$$

(EQ 164)

That is,

$$p(t) = B_0(t)p(0) + B_1(t)C_1 + B_2(t)C_2 + B_3(t)p(1),$$

(EQ 165)

where $B_0(t)$, $B_1(t)$, $B_2(t)$, and $B_3(t)$ are Bezier curves' *blending functions*, because they blend the four boundary constraint points to obtain each position along the curve.

As shown in Fig. 6.4, when $t=0$, only $B_0(0)$ is nonzero, and therefore only $P(0)$ has an influence on the curve. When $t=1$, only $B_3(1)$ is nonzero, and therefore only $P(1)$ has an influence on the curve. For all $0<t<1$, all boundary constraints have influences on the curve. Because the tangent vectors at the end points are specified by the 4 constraints as constants, if we connect multiple Bezier curves, we can specify C^1 or G^1 continuity

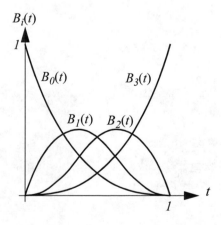

Fig. 6.4 **Bezier blending functions**

conditions, but we cannot specify C^2 or G^2 because the second derivatives do not exist.

Bezier curve has some important properties. If we use the four constraint points to form a convex hull in 3D (or convex polygon in 2D), the curve is cotangent to the two opposite edges defined by the $p(0)C_1$ and $C_2p(1)$ pairs. A convex hull, simply put, is a polyhedron with all of its vertices on only one side of each surface of the polyhedron. A cubic Bezier curve is just a weighted average of the four constraint points, and it is completely contained in the convex hull of the 4 control points. The sum of the four blending functions is equal to 1 for any t, and each polynomial is everywhere positive except at the two ends. As you can see, if we specify the constraint points on a line, according to the convex-hull property, the cubic Bezier curve is reduced to a line.

We often express Bezier curve equation in matrix form:

$$p(t) = \begin{bmatrix} t^3 & t^2 & t & 1 \end{bmatrix} \begin{bmatrix} -1 & 3 & -3 & 1 \\ 3 & -6 & 3 & 0 \\ -3 & 3 & 0 & 0 \\ 1 & 0 & 0 & 0 \end{bmatrix} \begin{bmatrix} p(0) \\ C_1 \\ C_2 \\ p(1) \end{bmatrix} \qquad \text{(EQ 166)}$$

That is,

$$p(t) = TM_bC, \qquad \text{(EQ 167)}$$

where M_b is called the Bezier matrix, and C includes the boundary constraints such that $C_0 = p(0)$ and $C_3 = p(1)$.

Bezier curves of general degree. Bezier curves can be easily extended into higher degrees. Given $n+1$ control point positions, we can blend them to produce the following:

$$p(t) = \sum_{k=0}^{n} C_k B_{k,n}(t), \qquad \text{(EQ 168)}$$

where the blending functions are called the Bernstein polynomials:

$$B_{k,n}(t) = C(n, k)t^k(1-t)^{n-k},$$ (EQ 169)

$$\text{and } C(n, k) = \frac{n!}{k!(n-k)!}.$$ (EQ 170)

OpenGL evaluators. OpenGL provides basic functions for calculating Bezier curves. Specifically, it uses *glMap1f()* to set up the interval (e.g., $0 \le t \le 1$), number of values (e.g., *3* for *xyz* or *4* for *xyzw*) to go from one control point to the next, degree of the equation (e.g., *4* for cubics), and control points (an array of points). Then, instead of calculating curve points and using *glVertex()* to specify the coordinates, we use *glEvaluCoord1()* to specify the coordinates at specified *t*'s, and the Bezier curve is calculated by the OpenGL system, as shown in Example *J5_4_Bezier.java*. A snapshot is in Fig. 6.5.

Fig. 6.5 Bezier curve

/* use OpenGL evaluators for Bezier curve */

```
import net.java.games.jogl.GL;
import net.java.games.jogl.GLDrawable;


public class J5_4_Bezier extends J5_3_Hermite {

  double ctrlpts[] =
            {0.0, -1.0, -0.5, -1.0, 1.0, -1.0,
          -1.0, -1.0, 1.0, 1.0, 0.05, 1.0};

  public void drawSphere() {

    int i;
```

```
  // specify Bezier curve vertex with:
  //   0<=t<=1, 3 values (x,y,z), and 4-1 degrees
  gl.glMap1d(GL.GL_MAP1_VERTEX_3, 0, 1, 3, 4, ctrlpts);
  gl.glEnable(GL.GL_MAP1_VERTEX_3);

  gl.glDisable(GL.GL_LIGHTING);

  gl.glLineWidth(3);
  gl.glColor4f(1f, 1f, 1f, 1f);

  gl.glBegin(GL.GL_LINE_STRIP);

  for (i = 0; i<=30; i++) {
   gl.glEvalCoord1d(i/30.0); // use OpenGL evaluator
  }

  gl.glEnd();

  // Highlight the control points
  gl.glPointSize(4);
  gl.glBegin(GL.GL_POINTS);
  gl.glColor4f(1f, 1f, 0f, 1f);
   gl.glVertex3d(ctrlpts[0], ctrlpts[1], ctrlpts[2]);
  gl.glVertex3d(ctrlpts[3], ctrlpts[4], ctrlpts[5]);
  gl.glVertex3d(ctrlpts[6], ctrlpts[7], ctrlpts[8]);
  gl.glVertex3d(ctrlpts[9], ctrlpts[10], ctrlpts[11]);
  gl.glEnd();

  // draw the convex hull as transparent
  gl.glEnable(GL.GL_BLEND);
  gl.glDepthMask(true);
  gl.glBlendFunc(GL.GL_SRC_ALPHA,
        GL.GL_ONE_MINUS_SRC_ALPHA);

  gl.glBegin(GL.GL_TRIANGLES);
  gl.glColor4f(0.9f, 0.9f, 0.9f, 0.3f);
  gl.glVertex3d(ctrlpts[0], ctrlpts[1], ctrlpts[2]);
  gl.glVertex3d(ctrlpts[3], ctrlpts[4], ctrlpts[5]);
  gl.glVertex3d(ctrlpts[9], ctrlpts[10], ctrlpts[11]);

  gl.glColor4f(0.9f, 0.0f, 0.0f, 0.3f);
  gl.glVertex3d(ctrlpts[0], ctrlpts[1], ctrlpts[2]);
  gl.glVertex3d(ctrlpts[9], ctrlpts[10], ctrlpts[11]);
  gl.glVertex3d(ctrlpts[6], ctrlpts[7], ctrlpts[8]);

  gl.glColor4f(0.0f, 0.9f, 0.0f, 0.3f);
  gl.glVertex3d(ctrlpts[0], ctrlpts[1], ctrlpts[2]);
  gl.glVertex3d(ctrlpts[6], ctrlpts[7], ctrlpts[8]);
```

```
gl.glVertex3d(ctrlpts[3], ctrlpts[4], ctrlpts[5]);

gl.glColor4f(0.0f, 0.0f, 0.9f, 0.3f);
gl.glVertex3d(ctrlpts[3], ctrlpts[4], ctrlpts[5]);
gl.glVertex3d(ctrlpts[6], ctrlpts[7], ctrlpts[8]);
gl.glVertex3d(ctrlpts[9], ctrlpts[10], ctrlpts[11]);

gl.glEnd();

gl.glDepthMask(false);

// for the background texture
gl.glBindTexture(GL.GL_TEXTURE_2D, STARS_TEX[0]);

}


public static void main(String[] args) {
  J5_4_Bezier f = new J5_4_Bezier();

  f.setTitle("JOGL J5_4_Bezier");
  f.setSize(WIDTH, HEIGHT);
  f.setVisible(true);
  }
}
```

6.4.4 Natural Splines

A spline is constructed from cubic curves with C^2 continuity. A natural cubic spline goes through all its control points. For $n+1$ control points, there are n cubic curves (segments). As in Equation 136 on page 153, a cubic curve equation has four parameters that define the curve. Therefore we need *4* constraints to decide the four parameters. For n cubic curves, we need *4n* constraints.

How many constraints we have already for a natural cubic spline? Well, for all cubic curves (segments) in a natural cubic spline, the two end points are known. There are n curves, therefore *2n* end points. Because the curves are connected with C^2 continuity, the first and second derivatives at the joints are equal. There are *n-1* joints, so there are *2n-2* constraint equations for the first derivatives and the second derivatives. Altogether we have *4n-2* constraints, but we need *4n* constraints in order to specify all curve segments of the natural cubic spline. We can add two assumptions such as the tangent vectors of the two end points of the spline.

Natural spline curves are calculated by solving a set of *4n* equations, which is time consuming. Also, changing one constraint (such as moving a control point) will result in changing the shape of all different segments, so all of the curve segments need to be calculated again. We call this global control. We would prefer a curve with local control, so changing a constraint only affects the curve locally. Hermite and Bezier curves are local control curves, but they only support C^1 continuity. In the next section, we introduce B-spline, which satisfies local control as well as C^2 continuity.

6.4.5 B-splines

A B-spline curve is a set of connected cubic curves based on control points that lie outside each of the curves. For *n+1* control points, there are *n-2* cubic curves (segments) on a B-spline:

$Q_3(t)$ is defined by $C_0C_1C_2C_3$,
$Q_4(t)$ is defined by $C_1C_2C_3C_4$,
...,
$Q_n(t)$ is defined by $C_{n-3}C_{n-2}C_{n-1}C_n$.

The cubic B-spline equation for $Q_i(t)$ is as follows:

$$p_i(t) = B_0(t)C_{i-3} + B_1(t)C_{i-2} + B_2(t)C_{i-3} + B_3(t)C_i \qquad \text{(EQ 171)}$$

where the blending functions, which are also called the *basis functions* because the B in B-spline stands for "basis", are

$$B_0(t) = \frac{1}{6}(1-t)^3, \qquad \text{(EQ 172)}$$

$$B_1(t) = \frac{1}{6}(3t^3 - 6t^2 + 4), \qquad \text{(EQ 173)}$$

$$B_2(t) = \frac{1}{6}(-3t^3 + 3t^2 + 3t + 1), \qquad \text{(EQ 174)}$$

$$\text{and } B_3(t) = \frac{1}{6}t^3. \tag{EQ 175}$$

As Bezier curves, the sum of the B-spline's blending functions is everywhere unity and each function is everywhere nonnegative, as shown in Fig. 6.6. That is, a B-spline curve segment is just a weighted average of the four control points and is contained in the convex hull of the four control points.

For two consecutive curve segments on a B-spline, their connection point is called a *knot*, which has corresponding knot value $t=1$ on the first segment and $t=0$ on the second segment. This type of B-spline is called *Uniform B-spline*, whose knot values are in equal unit value. We have $p_i(1)$ and $p_{i+1}(0)$:

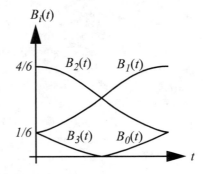

Fig. 6.6 B-spline blending functions

$$p_i(1) = 0C_{i-3} + \frac{1}{6}C_{i-2} + \frac{2}{3}C_{i-1} + \frac{1}{6}C_i, \tag{EQ 176}$$

$$p_{i+1}(0) = \frac{1}{6}C_{i-2} + \frac{2}{3}C_{i-1} + \frac{1}{6}C_i + 0C_{i+1}. \tag{EQ 177}$$

So the two end points meet at the knot:

$$p_i(1) = p_{i+1}(0) = \frac{1}{6}C_{i-2} + \frac{2}{3}C_{i-1} + \frac{1}{6}C_i. \tag{EQ 178}$$

That is, the knot is constrained by three control points as in Equation 178, while a B-spline curve segment is constrained by four control points wherever not on the knots. This is also obvious from Fig. 6.6.

We can calculate the first derivatives at the knots,

$$p'_i(1) = 0C_{i-3} + \left(-\frac{1}{2}\right)C_{i-2} + 0C_{i-1} + \frac{1}{2}C_i$$ (EQ 179)

$$p'_{i+1}(0) = \left(-\frac{1}{2}\right)C_{i-2} + 0C_{i-1} + \frac{1}{2}C_i + 0C_{i+1}$$ (EQ 180)

So the two end points' tangent vectors are equal. We can further calculate the second derivatives and see that B-splines are C^2 continuity at their knots, which is the same as natural cubic splines. Unlike natural cubic splines, B-splines do not go through the control points, and moving one control point to a different position affects only four curve segments at most. That is, B-spline curves are local-control, while natural cubic spline curves are global-control. If we use a control point twice in the equations (e.g., $C_i = C_{i+1}$), then the curves are pulled closer to this point. Using a control point three times will result in a line segment.

We can write B-spline equation in matrix form:

$$p_i(t) = \begin{bmatrix} t^3 & t^2 & t & 1 \end{bmatrix} \frac{1}{6} \begin{bmatrix} -1 & 3 & -3 & 1 \\ 3 & -6 & 3 & 0 \\ -3 & 0 & 3 & 0 \\ 1 & 4 & 1 & 0 \end{bmatrix} \begin{bmatrix} C_{i-3} \\ C_{i-2} \\ C_{i-1} \\ C_i \end{bmatrix}$$ (EQ 181)

That is,

$$p_i(t) = TM_{Bs}C$$ (EQ 182)

where M_{Bs} is called the B-spline matrix, and C represents the corresponding boundary constraints. Each curve is defined on its own domain ($0 \le t \le 1$). We can adjust the parameters so that the parameter domains for the various curve segments are sequential: $t_i \le t \le t_{i+1}$, $t_{i+1} - t_i = 1$, and $3 \le i \le n$. Here the knots are spaced at unit intervals of parameter t, and the B-splines are called Uniform B-splines. If t is not spaced evenly, we have Non-uniform B-splines, which is discussed in the next section.

B-splines of general degree. B-splines can be easily extended into higher degrees. Given $n+1$ control point positions, we can blend them to produce the following:

$$p(t) = \sum_{k=0}^{n} C_k B_{k,d}(t), \qquad \textbf{(EQ 183)}$$

where the blending functions are $(d-1)$ degree polynomials where $2 \le d \le n+1$:

$$B_{k,1}(t) = \begin{cases} 1, \text{ when } t_i \le t < t_{i+1} \\ 0, \text{ otherwise} \end{cases}, \qquad \textbf{(EQ 184)}$$

and
$$B_{k,d}(t) = \frac{t - t_k}{t_{k+d-1} - t_k} B_{k,d-1}(t) + \frac{t_{k+d} - t}{t_{k+d} - t_{k+1}} B_{k+1,d-1}(t). \qquad \textbf{(EQ 185)}$$

For an arbitrary n and d, we need knot value $t = 0$ up to $t = n + d$ to calculate the blending functions. In other words, we need a knot vector of $n + d$ values. For a cubic Uniform B-spline with 4 control points, $n = 4$ and $d = 4$, so we need to provide a uniform knot vector of 8 values: [0 1 2 3 4 5 6 7]. So the cubic Uniform B-spline we discussed above is just a special case here.

6.4.6 Non-uniform B-splines

If the parameter interval between successive knot values are not uniform, we have a knot vector, for example, [0 0 1 3 4 7 7]. The number of repeating knot values is the *multiplicity* of the curve. With such a knot vector, the blending function will be calculated resulting in different equations by Equation 184 and Equation 185. The multiplicity also reduces the continuity of the curve at the repeating knots by the number of repeating knot values, and the curve segments are shrunk into a point for the repeating knots. This is the primary advantage of Non-uniform B-splines.

If the continuity is reduced to C^0 with multiplicity 3, the curve interpolates a control point. For example, for a cubic B-spline with 4 control points, if the knot vector is [0 0 0 0 1 1 1 1], the curve goes through the first and the last control points, which is a Bezier curve. So a Bezier curve is a special case of a B-spline. For multiple curve segments with multiplicity 4, the curve segments can be dissected into pieces.

6.4.7 NURBS

3D models are transformed by MODELVIEW and PROJECTION matrices in homogeneous coordinates. If we apply perspective projection to the control points and then generate the curve using the above (non-rational) Hermite, Bezier, or B-spline equations, the generated curves change their shapes. In other words, they are variant under perspective projection. This problem can be solved by using rational curve equations, which can be considered as curves in homogeneous coordinates projected into 3D coordinates. We extend a curve in homogeneous coordinates as:

$$Q_h(t) = (x(t), y(t), z(t), w(t)). \tag{EQ 186}$$

Then, a rational curve in 3D coordinates is as:

$$Q(t) = \left(\frac{x(t)}{w(t)}, \frac{y(t)}{w(t)}, \frac{z(t)}{w(t)} \right). \tag{EQ 187}$$

If the rational equations are Non-uniform B-splines, they are called *NURBS* (Non-uniform Rational B-splines):

$$p(t) = \frac{\sum\limits_{k=0}^{n} \omega_k C_k B_{k,d}(t)}{\sum\limits_{k=0}^{n} \omega_k B_{k,d}(t)}. \tag{EQ 188}$$

where ω_k are user-specified weight factors for the control points. When all the weight factors are set to 1, the rational form is reduced to non-rational form, so non-rational equations are special cases of rational equations.

In addition to being invariant under perspective transformation, NURBS can be used to obtain various conics by choosing specific weight factors and control points. The GLU library provides NURBS functions built on top of the OpenGL evaluator commands for both NURBS curves and surfaces.

6.5 Bi-cubic Surfaces

As discussed before, cubic Hermite, Bezier, and B-spline curve equations are

$$p(t) \;=\; TM_hP\,, \hspace{3cm} \textbf{(EQ 189)}$$

$$p(t) \;=\; TM_bC\,, \hspace{3cm} \textbf{(EQ 190)}$$

$$\text{and}\, p(t) \;=\; TM_{Bs}C_{Bs} \;\text{ for one segment.} \hspace{1.5cm} \textbf{(EQ 191)}$$

Their differences here are really their matrices and constraint parameters. For a curve, if its constraints are themselves variables, the curve can be considered moving in 3D and changing its shape according to the variations of the constraints, and sweeping out a curved surface. If the constraints are themselves cubic curves, we have bi-cubic surfaces.

6.5.1 Hermite Surfaces

Let us assume that s and t are independent parameters, and our original Hermite curve equation with variable s has its constraints of variable t. We have bi-cubic Hermite surface equation as follows:

$$p(s, t) = SM_h \begin{bmatrix} p(0, t) \\ P(1, t) \\ \dfrac{\partial}{\partial s}p(0, t) \\ \dfrac{\partial}{\partial s}p(1, t) \end{bmatrix} = SM_h \begin{bmatrix} TM_h \begin{bmatrix} p(0, 0) \\ P(0, 1) \\ \dfrac{\partial}{\partial t}p(0, 0) \\ \dfrac{\partial}{\partial t}p(0, 1) \end{bmatrix} \\ TM_h \begin{bmatrix} p(1, 0) \\ P(1, 1) \\ \dfrac{\partial}{\partial t}p(1, 0) \\ \dfrac{\partial}{\partial t}p(1, 1) \end{bmatrix} \\ TM_h \begin{bmatrix} \dfrac{\partial}{\partial s}p(0, 0) \\ \dfrac{\partial}{\partial s}P(0, 1) \\ \dfrac{\partial^2}{\partial s\partial t}p(0, 0) \\ \dfrac{\partial^2}{\partial s\partial t}p(0, 1) \end{bmatrix} \\ TM_h \begin{bmatrix} \dfrac{\partial}{\partial s}p(1, 0) \\ \dfrac{\partial}{\partial s}P(1, 1) \\ \dfrac{\partial^2}{\partial s\partial t}p(1, 0) \\ \dfrac{\partial^2}{\partial s\partial t}p(1, 1) \end{bmatrix} \end{bmatrix}.$$

(EQ 192)

Because matrix expression can be reversed under transposition: $MN = N^T M^T$, we have the following

$$p(s, t) = SM_h \begin{bmatrix} p(0, 0) & P(0, 1) & \frac{\partial}{\partial t}p(0, 0) & \frac{\partial}{\partial t}p(0, 1) \\ p(1, 0) & P(1, 1) & \frac{\partial}{\partial t}p(1, 0) & \frac{\partial}{\partial t}p(1, 1) \\ \frac{\partial}{\partial s}p(0, 0) & \frac{\partial}{\partial s}P(0, 1) & \frac{\partial^2}{\partial s \partial t}p(0, 0) & \frac{\partial^2}{\partial s \partial t}p(0, 1) \\ \frac{\partial}{\partial s}p(1, 0) & \frac{\partial}{\partial s}P(1, 1) & \frac{\partial^2}{\partial s \partial t}p(1, 0) & \frac{\partial^2}{\partial s \partial t}p(1, 1) \end{bmatrix} M_h^T T^T \quad \textbf{(EQ 193)}$$

That is,

$$p(s, t) = SM_h P_h M_h^T T^T \quad \textbf{(EQ 194)}$$

Therefore, for a Hermite bi-cubic surface, we need to specify 16 constraints for an x, y, or z parametric equation, respectively. There are 4 end points on the surface patch, 8 tangent vectors in s or t directions at the 4 end points, and 4 "twists" at the 4 end points, which you can think to be the rate of a tangent vector in s direction twists (changes) along the t direction, or vice versa. Just like Hermite curves, Hermite surface patches can be connected with C^1 or G^1 continuity. We just need to specify the connecting end points' tangent vectors and twists equal or proportional.

For lighting or other purposes, the normal at any point (s, t) on the surface can be calculated by the cross-product of the s and t tangent vectors:

$$\frac{\partial}{\partial s}Q(s, t) \times \frac{\partial}{\partial t}Q(s, t) \quad \textbf{(EQ 195)}$$

6.5.2 Bezier Surfaces

Bi-cubic Bezier surfaces can be derived the same way as above:

$$p(s, t) = SM_b CM_b^T T^T,$$

(EQ 196)

where the control points (as shown in Fig. 6.7) are

$$C = \begin{bmatrix} C_{00} & C_{01} & C_{02} & C_{03} \\ C_{10} & C_{11} & C_{12} & C_{13} \\ C_{20} & C_{21} & C_{22} & C_{23} \\ C_{30} & C_{31} & C_{32} & C_{33} \end{bmatrix}.$$

(EQ 197)

As their corresponding curves, Bezier surfaces are C^1 or G^1 continuity. Also, Bezier surfaces can be easily extended into higher degrees, and OpenGL implements two-dimensional evaluators for Bezier surfaces of general degree, as discussed below.

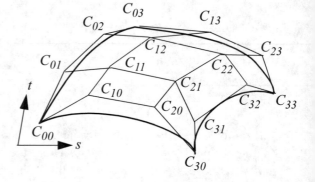

Fig. 6.7 Bi-cubic Bezier surface control points

Bezier surfaces of general degree. Given $(n + 1)(m + 1)$ control point positions C_{ij}, where $0 \le i \le n$ and $0 \le j \le m$, we can blend them to produce the following:

$$p(s, t) = \sum_{i=0}^{n} \sum_{j=0}^{m} C_{ij} B_{i, n}(s) B_{j, m}(t),$$

(EQ 198)

where the blending functions are the Bernstein polynomials discussed in Equation 169 and Equation 170 on page 161.

OpenGL evaluators. OpenGL provides basic functions for calculating Bezier surfaces of general degree. Specifically, it uses *glMap2f()* to set up the interval (e.g., $0 \leq s,t \leq 1$), number of values in *s* or *t* directions to skip to the next value (e.g., *3* for *xyz* or *4* for *xyzw* in *s* direction, and *12* for *xyz* or *16* or *xyzw* in *t* direction), degree of the equation (e.g., *4* for cubics), and control points (an array of points). Then, instead of calculating curve points and using *glVertex()* to specify the coordinates, we use *glEvaluCoord2(s, t)* to specify the coordinates at specified position, and the Bezier surface is calculated by the OpenGL system, as shown in Example *J5_5_BezierSurface.java*. A snapshot is in Fig. 6.8.

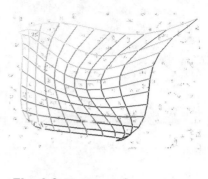

Fig. 6.8 Bezier surfaces

In OpenGL, *glMap*()* is also used to interpolate colors, normals, and texture coordinates.

/* draw a Bezier surface using 2D evaluators */

```java
import net.java.games.jogl.GL;


public class J5_5_BezierSurface extends J5_4_Bezier {
  double ctrlpts[] = { // C00, C01, C02, C03
          -1.0, -1.0, 1, -1.0, -0.75, -1.0,
          -1.0, 0.75, 1.0, -1.0, 1, -1.0,
          // C10, C11, C12, C13
          -0.75, -1.0, -1, -0.75, -0.75, 0,
          -0.75, 0.75, -5.0, -0.75, 1, 1.0,
          // C20, C21, C22, C23
          0.75, -1.0, 1, 0.75, -0.75, 0,
          0.75, 0.75, 1.0, 0.75, 1, -1.0,
          // C30, C31, C32, C33
          1, -1.0, -1, 1, -0.75, 1.0,
          1, 0.75, -1.0, 1, 1, 1.0,
  };

  public void drawSphere() {
    int i, j;

    // define and invoke 2D evaluator
```

```
gl.glMap2d(GL.GL_MAP2_VERTEX_3, 0, 1, 3, 4,
      0, 1, 12, 4, ctrlpts);
gl.glEnable(GL.GL_MAP2_VERTEX_3);

gl.glDisable(GL.GL_LIGHTING);
for (j = 0; j<=10; j++) {
 gl.glBegin(GL.GL_LINE_STRIP);
 for (i = 0; i<=10; i++) {
  gl.glColor3f(i/10f, j/10f, 1f);
  // use OpenGL evaluator
  gl.glEvalCoord2d(i/10.0, j/10.0);
 }
 gl.glEnd();
 gl.glBegin(GL.GL_LINE_STRIP);
 for (i = 0; i<=10; i++) {
  gl.glColor3f(i/10f, j/10f, 1f);
  // use OpenGL evaluator
  gl.glEvalCoord2d(j/10.0, i/10.0);
 }
 gl.glEnd();
}

// Highlight the knots: white
gl.glColor3f(1, 1, 1);
gl.glBegin(GL.GL_POINTS);
for (j = 0; j<=10; j++) {
 for (i = 0; i<=10; i++) {
  gl.glEvalCoord2d(i/10.0, j/10.0);
 }
}
gl.glEnd();

// for the background texture
gl.glBindTexture(GL.GL_TEXTURE_2D, STARS_TEX[0]);
}


public static void main(String[] args) {
 J5_5_BezierSurface f = new J5_5_BezierSurface();

 f.setTitle("JOGL J5_5_BezierSurface");
 f.setSize(WIDTH, HEIGHT);
 f.setVisible(true);
}
}
```

6.5.3 B-spline Surfaces

Bi-cubic B-spline surfaces can be derived the same way as above, respectively:

$$p(s, t) = SM_{Bs}C_{Bs}M_{Bs}^T T^T. \qquad \text{(EQ 199)}$$

As their corresponding curves, Bezier surfaces are C^1 or G^1 continuity, and B-spline surfaces are C^2 or G^2 continuity.

The GLU library provides a set of NURBS functions built on OpenGL evaluator commands that includes lighting and texture mapping functions, which is convenient for applications involving NURBS curves and surfaces.

6.6 Review Questions

1. Check out glPolygonMode() and draw models in points, lines, and surfaces in J5_1_Quadrics.java.

2. Please specify the names of the 3D models that are available in GLUT and GLU.

3. What are the models available for texture mapping in GLUT and GLU?

4. Prove that the sum of the Bezier blending functions is everywhere unity and each function is everywhere nonnegative.

5. Prove that the sum of the B-spline blending functions is everywhere unity and each function is everywhere nonnegative.

6. Compare Bezier and B-spline curves. Please list their properties separately. Then, discuss their similarities and differences.

7. Which of the following is wrong:

    a. Bezier curves are C^2 continuity   b. A natural cubic spline is C^1 continuity

    c. B-splines are C^2 continuity   d. Hermite curves are C^1 continuity

8. Compared with B-spline, which of the following is true:

    a. Natural spline is simpler to calculate   b. Bezier curves are global control

    c. Hermite curve interpolates its end points   d. They are all C^2 curves with segments

9. Which of the following is true about B-spline:

    a. Using the same control points multiple times is the same as increasing multiplicity.
    b. All B-splines are invariant under perspective transformation.
    c. Conics can be generated using certain B-splines.
    d. Increasing multiplicity will reduce the curve into line segments.

10. How many constraints are there for a bi-cubic Hermite surface patch? How many control points are there for a bi-cubic B-spline surface patch?

11. Calculate the Bezier cubic curve equation Q(X(t), Y(t), Z(t)) given $P_1(0, 0, 0)$, $P_2(1, 1, 1)$, $P_3(1, 0, 0)$, and $P_4(0, 1, 1)$. You need only to give the results. (Hint: $R_1 = 3*(P_2-P_1)$, $R4=3*(P_4-P_3)$)

$X(t) = ($_____$)t^3 + ($_____$)t^2 + ($_____$)t + ($_____$)$

$Y(t) = ($_____$)t^3 + ($_____$)t^2 + ($_____$)t + ($_____$)$

$Z(t) = ($_____$)t^3 + ($_____$)t^2 + ($_____$)t + ($_____$)$

12. Given curve surface equation $Q(s^3 t^3 + s^2 + t + 1, s^3 + s + t + 1, s^3 t^3 + t + 1)$. **Please find the tangent plane at (0, 1).**

Plane equation: _____

6.7 Programming Assignments

1. Check out glPolygonMode() and draw models in points, lines, and surfaces in J5_1_Quadrics.java.

2. As mentioned in the text, we can create a sphere on a display through subdivision, through a sphere's equation, or through a rotation of a circle. There are many ways to store a 3D model and display it. Explain in detail what are exactly saved in the computer for a sphere model and the algorithms used to display the model. Implement the algorithms accordingly.

3. A super ellipsoid is represented as follows. Please draw the 3D model at ($a = 0, 1, 2, 3$) and ($b = 0, 1, 2, 3$) with different combinations:

$$x = r_x(\cos\phi)^a(\cos\theta)^b, \quad 0 \le \phi \le \pi,$$
                                                     (EQ 200)

$$y = r_y(\cos\phi)^a(\sin\theta)^b, \ 0 \le \theta \le 2\pi, \qquad \text{(EQ 201)}$$

$$\text{and } z = r_z(\sin\phi)^a. \qquad \text{(EQ 202)}$$

4. Draw two Hermite curves with C^1 continuity. Build an interactive system so that the constraints are interactively specified.

5. Draw a uniform non-rational B-spline with multiple control points. Again, the control points are interactively specified.

6. Draw a non-uniform non-rational B-spline, and demonstrate its difference and advantage over Uniform Non-rational B-spline.

7. Draw a B-spline curve surface with 4 patches. Allow the control points to be interactively specified. Learn GLU NURBS functions and use them to draw a surface.

7

Vertex Shading, Pixel Shading, and Parallel Processing

Chapter Objectives:

- Briefly introduce GPUs, vertex shaders, pixel shaders, and parallel programming

7.1 Introduction

Graphics hardware has evolved significantly in recent years. Today, every computer has a graphics processing unit (GPU) or a graphics card that includes new parallel processing capabilities with programmable functions. Some GPUs are much more powerful than CPUs not only on graphics functions, but also on computing capabilities. The general-purpose GPU (GPGPU) is towards employing GPU for parallel computing applications other than graphics applications. Here our focus is on introducing basic GPU transformation, shading, and texture mapping capabilities.

In the past 10 years, GPUs have improved their performance more than 100 times. This evolution has been gradually replacing individual pipeline stages with increasingly programmable units. A vertex shader is a graphics processing function operating on vertex data for position (transformation), color (lighting), and texture. Therefore, vertex shading is the process carried out on a vertex shader, a programmable unit replacing the fixed graphics transformation and viewing pipeline unit. The vertices computed by vertex shaders are typically passed to geometry shaders, which can generate new graphics primitives from the original primitive assembled after vertex shading. Geometry shaders can be used to add and remove vertices or volumetric detail to existing meshes. A pixel shader is a programmable unit

J.X. Chen, *Guide to Graphics Software Tools*, doi: 10.1007/978-1-84800-901-1_7,
© Springer-Verlag London Limited 2008

that operates on pixel data, usually for additional level of complexity on bump mapping, shadows, and other effects. Here our focus is on vertex and pixel shaders.

Historically, GPUs have had dedicated units for different types of operations in the rendering pipeline, such as vertex transformation and shading and pixel texture mapping. With the unified architecture, a single floating point shader core with multiple independent processors are designed to handle any type of shading operations, including vertex shading and pixel shading. Today, they are flexible general-purpose computational engines instead of fixed-function 3D graphics pipeline. The processing methods and power has been changing and improving all the time. Along with the GPU improvements, graphics libraries (OpenGL and Direct3D) have been extended to include GPUs functions through OpenGL's Shading Language (GLSL) and DirectX's High Level Shading Language (HLSL). A new shading language Cg has been developed from nVidia for programming their GPU functions, and a latest programming language CUDA (Compute Unified Device Architecture) is a new hardware and software programming system for issuing and managing computations on the GPUs as a data-parallel computing device without the need of mapping them to a graphics API.

7.2 Programmable Pipelines

GPU hardware is complex and evolving, but we can conceptually describe it as in Fig. 7.1. Traditional graphics pipeline's transformation, viewing, and lighting fixed hardware components are replaced by the vertex shader, a programmable component that deal with vertex position, normal, color, texture coordinates, and others. At the fragment level, pixel shader is an addition to address advanced lighting and texture mapping, so true Phong shading, bump mapping, and many other functions can be implemented in real-time. Pixel shader programs are small programs that are executed on individual pixels in parallel.

GPU's are specialized hardware faster for graphics functions. They are programming units by assembly languages or special shading languages, like Cg, GLSL, or HLSL. The main programs still run on CPU. The shading languages are called at runtime for GPUs to work accordingly. Although the shading languages are designed to be similar to C programming language, they are limited in their capabilities to current available functions, which will be discussed in more detail. GPUs and their corresponding programming software system are evolving.

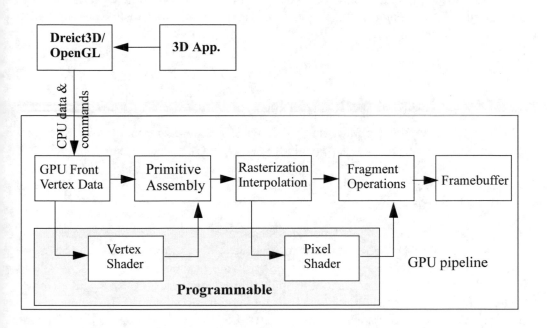

Fig. 7.1 A GPU programmable pipeline

As shown in Fig. 7.1, first, the vertex data are transformed into device coordinates through transformation and viewing, lighting colors are calculated on the vertices, and texture coordinates are generated on the vertices. These used-to-be fixed operations are now replaced by the programmable vertex shader operations.

Then, the Primitive Assembly stage will integrate transformed vertices into primitives (points, lines, triangles, or polygons) for clipping and then scan-conversion, or rasterization.

After that, Rasterization Interpolation will break a primitive into pixel values through interpolations, including vertex position and color values. The term "fragment" is used for each pixel's associated values because a primitive is broken into fragments during scan-conversion.

Finally, at the fragment level, Pixel Shader will be able to integrate color and texture values into a final color for each pixel, which is then stored in the corresponding location in the frame buffer.

7.3 GLSL, Cg, and HLSL

Corresponding to the graphics hardware, there are three major graphics shading programming languages that are popular today. OpenGL's shading language (GLSL), nVidia's Cg, and Direct X's High Level Shading Language (HLSL). These shading languages reduce the difficulties of programming graphics hardware in low-level assembly languages.

GLSL, also called GLslang, is OpenGL's shading language based on C programming language. It is an OpenGL standard to give developers more direct control of the graphics pipeline without having to use hardware-dependent languages. It allows cross-platform hardware compatibility on different operating systems and graphics cards. A graphics card supports GLSL if the vendor includes the GLSL compiler in the card's driver. Most graphics cards support GLSL.

Cg is a high-level shading language developed by NVIDIA for programming vertex and pixel shaders. It is very similar to Microsoft's HLSL because they are developed in parallel. The main program is in C or Java, and the GPU is programmed in Cg. The Cg compiler outputs DirectX or OpenGL shader programs. HLSL is developed by Microsoft for use with the Microsoft Direct3D (DirectX) API.

The shading languages are closely related to GPU hardware. Therefore, they are limited to the hardware capabilities. We cannot consider them as general purpose programming languages. Instead, we have to rely on the special hardware configuration and availability.

7.3.1 Cg Basics

In this section, we introduce some basics in Cg programming through a few simple examples. Please refer to nVidia company's Cg Homepage `http://developer.nvidia.com/page/cg_main.html` and *The Cg Tutorial* by Randima Fernando and Mark J. Kilgard for more detail. For easier explanation purpose, we name the CPU and traditional fixed graphics pipeline program to be JOGL program, and the corresponding shader programs to be vertex programs or pixel programs.

7.3.2 A Vertex Program

In the following program *J6_1_Cg.java* in JOGL, we extend example *J1_5_Circle* to invoke a vertex program *J6_1_VP.cg*. A vertex program is a coding on a vertex shader we discussed above.

/*Cg Example: set up vertex program */

```
import com.sun.opengl.cg.*;
import javax.media.opengl.*;


public class J6_1_Cg extends J1_5_Circle {

      CGcontext cgcontext;
      CGprogram vertexprog;

      // 1. Vertex profile: hardware specification/support
      static final int VERTEXPROFILE=CgGL.CG_PROFILE_ARBVP1;

   public void init(GLAutoDrawable glDrawable) {

     super.init(glDrawable);

     if(!CgGL.cgGLIsProfileSupported(VERTEXPROFILE))
     {
      System.out.println("Profile not supported");
      System.exit(1);
     }

      // 2. Create Cg context for setting up the environment
      cgcontext=CgGL.cgCreateContext();


      // 3. Create vertex program from file with the profile
      CgGL.cgGLSetOptimalOptions(VERTEXPROFILE);
      vertexprog=CgGL.cgCreateProgramFromFile(cgcontext,
  CgGL.CG_SOURCE, "J6_1_VP.cg", VERTEXPROFILE, null, null);
      CgGL.cgGLLoadProgram(vertexprog);
     }
```

```
public void display(GLAutoDrawable drawable) {

    // 4. Enable the profile and binding the vertex program
    CgGL.cgGLEnableProfile(VERTEXPROFILE);
    CgGL.cgGLBindProgram(vertexprog);

    drawCircle(drawable);

    // 5. Disable the profile
    CgGL.cgGLDisableProfile(VERTEXPROFILE);
}

public void drawCircle(GLAutoDrawable drawable) {

    super.display(drawable);
}

public static void main(String[] args) {
    J6_1_Cg f = new J6_1_Cg();

  f.setTitle("JOGL J6_1_Cg");
  f.setSize(WIDTH, HEIGHT);
  f.setVisible(true);
 }
}
```

The above JOGL program is a simplest that invokes a Cg vertex program. The added Cg functions are explained as follows.

1. There are different vertex profiles for compiling the program. Each profile corresponds to the GPU hardware and version. We choose a profile "ARBVP1", which has basic multivendor vertex programmability on OpenGL platform. The examples here can be compiled on a broad range of hardware. Other profiles are more capable depending on the graphics hardware.

2. We need to create a Cg context in order to serve as a "container" for the Cg programs.

3. We specify and link the corresponding vertex program *J6_1_VP.cg* with the JOGL program. *cgGLSetOptimalOptions* is to specify optimal compilation of Cg into assembly code. *cgCreateProgramFromFile* links the vertex program with the JOGL program. It causes the vertex program to be compiled at runtime.

4. Enabling the profile activates the GPU for the specified profile. The vertex program Binding the vertex program is to link the GPU with the vertex program, so that the corresponding parameters will be sent to the vertex program for execution at runtime.

5. Disabling the profile will return the control to the JOGL program. In the hardware, the control and function will return to traditional fixed graphics pipeline.

In summary, we choose a vertex profile so that specific GPU hardware and Cg vertex functions are defined. To initialize Cg, we need to set up a Cg context. After that, we link and specify to compile a specific vertex program. After that, we enable the profile and bind the vertex program to start GPU vertex program at runtime. The vertex program and GPU hardware are disengaged after disabling the profile.

The vertex program, which trivially scale the 2D coordinates, is as follows. We should know that a vertex position is not transformed by the current MODELVIEW or PROJECTION matrices by default. Therefore, we have to scale the vertices in order for the circle to appear in the display window.

// Vertex Program: J6_1_VP.cg: update position and color

```
void main(
in  float4 iPosition    :    POSITION,
in  float4 iColor       :    COLOR,
out float4 oPosition    :    POSITION,
out float4 oColor       :    COLOR
) {
  oPosition.xyz = iPosition.xyz/100;
   // division operator on vector
   oColor=iColor;
}
```

There are new concepts in the vertex program. First, "float4" represents a vector type of 4 components for color, position, and so on. Then, the *semantics* of upper case POSITION and COLOR after the colon symbols represent actual hardware registers and connections. The "in" symbols, which are optional, represent input values (vertex position and color) from fixed graphics pipeline to the vertex shader (through registers). The "out" symbols represent output values (vertex position and color) from the vertex shader to the graphics pipeline through registers for primitive assembly. "oPosition.xyz" represents the first 3 components of "oPosition". The 4th component is "oPosition.w". In Cg, this is part of the swizzling operation. For example, vector1.xyz = vector2.yxz represents assignments of vector1.x = vector2.y, vector1.y = vector2.x, and vector1.z = vector2.z. Also, "iPosition.xyz/100" is a division operator on the vector. Cg comes with many standard library functions.

In the vertex shader, the vertex program can manipulate the vertex position and color. In our example, we scale the 2D vertex position and return the original vertex color.

7.3.3 Transformation and Viewing

Transformation, viewing, and projection on the vertices are now performed in the vertex shader. In other words, the MODELVIEW and PROJECTION matrices need to be manually used to transform a vertex in the vertex shader. Cg allows retrieving the matrix, which is the product of MODEVIEW and PROJECTION matrices. In the JOGL program, we specify modelViewProjection to be the parameter name in the vertex program and set its value to the current MODELVIEW and PROJECTION matrix at runtime for the vertex program.

/* Cg Example: ModelviewProjection matrix */

```
import com.sun.opengl.cg.*;
import javax.media.opengl.*;

public class J6_2_Cg extends J6_1_Cg {

    static CGparameter modelviewprojection;


  public void init(GLAutoDrawable glDrawable) {

    super.init(glDrawable);

    vertexprog=CgGL.cgCreateProgramFromFile(cgcontext,
  CgGL.CG_SOURCE, "J6_2_VP.cg", VERTEXPROFILE, null, null);
    CgGL.cgGLLoadProgram(vertexprog);

    // modelview and projection matrix
```

```
    modelviewprojection=CgGL.cgGetNamedParameter(vertexprog,
"modelViewProjection");
  }


  public void display(GLAutoDrawable drawable) {

    CgGL.cgGLEnableProfile(VERTEXPROFILE);
    CgGL.cgGLBindProgram(vertexprog);
    // retrieve the current modelview and projection matrix
        CgGL.cgGLSetStateMatrixParameter(modelviewprojection,
CgGL.CG_GL_MODELVIEW_PROJECTION_MATRIX,
CgGL.CG_GL_MATRIX_IDENTITY);

    drawCircle(drawable);

    CgGL.cgGLDisableProfile(VERTEXPROFILE);
  }


  public static void main(String[] args) {
    J6_2_Cg f = new J6_2_Cg();

  f.setTitle("JOGL J6_2_Cg");
  f.setSize(WIDTH, HEIGHT);
  f.setVisible(true);
  }
}
```

cgGLSetStateMatrixParameter will retrieve the current MODELVIEW and PROJECTION matrix and send it to the vertex program, which transform the vertices into normalized coordinates in clip space as in the fixed transformation and viewing graphics pipeline, as shown below.

// J6_2_VP.cg Vertex Program: transformation and viewing

```
void main(
    float4 iPosition    :    POSITION,
    float4 iColor       :    COLOR,
out float4 position     :    POSITION,
out float4 color        :    COLOR,
uniform float4x4             modelViewProjection
) {
  position = mul(modelViewProjection, iPosition);
```

```
    color=iColor;
}
```

In *J6_2_VP.cg*, "uniform" stands for an allocated value by the JOGL program for the vertex program. The value can be changed by the JOGL program, but stays the same in the vertex program. "float4x4" represents a 4 by 4 matrix. "mul" will multiply the matrices together, which is one of the many built-in standard library functions.

7.3.4 A Fragment Program

Similarly, we can set up a pixel shader program (fragment program) as follows. Setting up the fragment program environment is similar to setting up the vertex program environment.

/* J6_3_Cg: Setting up Fragment Program */

```
import com.sun.opengl.cg.*;
import javax.media.opengl.*;


public class J6_3_Cg extends J6_2_Cg {

  CGprogram fragmentprog;
  static final int FRAGMENTPROFILE=CgGL.CG_PROFILE_ARBFP1;


  public void init(GLAutoDrawable glDrawable) {

   super.init(glDrawable);

   if(!CgGL.cgGLIsProfileSupported(FRAGMENTPROFILE))
   {
    System.out.println("Fragment profile not supported");
    System.exit(1);
   }

   CgGL.cgGLSetOptimalOptions(FRAGMENTPROFILE);
          fragmentprog=CgGL.cgCreateProgramFromFile(cgcontext,
   CgGL.CG_SOURCE, "J6_3_FP.cg", FRAGMENTPROFILE, null, null);
   CgGL.cgGLLoadProgram(fragmentprog);

  }
```

```
public void display(GLAutoDrawable drawable) {
    CgGL.cgGLEnableProfile(VERTEXPROFILE);
    CgGL.cgGLBindProgram(vertexprog);
    CgGL.cgGLSetStateMatrixParameter(modelviewprojection,
CgGL.CG_GL_MODELVIEW_PROJECTION_MATRIX,
CgGL.CG_GL_MATRIX_IDENTITY);

    CgGL.cgGLEnableProfile(FRAGMENTPROFILE);
    CgGL.cgGLBindProgram(fragmentprog);


    drawCircle(drawable);


    CgGL.cgGLDisableProfile(VERTEXPROFILE);
     CgGL.cgGLDisableProfile(FRAGMENTPROFILE);

  }


public static void main(String[] args) {
    J6_3_Cg f = new J6_3_Cg();

  f.setTitle("JOGL J6_3_Cg");
  f.setSize(WIDTH, HEIGHT);
  f.setVisible(true);
  }
}
```

In the fragment program, we modify the color for immediate output. The vertex colors of a primitive are interpolated along edges and then horizontal scan-lines for the pixels, so each fragment has an input color, which may be different from other fragments' colors.

// J6_3_FP.cg Fragment Program: color manipulation

```
void main(
    float4 iColor     :     COLOR,
out float4 color      :     COLOR
) {
   color.rgb =iColor.rgb/2;
}
```

We can use "uniform" variables to pass information from the JOGL program to a Cg program. The following program generates random triangle colors in the JOGL program. The color is sent to the vertex program through a "uniform" variable.

/* Cg Example: uniform random colors */

```
import com.sun.opengl.cg.*;
import javax.media.opengl.*;


public class J6_4_Cg extends J6_3_Cg {

    static CGparameter vertexColor;

    public void init(GLAutoDrawable glDrawable) {

        super.init(glDrawable);

        vertexprog = CgGL.cgCreateProgramFromFile(cgcontext,
CgGL.CG_SOURCE,
                "J6_4_VP.cg", VERTEXPROFILE, null, null);
        CgGL.cgGLLoadProgram(vertexprog);

        modelviewprojection =
CgGL.cgGetNamedParameter(vertexprog,
                "modelViewProjection");
        vertexColor    =    CgGL.cgGetNamedParameter(vertexprog,
"vColor");

    }


    public void drawtriangle(float[] v1, float[] v2, float[]
v3) {
        float color[] = new float[4];

        // generate a random color and set it to vertexColor
        color[0] = (float) Math.random();
        color[1] = (float) Math.random();
        color[2] = (float) Math.random();
        color[3] = 0;
        CgGL.cgSetParameter4fv(vertexColor, color, 0);


        gl.glBegin(GL.GL_TRIANGLES);
        gl.glVertex3fv(v1, 0);
        gl.glVertex3fv(v2, 0);
```

```
        gl.glVertex3fv(v3, 0);
        gl.glEnd();
    }

    public static void main(String[] args) {
        J6_4_Cg f = new J6_4_Cg();

        f.setTitle("JOGL J6_4_Cg");
        f.setSize(WIDTH, HEIGHT);
        f.setVisible(true);
    }
}
```

// J6_4_VP.cg Vertex Program: uniform vertex color

```
void main(
    float4 iPosition        :        POSITION,
    float4 iColor           :        COLOR,
out float4 position         :        POSITION,
out float4 color            :        COLOR,
uniform float4x4                     modelViewProjection,
uniform float4                       vColor
) {
    position = mul(modelViewProjection, iPosition);
    color=vColor;
}
```

If "uniform" is not used, then a variable is either a semantic from the system or is defined explicitly through assignment as: float4 white = float4(1, 1, 1, 1). For example, the following fragment program assigns a constant color:

// J6_5_FP.cg Fragment Program: white color

```
void main(
    float4 iColor       :        COLOR,
out float4 color        :        COLOR,
uniform float4                   fColor
) {
    float4 white = float4(1,1,1,1);
    color =white;
}
```

7.4 Parallel Processing and Cuda

Nvidia's CUDA (Compute Unified Device Architecture) is a programming language for developing multi-core and parallel processing applications on GPUs, specifically Nvidia's 8-series GPUs (and their successors in the future). The general architecture is shown in Fig. 7.2. Before CUDA, accessing the computational power in GPU for non-graphics applications is tricky. The GPU could only be programmed through a graphics API, so all users have to learn graphics before using it for parallel computing. GPU programs can only read (gather) data from DRAM instead of write (scatter) data to the DRAM, limiting the application flexibility. CUDA is built to avoid the limitations.

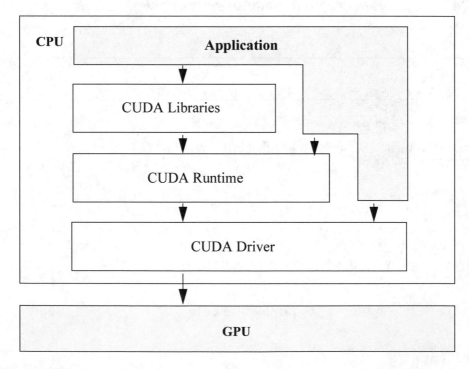

Fig. 7.2 CUDA software stack

When programming with CUDA, the GPU is viewed as a compute device capable of executing a very high number of threads in parallel. We can copy data between fast

DRAM memories through optimized API calls and high-performance Direct Memory Access (DMA) engines. The details of CUDA is described in nVidia's *CUDA Programming Guide.* (`http://www.nvidia.com/object/cuda_develop.html`)

The new GPUs are designed with more transistors devoted to data processing rather than data caching and flow control, as schematically shown in Fig. 7.3.

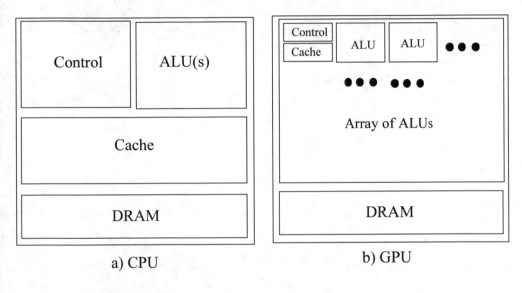

a) CPU   b) GPU

Fig. 7.3 **GPU has more transistors for data processing**

CUDA provides general DRAM memory gather and scatter operations, which correspond to memory read and write at any location in DRAM similar to be on a CPU. CUDA also provides a parallel data cache or on-chip shared memory that threads can share data, as shown in Fig. 7.4.

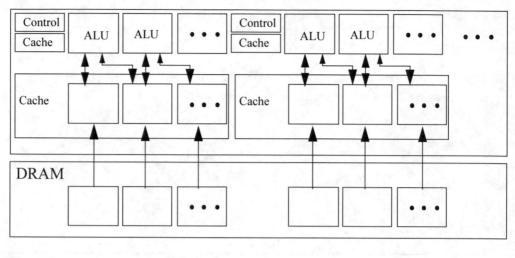

Fig. 7.4 GPU shared cache memory

Here we only give a short introduction to CUDA. To learn the technical details, please refer to `http://www.nvidia.com/object/cuda_develop.html`.

7.5 Introduction

Cg provides parallelism and flexibility in transformation, lighting, and texture mapping on vertex and pixel shaders. Specifically, lighting in the traditional fixed pipeline is completely replaced by vertex or pixel shader programs, which are more flexible and fragment shading can be achieved in real-time with parallel processing. In texture mapping, it is now possible to achieve bump mapping and other effects on the pixel shader in real time. In this chapter, we discuss some basics in using vertex and pixel shaders for lighting and texture mapping in Cg.

7.6 Per-Vertex Lighting

Lighting in OpenGL is calculated after MODELVIEW transformation automatically. However, in GPU programming, all transformation calculations have to be carried out manually. Therefore, for fixed lighting, it is simpler to calculate lighting in the world space. That is, we calculate lighting before MODELVIEW transformation. This requires using the vertex positions before transformation as well. In some existing applications, we cannot assume world space light source positions, because light sources can be transformed by the MODELVIEW matrix in the applications.

If we port an existing program with movable light source transformed by the MODELVIEW matrix, we have to transform the light source by the MODELVIEW matrix before sending its coordinates to the vertex shader. As an alternative, we can send the matrix that transforms the light source to the vertex shader to transform the light source in the vertex shader. At the same time, we have to transform the vertices and the vertices' normals in the vertex shader as well. Therefore, we have to send three matrices to the vertex shader: the MODELVIEW and PROJECTION matrix that transforms the vertex position for primitive assembly, the MODELVIEW matrix that transforms the vertex position, and the inverse transpose of the MODELVIEW matrix that transforms the vertex normal for lighting calculations:

```
static CGparameter
modelviewprojection, // modelviewProjection matrix
modelview, // modelview matrix
inversetranspose,
//inverse transpose of the modelview matrix
```

Finally, we have to implement a lighting model for calculating the final lighting result on a vertex. We will explain some technical details below.

7.6.1 Vertex and Light Source Transformation

After MODELVIEW transformation, a vertex or light source is said to be transformed from the object space to the eye space. There are limited number of light sources, so it is better to calculate the transformation in the JOGL program. There are many vertices with different current matrices. Therefore, it is better to calculate this transformation in the vertex shader:

```
float4 vPosition = mul(modelView, iPosition);
```

We should retrieve the current MODELVIEW matrix in the JOGL program for the corresponding objects and send it to the vertex shader at where we specify the vertices. That is, before an object is drawn after the last transformation command, we should retrieve the current matrix.

There are limited number of light sources. Therefore, for a light source we can retrieve its transformed position in JOGL program and send the transformed light source position to the vertex shader. For example, if the light source is transformed from the origin, we can retrieve its transformed position as follows:

```
gl.glGetFloatv(GL.GL_MODELVIEW_MATRIX, currM, 0);
sphereC[0] = currM[12];
sphereC[1] = currM[13];
sphereC[2] = currM[14];
CgGL.cgSetParameter3fv(myLightPosition, sphereC, 0);
```

7.6.2 Vertex Normal Transformation

A vertex normal is transformed by the transpose of the inverse of the current matrix that transforms the vertex. It is also named the inverse transpose of the MODELVIEW matrix. This can be derived as follows. A plane equation in general form is as follows:

$$ax + by + cz + d = 0 \qquad\qquad \textbf{(EQ 203)}$$

Given a vertex point $P(x, y, z, 1)$ and a normal $N(a, b, c, d)$ in homogeneous coordinates, the plane equation can be represented in matrix multiplication:

$$NP^T = 0 \qquad\qquad \textbf{(EQ 204)}$$

where P^T is the transpose of P so it is a vertical column. For a MODELVIEW matrix M that transforms the point, we have the following equivalent plane equation:

$$NM^{-1}MP^T = 0 \qquad\qquad \textbf{(EQ 205)}$$

where

$$M^{-1}M = I \qquad\qquad \textbf{(EQ 206)}$$

That is, for the transformed vertex point MP^T, we have a corresponding transformed normal NM^{-1}. Expressing in standard matrix multiplication form, we need to have the transpose of N on the right hand side:

$$\left(NM^{-1}\right)^T = \left(M^{-1}\right)^T (N)^T. \qquad \text{(EQ 207)}$$

That is, for a MODELVIEW matrix M that transforms the point, the inverse transpose of M transforms the corresponding normal. Therefore, whenever we retrieve the current matrix for vertex transformation, we should retrieve the inverse transpose of the current matrix as well for normal transformation:

```
CgGL.cgGLSetStateMatrixParameter(modelview,
    CgGL.CG_GL_MODELVIEW_MATRIX,
    CgGL.CG_GL_MATRIX_IDENTITY);
CgGL.cgGLSetStateMatrixParameter(inversetranspose,
    CgGL.CG_GL_MODELVIEW_MATRIX,
    CgGL.CG_GL_MATRIX_INVERSE_TRANSPOSE);
CgGL.cgGLSetStateMatrixParameter(modelviewprojection,
    CgGL.CG_GL_MODELVIEW_PROJECTION_MATRIX,
    CgGL.CG_GL_MATRIX_IDENTITY);
```

7.6.3 OpenGL Lighting Model

Here we discuss a simplified single light source situation. As we have discussed in Chapter 3, for a single light source the final vertex color is an integration of all the lighting components:

$$I_\lambda = I_{\lambda e} + I_{\lambda a} + I_{\lambda d} + I_{\lambda s}. \qquad \text{(EQ 208)}$$

where

$$I_{\lambda e} = M_{\lambda emission}, \qquad \text{(EQ 209)}$$

$$I_{\lambda a} = L_{\lambda a} M_{\lambda a}, \qquad \text{(EQ 210)}$$

$$I_{\lambda d} = L_{\lambda d} M_{\lambda d}(\boldsymbol{n} \bullet \boldsymbol{L}),$$

(EQ 211)

$$I_{\lambda s} = L_{\lambda s} M_{\lambda s}\left(\frac{\boldsymbol{n} \bullet (\boldsymbol{L} + \boldsymbol{V})}{|\boldsymbol{L} + \boldsymbol{V}|}\right)^{shininess}$$

(EQ 212)

Therefore, we need to send the following parameters to the vertex shader:

```
static CGparameter
myLa, //light source ambient
myLd, //light source diffuse
myLs, //light source specular
myLightPosition, // light source position
myEyePosition,
myMe, // material emission
myMa, // material ambient
myMd, // material diffuse
myMs, // material specular
myShininess; // material shininess
```

In the OpenGL lighting model, the vertex position is transformed to the eye space by the MODELVIEW matrix:

```
float4 vPosition = mul(modelView, iPosition);
float3 P = vPosition.xyz;
```

The light source direction is from the current vertex to the light source position:

```
float3 L = normalize(lightPosition - P);
```

The emission and ambient components are straight forward:

```
float3 Ie = Me;
float3 Ia = La*Ma;
```

The diffuse component is set to zero if the angle between the light source and vertex normal is bigger than 90 degree. Again, "max" and "dot" are Cg standard library functions:

```
float cosNL = max(dot(N, L), 0);
float3 Id = Md * Ld * cosNL;
```

For the specular component, the viewpoint direction is from the viewpoint (eyePosition) to the vertex position:

```
float3 V = normalize(eyePosition - P);
float3 H = normalize(L + V);
```

Also, if there is no diffuse component, there should have no specular component as well. Otherwise, it may have a trail of specular reflection on certain vertices where there is no diffuse reflection already, creating an obvious wrong lighting situation:

```
float cosNH = max(dot(N, H), 0);
if (cosNL==0) cosNH = 0; // condition in Cg
float3 Is = Ms * Ls * pow(cosNH, shininess);
```

Finally, we have the single lighting model in the vertex shader:

```
oColor.xyz = Ie + Ia + Id + Is;
oPosition = mul(modelViewProjection, iPosition);
```

Putting all above together, we have the following JOGL program and its corresponding vertex program for vertex lighting. A snapshot of the result is shown in Fig. 7.5.

Fig. 7.5 **A vertex shader lighting with a movable light source**

/*Cg Example: Vertex Program -- vertex lighting */

```
import com.sun.opengl.cg.*;
import com.sun.opengl.util.GLUT;
import javax.media.opengl.*;


public class J7_1_Cg extends J3_10_Lights {
    CGcontext cgcontext;
    CGprogram vertexprog;
    static CGparameter
    modelviewprojection, // modelviewProjection matrix
    modelview, // modelview matrix
    inversetranspose,
    //inverse transpose of the modelview matrix
    myLa, //light source ambient
    myLd, //light source diffuse
    myLs, //light source specular
    myLightPosition, // light source position
    myEyePosition,
    myMe, // material emission
    myMa, // material ambient
    myMd, // material diffuse
    myMs, // material specular
```

```
myShininess; // material shininess

static final int VERTEXPROFILE = CgGL.CG_PROFILE_ARBVP1;

public void init(GLAutoDrawable glDrawable) {

    super.init(glDrawable);

    if (!CgGL.cgGLIsProfileSupported(VERTEXPROFILE)) {
        System.out.println("Profile not supported");
        System.exit(1);
    }

    cgcontext = CgGL.cgCreateContext();

    CgGL.cgGLSetOptimalOptions(VERTEXPROFILE);
    vertexprog = CgGL.cgCreateProgramFromFile(cgcontext,
CgGL.CG_SOURCE,
            "J7_1_VP.cg", VERTEXPROFILE, null, null);
    CgGL.cgGLLoadProgram(vertexprog);

    // matrices:
    modelview = CgGL.cgGetNamedParameter(vertexprog,
"modelView");
    modelviewprojection =
CgGL.cgGetNamedParameter(vertexprog,
            "modelViewProjection");
    inversetranspose = CgGL.cgGetNamedParameter(vertexprog,
"inverseTranspose");

    //Light source properties
    myLa = CgGL.cgGetNamedParameter(vertexprog, "La");
    myLd = CgGL.cgGetNamedParameter(vertexprog, "Ld");
    myLs = CgGL.cgGetNamedParameter(vertexprog, "Ls");
    myLightPosition = CgGL.cgGetNamedParameter(vertexprog,
            "lightPosition");
    myEyePosition = CgGL.cgGetNamedParameter(vertexprog,
            "eyePosition");

    //Material properties
    myMe = CgGL.cgGetNamedParameter(vertexprog, "Me");
    myMa = CgGL.cgGetNamedParameter(vertexprog, "Ma");
    myMd = CgGL.cgGetNamedParameter(vertexprog, "Md");
    myMs = CgGL.cgGetNamedParameter(vertexprog, "Ms");
    myShininess = CgGL.cgGetNamedParameter(vertexprog,
            "shininess");

    gl.glEnable(GL.GL_LIGHTING);
    gl.glEnable(GL.GL_NORMALIZE);
```

```
        gl.glEnable(GL.GL_LIGHT0);

        // set up light source properties
        gl.glLightfv(GL.GL_LIGHT0, GL.GL_AMBIENT, blackish, 0);
        CgGL.cgSetParameter4fv(myLa, blackish, 0);

        gl.glLightfv(GL.GL_LIGHT0, GL.GL_DIFFUSE, white, 0);
        CgGL.cgSetParameter4fv(myLd, white, 0);

        gl.glLightfv(GL.GL_LIGHT0, GL.GL_SPECULAR, white, 0);
        CgGL.cgSetParameter4fv(myLs, white, 0);
    }

public void display(GLAutoDrawable drawable) {

        CgGL.cgGLEnableProfile(VERTEXPROFILE);
        CgGL.cgGLBindProgram(vertexprog);

        displayRobot(drawable);

        CgGL.cgGLDisableProfile(VERTEXPROFILE);
    }

public void displayRobot(GLAutoDrawable drawable) {
        myMaterialColor(blackish, yellish, white, black);
        super.display(drawable);
    }


public void drawSolar(float E, float e, float M, float m) {

        myMaterialColor(blackish, whitish, white, black);

        gl.glPushMatrix();
        gl.glRotatef(e, 0, 1, 0);
        // rotating around the "sun"; proceed angle
        gl.glRotatef(tiltAngle, 0, 0, 1); // tilt angle
        gl.glTranslatef(0, 1.5f * E, 0);

        gl.glPushMatrix();
        gl.glTranslatef(0, E, 0);
        gl.glScalef(E, E, E);

        myMaterialColor(blackish, white, white, black);
        drawSphere();
        gl.glPopMatrix();

        gl.glPushMatrix();
```

```
        gl.glScalef(E / 2, 1.5f * E, E / 2);
        gl.glRotatef(90, 1, 0, 0); // orient the cone

        myMaterialColor(blackish, red, white, black);
        drawCone();
        gl.glPopMatrix();

        gl.glTranslatef(0, E / 2, 0);
        gl.glRotatef(m, 0, 1, 0); // 1st moon
        gl.glPushMatrix();
        gl.glTranslatef(2 * M, 0, 0);
        gl.glLineWidth(1);
        gl.glScalef(E / 4, E / 4, E / 4);

        gl.glLightfv(GL.GL_LIGHT1, GL.GL_POSITION, origin, 0);

        // retrieve transformed light source position
        gl.glGetFloatv(GL.GL_MODELVIEW_MATRIX, currM, 0);
        sphereC[0] = currM[12];
        sphereC[1] = currM[13];
        sphereC[2] = currM[14];
        CgGL.cgSetParameter3fv(myLightPosition, sphereC, 0);

        // set up a fixed viewpoint
        sphereC[0] = 0;
        sphereC[1] = 0;
        sphereC[2] = 100;
        CgGL.cgSetParameter3fv(myEyePosition, sphereC, 0);

        myMaterialColor(whitish, white, white, whitish);
        drawSphere();
        gl.glPopMatrix();
        gl.glPopMatrix();
    }

    public void myMaterialColor(float myA[], float myD[], float
myS[],
        float myE[]) {

        gl.glMaterialfv(GL.GL_FRONT, GL.GL_AMBIENT, myA, 0);
        gl.glMaterialfv(GL.GL_FRONT, GL.GL_DIFFUSE, myD, 0);
        gl.glMaterialfv(GL.GL_FRONT, GL.GL_SPECULAR, myS, 0);
        gl.glMaterialfv(GL.GL_FRONT, GL.GL_EMISSION, myE, 0);

        // set up material properties
        CgGL.cgSetParameter4fv(myMe, myE, 0);
        CgGL.cgSetParameter4fv(myMa, myA, 0);
        CgGL.cgSetParameter4fv(myMd, myD, 0);
        CgGL.cgSetParameter4fv(myMs, myS, 0);
```

```
        CgGL.cgSetParameter1f(myShininess, 50);
}


public void drawSphere() {

    // retrieve matrices at where vertices are transformed
    CgGL.cgGLSetStateMatrixParameter(modelview,
        CgGL.CG_GL_MODELVIEW_MATRIX,
CgGL.CG_GL_MATRIX_IDENTITY);
    CgGL.cgGLSetStateMatrixParameter(inversetranspose,
        CgGL.CG_GL_MODELVIEW_MATRIX,
        CgGL.CG_GL_MATRIX_INVERSE_TRANSPOSE);
    CgGL.cgGLSetStateMatrixParameter(modelviewprojection,
        CgGL.CG_GL_MODELVIEW_PROJECTION_MATRIX,
        CgGL.CG_GL_MATRIX_IDENTITY);

    super.drawSphere();
}

public void drawCylinder() {

    // retrieve matrices at where vertices are transformed
    CgGL.cgGLSetStateMatrixParameter(modelview,
        CgGL.CG_GL_MODELVIEW_MATRIX,
CgGL.CG_GL_MATRIX_IDENTITY);
    CgGL.cgGLSetStateMatrixParameter(inversetranspose,
        CgGL.CG_GL_MODELVIEW_MATRIX,
        CgGL.CG_GL_MATRIX_INVERSE_TRANSPOSE);
    CgGL.cgGLSetStateMatrixParameter(modelviewprojection,
        CgGL.CG_GL_MODELVIEW_PROJECTION_MATRIX,
        CgGL.CG_GL_MATRIX_IDENTITY);
    super.drawSphere();
}

public void drawCone() {

    // retrieve matrices at where vertices are transformed
    CgGL.cgGLSetStateMatrixParameter(modelview,
        CgGL.CG_GL_MODELVIEW_MATRIX,
CgGL.CG_GL_MATRIX_IDENTITY);
    CgGL.cgGLSetStateMatrixParameter(inversetranspose,
        CgGL.CG_GL_MODELVIEW_MATRIX,
        CgGL.CG_GL_MATRIX_INVERSE_TRANSPOSE);
    CgGL.cgGLSetStateMatrixParameter(modelviewprojection,
        CgGL.CG_GL_MODELVIEW_PROJECTION_MATRIX,
        CgGL.CG_GL_MATRIX_IDENTITY);
    super.drawCone();
}
```

```
    public static void main(String[] args) {
        J7_1_Cg f = new J7_1_Cg();

        f.setTitle("JOGL J7_1_Cg");
        f.setSize(WIDTH, HEIGHT);
        f.setVisible(true);
    }
}
```

The corresponding vertex shader program is as follows:

// J7_1_VP.cg Vertex Program: vertex lighting

```
void main(
    float4 iPosition: POSITION,
    float4 iNormal  : NORMAL,
out float4 oPosition : POSITION,
out float4 oColor : COLOR,
uniform float4x4 modelView,
uniform float4x4 modelViewProjection,
uniform float4x4 inverseTranspose,
uniform float3    La,
uniform float3    Ld,
uniform float3    Ls,
uniform float3    lightPosition,
uniform float3    eyePosition,
uniform float3    Me,
uniform float3    Ma,
uniform float3    Md,
uniform float3    Ms,
uniform float     shininess
) {
  //calculate light source direction
  float4 vPosition = mul(modelView, iPosition);
  float3 P = vPosition.xyz;
  float3 L = normalize(lightPosition - P);

  //calculate vertex normal
  float4 hN = mul(inverseTranspose, iNormal);
  float3 N = normalize(hN.xyz);

  //calculate emission and ambient components
  float3 Ie = Me;
```

```
float3 Ia = La*Ma;

// calculate diffuse component
float cosNL = max(dot(N, L), 0);
float3 Id = Md * Ld * cosNL;

// calculate specular component
float3 V = normalize(eyePosition - P);
float3 H = normalize(L + V);
float cosNH = max(dot(N, H), 0);
if (cosNL==0) cosNH = 0;
float3 Is = Ms * Ls * pow(cosNH, shininess);

// final color assembly and vertex position in clip space
oColor.xyz = Ie + Ia + Id + Is;
oPosition = mul(modelViewProjection, iPosition);
}
```

On top of that, we can see that it is easy to have light source attenuation effect, spot light effect, multiple light sources, and other lighting calculations.

The advantage of GPU lighting is mainly on fragment lighting, which we will introduce below.

7.7 Per-Fragment Lighting

As we know, the vertex positions and colors calculated in the vertex shader are interpolated across a primitive after the primitive assembly. Therefore, the pixel shader receives the interpolated values for each pixel. For fragment lighting, we need to have the vertex position and normal in the eye space interpolated across a primitive as well. This can be achieved by two new semantics TEXCOORD0 and TEXCOORD1. The output in the vertex shader to TEXCOORD0 and TEXCOORD1 are values on the corresponding vertex, which are then interpolated across the primitive after primitive assembly and passed on to the pixel shader as input TEXCOORD0 and TEXCOORD1, respectively. Therefore, we still calculate vertex position and normal transformations into the eye space in the vertex shader, but we send them to the pixel shader through TEXCOORD0 and TEXCOOD1 for actual lighting calculation:

// J7_2_VP.cg Vertex Program: fragment lighting

```
void main(
    float4 iPosition  : POSITION,
    float4 iNormal   : NORMAL,
out float4 oPosition : POSITION,
out float4 vPosition : TEXCOORD0,
out float4 vNormal   : TEXCOORD1,

uniform float4x4 modelView,
uniform float4x4 modelViewProjection,
uniform float4x4 inverseTranspose
) {
  vPosition = mul(modelView, iPosition);
  vNormal = mul(inverseTranspose, iNormal);
  vNormal.xyz = normalize(vNormal.xyz);
  oPosition = mul(modelViewProjection, iPosition);
}
```

Since the lighting is calculated in the pixel shader, we should send all the lighting parameters to it:

```
        myLa = CgGL.cgGetNamedParameter(fragmentprog, "La");
        myLd = CgGL.cgGetNamedParameter(fragmentprog, "Ld");
        myLs = CgGL.cgGetNamedParameter(fragmentprog, "Ls");
        myLightPosition =
CgGL.cgGetNamedParameter(fragmentprog, "lightPosition");
        myEyePosition = CgGL.cgGetNamedParameter(fragmentprog,
            "eyePosition");
        myMe = CgGL.cgGetNamedParameter(fragmentprog, "Me");
        myMa = CgGL.cgGetNamedParameter(fragmentprog, "Ma");
        myMd = CgGL.cgGetNamedParameter(fragmentprog, "Md");
        myMs = CgGL.cgGetNamedParameter(fragmentprog, "Ms");
        myShininess = CgGL.cgGetNamedParameter(fragmentprog,
            "shininess");
```

Lighting calculation in the pixel shader is the same as the calculation in the vertex shader in the previous example, except that the position and normal are provided already, which are interpolated from the vertex transformation results.

// J7_2_VP.cg Fragment Program: fragment lighting

```
void main(
    float4 iPosition  :  TEXCOORD0,
    float4 iNormal    :   TEXCOORD1,
out float4 oColor : COLOR,
        uniform float3 La,
        uniform float3 Ld,
        uniform float3 Ls,
        uniform float3 lightPosition,
        uniform float3 eyePosition,
        uniform float3 Me,
        uniform float3 Ma,
        uniform float3 Md,
        uniform float3 Ms,
        uniform float shininess
) {
    //interpolated position and normal values
    float3 P = iPosition.xyz;
    float3 N = normalize(iNormal.xyz);
    float3 L = normalize(lightPosition - P);

    //calculate emission and ambient components
    float3 Ie = Me;
    float3 Ia = La*Ma;

    // calculate diffuse component
    float cosNL = max(dot(N, L), 0);
    float3 Id = Md * Ld * cosNL;

    // calculate specular component
    float3 V = normalize(eyePosition - P);
    float3 H = normalize(L + V);
    float cosNH = max(dot(N, H), 0);
    if (cosNL==0) cosNH = 0;
    float3 Is = Ms * Ls * pow(cosNH, shininess);

    oColor.xyz = Ie + Ia + Id + Is;
}
```

The complete JOGL program is as follows. A snapshot of the result is shown in Fig. 7.6. You may notice the detailed pixel-level lighting in this example, compared to the corresponding vertex-level lighting in Fig. 7.5.

Fig. 7.6 A pixel shader lighting with a movable light source

/*Cg Example: fragment lighting */

```java
import com.sun.opengl.cg.*;
import javax.media.opengl.*;

public class J7_2_Cg extends J7_1_Cg {
  CGprogram fragmentprog;
  static final int FRAGMENTPROFILE=CgGL.CG_PROFILE_ARBFP1;

   public void init(GLAutoDrawable glDrawable) {

      super.init(glDrawable);

      if (!CgGL.cgGLIsProfileSupported(FRAGMENTPROFILE)) {
         System.out.println("Fragment profile not
supported");
         System.exit(1);
      }

      CgGL.cgGLSetOptimalOptions(VERTEXPROFILE);
      vertexprog = CgGL.cgCreateProgramFromFile(cgcontext,
CgGL.CG_SOURCE,
            "J7_2_VP.cg", VERTEXPROFILE, null, null);
```

```java
        CgGL.cgGLLoadProgram(vertexprog);

        // matrix transformation in Vertex Shader
        modelview = CgGL.cgGetNamedParameter(vertexprog,
"modelView");
        modelviewprojection =
CgGL.cgGetNamedParameter(vertexprog,
            "modelViewProjection");
        inversetranspose = CgGL.cgGetNamedParameter(vertexprog,
"inverseTranspose");

        CgGL.cgGLSetOptimalOptions(FRAGMENTPROFILE);
        fragmentprog = CgGL.cgCreateProgramFromFile(cgcontext,
CgGL.CG_SOURCE,
            "J7_2_FP.cg", FRAGMENTPROFILE, null, null);
        CgGL.cgGLLoadProgram(fragmentprog);

        // lighting calculation in Pixel Shader
        myLa = CgGL.cgGetNamedParameter(fragmentprog, "La");
        myLd = CgGL.cgGetNamedParameter(fragmentprog, "Ld");
        myLs = CgGL.cgGetNamedParameter(fragmentprog, "Ls");
        myLightPosition =
CgGL.cgGetNamedParameter(fragmentprog,
            "lightPosition");
        myEyePosition = CgGL.cgGetNamedParameter(fragmentprog,
            "eyePosition");
        myMe = CgGL.cgGetNamedParameter(fragmentprog, "Me");
        myMa = CgGL.cgGetNamedParameter(fragmentprog, "Ma");
        myMd = CgGL.cgGetNamedParameter(fragmentprog, "Md");
        myMs = CgGL.cgGetNamedParameter(fragmentprog, "Ms");
        myShininess = CgGL.cgGetNamedParameter(fragmentprog,
            "shininess");

        gl.glEnable(GL.GL_LIGHTING);
        gl.glEnable(GL.GL_NORMALIZE);

        gl.glEnable(GL.GL_LIGHT0);

        gl.glLightfv(GL.GL_LIGHT0, GL.GL_AMBIENT, blackish, 0);
        CgGL.cgSetParameter4fv(myLa, blackish,0);

        gl.glLightfv(GL.GL_LIGHT0, GL.GL_DIFFUSE, white, 0);
        CgGL.cgSetParameter4fv(myLd, white, 0);

        gl.glLightfv(GL.GL_LIGHT0, GL.GL_SPECULAR, white, 0);
        CgGL.cgSetParameter4fv(myLs, white, 0);
    }

    public void display(GLAutoDrawable drawable) {
```

```
        CgGL.cgGLEnableProfile(VERTEXPROFILE);
        CgGL.cgGLBindProgram(vertexprog);
        CgGL.cgGLEnableProfile(FRAGMENTPROFILE);
        CgGL.cgGLBindProgram(fragmentprog);

        displayRobot(drawable);

        CgGL.cgGLDisableProfile(VERTEXPROFILE);
        CgGL.cgGLDisableProfile(FRAGMENTPROFILE);
    }


    public static void main(String[] args) {
        J7_2_Cg f = new J7_2_Cg();

        f.setTitle("JOGL J7_2_Cg");
        f.setSize(WIDTH, HEIGHT);
        f.setVisible(true);
    }
}
```

7.8 Per-Fragment Texture Mapping

7.8.1 Texture Coordinates

A vertex's texture coordinates are specified at each vertex, which are sent to the vertex shader through semantics TEXCOORD0. This is default similar to the vertex position and color. Unlike vertex position, which needs to be transformed by the current matrices, texture coordinates are fixed values at the vertices.

We can then pass the texture coordinates to the pixel shader as the vertex position and normal through a TEXCOORD semantics. For example, we can send it through TEXCOORD2, which will interpolate the texture coordinates for the pixels (fragments) across the corresponding primitive at the primitive assembly stage.

// J7_3_VP.cg Vertex Program: fragment texture mapping

```
void main(
```

```
    float4 iPosition   :   POSITION,
    float4 iNormal   :   NORMAL,
    float2 iTexCoord   :   TEXCOORD0,// input texture coord.

out float4 oPosition :   POSITION,
out float4 vPosition :   TEXCOORD0,
out float4 vNormal   :   TEXCOORD1,
out float2 oTexCoord :   TEXCOORD2,// output to pixel shader

uniform float4x4 modelView,
uniform float4x4 modelViewProjection,
uniform float4x4 inverseTranspose
) {
 vPosition = mul(modelView, iPosition);
 vNormal = mul(inverseTranspose, iNormal);
 vNormal.xyz = normalize(vNormal.xyz);
 oTexCoord = iTexCoord;
 oPosition = mul(modelViewProjection, iPosition);
}
```

7.8.2 Texture Objects

In the JOGL program, the current texture object (through glBindTexture) needs to be sent to the Pixel Shader for texel retrieval. The command to do so is:

```
    gl.glBindTexture(GL.GL_TEXTURE_2D, EARTH_TEX[0]);
    CgGL.cgGLSetTextureParameter(imgtexure, EARTH_TEX[0]);
    CgGL.cgGLEnableTextureParameter(imgtexure);
```

where "imgtexture" is a CGparameter:

```
    static CGparameter imgtexure; // texture object name

    // texture object name for Pixel Shader
    imgtexure = CgGL.cgGetNamedParameter(fragmentprog,
        "imgTexure");
```

In the Fragment program, texture is retrieved from library function tex2D:

```
 // retrieve texture from imgTexture at iTexCoord
  float4 texColor = tex2D(imgTexture, iTexCoord);
```

Here "imgTexture" needs to be a "uniform sampler2D" type with semantics TEX0:

```
uniform sampler2D imgTexure: TEX0,
```

which means that it is a 2D texture for texel retrieval. There are 1D, 3D, CUBE, and other type of built-in sampling application types.

7.8.3 Texture and Lighting Blending

Cg library function has a linear interpolation function "lerp", which interpolates two values according to the specified blending factor. For example,

```
oColor = lerp(texColor, oColor, α);
```

is equivalent to:

```
oColor = (1 - α)*texColor + α*oColor;
```

Therefore, we can calculate a fragment lighting color and blend it with the fragment texel color. The complete Pixel Shader program that calculates lighting and texture blending is as follows. A snapshot of the result is shown in Fig. 7.7.

Fig. 7.7 A pixel shader texture mapping and lighting

// J7_3_VP.cg Fragment Program: fragment texture mapping with lighting

```
void main(
    float4 iPosition: TEXCOORD0,
    float4 iNormal  : TEXCOORD1,
    float2 iTexCoord: TEXCOORD2,

out float4 oColor :   COLOR,
uniform sampler2D imgTexture: TEX0, //2D texture object
        uniform float3 La,
        uniform float3 Ld,
        uniform float3 Ls,
        uniform float3 lightPosition,
        uniform float3 eyePosition,
        uniform float3 Me,
        uniform float3 Ma,
        uniform float3 Md,
        uniform float3 Ms,
        uniform float shininess
) {
  float3 P = iPosition.xyz;
```

```
float3 N = normalize(iNormal.xyz);
float3 L = normalize(lightPosition - P);

//calculate emission and ambient components
float3 Ie = Me;
float3 Ia = La*Ma;

// calculate diffuse component
float cosNL = max(dot(N, L), 0);
float3 Id = Md * Ld * cosNL;

// calculate specular component
float3 V = normalize(eyePosition - P);
float3 H = normalize(L + V);
float cosNH = max(dot(N, H), 0);
if (cosNL==0) cosNH = 0;
float3 Is = Ms * Ls * pow(cosNH, shininess);

oColor.xyz = Ie + Ia + Id + Is;

// retrieve texture from imgTexture at iTexCoord
float4 texColor = tex2D(imgTexure, iTexCoord);

// blending of texColor with oColor
oColor = lerp(texColor, oColor, 0.6);
}
```

7.9 Per-Fragment Bump Mapping

In bump mapping, we can send the bump map, which is an array of normal vectors, as texture to the pixel shader. The bump map is also called a normal map. If we want to have texture mapping as well, we need to send the bump map object and the texture object to the pixel shader as well.

7.9.1 Bump Map Texture Coordinates

The bump map's coordinates correspond to the texture coordinates. As we have discussed already in texture mapping, a vertex's texture coordinates are sent to the vertex shader through semantics TEXCOORD0. We can then pass the texture coordinates to the pixel shader through a TEXCOORD semantics, which will interpolate the texture coordinates for the fragments across the corresponding primitive after the primitive assembly stage. That is, the texture coordinates will serve as indices to both of the bump map and the texture map.

7.9.2 Bump Map Object

In the JOGL program, the current bump map object (through glBindTexture) needs to be sent to the pixel shader for normal retrieval. First, we need to initialize the bump map as a texture:

```
void initTexture() {

    // initialize bumpmap texture obj
    gl.glGenTextures(1, IntBuffer.wrap(NORMAL_TEX));
    gl.glBindTexture(GL.GL_TEXTURE_2D, NORMAL_TEX[0]);
    gl.glTexParameteri(GL.GL_TEXTURE_2D,
            GL.GL_TEXTURE_MIN_FILTER,
            GL.GL_LINEAR);
    gl.glTexParameteri(GL.GL_TEXTURE_2D,
            GL.GL_TEXTURE_MAG_FILTER,
            GL.GL_LINEAR);
    readImage("NORMAL.jpg");

    gl.glTexImage2D(GL.GL_TEXTURE_2D, 0, GL.GL_RGB8,
        imgW, imgH, 0, GL.GL_BGR, GL.GL_UNSIGNED_BYTE,
        ByteBuffer.wrap(img));
    super.initTexture();
}
```

Then, we need to bind the bump map texture name:

```
CgGL.cgGLSetTextureParameter(normalmap, NORMAL_TEX[0]);
            CgGL.cgGLEnableTextureParameter(normalmap);
```

where "normalmap" is a CGparameter:

```
static CGparameter normalmap; // bump map object name

// texture object name for Pixel Shader
normalmap = CgGL.cgGetNamedParameter(fragmentprog,
    "normalMap");
```

In the fragment program, bump map is retrieved from library function tex2D:

```
// retrieve bump map vector from normalMap at iTexCoord
  float4 texColor = tex2D(normalMap, iTexCoord);
```

For a normalized normal n, its x, y, z values are negative one to positive one. So we can add one and then divide the result by two to store the values ($RGB = (n+1)/2$) in bump map and multiply by two and subtract one when we retrieve it ($n = RGB*2 -1$):

```
  float4 texColor1 = tex2D(normalMap, iTexCoord);
  float3 N = texColor1.xzy*2 - 1;
```

7.9.3 Normal Calculations

We need to transform the normals from the world space (global coordinates) into the texture space (tangent space), because we are attaching the normal map tangent to the surface at the point of lighting calculation. First, we define an arbitrary vector T. T can be aligned with the texture coordinates across the vertices as follows:

```
  float4 T = float4(iTexCoord.x, iTexCoord.y, 0, 0);
```

Because the normal is transformed to eye space, we need to transform T into eye space as well:

```
  float4 N = mul(inverseTranspose, iNormal);
  float4 tN = mul(inverseTranspose, T);
```

Therefore, by two cross products we can find TNB as follows:

```
  nNormal  = N.xyz;
  tNormal  = tN.xyz;
  bNormal  = cross(tNormal, nNormal);
  tNormal  = cross(nNormal, bNormal);
  tNormal  = normalize(tNormal);
  nNormal  = normalize(nNormal);
  bNormal  = normalize(bNormal);
```

The vertex program in the vertex shader includes calculating vertex position, normal, and TNB vectors and transforming them into eye space. Also, the texture coordinates are passed along as well. These values will be interpolated in the primitive and send to the pixel shader. The complete vertex program is as follows:

// J7_4_VP.cg Vertex Program: bump mapping

```
void main(
    float4 iPosition        :   POSITION,
    float4 iNormal          :   NORMAL,
    float2 iTexCoord        :   TEXCOORD0,
out float4 oPosition        :   POSITION,
out float2 oTexCoord        :   TEXCOORD0,
out float4 vPosition        :   TEXCOORD1,
out float3 nNormal      : TEXCOORD2,
out float3 tNormal      : TEXCOORD3,
out float3 bNormal      : TEXCOORD4,

uniform float4x4 modelView,
uniform float4x4 modelViewProjection,
uniform float4x4 inverseTranspose
) {
  vPosition = mul(modelView, iPosition);
  float4 T = float4(iTexCoord.x, iTexCoord.y, 0, 0);
  float4 tN = mul(inverseTranspose, T);
  float4 N = mul(inverseTranspose, iNormal);

  nNormal = N.xyz;
  tNormal = tN.xyz;
  bNormal = cross(tNormal, nNormal);
  tNormal = cross(nNormal, bNormal);
  tNormal = normalize(tNormal);
  nNormal = normalize(nNormal);
  bNormal = normalize(bNormal);

  oTexCoord = iTexCoord;
  oPosition = mul(modelViewProjection, iPosition);
}
```

7.9.4 Fragment Lighting Calculations

In the Pixel Shader, we need to retrieve pixel position and normal. At the same time, we need to transform the light source direction to the tangent space. Transforming the light source direction into tangent space can be done by the following coordinates transformation:

```
float3 Lg = normalize(lightPosition - P);
float3 L = float3(dot(tNormal, Lg),
        dot(nNormal, Lg),dot(bNormal, Lg)) ;
```

The complete fragment program is as follows. A snapshot of the result is shown in Fig. 7.8.

Fig. 7.8 A pixel shader bump mapping, texture mapping, and lighting

// J7_4_FP.cg Fragment Program: fragment bump mapping

```
void main(
    float2 iTexCoord          : TEXCOORD0,
    float4 iPosition          : TEXCOORD1,
    float3 nNormal            : TEXCOORD2,
    float3 tNormal            : TEXCOORD3,
    float3 bNormal            : TEXCOORD4,
out float4 oColor             : COLOR,
uniform sampler2D imgTexture  : TEX0,
uniform sampler2D normalMap   : TEX0,
        uniform float3 La,
        uniform float3 Ld,
        uniform float3 Ls,
        uniform float3 lightPosition,
```

```
            uniform float3 eyePosition,
            uniform float3 Me,
            uniform float3 Ma,
            uniform float3 Md,
            uniform float3 Ms,
            uniform float shininess
) {
  // retrieve bump map vector at iTexCoord
  float4 texColor1 = tex2D(normalMap, iTexCoord);
  float4 texColor2 = tex2D(imgTexture, iTexCoord);

  // retrieve pixel position and normal
  float3 N = texColor1.xzy*2 - 1;
  float3 P = iPosition.xyz;

// transform light source direction to tangent space
float3 Lg = normalize(lightPosition - P);
float3 L = float3(dot(tNormal, Lg),
        dot(nNormal, Lg),dot(bNormal, Lg)) ;

// calculate emission and ambient components
float3 Ie = Me;
float3 Ia = La*Ma;

// calculate diffuse component
float cosNL = max(dot(N, L), 0);
float3 Id = Md * Ld * cosNL;

// calculate specular component
float3 V = normalize(eyePosition - P);
float3 H = normalize(L + V);
float cosNH = max(dot(N, H), 0);
if (cosNL==0) cosNH = 0;
float3 Is = Ms * Ls * pow(cosNH, shininess);

oColor.xyz = Ie + Ia + Id + Is;
oColor = lerp(oColor, texColor2, 0.5);
}
```

7.10 Review Questions

1. What are the possible default values sent from the JOGL program to the vertex shader?

2. What are the possible default values sent from the JOGL program to the pixel shader?

3. What are the values that are calculated in parallel in the vertex shader?

4. What are the values that are calculated in parallel in the pixel shader?

5. If we calculate lighting on a vertex shader, what parameters and when these parameters are needed to be send to the vertex shader?

6. What is the main difference between Cg and CUDA?

7. If we can read texture in the vertex shader, we can achieve displacement mapping by providing a height map as a texture. Please describe how to achieve displacement mapping and find if there are graphics cards that allow texture access on the vertex shader.

8. In the pixel shader, we can have displacement of pixel positions for lighting calculation. This will allow self-shadow and other surface details, including texture coordinates retrieval. Please consider what can be used for pixel position displacement and what can be changed due to the pixel position displacement.

7.11 Programming Assignments

1. Please design a fixed point light source and calculate the lighting in the vertex shader for each vertex.

2. Please design a fixed point light source and calculate the lighting in the pixel shader.

3. Please implement a displacement mapping in the vertex shader.

4. Please implement a cubic mapping in the pixel shader.

5. Please implement parallax or relief mapping in the fragment shader.

8
Programming in Java3D

Chapter Objectives:

- Briefly introduce scene graph structure and Java3D programming

8.1 Introduction

Java3D is another API by Sun Microsystems that provides 3D graphics capabilities to Java applications. It is built on OpenGL and therefore has higher level of abstractions and architectures than OpenGL/JOGL. Java3D programmers work with high-level constructs, called *scene graphs*, for creating and manipulating 3D geometric objects. The details of rendering are handled automatically. Java3D programs can be stand-alone applications as well as applets in browsers that have been extended to support Java3D. A comprehensive tutorial, advanced books, and other information are available at `http://java.sun.com/products/java-media/3D/collateral/`

In this chapter, we provide a shortcut to scene graph structure and Java3D programming.

8.2 Scene Graph

A 3D virtual environment, or universe, is constructed by graphics models and their relations. A group of graphics models and their relations can be represented by an abstract tree structure, called scene graph, where nodes are models and link arcs

J.X. Chen, *Guide to Graphics Software Tools*, doi: 10.1007/978-1-84800-901-1_8,
© Springer-Verlag London Limited 2008

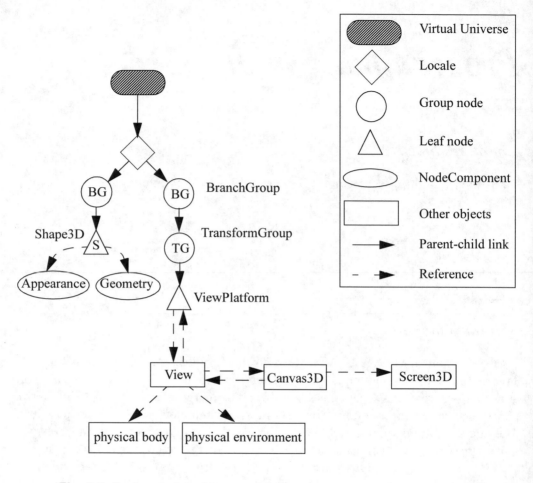

Fig. 8.1 Scene graph and its notations

represent relations. A Java3D virtual universe is created from a scene graph, as shown in Fig. 8.1.

The *nodes* in the scene graph are the objects or the instances of Java3D classes. The *arcs* represent the two kinds of relationships between nodes: parent-child or reference. A *Group node* can have any number of children but only one parent. A *Leaf node* has no children. A *Reference* associates a NodeComponent with a Leaf node. A *NodeComponent* specifies the geometry, appearance, texture, or material properties of a Leaf node (Shape3D object). A NodeComponent is not part of the scene graph tree and may be referenced by several Leaf nodes. All other objects following reference links are not part of the scene graph tree either. All nodes in the scene graph are accessible following solid arcs from the *Locale object*, which is the root. The arcs of a tree have no cycles, therefore there is only one path from the root to a leaf, which is called a *scene graph path*. Each scene graph path completely specifies the state information of its leaf. That is, the transformations and visual attributes of a leaf object depend only on its scene graph path. The scene graph, NodeComponents, references, and other objects all together form a virtual universe.

In Fig. 8.1, there are two scene graph branches. The branch on the right is for setting up viewing transformations, which is mostly the same for many different applications and is called a view branch. The branch on the left is for building up 3D objects and their attributes and relations in the virtual universe. Sometimes we call the object branch the scene graph and ignore the view branch, because the object branch is the major part in building and manipulating a virtual universe.

8.2.1 Setting Up Working Environment

To install and run Java3D, we need to install Java Development Kit first. In addition, a Java IDE is also preferred to speed up coding. At the beginning of this book, we have installed Java, JOGL, and Eclipse or JBuilder IDE. Now, we need to download and install Java3D SDK from:

`http://java.sun.com/products/java-media/3D/download.html`

For Windows platform, we should download the Java3D for Windows (OpenGL Version) SDK for the JDK (includes Runtime). We should install Java3D in the JDK that our IDE uses. If necessary, we can install multiple times into different version of JDKs that we use for different IDEs, such as JBuilder, which comes with its own JDK. Once we install the downloaded software, we are ready to edit and execute our sample programs.

After downloading Java3D SDK, you may download Java3D API specification as well, which includes online references to all Java3D objects as well as basic concepts and example programs. After going through this introduction, you may extend your knowledge on Java3D and use the online material to implement many more applications quickly.

Example Java3D_0.java in the following constructs a simple virtual universe as in Fig. 8.1 except that, for simplicity purposes, it uses a ColorCube object to replace the Shape3D leaf object and its appearance and geometry NodeComponents. ColorCube is designed to make a testbed easy. The result is as shown in Fig. 8.2. Here we only see the front face of the ColorCube object.

Fig. 8.2 Draw a color cube

/* draw a cube in Java3D topdown approach */

```
import java.awt.*;
import java.awt.event.*;
import javax.media.j3d.*;
import com.sun.j3d.utils.geometry.ColorCube;
import javax.vecmath.Vector3f;
import com.sun.j3d.utils.universe.*;


public class Java3D_0 extends Frame {

 Java3D_0() {

   //1. Create a drawing area canvas3D
   setLayout(new BorderLayout());
   GraphicsConfiguration gc =
     SimpleUniverse.getPreferredConfiguration();
   Canvas3D canvas3D = new Canvas3D(gc);
   add(canvas3D);

   // Quite window with disposal
   addWindowListener(new WindowAdapter()
     {public void windowClosing(WindowEvent e)
        {dispose(); System.exit(0);}
     }
   );

   //2. Construct ViewBranch topdown
   BranchGroup viewBG = createVB(canvas3D);

   //3. Construct sceneGraph: a color cube
```

```
BranchGroup objBG = new BranchGroup();
objBG.addChild(new ColorCube(0.2));

//4. Go live under locale in the virtualUniverse
VirtualUniverse universe = new VirtualUniverse();
Locale locale = new Locale(universe);
locale.addBranchGraph(viewBG);
locale.addBranchGraph(objBG);
}

BranchGroup createVB(Canvas3D canvas3D) {

//5. Initialize view branch
BranchGroup viewBG = new BranchGroup();
TransformGroup viewTG = new TransformGroup();
ViewPlatform myViewPlatform = new ViewPlatform();
viewBG.addChild(viewTG);
viewTG.addChild(myViewPlatform);

//6. Move the view branch to view object at origin
Vector3f transV = new Vector3f(0f, 0f, 2.4f);
Transform3D translate = new Transform3D();
translate.setTranslation(transV);
viewTG.setTransform(translate);

//7. Construct view for myViewPlatform
View view = new View();
view.addCanvas3D(canvas3D);
view.setPhysicalBody(new PhysicalBody());
view.setPhysicalEnvironment(new PhysicalEnvironment());
view.attachViewPlatform(myViewPlatform);

return (viewBG);
}


public static void main(String args[]) {

Java3D_0 frame = new Java3D_0();

frame.setSize(500,500);
frame.setVisible(true);
}
}
```

8.2.2 Drawing a ColorCube Object

The above Example *Java3D_0.java* is a Java application that draws a colored cube using Java3D. Our future examples are built on top of this first example. Here we explain the example in detail. We only need to understand the following:

1. We create `canvas3D` that corresponds to the default display device with a Screen3D object implied.

2. With `canvas3D`, we construct the view branch under the BranchGroup node, `viewBG`, which will be a child under `locale`. The detail of creating the view branch will be discussed later in this section.

3. We create the object branch under `objBG`, which is a ColorCube object under the group node.

4. We create `universe` and its associated `locale`, and add the view branch and the object branch to form the virtual universe completely. Whenever a branch is attached to the Locale object, all the branch's nodes are considered to be *live*. When an object is live, it's parameters cannot be changed unless through special means that we will discuss later.

5. Here in the subroutine we initialize the view branch. Under the BranchGroup `viewBG`, we have TransformGroup `viewTG`. Under `viewTG`, we have `myViewPlatform`, which a View object (`view`) corresponding to `canvas3D` will be attached to.

6. The purpose of `viewTG` is to move the viewpoint along positive z axis to look at the origin in perspective projection. Here we translate `myViewPlatform` along positive z axis, which sets the viewpoint to be centered at $(0, 0, 2.41)$ looking in the negative z direction toward the origin, and the view plane at the origin is a square from $(-1, -1, 0)$ to $(1, 1, 0)$.

7. We construct the View object `view` and attach it with `myViewPlatform`. The View object contains all default parameters needed in rendering a 3D scene from one viewpoint as specified above. The technical details are ignored in this introduction. The PhysicalBody object contains a specification of the user's head. The PhysicalEnvironment object is used to set up input devices (sensors) for head-tracking and other uses in immersive virtual environment.

In summary, we construct a virtual universe as shown in Fig. 8.1. The object branch specifies a ColorCube object from (-0.2, -0.2, -0.2) to (0.2, 0.2, 0.2). The view branch specifies a perspective projection with a viewpoint at (0, 0, 2.41) and view plane cross section at the origin from (-1, -1, 0) to (1, 1, 0). Each scene graph path, as we can see now, is like a series of OpenGL commands for setting up viewing or drawing a hierarchical scene. The details of rendering are handled automatically by the Java3D runtime system. The Java3D renderer is capable of optimizing and rendering in parallel. Therefore, in Java3D, we build a virtual universe with hierarchical structure, which is composed of nodes or instances of Java3D classes, in a scene graph tree structure.

8.3 The SimpleUniverse

Because the view branch is mostly the same for many different applications, Java3D provides a SimpleUniverse class that can be used to construct the view branch automatically, as shown in Fig. 8.3. This way we can simplify the code dramatically and focus on generating object scene graph. However, we lost the flexibility of modifying and controlling View, ViewPlatform, PhysicalBody, and PhysicalEnvironment directly, which are useful under special applications. Here we ignore them for simplicity purposes, because we can use SimpleUniverse to construct a testbed with all default components in a virtual universe. We focus our attention on generating a scene graph with more contents and controls here.

Example *Java3D_1_Hello.java* generates the same result as *Java3D_0.java*, as shown in Fig. 8.2 below. The difference is that here it uses the SimpleUniverse object simpleU to construct a virtual universe, including the Locale object and the view branch, which simplifies the code significantly.

/*draw a cube in Java3D topdown approach */

```
import java.awt.*;
import java.awt.GraphicsConfiguration;
import com.sun.j3d.utils.universe.*;
import com.sun.j3d.utils.geometry.*;
import javax.media.j3d.*;
import java.awt.event.*;

// renders a single cube.
```

```java
public class Java3D_1_Hello extends Frame {

 Java3D_1_Hello() {

  //1. Create a drawing area canvas3D
  setLayout(new BorderLayout());

  GraphicsConfiguration gc =
    SimpleUniverse.getPreferredConfiguration();

  Canvas3D canvas3D = new Canvas3D(gc);
  add(canvas3D);

  //2. Create a simple universe with standard view branch
  SimpleUniverse simpleU = new SimpleUniverse(canvas3D);

  //3. Move the ViewPlatform back to view object at origin
simpleU.getViewingPlatform().setNominalViewingTransform();

  //4. Construct sceneGraph: object branch group
  BranchGroup objBG = createSG();

  //5. Go live under simpleUniverse
  simpleU.addBranchGraph(objBG);

  // exit windows with proper disposal
  addWindowListener(new WindowAdapter() {
   public void windowClosing(WindowEvent e) {
    dispose();
    System.exit(0);
   }
  }
  );
 }


 BranchGroup createSG() {
  BranchGroup objBG = new BranchGroup();

  objBG.addChild(new ColorCube(0.2));
  return (objBG);
 }

 public static void main(String[] args) {

  Java3D_1_Hello frame = new Java3D_1_Hello();

  frame.setSize(500, 500);
```

```
    frame.setVisible(true);
  }
}
```

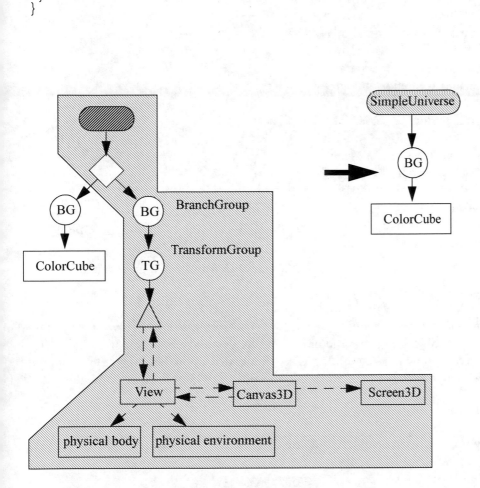

Fig. 8.3 **A SimpleUniverse generates a view branch automatically**

In the above, the method *setNominalViewingTransform()* sets the viewpoint at 2.41 meters. The default viewing volume and projection are the same as the previous example.

8.4 Transformation

In the following, we add a TransformGroup node as shown in Fig. 8.4a, which is named `objTransform` in the program. Here the transformation includes a rotation around *y* axis, and then a translation along *x* axis. The result is shown in Fig. 8.4b. As we mentioned earlier, a scene graph path determines the leaf object's state completely. Here, the ColorCube object will be transformed by the matrix built in `objTransform` and then sent to the display.

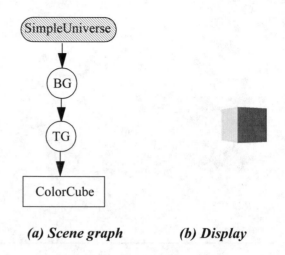

(a) Scene graph   *(b) Display*

Fig. 8.4 A transformation group node

BranchGroup objects can be *compiled*, as the method calls *objRoot.compile()* in Example *Java3D_2_Transform.java* below. Compiling a BranchGroup object converts the object and its descendants to a more efficient form for the Java3D renderer. Compiling is recommended as the last step before making it live at the highest level of a BranchGroup object, which is right under the Locale object.

/* draw a cube with transformation */

```
import com.sun.j3d.utils.geometry.*;
import javax.media.j3d.*;
import javax.vecmath.Vector3f;


public class Java3D_2_Transform extends Java3D_1_Hello {

  // Construct sceneGraph: object branch group
  BranchGroup createSG() {

    // translate object has composite transformation matrix
    Transform3D rotate = new Transform3D();
```

```
Transform3D translate = new Transform3D();
rotate.rotY(Math.PI/8);

// translate object actually saves a matrix expression
Vector3f transV = new Vector3f(0.4f, 0f, 0f);
translate.setTranslation(transV);

translate.mul(rotate); // final matrix: T*R

TransformGroup objTransform = new TransformGroup(
    translate);
objTransform.addChild(new ColorCube(0.2));

BranchGroup objRoot = new BranchGroup();
objRoot.addChild(objTransform);

// Let Java3D perform optimizations on this scene graph.
objRoot.compile();

return objRoot;
} // end of CreateSceneGraph method

public static void main(String[] args) {

Java3D_2_Transform frame = new Java3D_2_Transform();

frame.setSize(999, 999);
frame.setVisible(true);
}
}
```

8.5 Multiple Scene Graph Branches

In the following, we add another BranchGroup, as shown in Fig. 8.5a. The result is shown in Fig. 8.5b. Here a ColorCube object is rotated around *y* axis, and then translated along positive *x* axis, while another ColorCube object is rotated around *x* axis, and then translated along negative *x* axis. The code is shown in Example *Java3D_3_Multiple.java*.

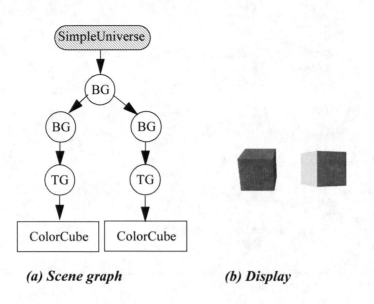

(a) Scene graph   *(b) Display*

Fig. 8.5 Multiple scene graph branches

As we mentioned before, a valid scene graph does not form a cycle, and each scene graph path determines the state of its leaf object completely. To draw two ColorCube objects exactly as in Fig. 8.5, we can form many different structures. For example, we can have the two TransformGroup nodes go directly under the root BranchGroup node; we can have the two BranchGroup nodes go directly under the Locale object, so each node is an independent root. A good hierarchical structure design will be easier for understanding and implementation.

/* draw two cubes with transformations */

```
import com.sun.j3d.utils.geometry.*;
import javax.media.j3d.*;
import javax.vecmath.Vector3f;

public class Java3D_3_Multiple extends Java3D_2_Transform {

  BranchGroup createSG() {
```

```
//1. construct two scene graphs
BranchGroup objRoot1 = createSG1();
BranchGroup objRoot2 = createSG2();

BranchGroup objRoot = new BranchGroup();
objRoot.addChild(objRoot1);
objRoot.addChild(objRoot2);

return objRoot;
}


BranchGroup createSG2() {

Transform3D rotate = new Transform3D();
Transform3D translate = new Transform3D();
rotate.rotY(Math.PI/8);

//2. translate and rotate matrices are mult. together
Vector3f transV = new Vector3f(0.4f, 0f, 0f);
translate.setTranslation(transV);
translate.mul(rotate);

TransformGroup objTransform = new TransformGroup(
  translate);
objTransform.addChild(new ColorCube(0.2));

BranchGroup objRoot = new BranchGroup();
objRoot.addChild(objTransform);
return objRoot;
}


BranchGroup createSG1() {

Transform3D rotate = new Transform3D();
Transform3D translate = new Transform3D();
rotate.rotX(Math.PI/8);

Vector3f transV = new Vector3f(-0.4f, 0f, 0f);
translate.setTranslation(transV);
translate.mul(rotate);

TransformGroup objTransform = new TransformGroup(
  translate);
objTransform.addChild(new ColorCube(0.2));

BranchGroup objRoot = new BranchGroup();
objRoot.addChild(objTransform);
```

```
    return objRoot;
  }


  public static void main(String[] args) {
   Java3D_3_Multiple frame = new Java3D_3_Multiple();
   frame.setSize(999, 999);
   frame.setVisible(true);
  }
}
```

8.6 Animation

Once a node is made live or compiled, the Java3D rendering system converts it to a more efficient internal representation so its values are fixed. In order to create animations, we need the capability to change values in a scene graph object after it becomes live. The list of values that can be modified is called the *capabilities* of the object. Each node has a set of capability bits. The values of these bits determine what capabilities exist for the node. The capabilities must be set before the node is either compiled or gone live.

As shown in Fig. 8.6, a behavior node is in reference to the transformation group node to modify its transformation and is added as a leaf child to it. Here the default transformation being modified is rotation around *y* axis by an interpolation of repeating values in an infinite loop. Example *Java3D_4_Animate.java* creates a scene graph as shown in Fig. 8.6, and an animation sequence is shown in Fig. 8.7.

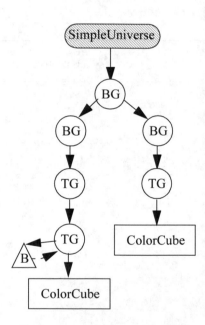

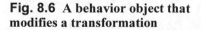

Fig. 8.6 A behavior object that modifies a transformation

Fig. 8.7 Animate a color cube

/* draw a cube with animation */

```
import com.sun.j3d.utils.geometry.*;
import javax.media.j3d.*;
import javax.vecmath.Vector3f;


public class Java3D_4_Animate extends Java3D_3_Multiple {

 BranchGroup createSG1() {

   Transform3D rotate = new Transform3D();
   Transform3D translate = new Transform3D();

   rotate.rotX(Math.PI/8);

   Vector3f transV = new Vector3f(-0.4f, 0f, 0f);
   translate.setTranslation(transV);

   translate.mul(rotate);

   TransformGroup objTransform = new TransformGroup(
     translate);

   BranchGroup objRoot = new BranchGroup();
   objRoot.addChild(objTransform);

   //1. Node closer to leaf object takes effect first
```

```
// Here objSpin transformation happens first,
//   then objTransform
TransformGroup objSpin = new TransformGroup();
objTransform.addChild(objSpin);
objSpin.addChild(new ColorCube(0.2));

//2. setCapability allows live change, and the default
//   change is rot on Y axis
objSpin.setCapability(TransformGroup.
           ALLOW_TRANSFORM_WRITE);

//3. Alpha provides a variable value of 0-1 for
// the angle of rotation; -1 means infinite loop
// 5000 means in 5 second alpha goes from 0 to 1
Alpha a = new Alpha(-1, 5000);

//4. rotator is a behavior node in reference to ojbSpin
// i.e., rotator links ojbSpin to alpha for rotation
RotationInterpolator rotator = new RotationInterpolator(
   a, objSpin);

//5. Bounding sphere specifies a region in which a
// behavior is active. Here a sphere centered at the
// origin with radius of 100 is created.
BoundingSphere bounds = new BoundingSphere();
rotator.setSchedulingBounds(bounds);

//6. rotator (behavior node) is child of objSpin (TG)
objSpin.addChild(rotator);

return objRoot;
}


public static void main(String[] args) {

Java3D_4_Animate frame = new Java3D_4_Animate();

frame.setSize(999, 999);
frame.setVisible(true);
}

}
```

Example *Java3D_4_Animate.java* animates a colored cube in Java3D. Here we explain some details in the code:

1. We create two transformation nodes, `objTransform` and `objSpin`, and `objSpin` is a child of `objTransform`. As in OpenGL, because `objSpin` is closer to the colored cube, it takes effect first. As we will see, `objSpin` is a dynamic rotation around y axis. After that, `objTransform` will rotate the colored cube on x axis and then translate it along negative x axis. The result is an animation and a snapshot is shown in Fig. 8.7.

2. Here we setCapability so we can modify the transformation matrix after `objSpin` becomes live. The default that we can write into the matrix is a rotation around y axis.

3. Here an Alpha object `a` is used to create a time varying value of 0 to 1 for controlling the angle of rotation. In *Alpha a = new Alpha(-1, 5000)*, "-1" means infinite loop and 5000 means in 5 seconds alpha goes from 0 to 1.

4. A RotationInterpolator object `rotator` is a behavior object that links `a` with `objectSpin` to change `objSpin` to a specific angle according to the current value of `a`. Because the value of `a` changes over time, the rotation changes as well. The default value of RotationInterpolator object is rotating around y axis from 0 to 360 degrees, and the colored cube will rotate 360 degrees every 5 second. You can check out RotationInterpolator Class to find out how to set up rotation around other axes.

5. Because behaviors are time consuming, for efficiency purposes, Java3D allows programmers to specify a spatial boundary, called a *scheduling region*, for a behavior to function. A behavior is not active unless the shape object is inside or intersects a Behavior object's scheduling region. Here Bounding sphere specifies a region in which a behavior is active, which is a sphere centered at the origin with radius of 1 as default.

6. The behavior object `rotator` is set to be one of the children of `objSpin`, as shown in the scene graph in Fig. 8.6.

8.7 Primitives

In general, we define a shape through a Shape3D object and its NodeComponent objects, as in Fig. 8.8. The Geometry node component defines the object's geometry, such as vertices and per-vertex colors. The Appearance node component defines the object's attributes, material color, texture, and other information that is not defined in geometry. For simplicity, we have only used the ColorCube class to define 3D objects, which have predefined geometry and appearance already. Here we introduce more basic primitives in Java3D, and construct a virtual universe in *Java3D_5_Primitives.java*, as in Fig. 8.9.

Fig. 8.8 Shape3D

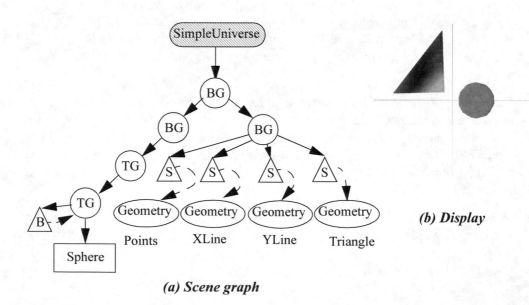

(a) Scene graph

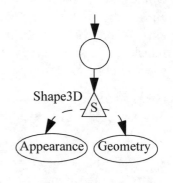

(b) Display

Fig. 8.9 Shapes and their geometries and appearances

The Java3D geometric utility classes create box, cone, cylinder, and sphere geometric primitives. Here a primitive object has pre-specified geometry, but the appearance can be specified, which has more flexibility than ColorCube. Each primitive class is actually composed of one or more Shape3D objects with their own Geometry node components, and in this example the Shape3D objects share one Appearance node component specified with the primitive. In our example in the left branch of the scene graph, we specify a sphere, and its default Appearance is white. In the right branch of the scene graph, we specify several Shape3D objects (points, lines, and triangles) with only their Geometry (coordinates and colors). The points and lines may not be obvious or visible in the display, but they exist.

/* draw multiple primitives */

```
import com.sun.j3d.utils.geometry.*;
import javax.media.j3d.*;
import javax.vecmath.*;


public class Java3D_5_Primitives extends Java3D_4_Animate {

  Color3f red = new Color3f(1.0f, 0.0f, 0.0f);
  Color3f green = new Color3f(0.0f, 1.0f, 0.0f);
  Color3f blue = new Color3f(0.0f, 0.0f, 1.0f);
  Color3f white = new Color3f(1.0f, 1.0f, 1.0f);

  //Create sphere (cone, etc) rotating around y axis
  BranchGroup createSG1() {

  Transform3D rotate = new Transform3D();
  Transform3D translate = new Transform3D();
  rotate.rotX(Math.PI/8);

  Vector3f transV = new Vector3f(0.4f, 0f, 0f);
  translate.setTranslation(transV);
  translate.mul(rotate);

  TransformGroup objTransform = new TransformGroup(
      translate);
  TransformGroup objSpin = new TransformGroup();
  BranchGroup objRoot = new BranchGroup();
  objRoot.addChild(objSpin);

  objSpin.addChild(objTransform);

  //1. draw a sphere, cone, box, or cylinder
```

```
    Appearance app = new Appearance();
    Sphere sphere = new Sphere(0.2f);
    sphere.setAppearance(app);
    objTransform.addChild(sphere);

//      Cone cone = new Cone(0.2f, 0.2f);
//      cone.setAppearance(app);
//      objSpin.addChild(cone);

//      Box box = new Box(0.2f, 0.2f, 0.2f, app);
//      box.setAppearance(app);
//      objSpin.addChild(box);

//      Cylinder cylinder = new Cylinder(0.2f, 0.2f);
//      cylinder.setAppearance(app);
//      objSpin.addChild(cylinder);


    objSpin.setCapability(TransformGroup.
            ALLOW_TRANSFORM_WRITE);

    Alpha a = new Alpha(-1, 5000);
    RotationInterpolator rotator =
      new RotationInterpolator(a, objSpin);
    BoundingSphere bounds = new BoundingSphere();

    rotator.setSchedulingBounds(bounds);
    objSpin.addChild(rotator);

    return objRoot;
}


// primitive points, lines, triangles, etc.
BranchGroup createSG2() {

    BranchGroup axisBG = new BranchGroup();

    //2. Create two points, may not be obviously visible
    PointArray points =
      new PointArray(2, PointArray.COORDINATES);
    axisBG.addChild(new Shape3D(points));

    points.setCoordinate(0, new Point3f(.5f, .5f, 0));
    points.setCoordinate(1, new Point3f(-.5f, -.5f, 0));

    //3. Create line for X axis
    LineArray xLine =
      new LineArray(2, LineArray.COORDINATES
```

```
                |LineArray.COLOR_3);
   axisBG.addChild(new Shape3D(xLine));

   xLine.setCoordinate(0, new Point3f(-1.0f, 0.0f, 0.0f));
   xLine.setCoordinate(1, new Point3f(1.0f, 0.0f, 0.0f));
   xLine.setColor(0, red);
   xLine.setColor(1, green);

   //4. Create line for Y axis
   LineArray yLine =
      new LineArray(2, LineArray.COORDINATES
               |LineArray.COLOR_3);
   axisBG.addChild(new Shape3D(yLine));

   yLine.setCoordinate(0, new Point3f(0.0f, -1.0f, 0.0f));
   yLine.setCoordinate(1, new Point3f(0.0f, 1.0f, 0.0f));
   yLine.setColor(0, white);
   yLine.setColor(1, blue);

   //5. Create a triangle
   TriangleArray triangle =
      new TriangleArray(3, TriangleArray.COORDINATES
               |TriangleArray.COLOR_3);
   axisBG.addChild(new Shape3D(triangle));

   triangle.setCoordinate(0, new Point3f(-.9f, .1f, -.5f));
   triangle.setCoordinate(1, new Point3f(-.1f, .1f, .0f));
   triangle.setCoordinate(2, new Point3f(-.1f, .7f, .5f));

   triangle.setColor(0, red);
   triangle.setColor(1, green);
   triangle.setColor(2, blue);

   return axisBG;
}


public static void main(String[] args) {

   Java3D_5_Primitives frame = new Java3D_5_Primitives();

   frame.setSize(999, 999);
   frame.setVisible(true);
}
}
```

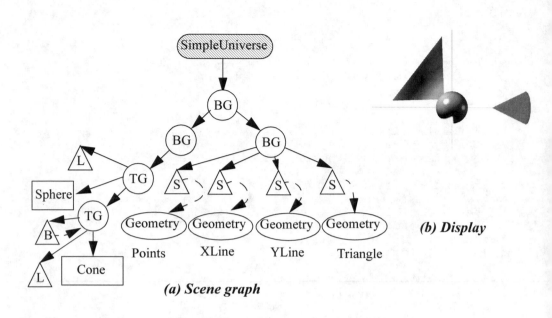

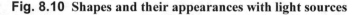

Fig. 8.10 Shapes and their appearances with light sources

8.8 Appearance

As we discussed earlier, Appearance class specifies attributes, material properties, textures, etc. As shown in Fig. 8.10a, here we implement a cone with coloring attribute (red), and a sphere with material properties (whitish) that work with light sources. There are two light sources in the environment. One light source is specified as a directional light facing the origin after transformation, is a sibling of the cone with the same color, and moves with the cone. The other light source is a white fixed point light source, which, according to its scene graph path, does not go through any transformation. The result is as shown in Fig. 8.10b.

/* draw objects with Appearance - light sources */

```
import com.sun.j3d.utils.geometry.*;
import javax.media.j3d.*;
import javax.vecmath.*;
```

```
public class Java3D_6_Appearance extends
  Java3D_5_Primitives {

static Color3f redish = new Color3f(0.9f, 0.3f, 0.3f);
static Color3f whitish = new Color3f(0.8f, 0.8f, 0.8f);
static Color3f blackish = new Color3f(0.2f, 0.2f, 0.2f);
static Color3f black = new Color3f(0f, 0f, 0f);

// primitive sphere (cone, etc) rotate around y axis
BranchGroup createSG1() {

  TransformGroup objSpin = new TransformGroup();
  BranchGroup objRoot = new BranchGroup();
  objRoot.addChild(objSpin);

  //1. set material attributes 4 the app. of an sphere
  Appearance app1 = new Appearance();
  Material mat = new Material();
  mat.setAmbientColor(blackish);
  mat.setDiffuseColor(whitish);
  mat.setEmissiveColor(black);
  mat.setShininess(200);
  app1.setMaterial(mat);

  // sphare at origin
  Sphere sphere =
   new Sphere(0.2f, Primitive.GENERATE_NORMALS, 80, app1);
  sphere.setAppearance(app1);
  objSpin.addChild(sphere);

  //2. specify a cone rotating around the sphere
  Transform3D rotate = new Transform3D();
  Transform3D translate = new Transform3D();
  rotate.rotZ(Math.PI/2);

  Vector3f transV = new Vector3f(0.7f, 0f, 0f);
  translate.setTranslation(transV);
  translate.mul(rotate);

  TransformGroup objTransform =
   new TransformGroup(translate);
  // objTransform is a child of objSpin
  objSpin.addChild(objTransform);
  // cone is a child of objTransform
  Cone cone = new Cone(0.2f, 0.4f);
  objTransform.addChild(cone);
```

```
//3. Set coloring attributes for appearance of a cone
Appearance app = new Appearance();
app.setColoringAttributes(
  new ColoringAttributes(redish, 1));
cone.setAppearance(app);

//4. Specify a light source that goes with the cone
BoundingSphere lightbounds = new BoundingSphere();
Vector3f light1Direction = new Vector3f(0f, 1f, 0.0f);
// facing origin as cone
DirectionalLight light1 = new DirectionalLight(
  redish, light1Direction);
light1.setInfluencingBounds(lightbounds);
// cone is a sibling, they go through same transform.
objTransform.addChild(light1);


//5. Specify another light source
PointLight light2 = new PointLight();
light2.setPosition(-1, 1, 1);
light2.setInfluencingBounds(lightbounds);
light2.setEnable(true);
objRoot.addChild(light2);

objSpin.setCapability(TransformGroup.
        ALLOW_TRANSFORM_WRITE);

Alpha a = new Alpha(-1, 5000);
RotationInterpolator rotator =
  new RotationInterpolator(a, objSpin);
BoundingSphere bounds = new BoundingSphere();
rotator.setSchedulingBounds(bounds);
objSpin.addChild(rotator);

return objRoot;
}


public static void main(String[] args) {
  Java3D_6_Appearance frame = new Java3D_6_Appearance();
  frame.setSize(999, 999);
  frame.setVisible(true);
}
}
```

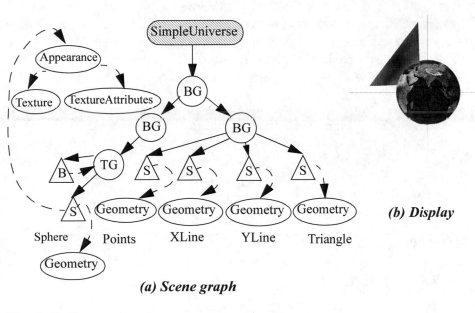

(a) Scene graph

(b) Display

Fig. 8.11 Texture mapping

8.9 Texture Mapping

Because texture mapping involves many options, here we go through the basic steps to make texture mapping available quickly. We just need to implement the following steps:

1. Prepare texture images: choose an image as a texture map. The image has to satisfy dimensions of power of 2 on the width and height as required by OpenGL texture mapping. A TextureLoader object loads JPEG, GIF, and other file formats.

2. Load the texture: once a TextureLoader object loads an image, the image can be used to "get texture" so the image is in texture representation.

3. Set the texture in Appearance bundle: Texture object is set in an appearance bundle referenced by the visual object.

4. Specify TextureCoordinates of Geometry: the programmer is allowed to specify the placement of the texture on the geometry through the texture coordinates. Texture coordinate specifications are made per geometry vertex. Each texture coordinate specifies a point of the texture to be applied to the vertex. When we create 3D objects, Java3D allows generating texture coordinates automatically.

Example *Java3D_7_Texture.java* demonstrates Java3D's texture capability. As shown in Fig. 8.11a, a Sphere object is specified. The sphere will be animated by its parent's behavior. At creation its geometry includes 3D coordinates and texture coordinates as well. Its texture map (image) and other attributes are specified with the Appearance node. TextureAttributes can be specified to define how the texture is applied to the Shape object, which we use default in this example.

/* **Java3D texture mapping** */

```
import javax.media.j3d.*;
import com.sun.j3d.utils.geometry.*;
import javax.media.j3d.*;
import com.sun.j3d.utils.image.TextureLoader;


public class Java3D_7_Texture extends Java3D_6_Appearance {

  BranchGroup createSG1() {

    TransformGroup objSpin = new TransformGroup();
    BranchGroup objRoot = new BranchGroup();

    objRoot.addChild(objSpin);

    //set material attributes 4 the app. of an sphere
    Appearance app = new Appearance();

    // Create Texture object
    TextureLoader loader =
      new TextureLoader("EARTH1.JPG", this);

    Texture earth = loader.getTexture();

    // Attach Texture object to Appearance object
    app.setTexture(earth);
```

```
// Create a sphere with texture
Sphere sphere =
   new Sphere(0.4f,Primitive.GENERATE_TEXTURE_COORDS,
        50,app);
objSpin.addChild(sphere);

objSpin.setCapability(TransformGroup.
        ALLOW_TRANSFORM_WRITE);

Alpha a = new Alpha(-1, 5000);
RotationInterpolator rotator =
   new RotationInterpolator(a, objSpin);

BoundingSphere bounds = new BoundingSphere();
rotator.setSchedulingBounds(bounds);

objSpin.addChild(rotator);

return objRoot;
}


public static void main(String[] args) {
  Java3D_7_Texture frame = new Java3D_7_Texture();

  frame.setSize(999, 999);
  frame.setVisible(true);
 }
}
```

8.10 Files and Loaders

In order to reuse constructed models and to transmit virtual universe across the Internet and on different platforms, 3D graphics files are created to save models, scenes, worlds, and animations. The relationships in an ordinary high-level 3D graphics tool are shown in Fig. 8.12. A 3D graphics tool is built on top of other 3D graphics tools or a low-level graphics library. Therefore, at the bottom of any graphics tool is a low-level graphics library. Low-level graphics libraries such as OpenGL or Direct3D are the rendering tools that actually draw 3D models into the display.

3D authoring tools are modeling tools that provide users with convenient methods to create, view, modify, and save models and virtual worlds, such as 3DStudio Max (3DS) and Alias Wavefront (OBJ). They free us from constructing complicated virtual universes and dealing with detailed specifications of 3D graphics file format definitions, which make our 3D virtual world construction job much easier. 3D authoring tools usually have good user interfaces,

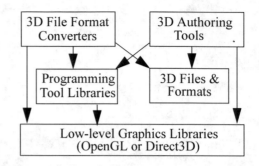

Fig. 8.12 Relationships in 3D graphics tool

which provide rich object editing tools (such as object extruding, splitting, and cutting, etc.) and flexible manipulation approaches. Using these tools, you can construct complicated 3D models conveniently even without knowing the 3D file formats.

3D graphics file formats are storage methods for virtual universes. Due to the complexities of a virtual universe, 3D file formats include many specifications about how 3D models, scenes, and hierarchies are stored. In addition, different applications include different attributes and activities and thus may require different file formats. Over the years, many different authoring tools are developed, and their corresponding 3D graphics file formats are in use today. DFX, VRML, 3DS, MAX, RAW, LightWave, POV, and NFF are probably the most commonly used formats.

Java3D has many loaders that are able to load virtual universes constructed from 3D modeling tools that are saved in 3D files. New loaders are in development and we can write custom loaders as well. The Java3D loaders define the interface for the loading mechanism, and users can develop file loader classes with the same interface as other loader classes. There are some loaders available at `http://java3d.j3d.org/ utilities/loaders.html`. For a current loader class and its usage, please check the Java3D home page.

8.11 Summary

Java3D is a comprehensive high-level 3D graphics API. In this chapter, we only covered the basic concept and some examples. Many important components in Java3D are not discussed here, such as advanced objects, rendering effects, and interaction. Our purpose is to build a scene graph structure concept in your knowledge, and demonstrate what a high-level graphics programming tool can bring. From here, you can build a hierarchical virtual universe and expand into many virtual environment related applications.

There are some other similar tools that exist as well, such as WorldToolKit and Vega. In the next chapter, we explain many graphics related tools and their applications, which are built on the basic graphics principle and programming we have covered so far.

8.12 Review Questions

1. Compare JOGL with Java3D; which of the following is appropriate:
  a. they are just two different 3D APIs with similar capabilities
  b. Java3D is a lower level programming environment
  c. JOGL is a runtime infrastructure for virtual objects and environments
  d. Java3D manipulates scene graphs in a hierarchy for a virtual world that JOGL doesn't perceive

2. Java3D is a fast runtime environment. Please provide three application examples where you would choose Java3D instead of JOGL.

3. Construct a scene graph for building a generalized solar system as in Chapter 4 with transparencies and texture.

4. VRML is a text based modeling language that is interpreted dynamically from the source files. A VRML browser can be implemented using Java3D. Please find a VRML file of about 100 lines of specifications and construct/sketch a scene graph from the VRML file.

8.13 Programming Assignments

1. Build a generalized solar system in Java3D. Compare the source code of this with JOGL implementation. What are the advantages and drawbacks of using Java3D?

2. Extend the above program to allow transparency and texture mapping, so the earth will be covered with earth texture, and the cones as light fields will be transparent.

3. Java3D works with an Internet browser. Try to set up and run your generalized solar system on a Web browser. Post a URL on your work.

4. Find a file loader online that would allow you to load and save a 3D model. Then, save your generalized solar system as a file. After that, download several models online and display them.

5. X3D is a scene description language in a text file format. There is a loader available for the X3D format at `http://java3d.j3d.org/utilities/loaders.html`. This loader also is capable of loading the majority of the VRML 97 specification, too. Please download it and use it to display some X3D and VRML models.

9
OpenGL Shading Language

Chapter Objectives:

- Introducing OpenGL Shader concepts - vertex and fragment shaders
- Texturing and lighting, image post-processing

9.1 Introduction

The OpenGL Shading Language (GLSL or GLslang) is the high level shading language used by OpenGL. It was originally introduced as an extension to OpenGL 1.4. In September, 2004, the OpenGL Architecture Review Board upgraded it to become part of the core specification with release 2.0. As with other shading languages, GLSL allows us to implement customized rendering processes that cannot be achieved using the normal rendering pipeline. One of the primary advantages of using OpenGL and GLSL is that it is supported on multiple platforms, including Windows, Apple Mac., and Linux. This chapter provides a brief introduction to using shaders in OpenGL using the OpenGL Shading Language. For more detailed information on the language specifications, we recommend the OpenGL 2.0 specification, which is available for download from www.opengl.org.

9.2 Anatomy of a GLSL Program

A GLSL program consists of a vertex shader and/or a fragment shader. The vertex shader is responsible for performing vertex transformations, normal transformations,

J.X. Chen, *Guide to Graphics Software Tools*, doi: 10.1007/978-1-84800-901-1_9, texture coordinate initialization, and material/color initialization. The fragment shader is responsible for performing texture lookups, lighting computations, and other effects such as fog. It is not necessary to have both a vertex shader and a fragment shader in a GLSL program. If either shader is missing, the fixed graphics pipeline will perform the corresponding task.

Fig. 9.1 shows the inputs and outputs for vertex and fragment shaders. The input to the vertex shader is a set of attribute and uniform variables that reflect the current OpenGL state. Attribute variables reflect vertex specific information, such as the vertex coordinate, normal vector, texture coordinates, and color. These values may be different for each vertex in a primitive. Uniform variables represent information that is the same for all vertices in a primitive. These include the modelview and projection matrices, clipping planes, material properties, and light sources.

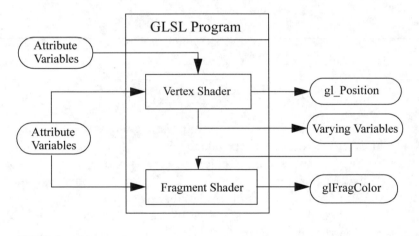

FIG 9.1 Shader program input and output

The output from a vertex shader generally consists of a special variable (gl_Position), and some varying variables. The special variable gl_Position defines the transformed position of the vertex. The varying variables can be used to define values that will be interpolated across the primitive as part of the rasterization process, and made available to the fragment shader. Of these, the most commonly used are the texture coordinates.

The input to the fragment shader consists of some varying variables (including the texture coordinates output by the vertex shader), and the same uniform variables accessible in the vertex shader.

The output from the fragment shader is primarily the special variable gl_FragColor. This defines the color of the fragment to be placed in the frame buffer.

9.3 GLSL Shader Basics

GLSL is a high level C style programming language with a few C++ type features. The following is a simple, though fully functional vertex shader.

```
void main()
{
   gl_Position = gl_ModelViewProjectionMatrix * gl_Vertex;
}
```

This sample shader actually performs all the tasks necessary to render a non-textured primitive. It transforms the input vertex, given by the attribute variable gl_Vertex, by the combined modelview-projection matrix, given by the uniform variable gl_ModelViewProjectionMatrix. It places the result in the special output variable gl_Position. If this vertex shader were used without a fragment shader, the fixed functionality pipeline would complete the task by performing all the necessary material and lighting calculations.

A similarly simple fragment shader would be as follows:

```
void main()
{
   gl_FragColor = vec4(1.0, 0.0, 0.0, 1.0);
}
```

Used in conjunction with the vertex shader above, this fragment shader will render a bright red by setting the special output variable gl_FragColor.

In the examples above, you will notice that we did not declare any of the variables that we used. This is because gl_Position, gl_ModelViewProjectionMatrix, gl_Vertex, and gl_FragColor, are all automatically defined for us by the language. gl_Position, gl_FragColor, and gl_Vertex are of type vec4, a vector of four floating point values. gl_ModelViewProjectionMatrix has a type of mat4, a 4 x 4 matrix of floating point values. There are a number of other implicitly defined input and output variables that we will discuss as we come across them in our code examples.

Also note the slightly unusual method of assigning a value to gl_FragColor. This is one of the mechanisms used for initializing vector values.

9.4 Compiling Shaders

Now that we know how to write basic vertex and fragment shaders, we need to know how to use them. The first step is to create the shaders. This is done using the glCreateShader function call as follows.

```
GLuint vertex_shader = glCreateShader(GL_VERTEX_SHADER);
GLuint fragment_shader = glCreateShader(GL_FRAGMENT_SHADER);
```

The glCreateShader function takes a single argument that defines the type of shader being created. This must be either GL_VERTEX_SHADER, or GL_FRAGMENT_SHADER. The return value is a handle that will be used later to create a complete shader program.

Next, we define the source code for each shader.

```
const GLchar* vertex_source =
" void main()
{
  gl_Position = gl_ModelViewProjectionMatrix * gl_Vertex;
}";

const GLchar* fragment_source =
" void main()
{
  gl_FragColor = vec4(1.0, 0.0, 0.0, 1.0);
}";
```

```
glShaderSource(vertex_shader, 1, &vertex_source, NULL);
glShaderSource(fragment_shader, 1, &fragment_source, NULL);
```

The glShaderSource function takes four arguments. The first argument is the handle of the shader created via glCreateShader. The third argument is a pointer to an array of strings that make up the source code for the shader, while the second argument gives the size of the array. Note that in our example, we pass all the source code through a single string, so our size value is 1. The fourth and final argument is a pointer to an array of integers that give the length of each string in the source array, and it should therefore be the same size as the source array. In our case, we use NULL, which means that the strings are null terminated.

Finally, we can compile the source code.

```
glCompileShader(vertex_shader);
glCompileShader(fragment_Shader);
```

It is usually a good idea to verify that the shaders have been compiled successfully. This function will need to be called once for each shader that is compiled:

```
GLint status;
glGetShader(vertex_shader, GL_COMPILE_STATUS, &status);

if(!status)
{
  printf("ERROR: Shader compilation error\n");
  exit (0);
}
```

In the next section, we show how to link the shaders together to create a program.

9.5 Linking Shaders

Now that the shaders have been compiled, we need to link them together to build a shader program. The first step is to create a shader program, as follows:

```
GLuint program = glCreateProgram();
```

The glCreateProgram function takes no arguments, and just returns a handle to the shader program. This handle will be used in the subsequent calls.

Next, we attach the shaders to the program:

```
glAttachShader(program, vertex_shader);
glAttachShader(program, fragment_shader);
```

The glAttachShader function takes two arguments. The first is the program handle, and the second is the shader handle, which is either a vertex shader or a fragment shader. Note that while a single shader should be attached only once to the program, you may attach multiple vertex and/or fragment shaders to a program, as long as only one of each has a "main" function. This allows you to assemble a program from a number of individually compiled shader "pieces".

Finally, we can link the program:

```
glLinkProgram(program);
```

This completes the process and makes the shader program ready for use. As with shader compilation, it is a good idea to verify the compilation status.

```
GLint status;
glGetProgram(program, GL_LINK_STATUS, &status);

if(!status)
{
  printf("ERROR: Program link failed\n");
  exit (0);
}
```

Note that some graphics drivers may actually defer compilation of the shader code until the link phase in order to make it easier to resolve function and variable references, so you may find compilation type errors (e.g., language syntax errors) only become evident when you link the shader program.

9.6 Executing Shaders

Shader programs are executed by drawing a primitive (a point, line, or triangle). The vertex shader will be executed once for each vertex defining the primitive. You can think of this as if each time you make a call to glVertex, the current OpenGL State is captured, and the vertex shader is executed.

Once all the vertices for a primitive have been defined, OpenGL will perform primitive assembly, followed by clipping, and then rasterization. For each fragment, or pixel that falls within the rendering window, the fragment shader will be executed.

Note that most modern graphics cards perform early Z rejection if depth buffering is enabled (which is generally the case). This means that the fragment shader will not be executed for any fragment whose depth value causes the fragment to be rejected during the final frame buffer operations.

Prior to drawing a primitive on which we wish to use our shader, we must configure OpenGL to use the shader. This is done through the glUseProgram function as follows.

```
glUseProgram(program);
```

All we need to do now is to draw an object - in this case, a teapot conveniently built into the GLUT library.

```
glViewport(0, 0, width, height);
glEnable(GL_DEPTH_TEST);

glClearColor(0.0, 0.0, 0.0, 0.0);
glClear(GL_COLOR_BUFFER_BIT | GL_DEPTH_BUFFER_BIT);
glMatrixMode(GL_PROJECTION);
glLoadIdentity();

glFrustum(-1.0, 1.0, -1.0, 1.0, 1.0, 100.0);

glMatrixMode(GL_MODELVIEW);
glLoadIdentity();
glTranslated(0.0, 0.0, -3.0);

glutSolidTeapot(1.5);

glutSwapBuffers();
```

The result is a rather two-dimensional looking red teapot. A snapshot is shown in Fig. 9.2.

We will look at improving this later by adding some lighting. But first, we need to introduce a few more features of the OpenGL shading language.

9.7 Varying Variables

A varying variable is a special variable that is interpolated across the polygon. The vertex shader sets the value of the varying variable once at each vertex. The hardware will then interpolate the value across the primitive, and the fragment shader can read the interpolated value. This can be used to interpolate texture coordinates and normal vectors. For example, suppose we wish to blend a color provided at each vertex uniformly across a polygon. We can set up our vertex shader as follows.

Fig. 9.2 GLUT teapot with a red shader

```
varying vec4 color;

void main()
{
  color = gl_Color;
  gl_Position = gl_ModelViewProjectionMatrix * gl_Vertex;
}
```

This vertex shader makes use of the gl_Color attribute variable, which is defined as part of the language and can be set in our program using the glColor function call. The corresponding fragment shader is as follows:

```
varying vec4 color;

void main()
{
  gl_FragColor = color;
}
```

We now use this shader to render a triangle, and use the glColor call to set the vertex shader input attribute gl_Color:

```
glBegin(GL_TRIANGLES);
glColor3f(1.0, 0.0, 0.0);
glVertex3f(-2.2, -2.0, 0.0);
glColor3f(0.0, 1.0, 0.0);
glVertex3f(2.2, -2.0, 0.0);
glColor3f(0.0, 0.0, 1.0);
glVertex3f(0.0, 2.2, 0.0);
glEnd();
```

Fig. 9.3 shows the result of this. This is, in fact, the same result that you would get if you rendered the triangle without any shaders.

9.8 Uniform Variables

Uniform variables can be used to pass additional information into the shaders from your program. Unlike attribute variables, the value of a uniform variable is fixed for each vertex in a primitive. Consider the following fragment shader:

Fig. 9.3 Color interpolation

```
uniform float density;

void main()
{
  float d = length(vec2(0.5, 0.5) - gl_TexCoord[0].xy);
  float c = sin(d * density);

  gl_FragColor = vec4(c, 0.0, 0.0, 1.0);
}
```

Here, the variable density is declared as a uniform variable. To supply a value for the uniform variable from your program, you can use the following code:

```
GLint density = glGetUniformLocation(program, "density");
glUniform1f(density, 20.0f);
```

The glGetUniformLocation function is used to obtain a handle for a named uniform variable. The first argument is the program handle returned from glCreateProgram. The second argument is the name of the variable.

Once you have a handle for the variable, the glUniform family of functions can be used to set a value for the variable. The specific function call depends upon the type of the variable. In this case, glUniform1f is used to set a scalar floating point value, but other functions include glUniform1i for scalar integers and glUniform2f for vec2 values.

Note that our shader also makes use of the built-in texture coordinate array gl_TexCoord. This array will automatically be populated for us when we supply texture coordinates in our calling code using the glTexCoord function call.

We can now render a quadrilateral with this shader as follows:

```
glBegin(GL_QUADS);

glTexCoord2f(0.0, 0.0);
glVertex3f(-2.0, -2.0, 0.0);

glTexCoord2f(1.0, 0.0);
glVertex3f(2.0, -2.0, 0.0);

glTexCoord2f(1.0, 1.0);
glVertex3f(2.0, 2.0, 0.0);

glTexCoord2f(0.0, 1.0);
glVertex3f(-2.0, 2.0, 0.0);

glEnd();
```

Fig. 9.4 shows the results of this shader.

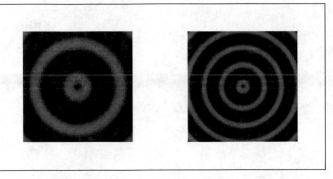

Fig. 9.4 Controlling shaders with uniform variables

9.9 Using Textures

Texture mapping is a very important feature in shaders and can be used to achieve a wide range of effects. In the fixed functionality pipeline, textures are generally thought of as two-dimensional pictures that are applied to a polygon surface using a limited set of modes or options. In a shader, we are free to use the texture values for many applications. They can be applied directly to a polygon surface, or used as pre-computed look-up values for more sophisticated algorithms.

To access a texture from a fragment shader, a sampler is used. The following simple fragment shader just wraps a texture directly on to the surface of the polygon being rendered.

```
uniform sampler2D tex;

void main()
{
   gl_FragColor = texture2D(tex, gl_TexCoord[0].xy);
}
```

The texture2D function is a built-in function used to perform a texture lookup. It takes a sampler and a texture coordinate as arguments, and returns the texture fragment at the given coordinate. Note that the sampler is declared as a uniform variable, which means that we must configure it from our program. This can be done as follows:

```
GLint tex = glGetUniformLocation(program, "tex");
glUniform1i(tex, 0);
```

Assuming that GL_TEXTURE0 is active, we draw a glut teapot again, which conveniently provides texture coordinates.

```
glFrontFace(GL_CW);
glEnable(GL_CULL_FACE);
glCullFace(GL_BACK);
glutSolidTeapot(1.5);
```

Fig. 9.5 shows the result of applying a world texture to the teapot.

9.10 Lighting

Lighting is a critical component of scene rendering. Without it, the resulting image looks flat, like the red teapot example we gave earlier. Even the application of textures does little to help bring out the depth of an object, as the previous example shows. In the following example, we simulate a relatively simple directional light source and apply it to the

Fig. 9.5 Texture mapping

teapot. A directional light source is one that is considered to be infinitely far away, so that rays from the light source are parallel. Our lighting computations will be performed in the fragment shader, and apart from the light and material properties, also require a normal vector at each fragment. This is set up in the vertex shader using a varying variable as follows.

```
varying vec3 normal;

void main()
```

```
{
  normal = gl_NormalMatrix * gl_Normal;

  gl_Position = gl_ModelViewProjectionMatrix * gl_Vertex;
}
```

The glutSolidTeapot function conveniently provides surface normals for each vertex. This is passed to our vertex shader via the gl_Normal attribute. We transform this into world coordinates using the gl_NormalMatrix, a uniform variable set up by OpenGL, and store it in a varying variable. This will be interpolated by the graphics hardware. We will use it in our fragment shader as follows.

```
varying vec3 normal;

void main()
{
  vec4 color = gl_FrontMaterial.emission
    + gl_FrontMaterial.ambient * gl_LightSource[0].ambient;

  vec3 n = normalize(normal);

  float NdotL = max(0.0,
    dot(n, normalize(gl_LightSource[0].position.xyz)));

  if(NdotL > 0.0)
  {
    color += gl_FrontMaterial.diffuse *
      gl_LightSource[0].diffuse * NdotL;

    vec3 halfV = normalize(
      gl_LightSource[0].halfVector.xyz);

    float NdotHV = max(0.0, dot(n,halfV));

    color += gl_FrontMaterial.specular *
      gl_LightSource[0].specular *
      pow(NdotHV, gl_FrontMaterial.shininess);
  }

  gl_FragColor = color;
}
```

In our fragment shader, we first compute the emission and ambient light components, both of which are independent of the surface normal and light direction.

gl_MaterialFront is a uniform variable data structure that defines the material properties of the front racing polygons. gl_LightSource is another uniform variable that contains information about the configured lights. Both of these are set up automatically by OpenGL using information that we provide in our program.

Note that since interpolation of vector values does not preserve the vector length, we must normalize the surface normal before computing the dot product with the light direction given via gl_LightSource[0].position. If the fragment is facing the light source (represented by a positive dot product), then the light will contribute diffuse and specular components to the final color.

The OpenGL specification defines the diffuse light contribution as the product of the material diffuse properties, the light source diffuse component, and the dot product of the surface normal and light direction. The specular light contribution is defined as the product of the material specular properties, the light source specular component, and the dot product of the surface normal and light half vector raised to the power of the shininess. The half vector is a vector with a direction half way between the eye direction and the light direction, which is automatically computed by OpenGL. The normalize, dot, max, and pow functions are built into the OpenGL shading language.

Next, we show how to set up the light and material properties in our program:

```
glEnable(GL_LIGHTING);
glEnable(GL_LIGHT0);

GLfloat diffuse_light[] = {0.6, 0.6, 0.6, 1.0};
GLfloat specular_light[] = {0.7, 0.7, 0.7, 1.0};
GLfloat ambient_light[] = {0.2, 0.2, 0.2, 1.0};
GLfloat position_light[] = {10.0, 20.0, 30.0, 1.0};

glLightfv(GL_LIGHT0, GL_DIFFUSE, diffuse_light);
glLightfv(GL_LIGHT0, GL_SPECULAR, specular_light);
glLightfv(GL_LIGHT0, GL_AMBIENT, ambient_light);
glLightfv(GL_LIGHT0, GL_POSITION, position_light);


GLfloat diffuse_color[] = {0.9, 0.0, 0.0};
GLfloat specular_color[] = {0.7, 0.0, 0.0};
GLfloat ambient_color[] = {0.1, 0.0, 0.0};
GLfloat emission_color[] = {0.1, 0.0, 0.0};
glMaterialfv(GL_FRONT, GL_DIFFUSE, diffuse_color);
glMaterialfv(GL_FRONT, GL_SPECULAR, specular_color);
glMaterialfv(GL_FRONT, GL_AMBIENT, ambient_color);
```

```
glMaterialfv(GL_FRONT, GL_EMISSION, emission_color);
glMaterialf(GL_FRONT, GL_SHININESS, 100.0);

glutSolidTeapot(1.5);
```

First, we must enable lighting, and specifically light number 0. We then configure the ambient, specular, and diffuse light components, and set the light source position. Because we are treating this as a directional light source, the position will actually be treated as a light direction. Next, we configure the material properties, including the ambient, specular, and diffuse properties, and the emission properties. Finally, we render the teapot. Fig. 9.6 shows the results of this shader program.

Fig. 9.6 Lighting

9.11 Advanced Shaders Techniques

9.11.1 Post Processing

So far, we have demonstrated how shaders can be used during the normal rendering process. Now we take a look at how shaders can be applied to the technique of image post processing.

In post processing, the scene is first rendered, and then captured in a texture. This texture is then processed using a customized shader to achieve a desired effect, such as sharpening, blurring, contrast enhancement, etc.

After rendering the scene, the next step in post processing is to capture the image. First, we must configure a texture in which to store the image.

```
GLuint frameBuffer;

glGenTextures(1, &frameBuffer);
glBindTexture(GL_TEXTURE_2D, frameBuffer);
```

```
glTexImage2D(GL_TEXTURE_2D, 0, GL_RGB,
   width, height, 0, GL_RGB, GL_UNSIGNED_BYTE, 0);
glTexParameteri(GL_TEXTURE_2D,
   GL_TEXTURE_MIN_FILTER,GL_NEAREST);
glTexParameteri(GL_TEXTURE_2D,
   GL_TEXTURE_MAG_FILTER, GL_NEAREST);
glTexParameteri(GL_TEXTURE_2D,
   GL_TEXTURE_WRAP_S, GL_CLAMP_TO_EDGE);
glTexParameteri(GL_TEXTURE_2D,
   GL_TEXTURE_WRAP_T, GL_CLAMP_TO_EDGE);
```

Note that this only needs to be done once. We can then capture the frame buffer, which must be done after rendering each frame.

```
glActiveTextureARB(GL_TEXTURE0);
glEnable(GL_TEXTURE_2D);
glBindTexture(GL_TEXTURE_2D, frameBuffer);
glCopyTexSubImage2D(GL_TEXTURE_2D, 0, 0, 0, 0, 0,
   width, height);
```

Now that we have the frame buffer captured, we need a way to process it using a shader. To do this, we render a screen aligned quadrilateral textured using the captured frame buffer texture. Since the quadrilateral covers the entire screen, our fragment shader will be executed once for each pixel. To simplify the task of rendering the quadrilateral, we use an orthographic projection.

```
glDisable(GL_LIGHTING);
glDisable(GL_DEPTH_TEST);
glDepthMask(GL_FALSE);

glMatrixMode(GL_PROJECTION);
glLoadIdentity();
glOrtho(0, width, 0, height, -1, 1);
glMatrixMode(GL_MODELVIEW);
glLoadIdentity();

glBegin(GL_QUADS);
glTexCoord2f(0.0, 0.0);
glVertex2i(0, 0);

glTexCoord2f(1.0, 0.0);
glVertex2i(width, 0);
```

```
glTexCoord2f(1.0, 1.0);
glVertex2i(width, height);

glTexCoord2f(0.0, 1.0);
glVertex2i(0, height);
glEnd();
```

As it stands, this program would capture the frame buffer, then render it onto a polygon covering the entire screen, resulting in an image that looks exactly the same as before. What we need now is a post processing shader to modify the image in some way. The following fragment shader simply discretizes the rgb components into 1/10th units.

```
uniform sampler2D frame;

void main()
{
  vec3 color = texture2D(frame, gl_TexCoord[0].xy).rgb;
  gl_FragColor.rgb = floor(color * 10) * 0.1;
}
```

The floor function rounds the individual components of the color vector down to the nearest integer value. Note that we must configure the uniform sample variable frame, which is exactly as we did in the teapot texturing example. This must be done before rendering the quadrilateral.

```
glUseProgram(postProgram);
GLint frame = glGetUniformLocation(postProgram, "frame");
glUniform1i(frame, 0);
```

where postProgram is the handle for the linked post processing shader program. Fig. 9.7 shows the unprocessed, and resulting processed images.

Fig. 9.7 The unprocessed (left) and processed (right) images

9.11.2 Depth-based Texture Processing

OpenGL provides us with the capabilities not only to capture the frame buffer as a texture, but also the depth buffer. This can be useful if we wish to implement some form of depth-based image post processing, such as adding a fog effect. To capture the depth buffer, we must first configure a texture.

```
GLuint depthBuffer;

glGenTextures(1, &depthBuffer);
glBindTexture(GL_TEXTURE_2D, depthBuffer);

glTexImage2D(GL_TEXTURE_2D, 0, GL_DEPTH_COMPONENT32,
   width, height, 0, GL_DEPTH_COMPONENT, GL_UNSIGNED_INT, 0);
glTexParameteri(GL_TEXTURE_2D,
   GL_TEXTURE_MIN_FILTER, GL_NEAREST);
glTexParameteri(GL_TEXTURE_2D,
   GL_TEXTURE_MAG_FILTER, GL_NEAREST);
glTexParameteri(GL_TEXTURE_2D,
   GL_DEPTH_TEXTURE_MODE, GL_LUMINANCE);
```

As with the texture used for capturing the frame buffer, this only needs to be done once. The depth buffer can then be captured after rendering the scene as follows.

```
glActiveTexture (GL_TEXTURE1);
glEnable(GL_TEXTURE_2D);
glBindTexture(GL_TEXTURE_2D, depthBufTexture);
glCopyTexSubImage2D(GL_TEXTURE_2D, 0, 0, 0, 0, 0,
   width, height);
```

To test this out, we can write a simple fragment shader that reads the depth value, and outputs it as a grayscale color.

```
uniform sampler2D depth;

void main()
{
   float z = texture2D(depth, gl_TexCoord[0].xy).r;
   gl_FragColor.rgb = vec3(z);
}
```

Note that the depth texture is effectively a grayscale texture, so it does not matter whether we access it using the red, green, or blue component. They will then have the same value.

We also need a couple of lines of code in our program to configure the depth texture.

```
GLint depth = glGetUniformLocation(postProgram, "depth");
glUniform1i(depth, 1);
```

This has the value 1, since we have configured the depth textures as active texture 1. Fig. 9.8 shows a view of the depth buffer.

One important point to note about the depth buffer is that the values are non-linear, having been transformed by the projection matrix. If we want to make use of the depth buffer, we need to be able to convert the values in the buffer back to real world depth values. Fortunately, this is relatively easy if we take a look at how a vertex is multiplied by the standard projection matrix.

Fig. 9.8 The depth buffer image

$$
\begin{bmatrix} x' \\ y' \\ z' \\ w' \end{bmatrix} = \begin{bmatrix} \dfrac{2n}{r-1} & 0 & \dfrac{r+1}{r-1} & 0 \\ 0 & \dfrac{2n}{t-b} & \dfrac{t+b}{t-b} & 0 \\ 0 & 0 & \dfrac{f+n}{n-f} & \dfrac{-2fn}{f-n} \\ 0 & 0 & -1 & 0 \end{bmatrix} \begin{bmatrix} x \\ y \\ z \\ 1 \end{bmatrix}, \qquad \text{(EQ 213)}
$$

where $n, f, t, l, b,$ and r, are the near, far, top, left, bottom and right clipping planes, respectively. The value that goes into the depth buffer is z'/w', which has a value of -1 at the near clipping plane and a value of $+1$ at the far clipping plane. However, the value is normalized into the range from 0 to 1 first. From the projection matrix, we can deduce that:

$$
z = \frac{P_{34}}{\dfrac{z'}{w'} + P_{33}} \qquad \text{(EQ 214)}
$$

where

$$P_{33} = \frac{f+n}{n-f}$$ **(EQ 215)**

$$P_{34} = \frac{-2fn}{f-n}$$ **(EQ 216)**

Given that we can obtain z'/w' from the depth buffer and both P_{33} and P_{34} can be computed based on the knowledge of the near and far clipping planes, we can easily compute the linear, real world depth value of a fragment. The following fragment shader does exactly that, given a near clipping plane distance of 1 and a far clipping plane distance of 100.

```
uniform sampler2D depth;

void main()
{
  float n = 1.0;
  float f = 100.0;

  float z = 2.0 * texture2D(depth, gl_TexCoord[0].xy).r - 1.0;
  float p34 = -2.0 * f * n / (f - n);
  float p33 = (f + n) / (n - f);

  z = p34 / (z + p33);
  z /= f;

  gl_FragColor.rgb = vec3(z);
}
```

Note that we first scale the normalized depth value read from the depth texture back into the correct range. The final division by f scales the linear depth value back into the 0-1 range needed for color components. Fig. 9.9 shows the resulting linear depth values displayed as a grayscale image.

9.11.3 Fog

Now that we know how to obtain real world depth values from the depth buffer, we can implement some depth-based post processing effects. Fog is one obvious example. The

Fig. 9.9 Linear depth values from the depth buffer

following fragment shader uses the computed real world depth value, and an exponential fog function to blend the original scene with a fog color.

```
uniform sampler2D frame;
uniform sampler2D depth;

void main()
{
  float n = 1.0;
  float f = 100.0;
  vec3 fog = vec3(0.8, 0.8, 0.8);

  float z = 2.0 * texture2D(depth, gl_TexCoord[0].xy).r - 1.0;
  float p34 = -2.0 * f * n / (f - n);
  float p33 = (f + n) / (n - f);

  z = p34 / (z + p33);

  vec3 color = texture2D(frame, gl_TexCoord[0].xy).rgb;
  color = mix(fog, color, exp(-z * 0.1));

  gl_FragColor.rgb = color;
}
```

The mix function is a built-in function that linearly blends two values based on a third value. We use it to blend the original scene color with the fog color, based on the computed fog density at each fragment. Fig. 9.10 shows applying fog in a post processing step.

So far, we have not achieved anything that the fixed functionality pipeline cannot do. However, we can take this effect one step further and use the true Euclidean distance from the viewpoint to the fragment, rather than just the depth value. This overcomes a major problem of fog as implemented by the fixed graphics pipeline: two objects can have the same depth value, yet significantly different Euclidean distances.

Fig. 9.10 Adding fog in a post processing step

To compute the Euclidean distance of a fragment, we need to know a bit more information about the view frustum. By setting up a vector pointing in the direction of the view frustum edges, we can use the hardware to interpolate this to provide us with a vector pointing in the direction of the fragment from the viewpoint. We modify our program to pass in the frustum edges via the built in attribute gl_Normal when we render the screen-aligned quadrilateral. The frustum edges are simply the coordinates of the near clipping plane coordinates.

```
glBegin(GL_QUADS);

glNormal3f(-1.0, -1.0, -1.0);
glTexCoord2f(0.0, 0.0);
glVertex2i(0, 0);

glNormal3f(1.0, -1.0, -1.0);
glTexCoord2f(1.0, 0.0);
glVertex2i(width, 0);

glNormal3f(1.0, 1.0, -1.0);
glTexCoord2f(1.0, 1.0);
glVertex2i(width, height);

glNormal3f(-1.0, 1.0, -1.0);
glTexCoord2f(0.0, 1.0);
```

```
glVertex2i(0, height);

glEnd();
```

We can then set up a vertex shader as follows:

```
varying vec3 fragmentDir;

void main()
{
  gl_Position = gl_ModelViewProjectionMatrix * gl_Vertex;
  gl_TexCoord[0] = gl_MultiTexCoord0;

  fragmentDir = gl_Normal;
}
```

This shader takes the frustum edges and sets up a varying variable, fragmentDir. The graphics hardware will interpolate this for us, providing a vector pointing in the direction of each fragment from the viewpoint. We modify our fragment shader as follows:

```
uniform sampler2D frame;
uniform sampler2D depth;

varying vec3 fragmentDir;

void main()
{
  float n = 1.0;
  float f = 100.0;
  vec3 fog = vec3(0.8, 0.8, 0.8);

  float z = 2.0 * texture2D(depth, gl_TexCoord[0].xy).r - 1.0;
  float p34 = -2.0 * f * n / (f - n);
  float p33 = (f + n) / (n - f);

  z = p34 / (z + p33);

  fragmentDir /= abs(fragmentDir.z);
  fragmentDir *= z;
  z = length(fragmentDir);

  vec3 color = texture2D(frame, gl_TexCoord[0].xy).rgb;
  color = mix(fog, color, exp(-z * 0.1));
```

```
    gl_FragColor.rgb = color;
}
```

We first scale the fragmentDir vector to give it a unit length in the Z axis, and then multiply it by the computed depth value. The result is a vector that gives the relative direction of the fragment from the viewpoint position. Thus the Euclidean distance of the fragment is simply the length of this vector. Fig. 9.11 shows the same scene rendered simply with depth based fog, and Euclidean fog.

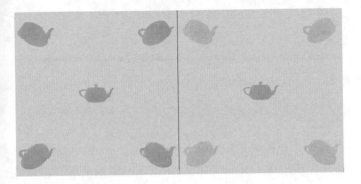
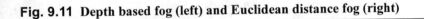

Fig. 9.11 Depth based fog (left) and Euclidean distance fog (right)

The teapots all lie at the same Z distance from the viewpoint and are therefore fogged the same amount when using only the Z depth for fog computations (left image). However, the off-axis teapots, are fogged more when using the Euclidean distance (right image).

Now suppose we want something more advanced than just plain homogeneous fog, for example, layered or heterogeneous fog, where the fog density is a function of the fragment location. In order to do this, we need to know the real world position of each fragment. It turns out that we can compute this from knowledge of the viewpoint location and orientation. If we provide the transformation representing the location and orientation of the viewpoint to the vertex shader, we can transform the frustum vertices to give us the location of each fragment relative to the camera in world coordinates. Adding this to the location of the viewpoint will then give the location of the fragment in world coordinates. All we need is a way to pass the viewpoint information to the vertex shader. For this, we can use the modelview matrix, since we do not really need it for rendering the screen aligned quadrilateral, and it is simpler than passing it as uniform variables. It also means we can use glTranslate and glRotate methods in our program to set up the viewpoint location and orientation. Our vertex shader can be written as follows:

```
varying vec3 fragmentDir;

void main(void)
{
  mat3 orientation;
  orientation[0] = gl_ModelViewMatrix[0].xyz;
  orientation[1] = gl_ModelViewMatrix[1].xyz;
  orientation[2] = gl_ModelViewMatrix[2].xyz;
  fragmentDir = orientation * (gl_Normal / abs(gl_Normal.z));

  gl_TexCoord[0] = gl_MultiTexCoord0;
  gl_Position = gl_ProjectionMatrix * gl_Vertex;
}
```

We extract the upper leftmost 3x3 of the modelview matrix to give the viewpoint orientation, and use this to transform the frustum vector after first normalizing it in the Z axis (the view direction). Once transformed, this will be normalized in the view direction in world coordinates, making computations in the fragment shader easier. Also note that we now compute gl_Position using gl_ProjectionMatrix, rather than gl_ModelViewProjectionMatrix. Since the modelview matrix for the screen aligned quadrilateral was the identity matrix, the end result is the same.

We also need to make some adjustments to the fragment shader.

```
uniform sampler2D frame;
uniform sampler2D depth;

varying vec3 fragmentDir;

void main()
{
  float n = 1;
  float f = 100;

  float z = 2.0 * texture2D(depth, gl_TexCoord[0].xy).r - 1.0;
  float p34 = -2.0 * f * n / (f - n);
  float p33 = (f + n) / (n - f);
```

```
z = p34 / (z + p33);
fragmentDir *= z;

vec3 cameraPos = gl_ModelViewMatrix[3].xyz;
vec3 fragmentPos = cameraPos + fragmentDir;

float fog = computeFog(fragmentPos, cameraPos);

vec3 color = texture2D(frame, gl_TexCoord[0].xy).rgb;

gl_FragColor.rgb = mix(fog, color, exp(-fog));;
}
```

Once we have computed the fragment depth, we scale the fragment direction vector to give the location of the fragment relative to the viewpoint in world coordinates. We then extract the camera location from the modelview matrix and use it to find the final fragment location.

Given that we now have the viewpoint and fragment locations, we can compute the amount of fog between the two locations, and use this to blend the fragment with the fog color. All we need now is an implementation for the computeFog function.

To compute the amount of fog between two points, we need to evaluate the integral of the fog density function along the line between the viewpoint and fragment. This turns out to be a remarkably complex problem for heterogeneous fog and beyond the scope of this chapter, so we provide a simpler method for layered fog.

Suppose the total fog between the viewpoint and the fragment is given by the integral F along the viewpoint-fragment vector.

$$F = \int_{viewpoint}^{fragment} f(u)\,du \qquad\qquad \textbf{(EQ 217)}$$

where $f(u)$ is the fog density at a given point u. Since the fog density is only dependent upon y, this can be simplified.

$$F = \frac{1}{\sin\theta_{fragment}} \int_{viewpoint}^{fragment} f(y)\,dy \qquad\qquad \textbf{(EQ 218)}$$

where $\theta_{fragment}$ is the angle of inclination of the viewpoint to the fragment vector. Thus the evaluation of the fog density function simplifies to a one dimensional integral. If we choose an analytical function for the fog density, it becomes relatively easy to evaluate. For example, if we choose a fog density function

$$f(y) = \frac{a}{y} \qquad \text{(EQ 219)}$$

then

$$\int_{viewpoint}^{fragment} \frac{a}{y} dy = [a\ln(y)]_{viewpoint}^{fragment} = a\ln(y_{fragment}) - a\ln(y_{viewpoint}) \qquad \text{(EQ 220)}$$

We can set up such a function in the fragment shader as follows:

```
float computeFog(in vec3 frag, in vec3 cam)
{
   float miny = 10.0;
   float maxy = 120.0;
   float a = 0.4;

   float len = length(frag - cam);
   float height = abs(frag.y - cam.y);
   float r_sin_theta = len / height;

   float fog = a * r_sin_theta * abs(
     log(clamp(frag.y, miny, maxy))
     - log(clamp(cam.y, miny, maxy)));

   fog = 1.0 - exp(-fog);
   return (fog);
}
```

The "miny", "maxy" and "a" values can be adjusted as necessary to achieve the desired effect. Fig. 9.12 shows the results of applying this technique to a somewhat more complicated scene, with both before and after images.

Fig. 9.12 Before (left) and after (right) post processing

A wide range of fog effects can be achieved simply by using different fog density functions and colors.

10
Direct3D Shader Programming

Chapter Objectives:

- Introduce basic Direct3D graphics principles and shader programming

10.1 Introduction

In this chapter, we introduce Direct3D programming basics and provide some examples of Direct3D 10 shader programming. The examples here are developed in Microsoft Visual Studio (2005) under Windows Vista in C++ and are compiled with DirectX SDK November 2007. Windows Vista is required to run the examples. We start from an empty example framework and add new components and shading effects incrementally.

The Direct3D 10 graphics pipeline has programmable stages generating graphics for real-time applications. The programmable stages are as follows:

- Input-Assembler Stage — supplying data (triangles, lines and points) to the pipeline.

- Vertex-Shader Stage — performing operations such as transformations, skinning, and lighting on a vertex.

- Geometry-Shader Stage — generating primitives. Given an input primitive, the Geometry Shader can discard the primitive or emit one or more new primitives.

J.X. Chen, *Guide to Graphics Software Tools*, doi: 10.1007/978-1-84800-901-1_10,
© Springer-Verlag London Limited 2008

- Stream-Output Stage — streaming primitive data from the pipeline to memory on its way to the rasterizer. Data can be streamed out and/or passed into the rasterizer. Data streamed out to memory can be recirculated back into the pipeline as input data or read-back from the CPU.

- Rasterizer Stage — clipping primitives, preparing primitives for the pixel shader and determining how to invoke pixel shaders.

- Pixel-Shader Stage — operating on the interpolated data and generating per-pixel data such as color.

- Output-Merger Stage — responsible for combining various types of output data.

In this chapter, instead of describing all the graphics components and details, we provide specific examples and code segments to explain how the graphics system works.

10.1.1 Setting Up Working Environment

Here we setup development environment and create an example framework for the examples. First, we should have a Direct3D 10 compatible video card and Microsoft Windows Vista operation system. Examples in this chapter have been tested on an NVIDIA 8600GT video card. Next, we need to search and download DirectX SDK (November 2007), needed for Direct3D programming from www.microsoft.com. After that, we setup Visual Studio (2005) for DirectX SDK including the header and library files required for writing the DirectX program as follows. Most of the code is generated automatically. We need only to modify and add a few code segments.

In Visual Studio 2005, select "Tools->Options" menu, browse to "Projects and Solutions->VC++ Directories", select "Include files" in "Show directories for:" combo box, add "$(DXSDK_DIR)include" to the directory list, select "Library files" in "Show directories for:", and add "$(DXSDK_DIR)lib\x86" to the directory list for a 32bit computer or add "$(DXSDK_DIR)lib\x64" to the directory list for a 64bit computer. DXSDK_DIR is a system-wide environment variable created by the DirectX SDK installation program. The variable holds the installation path for DirectX SDK. Now we are ready for programming.

10.1.2 An Example Framework

We can create an example framework project as follows. First, in Visual Studio 2005, we select "File->New->Project" menu to create a new project. In the "New Project" window, select "Win32" under "Visual C++" in the left "Project types" tree list window, then select "Win32 Project" in the right "Templates" window. At the bottom of the "New Project" window, enter "ExampleFramework" in the "Name" field, click on the "Browse" button to select a folder for the new project, and click on "OK" to continue. A "Win32 Application Wizard" window will be opened. Simply click on "Finish" to use the default setting. If we compile and run the application, we should see an empty window with standard Windows menu and controls. Then we can initialize Direct3D.

The minimal Direct3D 10 application includes setting up a window, creating a Direct3D device object, and displaying a color in the window. Most of the code for setting up the window for the example framework is already generated. We need only to add a few methods as follows. The code for creating a Direct3D device object is in the method InitD3D10Device. The method accepts a handle for the current window, creates a device and a swap chain, creates a render target view, and finally sets up a viewport.

The device object is used by the application to perform rendering. It contains methods to create resources needed for rendering into a buffer, including the swap chain for taking care of the buffers and displaying the content on the actual monitor screen. The swap chain contains two or more buffers (the front buffer and the back buffer). To create the swap chain, we fill in a DXGI_SWAPCHAIN_DESC structure that describes the swap chain. The following code lists the DXGI_SWAPCHAIN_DESC structure used in our example framework.

```
// Create a swap chain
DXGI_SWAP_CHAIN_DESC swapChainDesc;
ZeroMemory(&swapChainDesc, sizeof(swapChainDesc));
swapChainDesc.BufferCount = 1;
swapChainDesc.BufferDesc.Width = width;
swapChainDesc.BufferDesc.Height = height;
swapChainDesc.BufferDesc.Format =
DXGI_FORMAT_R8G8B8A8_UNORM;
swapChainDesc.BufferDesc.RefreshRate.Numerator = 60;
swapChainDesc.BufferDesc.RefreshRate.Denominator = 1;
swapChainDesc.BufferUsage =
DXGI_USAGE_RENDER_TARGET_OUTPUT;
swapChainDesc.OutputWindow = hWnd;
```

```
swapChainDesc.SampleDesc.Count = 1;
swapChainDesc.SampleDesc.Quality = 0;
swapChainDesc.Windowed = TRUE;
```

In the above code, BufferCount tells the number of buffers in the swap chain in addition to the front buffer. In the full screen mode, a dedicated front buffer is required. In the windowed mode, a dedicated front buffer is not required and the desktop will be the front buffer. Since all our examples are in the windowed mode, we use a single buffer as the back buffer. BufferDesc specifies the back buffer display mode including the size of the display area, the refresh rate, and the display format. We set the back buffer to have the same size as our window area. We use a 4-component 32-bit unsigned-integer format, DXGI_FORMAT_R8G8B8A8_UNORM, with values normalized between 0 and 1 as the back buffer display format. We also set refresh rate to be 60 Hz. BufferUsage tells the CPU access options for the back buffer. The back buffer can be used for the shader input or for the render target output. In this example, we set back buffer usage to be the render target output. In the later examples, we also set the back buffer usage to be the shader input. Finally we set the default non-anti-aliasing sampler mode in SampleDesc.

We use the following code to create both the Direct3D device and the swap chain:

```
D3D10CreateDeviceAndSwapChain(NULL,
D3D10_DRIVER_TYPE_HARDWARE, NULL, createDeviceFlags,
D3D10_SDK_VERSION, &swapChainDesc, &g_pSwapChain,
&g_pD3D10Device);
```

Next we create a render target view to bind the back buffer to the graphics pipeline. A back buffer can be a texture buffer. A render target view is required to bind a texture buffer for rendering. In the following code segment, we first call the GetBuffer method to obtain the back buffer object in the swap chain created above. Then we call the CreateRenderTargetView method to create a render target using the back buffer object. Finally we call OMSetRenderTargets to bind the render target view to the graphics pipeline for rendering.

```
// Create a render target view
    ID3D10Texture2D *pBuffer;
    g_pSwapChain->GetBuffer(0, __uuidof(ID3D10Texture2D),
(LPVOID*)&pBuffer);
```

```
    g_pD3D10Device->CreateRenderTargetView(pBuffer, NULL,
&g_pD3D10RenderTargetView);
    pBuffer->Release();

    g_pD3D10Device->OMSetRenderTargets(1,
&g_pD3D10RenderTargetView, NULL);
```

By default, Direct3D 10 does not create any viewport. In our example, we set up a viewport that uses the entire window client area. In the following code, we set the top left corner of the viewport to be (0, 0) and width and height to be identical to the render target size.

```
// Setup the viewport
D3D10_VIEWPORT viewport;
viewport.Width = width;
viewport.Height = height;
viewport.MinDepth = 0.0f;
viewport.MaxDepth = 1.0f;
viewport.TopLeftX = 0;
viewport.TopLeftY = 0;
g_pD3D10Device->RSSetViewports(1, &viewport);
```

Now we have finished the InitD3DDevice method. In the method we have created some resources including swap chain, render target view, and Direct3D device. We need to release these created resources before exiting the application. The release task is done in the DestoryD3D10Device method as follows:

```
void DestoryD3D10Device()
{
if(g_pD3D10Device) g_pD3D10Device->ClearState();
    if(g_pD3D10RenderTargetView) g_pD3D10RenderTargetView-
>Release();
    if(g_pSwapChain) g_pSwapChain->Release();
    if(g_pD3D10Device) g_pD3D10Device->Release();
}
```

In this example, we render a simplest scene possible, which is to fill the current window with a single color. We implement rendering in the RenderScene() method:

```
void RenderScene()
{
```

```
    // Clear the back buffer
    float bgColor[4] = { 0.0f, 0.0f, 0.0f, 1.0f};
    g_pD3D10Device-
  >ClearRenderTargetView(g_pD3D10RenderTargetView, bgColor);

    g_pSwapChain->Present(0, 0);
}
```

We first call the ClearRenderTargetView method to clear the render target view to black. Then we call the swap chain's Present method to display the swap chain back buffer to the screen.

The last thing we need to do is to modify the main message loop in the WinMain method in order to enable Direct3D rendering:

```
// Main message loop:
MSG msg = {0};
while (WM_QUIT != msg.message){
    if (PeekMessage(&msg, NULL, 0, 0, PM_REMOVE)){
        if (!TranslateAccelerator(msg.hwnd, hAccelTable,
&msg)){
            TranslateMessage(&msg);
            DispatchMessage(&msg);
        }
    }
    else{
        RenderScene();
    }
}
```

Here we call the PeekMessage() method to see if there's any message that needs to be handled. When there are no messages left, we call RenderScene() for display.

10.2 Rendering Primitives

Here we extend our framework to render primitives, including points, lines, and triangles. We first create a series of 3D positions for primitives and then we animate the primitives by modifying primitive positions and colors in the vertex shader.

10.2.1 Creating Primitives

In the InitD3D10Device method we add some new code segments to enable shader rendering. We create an effect object from the effect file and obtain rendering techniques from the created effect object. We also create vertices for primitives and an input layout that tells the graphics pipeline the format of the vertices.

```
// Create the effect object
D3DX10CreateEffectFromFile(L"Example01.fx", NULL, NULL,
"fx_4_0", dwShaderFlags, 0, g_pD3D10Device, NULL, NULL,
&g_pD3D10Effect, NULL, NULL);

// Obtain the effect technique
g_pD3D10Technique = g_pD3D10Effect-
>GetTechniqueByName("RenderScene");

// Prepare time variable for animation
g_pTimeVariable = g_pD3D10Effect-
>GetVariableByName("t_time")->AsScalar();

// Define the input layout
D3D10_INPUT_ELEMENT_DESC inputLayout[] = {
  { "POSITION", 0, DXGI_FORMAT_R32G32B32_FLOAT, 0, 0,
D3D10_INPUT_PER_VERTEX_DATA, 0 },
};

// Create the input layout
UINT numElements = 1;
D3D10_PASS_DESC PassDesc;
g_pD3D10Technique->GetPassByIndex(0)->GetDesc(&PassDesc);
g_pD3D10Device->CreateInputLayout(inputLayout, numElements,
PassDesc.pIAInputSignature, PassDesc.IAInputSignatureSize,
&g_pD3D10VertexLayout);

// Set the input layout
g_pD3D10Device->IASetInputLayout(g_pD3D10VertexLayout);

// prepare positions for primitive vertices
CreateVertexBuffer();

SetPrimitiveTopology(g_currentPrimitiveTopo);
```

In the above code, we first create an effect object from an ASCII effect file (Example01.fx). The effect file includes shader programs (or simply shaders) and techniques needed for rendering and animation. In this example, we use shaders to modify the primitive positions and colors at run time. Although we could achieve the same by writing C++ code in the application to modify the primitive positions and colors, shaders provide more flexibility and efficiency. In this work, we will differentiate the C++ application program and the shader programs by simply calling them the application and the shaders. Below is the code to create the effect object. We will explain the effect file in detail later.

```
D3DX10CreateEffectFromFile(L"Example01.fx", NULL, NULL,
"fx_4_0", dwShaderFlags, 0,
                g_pD3D10Device, NULL, NULL, &g_pD3D10Effect,
NULL, NULL);
```

A rendering technique specifies the states of the vertex shader, geometry shader, pixel shader, sampler, texture, and others to carry out rendering. Normally an effect file defines one or more rendering techniques. In the file Example01.fx, we define a technique named "RenderScene". We call the ID3D10Effect::GetTechniqueByName() method and use "RenderScene" as the name to obtain the technique object. Later we will use this technique to do the actual rendering.

```
g_pD3D10Technique = g_pD3D10Effect-
>GetTechniqueByName("RenderScene");
```

A vertex has a position as well as other optional attributes such as color, normal, and texture coordinates. In this example, we use only the position attribute for a vertex. In order to send primitive vertex position into the GPU, we need to define the vertex format in our application. In Direct3D 10, a vertex format is defined using a C structure. The structure has fields for different vertex attributes. Since we only use vertex position in this example, we define our vertex format structure with a single D3DXVECTOR3 field.

```
struct Vertex
{
  D3DXVECTOR3 Pos;
};
```

Next we create a buffer in the system memory to store the primitive vertices. The buffer will be sent to the GPU for rendering. Since the buffer is just a chunk of memory, we need to tell the GPU how to extract attributes from the buffer. This is done by creating an input layout. An input layout is a Direct3D object that describes the structure of vertices in a way that can be understood by the GPU. We define an input layout by creating a D3D10_INPUT_ELEMENT_DESC array. Inside the array, each element corresponds to a vertex attribute and has seven fields:

1. SemanticName: a string containing a word that describes the nature or purpose of this element predefined by the shader system, such as POSITION, COLOR, etc.

2. SemanticIndex: a supplement to semantic name. A vertex may have multiple attributes of the same nature. For example, it may have 2 sets of texture coordinates or 2 sets of colors. Instead of using semantic names that have numbers appended, such as "COLOR0" and "COLOR1", the two elements can share a single semantic name, "COLOR", with different semantic indices 0 and 1.

3. Format: the data type to be used for this element. For instance, a format of DXGI_FORMAT_R32G32B32_FLOAT has three 32-bit floating point numbers, making the element 12-bytes long. A format of DXGI_FORMAT_R16G16B16A16_UINT has four 16-bit unsigned integers, making the element 8-bytes long.

4. InputSlot: the position of the vertex buffer. A Direct3D 10 application sends vertex data to the GPU via the use of a vertex buffer. Multiple (16) vertex buffers can be fed to the GPU simultaneously. Each vertex buffer is bound to an input slot number ranging from 0 to 15. The InputSlot field tells the GPU which vertex buffer it should fetch for this element.

5. AlignedByteOffset: an offset in the vertex buffer. The vertex buffer is simply a chunk of memory. The AlignedByteOffset field tells the GPU where in that chunk of memory it should start fetching for this element.

6. InputSlotClass: This field has the value D3D10_INPUT_PER_VERTEX_DATA. When an application uses instancing, it can set an input layout's InputSlotClass to D3D10_INPUT_PER_INSTANCE_DATA. For our examples, we will use D3D10_INPUT_PER_VERTEX_DATA exclusively.

7. InstanceDataStepRate: This field is used for instancing. Since we are not currently using instancing, this field is not used and is set to 0.

Since our sample vertex has only one attribute, position, the array has only one element.

```
// Define the input layout
D3D10_INPUT_ELEMENT_DESC inputLayout[] =
{
  { "POSITION", 0, DXGI_FORMAT_R32G32B32_FLOAT, 0, 0,
D3D10_INPUT_PER_VERTEX_DATA, 0 },
};
```

Finally, we call the ID3D10Device::CreateInputLayout() method to actually create a vertex layout object. The CreateInputLayout() method requires a list of parameters from the vertex shader, namely the input signature. We do this by first calling the technique's GetPassByIndex() method to obtain a pass object, which represents the first rendering pass of the technique. Rendering in passes is the process of rendering different attributes of the scene separately. Although we do not use multi-pass rendering here, Direct3D provides such a mechanism. Then, we call the pass object's GetDesc() method to obtain a pass description structure. Within this structure is a field named pIAInputSignature that is a pointer to the binary data representing the input signature of the vertex shader used in this pass. We call ID3D10Device::IASetInputLayout() to create a vertex layout object as the active vertex layout. The code to do all of these is shown below:

```
// Create the input layout
D3D10_PASS_DESC PassDesc;
// get pass description structure containing input signature
g_pD3D10Technique->GetPassByIndex(0)->GetDesc(&PassDesc);
g_pD3D10Device->CreateInputLayout(inputLayout, numElements,
PassDesc.pIAInputSignature, PassDesc.IAInputSignatureSize,
&g_pD3D10VertexLayout);

// Set the input layout
g_pD3D10Device->IASetInputLayout(g_pD3D10VertexLayout);
```

In the CreateVertexBuffer() method we create the actual data for the primitive position and send these data to the graphics pipeline for rendering. In the method, we store actual vertices data in the vertex buffer object and send the object to the graphics pipeline. To create a vertex buffer in Direct3D 10, we fill in two structures, D3D10_BUFFER_DESC and D3D10_SUBRESOURCE_DATA, and then call ID3D10Device::CreateBuffer() to finish the buffer creation. D3D10_BUFFER_DESC describes the vertex buffer object to be created, and D3D10_SUBRESOURCE_DATA describes the actual data that will be copied to the vertex buffer during creation. After the vertex buffer is created, we call ID3D10Device::IASetVertexBuffers() to bind it to the device.

We create actual vertices data for point, line list, line strip, triangle list, and triangle strip. Instead of creating multiple vertex buffers, we put all these vertices in one single buffer and use offset and vertex count to render different primitives. The first step is to create a vertex array using the following code:

```
Vertex vertices[g_totalVertexNum];
```

The global variable g_totalVertexNum stores the total number of vertices for all primitives. We use two pre-defined array to store the vertex number and the starting offset for each type of primitives in the vertex array.

```
int g_primitiveVertexNum[] = {180, 18, 19, 36, 39};
int g_primitiveOffset[] = {0, 180, 198, 217, 253};
```

We use another global variable g_currentPrimitiveTopo to indicate which type of primitives will be displayed on the screen. The possible values of g_currentPrimitiveTopo are:

```
POINTLIST = 0,
LINELIST = 1,
LINESTRIP = 2,
TRIANGLELIST = 3,
TRIANGLESTRIP = 4,
```

For example, if g_currentPrimitiveTopo equals 1, then 18 vertices starting from the 180th element in the vertex array will be used to display a line list on the screen. If g_currentPrimitiveTopo equals 2, then 19 vertices starting from the 198th element in the vertex array will be used to display a line strip on screen.

To allow users to select different primitives for rendering, we modify the system-generated WndProc() method to handle the WM_KEYDOWN message. Whenever users press the space key on the keyboard, we increment g_currentPrimitiveTopo by one and call SetPrimitiveTopology() to set the current drawing primitive type. We also change the window title string to match the current type of primitive. The SetPrimitiveTopology() method is a simple, convenient method to set the current drawing primitive type based on g_currentPrimitiveTopo. We call the ID3DDevice::IASetPrimitiveTopology() method to set the current drawing type.

Next we change the RenderScene() method to do the actual rendering. We start by calling ID3D10EffectTechnique::GetDesc() in the technique object obtained in InitD3D10Device() to receive a D3D10FX_TECHNIQUE_DESC structure which describes the technique. The member, Passes, indicates the number of rendering passes the technique contains. To correctly render using this technique, we should loop though all passes. Within the loop, we must first call the technique's GetPassByIndex() method to obtain the current pass object, then call its Apply() method to bind the associated shaders and render states to the graphics pipeline. The ID3D10Device::Draw() method commands the GPU to render using the current vertex buffer, vertex layout, and primitive topology. The first parameter in Draw() is the number of vertices used to draw and the second parameter is the index of the first vertex to draw. The entire rendering code is listed below:

```
// do actual rendering
D3D10_TECHNIQUE_DESC techDesc;
g_pD3D10Technique->GetDesc(&techDesc);
for(UINT p = 0; p < techDesc.Passes; ++p)
{
  g_pD3D10Technique->GetPassByIndex(p)->Apply(0);
  g_pD3D10Device-
>Draw(g_primitiveVertexNum[g_currentPrimitiveTopo],
g_primitiveOffset[g_currentPrimitiveTopo]);
  }
```

When we press the space bar, it will loop through rendering points, lines, and triangles. Fig. 10.1 is a snapshot of rendering the triangles.

10.2.2 Animation Using Shaders

In this example, we use shaders for primitive animations. We write shaders in an effect file Example01.fx as below:

Fig. 10.1 Rendering triangles

//File: Example01.fx

```
//global variable for current frame time
floatg_time;

//vertex shader output structure
struct PS_INPUT
{
  float4 pos : SV_POSITION;
```

```
    float4 color : COLOR0;
};

//vertex shader program
PS_INPUT VS(float4 pos : POSITION)
{
    //set output to be zero
    PS_INPUT output = (PS_INPUT)0;
    output.pos = pos;
    //change vertex x and y coordinates based on current framme
time
    output.pos.xy *= abs(sin(g_time * 0.5));

    //create vertex color based on vertex position
    output.color.x = 1.0 - output.pos.x * output.pos.x;
    output.color.y = 1.0 - output.pos.y * output.pos.y;
    output.color.z = 0.0;
    output.color.w = 1.0;

    //pass vertex information to pixel shader
    return output;
}

//pixel shader program
float4 PS(PS_INPUT input) : SV_Target
{
    //return interpolated pixel color
    return input.color;
}

//default technique
technique10 RenderScene
{
    //the only pass object
    pass P0
    {
        //we use vertex shader and pixel shader, geometry shader
is a new feature and is optional
        SetVertexShader(CompileShader(vs_4_0, VS()));
        SetGeometryShader(NULL);
        SetPixelShader(CompileShader(ps_4_0, PS()));
    }
}
```

Effect files are written using high-level shading language (HLSL). In this chapter, our effect files have three different parts: global variables, shaders, and techniques. Just like a C program, we first declare global variables at the top of the file, which are used to send values from the application to the shaders. Normally these variables will be initialized by the application and then used in the shaders. The global variables are similar to the constants and variables in a C++ program. In this example, we use one global variable: g_time. The variable is used to record the frame time for primitive animation. The application will set the value for this variable at each frame while the shader will use the value to animate the primitives.

To access the variable, we call the ID3D10Effect::GetVariableByName() method, which is in the InitD3D10Device() method, to obtain an interface to the variable in the application. The method accepts a string parameter for the variable name. In the application, we use an ID3D10EffectScalarVariable type pointer variable g_pTimeVariable to hold the interface returned by the method. Below is the code to get access to the g_time global variable in the effect file.

```
//get the only one global variable in effect file
g_pTimeVariable = g_pD3D10Effect-
>GetVariableByName("g_time")->AsScalar();
```

The data type of variable g_time in the effect file is a floating point number, so we call the AsScalar() method to get the interface. In future examples, we will see that it is possible to have other type of variables in the effect file, such as a vector or matrix. We need to use a corresponding method such as AsVector() or AsMatrix() to get access to these types of variables.

Also, just like the C++ function scope rules, variables in the effect file declared outside of the scope of the effect functions are visible throughout the effect; variables declared inside of an effect function are only visible within that function.

We set the value for the time variable in the application in the RenderScene() method:

```
//set time
long timeCurrent = GetTickCount();
float t = (timeCurrent - g_timeStart) / 1000.0f;
g_pTimeVariable->SetFloat(t);
```

The second part in our effect is the shaders, which are small executable programs. The Direct3D 10 pipeline uses three different kinds of shaders. A vertex shader works on vertex data, where each vertex input yields a vertex output. A geometry shader works on the primitive data; each primitive input may produce zero, one, or many output primitives. A pixel shader works on pixel data, and each pixel input produces a pixel output unless the pixel is culled. Shaders are written as local functions following C style function rules.

In this example, we use only the vertex and pixel shaders. In the vertex shader, we alter vertex x and y coordinates for animation. We also calculate vertex color depending on vertex coordinates. Then the vertex shader output (vertex positions and colors) are interpolated for pixel shader processing. In this example, the pixel shader output is simply the interpolated pixel color.

To pass the vertex shader output into the pixel shader, we define the vertex shader output structure. The structure has two fields, for position and color. Both of these fields are 4-element floating point vectors.

```
//vertex shader output structure
struct PS_INPUT
{
   float4 pos : SV_POSITION;
   float4 color : COLOR0;
};
```

The input to the vertex shader is the vertex position and the output is a PS_INPUT structure. The program is listed below:

```
//vertex shader program
PS_INPUT VS(float4 pos : POSITION)
{
    //set output to be zero
    PS_INPUT output = (PS_INPUT)0;
    output.pos = pos;
    //change vertex x and y coordinates based on current frame
time
    output.pos.xy *= abs(sin(g_time * 0.5));

    //create vertex color based on vertex position
    output.color.x = 1.0 - output.pos.x * output.pos.x;
    output.color.y = 1.0 - output.pos.y * output.pos.y;
    output.color.z = 0.0;
    output.color.w = 1.0;

    //pass vertex data to pixel shader
    return output;
}
```

The code for the pixel shader is listed below. We simply return the interpolated pixel color.

```
//pixel shader program
float4 PS(PS_INPUT input) : SV_Target
{
    //return interpolated pixel color
    return input.color;
}
```

In Example01.fx, we define a technique named RenderScene, which includes a collection of rendering passes. The code for the RenderScene technique is listed below:

```
//default technique
technique10 RenderScene
{
    //the only pass object
    pass P0
    {
        //we use vertex shader and pixel shader
        //geometry shader is a new feature and is optional
        SetVertexShader(CompileShader(vs_4_0, VS()));
        SetGeometryShader(NULL);
        SetPixelShader(CompileShader(ps_4_0, PS()));
    }
}
```

In the above code, we tell Direct3D to compile the vertex and pixel shaders. Since we do not use the geometry shader here, we simple pass a NULL into the pipeline for the geometry shader.

Now we can run Example01.exe and see different primitives rendered on the screen with animated positions and colors.

10.3 Pixel Lighting

In this example we discuss how to implement pixel lighting. We calculate light components for each pixel in the pixel shader. Compared to vertex lighting, pixel lighting provides a smoother and more realistic shading effect.

We use three light sources and a cube to display the lighting effect. The cube rotates around its center and the light sources orbit around the cube. The light sources are rendered as single colored cubes. We transform and scale the center cube to draw three smaller cubes as light sources. Lighting effects implemented in this example are directional light, directional light with specular, point light, point light with specular, spot light, spot light with specular, and hemisphere lighting. Similar to previous example, users can select different lighting effects by pressing the space key on the keyboard.

10.3.1 Creating Depth Stencil View

Since we have lights orbiting around the center cube, we use the depth buffer to keep track of the depth of every pixel drawn to the screen in order to provide correct rendering results. We first create a depth buffer (namely, a DepthStencil texture). Then we create a DepthStencilView of the depth buffer to bind the depth buffer to the graphics pipeline. Below is the code to create a depth buffer and a DepthStencilView. We fill in a D3D10_TEXTURE2D_DESC structure to create a texture. The BindFlags parameter has been set to D3D10_BIND_DEPTH_STENCIL so that Direct3D knows that the texture will be used as a depth buffer. Then we fill in a D3D10_DEPTH_STENCIL_VIEW_DESC structure to create a DepthStencil view. In Direct3D 10, texture resources are accessed with a view, which is a mechanism for hardware to interpret a resource in the memory. A view is an object that tells the device how a texture should be accessed during rendering.

```
// Create depth stencil texture
D3D10_TEXTURE2D_DESC depthDesc;
depthDesc.Width = width;
depthDesc.Height = height;
depthDesc.MipLevels = 1;
depthDesc.ArraySize = 1;
depthDesc.Format = DXGI_FORMAT_D32_FLOAT;
depthDesc.SampleDesc.Count = 1;
depthDesc.SampleDesc.Quality = 0;
depthDesc.Usage = D3D10_USAGE_DEFAULT;
depthDesc.BindFlags = D3D10_BIND_DEPTH_STENCIL;
depthDesc.CPUAccessFlags = 0;
depthDesc.MiscFlags = 0;
g_pD3D10Device->CreateTexture2D(&depthDesc, NULL,
&g_pD3D10DepthStencil);
// Create the depth stencil view
D3D10_DEPTH_STENCIL_VIEW_DESC dsvDesc;
dsvDesc.Format = depthDesc.Format;
```

```
dsvDesc.ViewDimension = D3D10_DSV_DIMENSION_TEXTURE2D;
dsvDesc.Texture2D.MipSlice = 0;
g_pD3D10Device->CreateDepthStencilView(g_pD3D10DepthStencil,
&dsvDesc, &g_pD3D10DepthStencilView);
```

We bind the depth stencil view to the graphics pipeline with the render target view at the same time by calling the OMSetRenderTargerts method. The third parameter of the OMSetRenderTargets method is a pointer to the depth stencil view. In the following code, we call the OMSetRenderTargets method to set both the render target view and the depth stencil view.

```
g_pD3D10Device->OMSetRenderTargets(1,
&g_pD3D10RenderTargetView, g_pD3D10DepthStencilView);
```

10.3.2 Creating Input Layout

In this example, in addition to vertex positions, we will add vertex normals into the graphics pipeline. We define our vertex layout structure with two D3DXVECTOR3 fields for the vertex positions and normals.

```
struct Vertex
{
    D3DXVECTOR3 Pos;
    D3DXVECTOR3 Normal;
};
```

Then we define the input layout by creating a D3D10_INPUT_ELEMENT_DESC array. Inside the array, each element corresponds to a vertex attribute. Since we use two vertex attributes, position and normal, the input layout array also has two elements. The first element is for the vertex position and the second is for the vertex normal. For the second element, we set 12 to the AlignedByteOffset field in the D3D10_INPUT_ELEMENT_DESC structure since the first element, vertex position, takes 12 bytes for three float point numbers. We use the following code to create the input layout and bind it to the graphics pipeline:

```
// Define the input layout
D3D10_INPUT_ELEMENT_DESC inputLayout[] ={
```

```
    { "POSITION", 0, DXGI_FORMAT_R32G32B32_FLOAT, 0, 0,
D3D10_INPUT_PER_VERTEX_DATA, 0 },
    { "NORMAL", 0, DXGI_FORMAT_R32G32B32_FLOAT, 0, 12,
D3D10_INPUT_PER_VERTEX_DATA, 0 },
};

// Create the input layout
UINT numElements = 2;
D3D10_PASS_DESC PassDesc;
g_pD3D10Technique->GetPassByIndex(0)->GetDesc(&PassDesc);
g_pD3D10Device->CreateInputLayout(inputLayout, numElements,
        PassDesc.pIAInputSignature,
PassDesc.IAInputSignatureSize, &g_pD3D10VertexLayout);

// Set the input layout
g_pD3D10Device->IASetInputLayout(g_pD3D10VertexLayout);
```

10.3.3 Creating Cube Geometry

Inside the CreateVertexBuffer() method, we create the vertex buffer for a cube. First, we create 24 vertices for the six faces of the cube, where each face includes four vertices. The vertex buffer includes the positions and the normals for the vertices.

```
// Create vertex buffer
   Vertex vertices[] =
   {
       //POSITIONNORMAL
       { D3DXVECTOR3(-1.0f, -1.0f, 1.0f), D3DXVECTOR3(-1.0f,
0.0f, 0.0f) },
       { D3DXVECTOR3(-1.0f, -1.0f, -1.0f), D3DXVECTOR3(-1.0f,
0.0f, 0.0f) },
       { D3DXVECTOR3(-1.0f, 1.0f, -1.0f), D3DXVECTOR3(-1.0f,
0.0f, 0.0f) },
       { D3DXVECTOR3(-1.0f, 1.0f, 1.0f), D3DXVECTOR3(-1.0f,
0.0f, 0.0f) },

       { D3DXVECTOR3(1.0f, -1.0f, 1.0f), D3DXVECTOR3(1.0f,
0.0f, 0.0f) },
       { D3DXVECTOR3(1.0f, -1.0f, -1.0f), D3DXVECTOR3(1.0f,
0.0f, 0.0f) },
       { D3DXVECTOR3(1.0f, 1.0f, -1.0f), D3DXVECTOR3(1.0f,
0.0f, 0.0f) },
       { D3DXVECTOR3(1.0f, 1.0f, 1.0f), D3DXVECTOR3(1.0f, 0.0f,
0.0f) },
```

```
    { D3DXVECTOR3(-1.0f, -1.0f, -1.0f), D3DXVECTOR3(0.0f, -
1.0f, 0.0f) },
    { D3DXVECTOR3(1.0f, -1.0f, -1.0f), D3DXVECTOR3(0.0f, -
1.0f, 0.0f) },
    { D3DXVECTOR3(1.0f, -1.0f, 1.0f), D3DXVECTOR3(0.0f, -
1.0f, 0.0f) },
    { D3DXVECTOR3(-1.0f, -1.0f, 1.0f), D3DXVECTOR3(0.0f, -
1.0f, 0.0f) },

    { D3DXVECTOR3(-1.0f, 1.0f, -1.0f), D3DXVECTOR3(0.0f,
1.0f, 0.0f) },
    { D3DXVECTOR3(1.0f, 1.0f, -1.0f), D3DXVECTOR3(0.0f,
1.0f, 0.0f) },
    { D3DXVECTOR3(1.0f, 1.0f, 1.0f), D3DXVECTOR3(0.0f, 1.0f,
0.0f) },
    { D3DXVECTOR3(-1.0f, 1.0f, 1.0f), D3DXVECTOR3(0.0f,
1.0f, 0.0f) },

    { D3DXVECTOR3(-1.0f, -1.0f, -1.0f), D3DXVECTOR3(0.0f,
0.0f, -1.0f) },
    { D3DXVECTOR3(1.0f, -1.0f, -1.0f), D3DXVECTOR3(0.0f,
0.0f, -1.0f) },
    { D3DXVECTOR3(1.0f, 1.0f, -1.0f), D3DXVECTOR3(0.0f,
0.0f, -1.0f) },
    { D3DXVECTOR3(-1.0f, 1.0f, -1.0f), D3DXVECTOR3(0.0f,
0.0f, -1.0f) },

    { D3DXVECTOR3(-1.0f, -1.0f, 1.0f), D3DXVECTOR3(0.0f,
0.0f, 1.0f) },
    { D3DXVECTOR3(1.0f, -1.0f, 1.0f), D3DXVECTOR3(0.0f,
0.0f, 1.0f) },
    { D3DXVECTOR3(1.0f, 1.0f, 1.0f), D3DXVECTOR3(0.0f, 0.0f,
1.0f) },
    { D3DXVECTOR3(-1.0f, 1.0f, 1.0f), D3DXVECTOR3(0.0f,
0.0f, 1.0f) },

};
```

Then we create an index buffer to specify which vertex is used in each triangle.

```
// Create index buffer
    DWORD indices[] =
    {
        3,1,0,    2,1,3,//face 0
        6,4,5,    7,4,6,//face 1
        10,8,9,   11,8,10,//face 2
        15,13,12,14,13,15,//face 3
        19,17,16,18,17,19,//face 4
```

```
        22,20,21,23,20,22//face5
};
```

For example, the first triangle is defined by points 3, 1, and 0. This means that the first triangle has vertices at: (-1.0f, 1.0f, 1.0f), (-1.0f, -1.0f, -1.0f), and (-1.0f, -1.0f, 1.0f) respectively. Each cube face has two triangles. In total, we define 12 triangles here.

The creation of the index buffer is very similar to the vertex buffer, where we specify parameters such as size and type in the structure, and call the CreateBuffer() method with type D3D10_BIND_INDEX_BUFFER.

```
bufferDesc.Usage = D3D10_USAGE_DEFAULT;
bufferDesc.ByteWidth = sizeof(DWORD) * 36;
bufferDesc.BindFlags = D3D10_BIND_INDEX_BUFFER;
bufferDesc.CPUAccessFlags = 0;
bufferDesc.MiscFlags = 0;
initData.pSysMem = indices;
g_pD3D10Device->CreateBuffer(&bufferDesc, &initData,
&g_pD3D10IndexBuffer);
```

Finally we call the ID3D10Device::IASetIndexBuffer() method to bind the index buffer to the graphics pipeline and call the ID3D10Device::IASetPrimitiveTopology() method to render the vertices as a triangle list.

10.3.4 Interfaces for Accessing Variables In Effect Object

We have eight variables, g_worldMatrix, g_viewMatrix, g_projectionMatrix, g_lightDirections, g_lightColors, g_solidLightColor, g_eyePosition, and g_lightingMode, in the effect object. Since Direct3D 10 removed some fixed graphics functions from the graphics pipeline, we use three matrix variables, g_worldMatrix, g_viewMatrix, and g_projectionMatrix, to send world, view, and projection transformation matrices to the graphics pipeline for shader programming. For directional lighting, the g_lightDirections variable sends the light direction into the graphics pipeline. For point lighting and spot lighting, the g_lightPositions variable sends the light position into the pipeline. The variable g_solidLightColor is used to send fixed light color into the graphics pipeline. In the example, we render lights as small cubes with fixed light colors. We calculate the specular light component using eye position with the g_eyePosition variable. The g_lightingMode variable defines the current lighting mode: directional, directional with specular, point, point with specular, spot, spot with specular, and hemisphere lighting.

10.3.5 Rendering the Scene

To render the scene, first, we clear the render target and depth stencil buffer for rendering. The following code ensures that depth values from previous frames do not incorrectly discard pixels in the current frame. In each frame, we set the depth buffer to the maximum value (1.0).

```
// Clear the depth buffer to 1.0 (max depth)
g_pD3D10Device-
>ClearDepthStencilView(g_pD3D10DepthStencilView,
D3D10_CLEAR_DEPTH, 1.0f, 0);
```

In the previous example, we implemented animation in the vertex shader by simply modifying the x and y coordinates. We need to do more in this example in order to implement orbiting and rotation. In the application, we set up the world matrix, view matrix, and projection matrix that are required to implement the 3D transformation. Before rendering, we initialize the world matrix as an identity matrix by calling the D3DXMatrixIdentity() method. Then we initialize the view matrix by calling the D3DXMatrixLookAtLH() method. The method creates a left-hand look-at matrix with three input parameters, the eye position, the camera look-at position, and the world up vector. We define the eye position in the global variable g_eyePosition, set the camera to look-at point (0,0,0), and use the positive y direction as the world up vector. We create a projection matrix by the D3DXMatrixPerspectiveFovLH() method, which requires four parameters, FOVy, Aspect, Zn, and Zf. FOVy is the field of view in the Y direction. Aspect is the ratio of view space width to height. Zn and Zf are the near and far Z values in the view space, respectively. The code for all these is listed below:

```
// Initialize the world matrices
   D3DXMatrixIdentity(&g_worldMatrix);

   // Initialize the view matrix
   D3DXVECTOR3 At(0.0f, 0.0f, 0.0f);
   D3DXVECTOR3 Up(0.0f, 1.0f, 0.0f);
   D3DXMatrixLookAtLH(&g_viewMatrix, &g_eyePosition, &At, &Up);

   // Initialize the projection matrix
   D3DXMatrixPerspectiveFovLH(&g_projectionMatrix,
 (float)D3DX_PI * 0.25f, width/(FLOAT)height, 0.1f, 100.0f);
```

```
// Pass world, view and projection matrix into shader
g_pWorldMatrixVariable->SetMatrix((float*)&g_worldMatrix);
g_pViewMatrixVariable->SetMatrix((float*)&g_viewMatrix);
g_pProjectionMatrixVariable-
>SetMatrix((float*)&g_projectionMatrix);
```

At run time, we update the world matrix for animation. In the RenderScene() method, we call D3DXMatrixRotationYawPitchRoll() to create a rotate world matrix based on the current frame time. The world matrix will be used to transform the center cube. The world matrix is set to have different rotation angles in the x, y, and z direction.

```
// Rotate cube around the origin point
D3DXMatrixRotationYawPitchRoll(&g_worldMatrix, t, t * 0.1f, t
* 0.1f);
// Pass world matrix into shader
g_pWorldMatrixVariable->SetMatrix((float*)&g_worldMatrix);
```

Since we use three lights orbiting around the center cube, we also need to update the light directions and positions at run time. We set the first light to rotate around the z axis, the second light to rotate around the x axis, and the third light to rotate around thee y axis. To rotate light directions, we first store initial light directions in a local variable lightDirs, which is an array of D3DVECTOR4 (a vector having four floating point numbers). Then we call the D3DXMatrixRotation() method and the D3DXVec3Transform method to rotate the light direction vectors.

```
// Setup lighting parameters
  D3DXVECTOR4 lightDirs[3] =
  {
    D3DXVECTOR4(-1.0f, 0.0f, 0.0f, 1.0f),
    D3DXVECTOR4(0.0f, -1.0f, 0.0f, 1.0f),
    D3DXVECTOR4(0.0f, 0.0f, -1.0f, 1.0f),
  };

  //rotate lights around the origin point
  D3DXMATRIX rotMat;

  //rotate 1st light around Z axis
  D3DXMatrixRotationZ(&rotMat, 2.5f*t);
   D3DXVec3Transform(&lightDirs[0],
 (D3DXVECTOR3*)&lightDirs[0], &rotMat);

  //rotate 2rd light around X axis
  D3DXMatrixRotationX(&rotMat, -2.0f*t);
```

```
   D3DXVec3Transform(&lightDirs[1],
(D3DXVECTOR3*)&lightDirs[1], &rotMat);

   //rotate 3rd light around Y axis
   D3DXMatrixRotationY(&rotMat, 1.5f*t);
   D3DXVec3Transform(&lightDirs[2],
(D3DXVECTOR3*)&lightDirs[2], &rotMat);
```

As mentioned before, we will render a rotating cube as well as three orbiting light sources. In this example, we use two techniques, RenderScene and RenderLight. The first technique is to render the lighting effect on the center cube. The second technique is to render single-colored cubes representing light sources.

```
// Obtain the technique
g_pD3D10Technique = g_pD3D10Effect-
>GetTechniqueByName("RenderScene");
// Obtain the technique to render light
g_pD3D10TechniqueRenderLight = g_pD3D10Effect-
>GetTechniqueByName("RenderLight");
```

The code to render the center cube is almost the same as the rendering code in the previous examples. The only difference is that we are using the DrawIndexed() method to draw indexed primitives. Using indices to the vertices saves repeating vertices in drawing primitives. Each index is referred to a vertex in the vertex buffer. The DrawIndexed() method accepts three parameters, IndexCount, StartIndexLocation, and BaseVertexLocation. IndexCount is the number of indices to draw. StartIndexLocation is the start of the first index. BaseVertexLocaton is the index of the first vertex. Below is the code for rendering the cube.

```
// Render the cube
D3D10_TECHNIQUE_DESC techDesc;
g_pD3D10Technique->GetDesc(&techDesc);
for(UINT p = 0; p < techDesc.Passes; ++p)
{
  g_pD3D10Technique->GetPassByIndex(p)->Apply(0);
  g_pD3D10Device->DrawIndexed(36, 0, 0);
}
```

We have three lights with red, green and blue colors. To render light sources, we use the same geometry for the center cube instead of creating new vertices for the light source cubes. We calculate the translation and scaling matrices to draw cubes with different sizes at different positions. We calculate the light positions based on light directions. Then we call the D3DXMatrixTranslation() method and the D3DXMatrixScaling() method to transform and scale the center cube. For each light, we update the world projection matrix to reflect translation and scaling. We also send red, green, and blue light colors to the graphics pipeline. Finally we use the second technique, g_pD3D10TechniqueRenderLight, to render light sources as single-color small cubes.

```
// Render lights use fix-colored cubes
   D3DXMATRIX tranMat;
   D3DXMATRIX scaleMat;
   D3DXVECTOR4 lightPos;

   for(int i = 0; i < 3; i++)
   {
      lightPos = lightDirs[i]*3.0f;
      D3DXMatrixTranslation(&tranMat, lightPos.x, lightPos.y,
lightPos.z);
      D3DXMatrixScaling(&scaleMat, 0.05f, 0.05f, 0.05f);
      tranMat = scaleMat*tranMat;

      // Update the world variable to reflect the current light
      g_pWorldMatrixVariable->SetMatrix((float*)&tranMat);
      g_pSolidLightColorVariable-
>SetFloatVector((float*)&g_lightColors[i]);

      g_pD3D10TechniqueRenderLight->GetDesc(&techDesc);
      for(UINT p = 0; p < techDesc.Passes; ++p)
      {
         g_pD3D10TechniqueRenderLight->GetPassByIndex(p)-
>Apply(0);
         g_pD3D10Device->DrawIndexed(36, 0, 0);
      }
   }
```

10.3.6 Lighting in Shaders

Now we will explain the effect file Example02.fx. The actual pixel lighting is done in the file using shaders.

The input to the vertex shader includes the vertex position and normal. In the vertex shader, we use the world, view, and projection matrices to transform vertex position for further processing in the graphics pipeline. In order to do lighting, we also transform the vertex position and normal into the world space, which are simply the vertex position and normal after the world transformation but before the view transformation.

We use TEXCOORD0 and TEXCOORD1 to pass the vertex world position and normal to the pixel shader. The shader input structures and the vertex shader are listed below.

```
//vertex shader input structure
struct VS_INPUT
{
  float4 Pos : POSITION;
  float3 Norm : NORMAL;
};
//pixel shader input structure
struct PS_INPUT
{
  float4 Pos : SV_POSITION;
  float3 Norm : TEXCOORD0;
  float3 PosWorld : TEXCOORD1;
};

// Vertex Shader program
PS_INPUT VS(VS_INPUT input)
{
  PS_INPUT output = (PS_INPUT)0;
  output.Pos = mul(input.Pos, g_worldMatrix);

  output.PosWorld = output.Pos.xyz;

  output.Pos = mul(output.Pos, g_viewMatrix);
  output.Pos = mul(output.Pos, g_projectionMatrix);

  output.Norm = mul(input.Norm, g_worldMatrix);

  return output;
}
```

10.3.7 Directional Pixel Lighting

Directional pixel lighting assumes the lighting source is a fixed direction at infinity. The Direct3D pipeline automatically interpolates vertex normals from the vertex shader to generate pixel normals. In the pixel shader, we add diffuse components of all the light sources together for the final lighting result.

```
for(int i = 0; i < lightCount; i++)
{
    float3 lightDir = normalize((float3)g_lightDirections[i]);
    finalColor += saturate(dot(lightDir, normal)) *
g_lightColors[i];
}
```

In the above code, the dot() function is an intrinsic function of HLSL. The function computes the dot product of the two input vectors. Function saturate() is another intrinsic function of HLSL. It clamps the input value to the range of 0 to 1. A snapshot is shown in Fig. 10.2.

10.3.8 Directional Pixel Light with Specular

We calculate the specular component if the cosine between the light direction and the surface normal is greater than 0.

Fig. 10.2 Rendering with 3 lights

```
float3 lightDir = normalize((float3)g_lightDirections[i]);
float NdotL = saturate(dot(lightDir, normal));

float4 diffuseColor = NdotL * g_lightColors[i];
float specular = 0;

if (NdotL > 0)//calculate specular component
{
    float3 reflection = normalize(reflect(-lightDir, normal));
    specular = pow(saturate(dot(reflection, viewDir)),
shininess);
}

finalColor += diffuseColor + specular;
```

In the above code, the reflect() function is an intrinsic HLSL function returning a reflection vector using an entering ray direction and a surface normal. Function pow() is also an intrinsic function returning the specified value raised to the specified power. In Direct3D, the reflection vector is calculated using a formula $R = L - 2N(L \bullet N)$, so we use the reversed light direction to calculate the reflection vector. Finally we add the specular component to the diffuse component to produce the final lighting effect. A snapshot is shown in Fig. 10.3

Fig. 10.3 **Pixel lighting with specular**

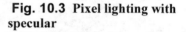

10.3.9 Point Pixel Lighting

Here we assume the light source is local at a position in the world space. In order to calculate point light intensity, we compute light direction for each pixel. In the pixel shader, we use the local variable lightDir to store light direction for the current pixel. The local light direction is the vector from the light position to the pixel's world space position. We also store in the local variable dist the distance from the current pixel to each light source for light source attenuation calculations.

```
for (int i = 0; i < 3; i++)
{
    lightDir[i] = lightPos[i] - input.PosWorld;
    dist[i] = length(lightDir[i]);
}
```

Light position is calculated using the following code:

```
for (int i = 0; i < 3; i++)
    lightPos[i] = g_lightDirections[i].xyz*3.0f;
```

We calculate point light attenuation based on the following formula

```
Att = 1/(k0+k1*d+k2*d);
```

where k0 is the constant attenuation, k1 is the linear attenuation, k2 is the quadratic attenuation, and d is the distance from the light source position to the pixel. In the pixel shader we define attenuation parameters as below:

```
//attenuation parameters for point light
float constAtt = 1.0;
float linearAtt = 0.005;
float quadAtt = 0.005;
```

It is possible to use different attenuation parameters at run time. To do this, we need to add more global variables for the attenuation parameters and pass different values into the pipeline at run time. Finally we multiply attenuation to each light source's diffuse color for point lighting. A snapshot of point pixel lighting is shown in Fig. 10.4:

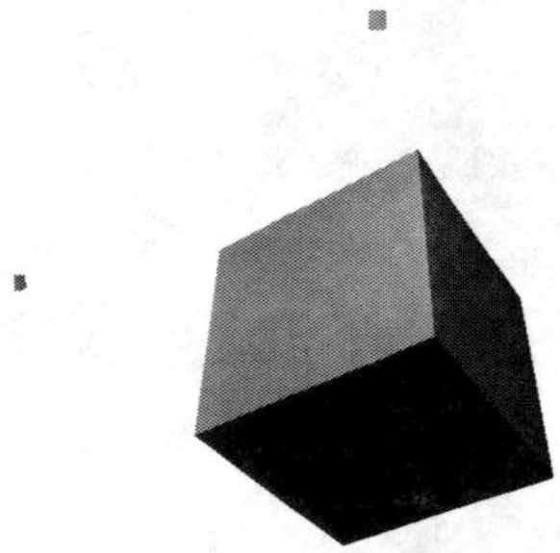

```
for(int i = 0; i < lightCount;
i++)
{
    //point light attenuation
    float att = 1.0/(constAtt +
linearAtt*dist[i] +
quadAtt*dist[i]*dist[i]);
    float NdotL =
saturate(dot(normalize(lightDir[i]), normal));//diffuse color

    finalColor += NdotL * g_lightColors[i] * att;
}
```

Fig. 10.4 Point pixel lighting

10.3.10 Point Pixel Lighting with Specular

Similar to directional lighting, we calculate the specular component based on the cosine between the light reflection vector and the eye viewing vector. We use the local light direction variable lightDir instead of the global variable g_lightDirections to calculate the specular component. A snapshot is shown in Fig. 10.5.

```
float3 reflection =
normalize(reflect(-
normalize(lightDir[i]),
normal));
specular =
pow(saturate(dot(reflection,
viewDir)), shininess);
```

Fig. 10.5 Point pixel lighting with specular

10.3.11 Spot Pixel Lighting

Compared to point lighting, a spot lighting has three new properties: a spot direction, which represents the axis of the light cone; an angle of the cone; and a decay rate, which measures how the light intensity decreases from the center to the walls of the cone. We add the following code to the point pixel lighting program to achieve spot lighting.

```
//cosine of the angle between g_lightDirection and lightDir
float spotDot = dot(normalize(-g_lightDirections[i]), -
normalize(lightDir[i]));
//cut off effect
float spotEffect = smoothstep(0.665, 0.67, spotDot);
```

In spot lighting, the global variable g_lightDirections stores the spot light directions. We calculate the cosine of the angle between the spot direction and the local light direction. Then we call smoothstep(), an intrinsic function, to simulate the spot light cut-off effect. This function accepts a range and a specified value. If the value is less than the lower bound of the range, the function returns 0. If the value is greater than the upper bound of the range, the function returns 1. We set the lower bound and upper bound to be (0.665, 0.67). The code to add the specular component is the same as in the point light. Finally we add the diffuse and specular components for the final lighting effect. A snapshot is shown in Fig. 10.6.

Fig. 10.6 Spot pixel lighting

10.3.12 Hemisphere Pixel Lighting

The idea behind hemisphere lighting is that we model the illumination as two hemispheres. The upper hemisphere is illuminated by the light source. The lower hemisphere is illuminated by a virtual light source. To compute the illumination at any point on the surface, we must compute the integral of the illumination received at that point:

```
Color = a*SkyColor + (1-a)*GroundColor;
```

where $a = 0.5 + (0.5*\cos(\theta))$, θ is the angle between the surface normal and the light source direction.

In the pixel shader, we specify the ground colors for three lights. We can add new global variables for ground colors and send different colors into the pixel shader at run time. The following code calculates hemisphere lighting for each light. A snapshot is shown in Fig. 10.7.

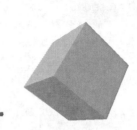

```
lightDir[i] = lightPos[i] -
input.PosWorld;
float NdotL =
dot(normalize(lightDir[i]),
normal);
float a = 0.5 + 0.5 * NdotL;
finalColor += (1 - a) *
groundColor[i] + a *
g_lightColors[i];
```

Fig. 10.7 Hemisphere lighting

10.4 Texture Mapping

Here, we show how to implement texture mapping in the shaders. This example includes single texture mapping, multi-texture mapping, texture mapping with light, texture animation, light mapping, and bump mapping. We also implement render-to-texture effect in this example.

In this example, we create a rotating cube in the scene and apply different textures onto the cube to show texture mapping as well as render-to-texture. The basic idea of render-to-texture is to draw the scene to a texture and then apply the texture to one or more objects in the scene.

10.4.1 Creating Views

We create two render target views (g_pD3D10RenderTargetView and g_pD3D10TextureRenderTargetView) in the example. g_pD3D10RenderTargetView is created from the swap chain back buffer. We use it to display the final rendering result. g_pD3D10TextureRenderTargetView is created from a separate 2D texture.

When using render-to-texture, we will render the scene to the second render target view and then use the rendering result as a texture for the final rendering result.

The following code creates the texture render target view.

```
texDesc.Format = DXGI_FORMAT_R8G8B8A8_UNORM;
texDesc.BindFlags =
D3D10_BIND_RENDER_TARGET|D3D10_BIND_SHADER_RESOURCE;
g_pD3D10Device->CreateTexture2D(&texDesc, NULL,
&g_pTextureRenderTarget);
g_pD3D10Device-
>CreateRenderTargetView(g_pTextureRenderTarget, NULL,
&g_pD3D10TextureRenderTargetView);
```

In the above, first we create a 2D texture with format DXGI_FORMAT_R8G8B8A8 _UNORM and bind flags D3D10_BIND_RENDER_TARGET | D3D10_BIND_ SHADER_RESOURCE. We specify D3D10_BIND_SHADER_RESOURCE in the bind flags so that we can access the texture in the shader.

In addition to the default depth stencil texture g_pD3D10DepthStencil, we have to create a second depth stencil texture, g_pD3D10TextureDepthStencil, for render-to-texture. These two depth stencil textures have the same format. We also create a second depth stencil view g_pD3D10TextureDepthStencilView, which has the same format as the default depth stencil view g_pD3D10DepthStencilView.

```
// Create depth stencil texture
  D3D10_TEXTURE2D_DESC depthDesc;
  depthDesc.Width = width;
  depthDesc.Height = height;
  depthDesc.MipLevels = 1;
  depthDesc.ArraySize = 1;
  depthDesc.Format = DXGI_FORMAT_D32_FLOAT;
  depthDesc.SampleDesc.Count = 1;
  depthDesc.SampleDesc.Quality = 0;
  depthDesc.Usage = D3D10_USAGE_DEFAULT;
  depthDesc.BindFlags = D3D10_BIND_DEPTH_STENCIL;
  depthDesc.CPUAccessFlags = 0;
  depthDesc.MiscFlags = 0;
 g_pD3D10Device->CreateTexture2D(&depthDesc, NULL,
&g_pD3D10DepthStencil);

 g_pD3D10Device->CreateTexture2D(&depthDesc, NULL,
&g_pD3D10TextureDepthStencil);
```

```
// Create the depth stencil view
D3D10_DEPTH_STENCIL_VIEW_DESC dsvDesc;
dsvDesc.Format = depthDesc.Format;
dsvDesc.ViewDimension = D3D10_DSV_DIMENSION_TEXTURE2D;
dsvDesc.Texture2D.MipSlice = 0;
g_pD3D10Device->CreateDepthStencilView(g_pD3D10DepthStencil,
&dsvDesc, &g_pD3D10DepthStencilView);
g_pD3D10Device-
>CreateDepthStencilView(g_pD3D10TextureDepthStencil,
&dsvDesc, &g_pD3D10TextureDepthStencilView);
```

10.4.2 Creating Input Layout

For texture mapping, we need to specify texture coordinates for each vertex. In this example, we define our vertex structure with five fields. The first three fields are used for the vertex position, texture coordinates, and normal. The last two fields are used for the vertex tangent vector and the binormal vector. These two fields are used in the bump mapping example. We will explain these two fields in the bump mapping section.

```
struct Vertex
{
    D3DXVECTOR3 Pos;
    D3DXVECTOR2 Tex;
    D3DXVECTOR3 Normal;
D3DXVECTOR3 Tangent;
    D3DXVECTOR3 Binormal;
};
```

Then we define the input layout by creating a D3D10_INPUT_ELEMENT_DESC array. Inside the array, each element corresponds to one vertex attribute. The first element is for the vertex position; the second is for the vertex texture coordinates; and the third is for the vertex normal. For the second element, we assign 12 to the AlignedByteOffset field in the D3D10_INPUT_ELEMENT_DESC structure since the first element, the vertex position, takes 12 bytes for the three float-point numbers. For the third element, we set 20 to the AlignedByteOffset field in the D3D10_INPUT_ELEMENT_DESC structure since the first element, the vertex position, and the second element, the texture coordinates take 20 bytes for the five float-point numbers. Similarly, the offset for the fourth and fifth elements are 32 and 48. Below is the code to create the input layout and bind it to the graphics pipeline.

```
// Define the input layout
   D3D10_INPUT_ELEMENT_DESC inputLayout[] =
   {
      { "POSITION", 0, DXGI_FORMAT_R32G32B32_FLOAT, 0, 0,
D3D10_INPUT_PER_VERTEX_DATA, 0 },
      { "TEXCOORD", 0, DXGI_FORMAT_R32G32_FLOAT, 0, 12,
D3D10_INPUT_PER_VERTEX_DATA, 0 },
      { "NORMAL", 0, DXGI_FORMAT_R32G32B32_FLOAT, 0, 20,
D3D10_INPUT_PER_VERTEX_DATA, 0 },
   { "TANGENT", 0, DXGI_FORMAT_R32G32B32_FLOAT, 0, 32,
D3D10_INPUT_PER_VERTEX_DATA, 0},
      { "BINORMAL", 0, DXGI_FORMAT_R32G32B32_FLOAT, 0, 48,
D3D10_INPUT_PER_VERTEX_DATA, 0}
   };

   // Create the input layout
UINT numElements = 5;
D3D10_PASS_DESC PassDesc;
   g_pD3D10Technique->GetPassByIndex(0)->GetDesc(&PassDesc);
   g_pD3D10Device->CreateInputLayout(inputLayout,
numElements,
      PassDesc.pIAInputSignature,
PassDesc.IAInputSignatureSize, &g_pD3D10VertexLayout);
```

10.4.3 Render-to-texture Function

At run time, we can press the "R" key on the keyboard to enable or disable render-to-texture. By default the example disables render-to-texture. The following code shows render-to-texture as well as normal texture mapping.

```
if (g_renderToTexture)//render to texture
   {
      g_pD3D10Device->OMSetRenderTargets(1,
&g_pD3D10TextureRenderTargetView,
g_pD3D10TextureDepthStencilView);
      g_pMainTexVariable->SetResource(g_pTextureMain);

      // Render scene to target texture
      for(UINT p = 0; p < techDesc.Passes; ++p)
      {
         g_pD3D10Technique->GetPassByIndex(p)->Apply(0);
         g_pD3D10Device->DrawIndexed(36, 0, 0);
      }
```

```
        g_pD3D10Device->OMSetRenderTargets(1,
&g_pD3D10RenderTargetView, g_pD3D10DepthStencilView);
        g_pMainTexVariable-
>SetResource(g_pTextureRenderTargetSRV);

        // Render scene again using render target as texture
        for(UINT p = 0; p < techDesc.Passes; ++p)
        {
            g_pD3D10Technique->GetPassByIndex(p)->Apply(0);
            g_pD3D10Device->DrawIndexed(36, 0, 0);
        }
    }
    else
    {
        g_pD3D10Device->OMSetRenderTargets(1,
&g_pD3D10RenderTargetView, g_pD3D10DepthStencilView);
        g_pMainTexVariable->SetResource(g_pTextureMain);

        // Render scene
        for(UINT p = 0; p < techDesc.Passes; ++p)
        {
            g_pD3D10Technique->GetPassByIndex(p)->Apply(0);
            g_pD3D10Device->DrawIndexed(36, 0, 0);
        }
    }
```

When the variable g_renderToTexture is true, we call OMSetRenderTargets() to use g_pD3D10TextureRenderTargetView and g_pD3D10TextureDepthStencilView. Then we call the DrawIndexed() method to render the scene into the render target texture. After the rendering complete, we call OMSetRenderTargets() again to switch back to the g_pD3D10RenderTargetView and g_pD3D10DepthStencilView. In this case, we change g_pMainTexVariable to use rendered texture g_pTextureRenderTargetSRV instead of the default wood texture. Then we call the DrawIndexed() method to render the scene with the rendered texture applied onto the cube. The final effect is the entire scene rendered to all faces of the cube.

When the variable g_renderToTexture is false, we simply call OMSetRenderTargets() to use the g_pD3D10RenderTargetView and g_pD3D10DepthStencilView. Then we call the DrawIndexed() method to render the scene to the screen using the default textures.

10.4.4 Texture Mapping in Shaders

Now we explain the Example03.fx file. Again, we start from defining global variables. The new variable types are Texture2D and SamplerState.

```
//texture objects
Texture2D g_texMain;
Texture2D g_texText;
Texture2D g_texLight;
Texture2D g_texBumpMap;

//texture sampler object
SamplerState g_linearSampler
{
  Filter = MIN_MAG_MIP_LINEAR;
  AddressU = Wrap;
  AddressV = Wrap;
};
```

In Direct3D 10, textures and samplers are independent objects. Each texture object implements texture sampling methods that take a sampler as an input parameter. A sampler tells the shaders how to sample the texture provided. In this example, we use a linear filter.

The input structures for the vertex shader and pixel shader are different from previous examples. Structure VS_INPUT has three elements: vertex position, texture coordinates, and normal. Structure PS_INPUT has four elements: pixel position, pixel texture coordinates, pixel surface normal, and interpolated vertex world space coordinates.

```
//vertex shader input structure
struct VS_INPUT
{
  float4 Pos : POSITION;
  float2 Tex : TEXCOORD;
float3 Norm : NORMAL;
float3 Tangent : TANGENT;
float3 Binormal : BINORMAL;
};

//pixel shader input structure
struct PS_INPUT
{
  float4 Pos : SV_POSITION;
  float2 Tex : TEXCOORD0;
```

```
    float3 Norm : TEXCOORD1;
  float3 PosWorld : TEXCOORD2;
  float3 Tangent : TEXCOORD3;
  float3 Binormal : TEXCOORD4;
  };
```

In the vertex shader, we transform the vertex position for Direct3D pipeline processing. We pass the transformed vertex position, texture coordinates, and world space vertex position and normal to the pixel shader. We also animate the cube by scaling vertices based on the current frame time.

```
  //scale geometry based on current frame time
  output.Pos.xyz *= sin(g_frameTime)*0.25 + 1.2;
```

In the pixel shader, we apply different texture mapping techniques depending on the value of the global variable g_textureMappingMode.

10.4.5 Simple Texture Mapping

In simple texture mapping, we apply a single texture onto the cube. Pixel color is determined by the texture object Sample() function. The Sample() function takes a sampler and the texture coordinates as input parameters and returns a color. A snapshot is shown in Fig. 10.8.

```
  finalColor +=
  g_texMain.Sample(g_linearSampler
  , input.Tex);
```

Fig. 10.8 Texture mapping

10.4.6 Multi-Texture Mapping

Multi-texture mapping in the pixel shader is quite straight forward. We simply add up the returned colors from the different texture objects' Sample() function to be the final pixel color. In this case, we added up the returned colors from the main wood texture and a text texture. The final effect is to draw the text on the wood texture. A snapshot is shown in Fig. 10.9.

```
finalColor +=
g_texMain.Sample(g_linearSampler
, input.Tex) +
g_texText.Sample(g_linearSampler
, input.Tex);
```

Fig. 10.9 Multi-texture mapping

10.4.7 Texture and Lighting

To combine lighting and texture mapping, we multiply the texture colors at the current pixel location with the calculated light colors. We implement a directional light with specular in the pixel shader. A snapshot is shown in Fig. 10.10.

```
//multi-texture
finalColor +=
g_texMain.Sample(g_linearSampler
, input.Tex) +
g_texText.Sample(g_linearSampler
, input.Tex);

//lighting
float3 light =
normalize((float3)g_lightDirecti
on);
float3 normal = normalize(input.Norm);
float NdotL = saturate(dot(light, normal));

//eye view dir
float3 viewDir = normalize(g_eyePosition - input.PosWorld);
```

Fig. 10.10 Multi-texture with lighting

```
//specular
float specular = 0;
if (NdotL > 0){
    float3 reflection = normalize(reflect(-light, normal));
    specular = pow(saturate(dot(reflection, viewDir)), 32);
}
finalColor *= NdotL * g_lightColor + specular;
```

10.4.8 Texture Animation

We could also use the pixel shader to create animation effects. In this section, we look at a shader that perturbs the texture coordinates in a time-varying fashion to achieve an oscillating effect. We can produce an animated effect to simulate a gelatinous surface or a "dancing" logo. The idea of the effect is to use a sine function in the pixel shader to perturb the texture coordinates before the texture sampling operation. The amount and frequency of the perturbation can be controlled through global variables sent from the application. In the example, we simply use a built-in constant and frequency in the pixel shader. The code that implements the effect is listed below. A snapshot is shown in Fig. 10.11.

Fig. 10.11 Texture animation

```
float2 freq = {3.5, 3.0};
float2 amplitude = {0.1, 0.1};
float2 wobbleTex = input.Tex;

//animated texture coordinates
float rad = sin((input.Tex.x + input.Tex.y - 1.0 +
g_frameTime) * freq.x);
wobbleTex.x += rad * amplitude.x;

rad = sin((input.Tex.x - input.Tex.y + g_frameTime) * freq.y);
wobbleTex.y += rad * amplitude.y;

//multi-texture
```

```
finalColor += g_texMain.Sample(g_linearSampler, wobbleTex) +
g_texText.Sample(g_linearSampler, wobbleTex);
```

10.4.9 Light Mapping

A light map is a texture map to simulate the effect of light sources. Like specular highlights, it can be used to improve the appearance of local light sources without resorting to excessive tessellation of the objects in the scene. To use a light map, a texture simulating the light's effect on the object is created, then applied to one or more objects in the scene. Appropriate texture coordinates are generated, and texture transformations can be used to position the light and to create moving or changing light effects.

In our example, we create a light map with two local lights. The texture object for the light map is g_texLight. We modulate the light map with the color of the geometry surfaces to simulate the effects of local lights. A snapshot is shown in Fig. 10.12.

```
finalColor +=
g_texMain.Sample(g_linearSampler
, input.Tex) +
g_texText.Sample(g_linearSampler
, input.Tex);
//modulate light map with
geometry surface intensity
finalColor *=
g_texLight.Sample(g_linearSample
r, input.Tex);
```

Fig. 10.12 Light mapping

10.4.10 Bump Mapping

Bump mapping modifies the surface normals by the normals in the bump map, which is saved as a texture, before lighting is applied. To achieve bump mapping, we need a surface normal, a light source, a viewing direction vector, and the bump map normal to calculate the bumping effect. The normal values in the bump map are in the tangent space, in which an unperturbed surface normal at each point is (0, 0, 1) and the corresponding point on the surface is at (0, 0, 0). To calculate lighting in the tangent space, we transform the light direction and view direction into the tangent space. We send two vectors, the tangent and binormal vectors, from the application to the shader. A tangent vector is in the tangent plane at the point of the surface being rendered and perpendicular to the normal at the point of the surface. A binormal vector is perpendicular to both the normal and the tangent vector. We use the surface normal, the tangent vector, and the binormal vector to form a transformation matrix in order to transform the light direction and the view direction to the tangent space.

In the bump map, the RGB color for the straight up normal is (0.5, 0.5, 1.0). This is why the bump map is a blueish color. In the pixel shader, we use the following code to calculate lighting for bump mapping. A snapshot is shown in Fig. 10.13.

First we normalize the surface normal, tangent vector, and binormal vector.

```
float3 normalWS =
normalize(input.Norm);
float3 tangentWS =
normalize(input.Tangent);
float3 binormalWS =
normalize(input.Binormal);
```

Fig. 10.13 Bump mapping

Then we construct a transformation matrix using the three vectors.

```
float3x3 worldToTangentMatrix = float3x3(tangentWS,
binormalWS, normalWS);
```

Then, we transform the light and view directions into the tangent space.

```
float3 light = normalize(mul((float3)g_lightDirection,
worldToTangentMatrix));
float3 viewDir = g_eyePosition - input.PosWorld;
viewDir = normalize(mul(worldToTangentMatrix, viewDir));
```

The perturbed normal is stored in the bump map.

```
float3 normal = g_texBumpMap.Sample(g_linearSampler,
input.Tex).xyz;
normal = normalize(normal*2 - 1);
```

Finally, we calculate lighting using the tangent space light direction and view direction, as well as perturbed normal.

```
// calculate lighting in tangent space
float NdotL = saturate(dot(light, normal));

float specular = 0;
if (NdotL > 0)
{
    float3 reflection = normalize(reflect(-light, normal));
    specular = pow(saturate(dot(reflection, viewDir)), 8);
}

finalColor *= NdotL * g_lightColor + specular;
```

10.5 Simulating Fixed Functional Fog

In this example we implement a standard fixed functional fog effect using the pixel shader. In the pixel shader, we calculate the fog component based on three different equations.

10.5.1 Linear Fog

The linear fog effect is calculated by the following fog equation:

$$fog = (fogend - pixel\_to\_eye\_distance)/(fogend - fogstart). \qquad \text{(EQ 221)}$$

We use the following code to implement the linear fog in the pixel shader:

```
float dist = length(eyePos - input.PosWorld);
fog = (fogEnd - dist)/(fogEnd - fogStart);
```

where fogEnd and fogStart are pre-defined variables of the fog range.

10.5.2 Exponential Fog

In achieving the exponential fog effect, we use an exponential function for fog density. With a negative exponential value, the function will model the diminishing of the original color as a function of distance. We use the following equation:

$$fog = e^{-(fogDensity*pixel\_to\_eye\_distance)}.$$

(EQ 222)

We use the following code to implement exponential fog in the pixel shader:

```
float dist = length(eyePos - input.PosWorld);
fog = 1.0 / pow(E, dist*fogDensity);
```

where the variable fogDensity is a pre-defined variable for the density of the fog.

10.5.3 Square Exponential Fog

The last fog effect is calculated using a slightly modified exponential function. We use the square of the product of fog density and the pixel-to-eye distance to change the exponential decay function.

```
float dist = length(eyePos - input.PosWorld);
fog = 1.0 / pow(E, dist*dist*fogDensity*fogDensity);
```

10.6 Cube Mapping

In this example we explain cube mapping using a new feature in Direct3D 10, the geometry shader. Traditionally, we needed to use multi-pass rendering technology to render six views of the scene sequentially in order to create cube mapping textures. With the geometry shader, we can render six views of the scene at the same time on the graphics hardware.

The basic idea of cube mapping is that we use the reflection vector from the surface of an object to look up the reflection color from an environment that is stored in a texture map with six subfaces. If environment mapping is done correctly, the result looks as if the object being rendered is shiny, reflecting its environment. We first render the scene into a cube map then apply the cube map onto objects.

10.6.1 Creating Geometry

In this example, we create a rotating center cube and six smaller cubes orbiting around the center cube. We create another large cube to render the background world. The background and the orbiting cubes will be reflected on the center cube. We use the same vertices for the center cube and the orbiting cubes. We create another set of vertices for the background cube, which has different texture coordinates and normals. In the vertex buffer, for each vertex we have three vectors (position, texture coordinates, and normal). For example, the first vertex is defined as follows:

```
//cube geometry
{ D3DXVECTOR3(-1.0f, -1.0f, 1.0f), D3DXVECTOR2(0.0f, 1.0f),
D3DXVECTOR3(-1.0f, 0.0f, 0.0f) },
```

10.6.2 Creating Resources for Cube Mapping

A cube map has six 2D textures that are organized to represent the inside faces of a cube. We use the following code to create six view matrices to render environment to a cube map.

```
// Generate cube map view matrices
    D3DXVECTOR3 eyePos = D3DXVECTOR3(0.0f, 0.0f, 0.0f);
    D3DXVECTOR3 lookAt = D3DXVECTOR3(0.0f, 0.0f, 0.0f);
    D3DXVECTOR3 upDir;

    lookAt = D3DXVECTOR3(1.0f, 0.0f, 0.0f);
    upDir  = D3DXVECTOR3(0.0f, 1.0f, 0.0f);
    D3DXMatrixLookAtLH(&g_cubeMapViewMat[0], &eyePos, &lookAt,
&upDir);

    lookAt = D3DXVECTOR3(-1.0f, 0.0f, 0.0f);
    upDir  = D3DXVECTOR3(0.0f, 1.0f, 0.0f);
    D3DXMatrixLookAtLH(&g_cubeMapViewMat[1], &eyePos, &lookAt,
&upDir);

    lookAt = D3DXVECTOR3(0.0f, 1.0f, 0.0f);
    upDir  = D3DXVECTOR3(0.0f, 0.0f, -1.0f);
    D3DXMatrixLookAtLH(&g_cubeMapViewMat[2], &eyePos, &lookAt,
&upDir);
```

```
    lookAt = D3DXVECTOR3(0.0f, -1.0f, 0.0f);
    upDir  = D3DXVECTOR3(0.0f, 0.0f, 1.0f);
    D3DXMatrixLookAtLH(&g_cubeMapViewMat[3], &eyePos, &lookAt,
&upDir);

    lookAt = D3DXVECTOR3(0.0f, 0.0f, 1.0f);
    upDir  = D3DXVECTOR3(0.0f, 1.0f, 0.0f);
    D3DXMatrixLookAtLH(&g_cubeMapViewMat[4], &eyePos, &lookAt,
&upDir);

    lookAt = D3DXVECTOR3(0.0f, 0.0f, -1.0f);
    upDir  = D3DXVECTOR3(0.0f, 1.0f, 0.0f);
    D3DXMatrixLookAtLH(&g_cubeMapViewMat[5], &eyePos, &lookAt,
&upDir);
```

These six view matrices point the camera to the positive and negative x faces, the positive and negative y faces, and the positive and negative z faces with the eye position at the scene center.

For cube mapping, we render the background scene into six faces of a cube mapping texture. In Direct3D 10, a render target view allows multiple render targets and depth stencil textures to be active at the same time. We create a render target view with six render target textures, each for one face of the cube map. We also create a depth stencil view having six depth stencil textures.

```
// Create cubic depth stencil texture.
    D3D10_TEXTURE2D_DESC texDesc;
    texDesc.Width = CUBEMAP_SIZE;
    texDesc.Height = CUBEMAP_SIZE;
    texDesc.MipLevels = 1;
    texDesc.ArraySize = 6;
    texDesc.SampleDesc.Count = 1;
    texDesc.SampleDesc.Quality = 0;
    texDesc.Format = DXGI_FORMAT_D32_FLOAT;
    texDesc.Usage = D3D10_USAGE_DEFAULT;
    texDesc.BindFlags = D3D10_BIND_DEPTH_STENCIL;
    texDesc.CPUAccessFlags = 0;
    texDesc.MiscFlags = D3D10_RESOURCE_MISC_TEXTURECUBE;
    g_pD3D10Device->CreateTexture2D(&texDesc, NULL,
&g_pCubeMapDS);

    // Create the depth stencil view for the entire cube
    D3D10_DEPTH_STENCIL_VIEW_DESC depthStencilDesc;
    depthStencilDesc.Format = DXGI_FORMAT_D32_FLOAT;
    depthStencilDesc.ViewDimension =
D3D10_DSV_DIMENSION_TEXTURE2DARRAY;
```

```
    depthStencilDesc.Texture2DArray.FirstArraySlice = 0;
    depthStencilDesc.Texture2DArray.ArraySize = 6;
    depthStencilDesc.Texture2DArray.MipSlice = 0;
    g_pD3D10Device->CreateDepthStencilView(g_pCubeMapDS,
&depthStencilDesc, &g_pCubeMapDSV);

// Create the cube map for env map render target
    texDesc.Format = DXGI_FORMAT_R16G16B16A16_FLOAT;
    texDesc.BindFlags = D3D10_BIND_RENDER_TARGET |
D3D10_BIND_SHADER_RESOURCE;
    texDesc.MiscFlags = D3D10_RESOURCE_MISC_GENERATE_MIPS |
D3D10_RESOURCE_MISC_TEXTURECUBE;
    texDesc.MipLevels = MIP_LEVELS;
    g_pD3D10Device->CreateTexture2D(&texDesc, NULL,
&g_pCubeMap);

    // Create the 6-face render target view
    D3D10_RENDER_TARGET_VIEW_DESC rtvDesc;
    rtvDesc.Format = texDesc.Format;
    rtvDesc.ViewDimension =
D3D10_RTV_DIMENSION_TEXTURE2DARRAY;
    rtvDesc.Texture2DArray.FirstArraySlice = 0;
    rtvDesc.Texture2DArray.ArraySize = 6;
    rtvDesc.Texture2DArray.MipSlice = 0;
    g_pD3D10Device->CreateRenderTargetView(g_pCubeMap,
&rtvDesc, &g_pCubeMapRTV);
```

Finally we create a shader resource view so that we can access the rendered cube map in the shaders for cube mapping.

```
    // Create the shader resource view for the cubic env map
    D3D10_SHADER_RESOURCE_VIEW_DESC srvDesc;
    ZeroMemory(&srvDesc, sizeof(srvDesc));
    srvDesc.Format = texDesc.Format;
    srvDesc.ViewDimension = D3D10_SRV_DIMENSION_TEXTURECUBE;
    srvDesc.TextureCube.MipLevels = MIP_LEVELS;
    srvDesc.TextureCube.MostDetailedMip = 0;
    g_pD3D10Device->CreateShaderResourceView(g_pCubeMap,
&srvDesc, &g_pCubeMapSRV);
```

10.6.3 Rendering the Scene

We call the SetupCubeMapRendering() method to setup the render target view and the depth stencil view for cube map rendering. Then we call RenderToCubeMap() to render the environment into the cube map that has six faces. After that, we call the

SetupSceneRendering() method to setup the render target view and the depth stencil view for regular scene rendering. We then render the center cube in the scene using the cube map texture as discussed in the following sections.

10.6.4 Rendering to Cube Map in Shaders

We have four techniques in the effect file Example05.fx. The first technique, RenderEnvBox, is used to render the background cube without lighting. The second technique, RenderCubeMap, is used to render the background cube and the orbiting cubes into the cube map. The third technique, RenderScene, is used to render orbiting cubes with lighting and texture mapping. The last technique, RenderSceneCubeMapped is used to render the center cube with cube mapping.

In the RenderCubeMap technique, we use VS_CubeMap, GS_CubeMap, and PS_CubeMap shaders to render the background cube and the orbiting cubes into the cube map. The vertex shader, VS_CubeMap, calculates the world space vertex positions of the background cube and the orbiting cubes and passes through their associated texture coordinates.

```
struct VS_INPUT
{
  float4 Pos  : POSITION;
  float2 Tex  : TEXCOORD;
  float3 Norm : NORMAL;
};
GS_CUBEMAP_INPUT VS_CubeMap(VS_INPUT input)
{
  GS_CUBEMAP_INPUT output = (GS_CUBEMAP_INPUT)0;

  output.Pos = mul(input.Pos, worldMat);
  output.Tex = input.Tex;

  return output;
}
```

The geometry shader, GS_CubeMap, runs once per primitive that VS_CubeMap has processed. In our example, it is used to render the primitives to the six faces of the cube map. The geometry shader output has a special field called RenderTargetIndex. The field has semantic type SV_RenderTargetArrayIndex, and this semantic enables the field to select the render target to which the primitive is emitted.

The geometry shader loops six times, once for each cube face. Inside the loop, the RenderTargetIndex field is set to be the loop control variable to make sure that in each iteration of the loop, the primitive is emitted to a corresponding render target. Another for-loop (the inner loop) runs three times per face to process three vertices for the input triangle primitive. We transform the input vertex position by the view and projection matrices. Each iteration of the outer for-loop uses a different view transformation matrix and emits vertices to a different render target. This renders one triangle onto six render target textures in a single pass without calling DrawIndexed() multiple times.

```
[maxvertexcount(18)]
void GS_CubeMap(triangle GS_CUBEMAP_INPUT input[3], inout
TriangleStream<PS_CUBEMAP_INPUT> CubeMapStream)
{
  for(int i = 0; i < 6; i++)
  {
    PS_CUBEMAP_INPUT output;
    output.RenderTargetIndex = i;
    for(int j = 0; j < 3; j++)
    {
      output.Pos = mul(input[j].Pos, viewMatCubeMap[i]);
      output.Pos = mul(output.Pos, projMat);
      output.Tex = input[j].Tex;
      CubeMapStream.Append(output);
    }
    CubeMapStream.RestartStrip();
  }
}
```

The pixel shader simply fetches the diffuse texture and applies it to the mesh.

10.6.5 Cube Mapping in Shaders

We use the RenderSceneCubeMapped technique to render the center cube with cube mapping. The vertex shader, VS_CubeMapped, transforms the vertex position and normal of the center cube.

In the pixel shader, PS_CubeMapped, we do cube mapping when the global variable cubeMapMode equals 0. We first calculate the cube map reflection ray:

```
//cube mapping
```

```
float3 cubeMapReflectRay = normalize(reflect(-viewDir,
normal));
```

Then we use the reflection ray to access the cube map texture:

```
finalColor += texCubeMap.Sample(samCube, cubeMapReflectRay);
```

The result of cube mapping is the reflection of environment on the center cube. A snapshot is shown in Fig. 10.14.

10.6.6 Cube Mapping with Refraction

In this example, we also implement refraction effect in addition to cube mapping. The final result is the combination of the reflected and refracted background.

We could use the build-in intrinsic function refract() to model refraction in the shaders. Given an entering ray, a surface normal, and a refraction index (a measure of how much the

Fig. 10.14 Cube mapping (texture by Emil Persson)

speed of light is reduced inside different materials), the refract function calculates the refracted vector. We then use the refracted vector to access a cube map to determine the surface color for a transparent object.

In the real world, most transparent objects present both reflection and refraction effects. This is known as the Fresnel effect. The Fresnel equations describe the reflection and refraction that occur at material boundaries. The Fresnel equations involve the angle of incidence, the polarization and wavelength of the light, and the refraction indices of the materials involved. Since our goal is to provide good enough results simulating reflection and refraction instead of accurate physical simulation, we use an approximation for the ratio between reflected light and refracted light developed by Christophe Schlick.

$$F = f + (1 - f)(1 - V \bullet N)^5,$$ **(EQ 223)**

where V is the view direction, N is the surface normal and f is the reflectance of the material when the angle between the view direction and the surface normal is:

$$f = \left(1 - \frac{n1}{n2}\right)^2 \Big/ \left(1 + \frac{n1}{n2}\right)^2 ,$$

(EQ 224)

where $n1$ and $n2$ are the refraction indices for materials 1 and 2. We use the following code in the pixel shader to perform the refraction calculation.

```
float eta = 0.66;
float3 cubeMapRefractRay = normalize(refract(-viewDir,
normal, eta));

float f = ((1.0 - eta) * (1.0 - eta)) / ((1.0 + eta) * (1.0 +
eta));
float ratio = f + (1.0 - f) * pow((1.0 - dot(viewDir,
normal)), 5.0);
finalColor += g_texCubeMap.Sample(g_samCube,
cubeMapReflectRay);
finalColor *= ratio;
finalColor += g_texCubeMap.Sample(g_samCube,
cubeMapRefractRay) * (1.0 - ratio);
```

We use the local variable eta for the ratio of the refraction indices. We calculate a refracted vector from the viewing direction, surface normal, and eta. Then we use Christophe Schlick's equation to calculate the ratio between the reflected light and the refracted light. Finally we mix reflected color and refracted color together for the final result. The refracted color is given by accessing the environment map using the refracted vector. A snapshot is shown in Fig. 10.15.

Fig. 10.15 Cube mapping with refraction (texture courtesy of Emil Persson)

10.6.7 Cube mapping with Separated Refraction

We modified our shader to create a special refraction effect, which is not necessarily accurate in physics.

We know light components with different wavelengths have different refractions. In this example we model our light to have three different wavelengths: red, green, blue. For each wavelength, we use a different ratio of refraction indices for the refraction vector calculation. By setting a slightly different ratio of refraction indices, we can get a slightly different refraction vector. Finally we combine the three light components together for the final result. A snapshot is shown in Fig. 10.16.

Fig. 10.16 Cube mapping with separated refraction (texture courtesy of Emil Persson)

```
float eta[3] = {0.65, 0.66,
0.69}, f[3], ratio[3];
float3 cubeMapRefractRay[3];
float4 cubeMapColor[3];

for (int i = 0; i < 3; i++)
{
    f[i] = ((1.0 - eta[i]) * (1.0 - eta[i])) / ((1.0 + eta[i])
* (1.0 + eta[i]));
    cubeMapRefractRay[i] = normalize(refract(-viewDir, normal,
eta[i]));
    ratio[i] = f[i] + (1.0 - f[i]) * pow((1.0 - dot(viewDir,
normal)), 5.0);
    cubeMapColor[i] = g_texCubeMap.Sample(g_samCube,
cubeMapRefractRay[i]);
}

finalColor += g_texCubeMap.Sample(g_samCube,
cubeMapReflectRay);

finalColor.x = finalColor.x * ratio[0] + cubeMapColor[0].x *
(1.0 - ratio[0]);
finalColor.y = finalColor.y * ratio[1] + cubeMapColor[1].y *
(1.0 - ratio[1]);
finalColor.z = finalColor.z * ratio[2] + cubeMapColor[2].z *
(1.0 - ratio[2]);
```

11
Advanced Topics

Chapter Objectives:

- Wrap up basic computer graphics principles and programming
- Briefly introduce some advanced graphics concepts and methods

11.1 Introduction

We have covered basic graphics principles and OpenGL programming. A graphics system includes a graphics library and its supporting hardware. Most of the OpenGL library functions are implemented in hardware, which would otherwise be very slow. Some advanced graphics functions built on top of the basic library functions, such as drawing curves and curved surfaces, are also part of the OpenGL library or the OpenGL Utility library (GLU). GLU is considered part of the OpenGL system to facilitate complex model construction and rendering.

On top of a graphics library, many graphics methods and tools (namely high level graphics packages) are developed for certain capabilities or applications. For example, mathematics on curve and surface descriptions are used to construct curved shapes, constructive solid geometry (CSG) methods are used to assemble geometric models through logical operations, recursive functions are used to generate fractal images, visualization methods are developed to understand certain types of data, simulation methods are developed to animate certain processes, etc. In this chapter, we wrap up the first part of the book by briefly introducing some advanced graphics concepts. In the second part of the book, we introduce and compile specific graphics tools in more detail.

J.X. Chen, *Guide to Graphics Software Tools*, doi: 10.1007/978-1-84800-901-1_11,
© Springer-Verlag London Limited 2008

11.2 Graphics Libraries

A *low-level graphics library* or package is a software interface to graphics hardware. All graphics tools or applications are built on top of a certain low-level graphics library. High-level graphics tools are usually easier to learn and use. An introductory computer graphics course mainly discusses the implementations and applications of low-level graphics library functions. A graphics programmer understands how to program in at least one graphics library. OpenGL, Direct3D, and PHIGS are well-known low-level graphics libraries. *OpenGL* and Direct3D are currently the most widely adopted 3D graphics APIs in research and applications.

A *high-level graphics library*, which is often called a *3D programming tool library* (e.g., OpenInventor, discussed in Chapter 12), provides the means for application programs to handle scene constructions, 3D file imports and exports, object manipulations, and display. It is an API toolkit built on top of a low-level graphics library. Most high-level graphics libraries are categorized as animation, simulation, or virtual reality tools.

11.3 Visualization

Visualization employs graphics to make pictures that give us insight into the abstract data and symbols. The pictures may directly portray the description of the data or completely present the content of the data in an innovative form. Users, when presented with a new computed result or some other collection of online data, want to see and understand the meaning as quickly as possible. They often prefer understanding through observing an image or 3D animation rather than from reading abstract numbers and symbols.

11.3.1 Interactive Visualization and Computational Steering

Interactive visualization allows visualizing the results or presentations interactively in different perspectives (e.g., angles, magnitude, layers, levels of detail, etc.), and thus helps the user to better understand the results on the fly. Interactive visualization systems are most effective when the results of models or simulations have multiple or dynamic forms, layers, or levels of detail, which help users interact with visual presentations and understand the different aspects of the results.

For scientific computation and visualization, the integration of computation, visualization, and control into one tool is highly desirable, because it allows users to interactively "steer" the computation. At the beginning of the computation, before any result is generated, a few important pieces of feedback will significantly help in choosing correct parameters and initial values. Users can visualize some intermediate results and key factors to steer the computation in the right direction. With *computational steering*, users are able to modify parameters in their systems as the computation progresses, and avoid errors or uninteresting output after long tedious computation. Computational steering is an important method for adjusting uncertain parameters, moving the simulation in the right direction, and fine tuning the results.

11.3.2 Data Visualization: Dimensions and Data Types

A visualization technique is applicable to certain data types (discrete, continual, point, scalar, or vector) and dimensions (1D, 2D, 3D, and multiple: *N*-D). *Scatter Data* represent data as discrete points on a line (1D), plane (2D), or in space (3D). We may use different colors, shapes, sizes, and other attributes to represent the points in higher dimensions beyond 3D, or use a function or a representation to transform the high dimensional data into 2D/3D. *Scalar Data* have scalar values in addition to dimension values. The scalar value is actually a special additional dimension that we pay more attention to. 2D diagrams like histograms, bar charts, or pie charts are 1D scalar data visualization methods. Both histograms and bar charts have one coordinate as the dimension scale and another as the value scale. Histograms usually have scalar values in confined ranges, while bar charts do not carry this information. Pie charts use a slice area in a pie to represent a percentage. 2D contours (iso-lines in a map) of constant values, 2D images (pixels of *x-y* points and color values), and 3D surfaces (pixels of *x-y* points and height values) are 2D scalar data visualization methods. Volume and iso-surface rendering methods are for 3D scalar data. A *voxel* (volume pixel) is a 3D scalar datum with (x, y, z) coordinates and an intensity or color value. *Vector Data* include directions in addition to scalar and dimension values. We use line segments, arrows, streamlines, and animations to present the directions.

- *Volume rendering* or visualization is a method for extracting meaningful information from a set of 2D scalar data. A sequence of 2D image slices of human body can be reconstructed into a 3D volume model and visualized for diagnostic purposes or for planning of treatment or surgery. For example, a set of volumetric data such as a deck of Magnetic Resonance Imaging (MRI) slices or Computed Tomography (CT) can be blended into a 2D X-ray image by firing rays through the volume and blending the voxels along the rays. This is a rather costly operation and the blending methods vary. The concept of volume rendering is also to extract the contours from given data slices. An iso-surface is a 3D constant intensity surface represented by triangle strips or higher-order surface patches within a volume. For example, the voxels on the surface of bones in a deck of MRI slices appear to have the same intensity value.

- From the study of turbulence or plasmas to the design of new wings or jet nozzles, flow visualization motivates much of the research effort in scientific visualization. Flow data are mostly 3D vectors or tensors of high dimensions. The main challenge of flow visualization is to find ways of visualizing multivariate data sets. Colors, arrows, particles, line convolutions, textures, surfaces, and volumes are used to represent different aspects of fluid flows (velocities, pressures, streamlines, streaklines, vortices, etc.).

- The visual presentation and examination of large data sets from physical and natural sciences often require the integration of terabyte or gigabyte distributed scientific databases with visualization. Genetic algorithms, radar range images, materials simulations, and atmospheric and oceanographic measurements are among the areas that generate large multidimensional multivariate data sets. The data vary with different geometries, sampling rates, and error characteristics. The display and interpretation of the data sets employ statistical analyses and other techniques in conjunction with visualization.

- The field of *information visualization* includes visualizing retrieved information from large document collections (e.g., digital libraries), the Internet, and text databases. Information is completely abstract. We need to map the data into a physical space that will represent relationships contained in the information faithfully and efficiently. This could enable the observers to use their innate abilities to understand through spatial relationships the correlations in the library. Finding a good spatial representation of the information at hand is one of the most challenging tasks in information visualization.

Many forms and choices exist for the visualization of 2D or 3D data sets, which are relatively easy to conceive and understand. For data sets that are more than 3D, visualization methods are challenging research topics. For example, the Linked micromap plots are developed to display spatially indexed data that integrate geographical and statistical summaries (http://www.netgraphi.com/cancer4/).

11.3.3 Parallel Coordinates

The *parallel coordinates* method represents d-dimensional data as values on d coordinates parallel to the x-axis equally spaced along the y-axis (Fig. 11.1, or the other way around, rotating 90 degrees). Each d-dimensional datum corresponds to the line segments between the parallel coordinates connecting the corresponding values. That is, each polygonal line of $(d-1)$ segments in the parallel coordinates represents a point in d dimensional space. Parallel coordinates provide a

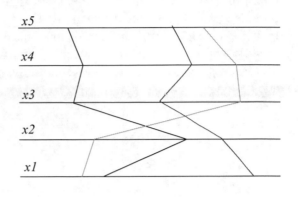

Fig. 11.1 Parallel coordinates: an example

means to visualize higher order geometries in an easily recognizable 2D representation. It also helps find the patterns, trends, and correlations in the data set.

The purpose of using parallel coordinates is to find certain features in the data set through visualization. Consider a series of points on a straight line in Cartesian coordinates: $y=mx+b$. If we display these points in parallel coordinates, the points on a line in Cartesian coordinates become line segments. These line segments intersect at a point. This point in the parallel coordinates is called the *dual* of the line in the Cartesian coordinates. The point~line duality extends to conic sections. An ellipse in Cartesian coordinates maps into a hyperbola in parallel coordinates, and vice versa. Rotations in Cartesian coordinates become translations in parallel coordinates, and vice versa.

Clustering is easily isolated and visualized in parallel coordinates. An individual parallel coordinate axis represents a 1D projection of the data set. Thus, separation between or among sets of data on one axis represents a view of the data of isolated clusters. The *brushing* technique is to interactively separate a cluster of data by painting it with a unique color. The brushed color becomes an attribute of the cluster. Different clusters can be brushed with different colors and relations among clusters can then be visually detected. Heavily plotted areas can be blended with color mixes and transparencies. Animation of the colored clusters through time allows visualization of the data evolution history.

The grand tour method is used to search for patterns by looking at the high-dimensional data from all different angles. That is, to project the data into all possible *d*-planes through generalized rotations. The purpose of the grand tour animation is to look for unusual configurations of the data that may reflect some structure from a specific angle. The rotation, projection, and animation methods vary depending on specific assumptions. There are visualization tools that include parallel coordinates and grand tours: ExplorN (`ftp://www.galaxy.gmu.edu/pub/software/ExplorN_v1.tar`), CrystalVision (`ftp://www.galaxy.gmu.edu/pub/software/CrystalVisionDemo.exe`), and XGobi (`http://www.research.att.com/areas/stat/xgobi/`).

11.4 Modeling and Rendering

Modeling is a process of constructing a virtual 3D graphics object (computer model, or model) from a real object or an imaginary entity. Creating graphics models requires a significant amount of time and effort. Modeling tools make creating and constructing complex 3D models fast and easy. A graphics model includes geometrical descriptions (particles, vertices, polygons, etc.) as well as associated graphics attributes (colors, shadings, transparencies, materials, etc.), which can be saved in a file using a standard (3D model) file format. Modeling tools help create virtual objects and environments for CAD (computer-aided design), visualization, virtual reality, simulation, education, training, and entertainment.

Rendering is a process of creating images from graphics models. 3D graphics models are saved in computer memory or hard-disk files. The term *rasterization* and *scan-conversion* are used to refer to low-level image generation or drawing. All modeling tools provide certain drawing capabilities to visualize the models generated. However, in addition to simply drawing (scan-converting) geometric objects, rendering tools often include lighting, shading, texture mapping, color blending, ray tracing, radiosity, and other advanced graphics capabilities. For example, the *RenderMan* Toolkit includes photorealistic modeling and rendering of particle systems, hair, and many other objects with advanced graphics functions such as ray tracing, volume display, motion blur, depth-of-field, and so forth. Many powerful graphics tools include modeling, rendering, animation, and other functions in one package.

Basic modeling and rendering methods were discussed in previous chapters. Here we introduce some advanced modeling and rendering techniques.

11.4.1 Curves and Surfaces

To describe a sphere, we can save a list of vertices on the surface of the sphere. However, it would be probably more efficient and accurate to save just the sphere equation and calculate the vertices of the surface when needed. Parametric mathematical equations are used to generate smooth curves and curved surfaces. Cubic parametric functions are the lowest-degree curve functions that are non-planar in 3D. Therefore, we can use Hermite, Bezier, B-spline, NURB, natural cubic spline, and other mathematical equations or methods, which are abundant in math or graphics books and literature.

11.4.2 Sweep Representations

We can create a 3D volume by sweeping a 2D area along a linear path normal to the area. *Sweeping* is implemented in most graphics modeling tools. The generated model contains many vertices that may be eliminated. Algorithms are developed to simplify models and measure the similarity between models. A model can also be represented with multiple levels of detail for use with fast animations and high-resolution rendering interchangeably.

11.4.3 Instances

In a hierachical model, there are parts that are exactly the same. For example, all four wheels of a car can be the same model. Instead of saving four copies of the model, we save just one primitive model and three *instances*, which are really pointers to the same primitive. If we modify the primitive, we know that the primitive and the instances are identically changed.

11.4.4 Constructive Solid Geometry

Constructive Solid Geometry (CSG) is a solid modeling method. A set of solid primitives such as cubes, cylinders, spheres, and cones are combined by union, difference, and intersection to construct a more complex solid model. In CSG, a solid model is stored as a tree with operators at the internal nodes and solid primitives at the leaves. The tree is processed in the depth-first search with a corresponding sequence of operations, and finally, rendering. CSG is a modeling method that is often used to create new and complex mechanical parts.

11.4.5 Procedural Models

Procedural models describe objects by procedures instead of using a list of primitives. Fractal models, grammar-based models, particle system models, and physically-based models are all procedural models. Procedural models can interact with external events to modify themselves. Also, very small changes in specifications can result in drastic changes of form.

11.4.6 Fractals

A *fractal* is a geometric shape that is substantially and recursively self-similar. Theoretically, only infinitely recursive processes are true fractals. Fractal models have been developed to render plants, clouds, fluid, music, and more. For example, a grammar model can be used to generate self-similar tree branches: T -> T | T[T] | (T)T | (T)[T] | (T)T[T], where square brackets denote a right branch and parentheses denote a left branch. We may choose a different angle, thickness, and length for the branch at a depth in the recursion with flowers or leaves at the end of the recursions.

11.4.7 Particle systems

Particle systems are used to model and render irregular fuzzy objects such as dust, fire, and smoke. A set of particles are employed to represent an object. Each individual particle generated evolves and disappears in space, all at different times depending on its individual animation. In general, a particle system and its particles have very similar parameters, but with different values:

- Position (including orientation in 3D space and center location x, y, and z)

- Movement (including velocity, rotation, acceleration, etc.)

- Color (RGB) and transparency (alpha)

- Shape (point, line, fractal, sphere, cube, rectangle, etc.)

- Volume, density, and mass

- Lifetime (only for particles)

- Blur head and rear pointers (only for particles)

The position, shape, and size of a particle system determine the initial positions of the particles and their range of movement. The movements of the particles are restricted within the range defined by their associated particle system. The shape of a particle system can be a point, line segment, fractal, sphere, box, or cylinder. The movement of a particle system is affected by internal or external forces, and the results of the rotations and accelerations of the particles as a whole. A particle system may change its shape, size, color, transparency, or some other attributes as it evolves. The lifetime defines how long a particle will be active. A particle has both a head position and a tail position. The head position is usually animated and the tail position follows along for motion blur.

In general, particle systems are first initialized with each particle having an original position, velocity, color, transparency, shape, size, mass, and lifetime. After the initialization, for each calculation and rendering frame, some parameters of the particles are updated using a rule base, and the resulting particle systems are rendered. Fig. 11.2 summarizes the applications that employ particle systems. Structured particle systems are often used to model trees, water drops, leaves, grass, rainbows, and clouds. Stochastic particle systems are often used to model fireworks, explosions, snow, and so forth. Oriented particle systems are often used to model deformable and rigid bodies such as cloth, lava flow, etc.

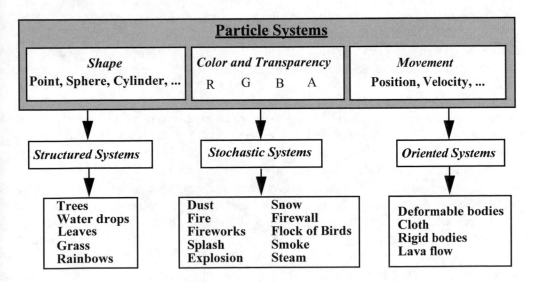

Fig. 11.2 Applications of particle systems in computer graphics

11.4.8 Image-based Modeling and Rendering

Image-based modeling or rendering uses images or photographs to replace geometric models. This technique achieves shorter modeling times, faster rendering speeds, and unprecedented levels of photorealism. It also addresses different approaches to turn images into models and then back into renderings, including movie maps, panoramas, image warping, light fields, and 3D scanning.

It has been observed that the rendering process can be accelerated significantly by reusing the images to approximate the new frames instead of rendering them from the geometric model directly. The rendering error introduced by the approximation, which determines whether or not an image must be refreshed, can be calculated by comparing the image to the object's geometry.

Given the view position and direction, we can use a texture image mapped onto a polygon with transparent background to replace a complex model such as a tree, building, or human avatar. The polygon is called a *billboard* or *poster* if it is always perpendicular to the view point.

We can integrate image-based rendering and model-based rendering in one application. For example, we can use images to render avatar body parts and employ geometrical transformations to move and shape the parts. A human-like avatar geometric model consists of joints and body segments. The 3D positions of these joints, governed by the movement mechanism or pre-generated motion data, uniquely define the avatar's gesture at a moment. The entire animation process is used to find the joint coordinates of each frame in terms of animation time.

If we project every segment of the 3D avatar separately onto the projection plane, the synthesis of these projected 2D images will be the final image of the 3D avatar we actually see on the screen, provided the segment depth values are taken into account appropriately. Therefore, avatar walking can be simulated by the appropriate transformations of the avatar segment images. From this point of view, the avatar's walking is the same as its segments' movements in the 3D space. Here, the basic idea is to reuse the snapshot segment images over several frames rather than rendering the avatar for each frame from the geometric model directly. The complicated human-like 3D avatar model is used only for capturing body segment images when they need to be updated. The subsequent animation frames are dynamically generated through 2D transformations and synthesis of the snapshot segment images.

11.5 Animation and Simulation

Computer *animation* is achieved by refreshing the screen display with a sequence of images at more than 24 frames per second. *Keyframe* animation is achieved by using pre-calculated keyframe images and in-between images, which may take a significant amount of time, and then displaying (playing back) the sequence of generated images in real time. Keyframe animation is often used for visual effects in films and TV commercials, where no interactions or unpredictable changes are necessary. Interactive animation, on the other hand, is achieved by calculating, generating, and displaying the images simultaneously on the fly. When we talk about *real-time animation*, we mean the virtual animation occurring in the same time frames as real world behavior. However, for graphics researchers, real-time animation often simply implies the animation is smooth or interactive. Real-time animation is often used in virtual environments for education, training, and 3D games. Many modeling and rendering tools are also animation tools, which are often associated with simulation.

Simulation, on the other hand, is a software system we construct, execute, and experiment with to understand the behavior of the real world or imaginary system, which often means a process of generating certain natural phenomena through scientific computation. The simulation results may be large datasets of atomic activities (positions, velocities, pressures, and other parameters of atoms) or fluid behaviors (volume of vectors and pressures). Computer simulation allows scientists to generate the atomic behavior of certain nanostructured materials for understanding material structure and durability and to find new compounds with superior quality. Simulation integrated with visualization can help pilots learn to fly and aid automobile designers in testing the integrity of the passenger compartment during crashes. For many computational scientists, simulation may not be related to any visualization at all. However, for many graphics researchers, simulation often simply means animation. Today, graphical simulation, or simply simulation, is an animation of a certain process or behavior that is often generated through scientific computation and modeling. Here we emphasize an integration of simulation and animation — the simulated results are used to generate graphics models and control animation behaviors. It is far easier, cheaper, and safer to experiment with a model through simulation than with a real entity. In fact, in many situations, such as training space-shuttle pilots and studying molecular dynamics, modeling and simulation are the only feasible methods to achieve the goals. *Real-time simulation* is an overloaded term. To computational scientists, it often means the simulation time is the actual time in which the physical process (under simulation) should occur. In automatic control, it means the output response time is fast enough for automatic feedback and control. In graphics, it often means that the simulation is animated at an interactive rate of human perception. The emphasis in graphics is more on responsiveness and smooth animation rather than strictly accurate timing of the physical process. In many simulation-for-training applications, the emphasis is on generating realistic behavior for interactive training environments rather than strictly scientific or physical computation.

11.5.1 Physics-Based Modeling and Simulation: Triangular Polyhedra

A *polyhedron* is an arbitrary 3D shape whose surface is a collection of flat polygons. A *regular* polyhedron is one whose faces and vertices all look the same. There are only five regular polyhedra: the *tetrahedron* — 4 faces with three equilateral triangles at a vertex; the *cube* — 6 faces with three squares at a vertex; the *octahedron* — 8 faces with four equilateral triangles at a vertex; the *dodecahedron* — 12 faces with three pentagons at a vertex; and the *icosahedron* — 20 faces with five equilateral triangles at a vertex. The regular polyhedron models can be found in many books and graphics packages. However, the complex polyhedron model requires effort to be constructed.

Physics-based modeling (also called physically-based modeling) is a modeling method that employs physics laws to construct models. Here, we use the physics-based modeling method to construct some polyhedra. Given an arbitrary number n, we construct a triangular polyhedron model of n vertices such that the distance from each vertex to the origin equals one, and the distances between the neighboring vertices are as far distant as possible. Let's assume that the radius of the polyhedron is one. The method includes the following steps:

1. Generate n arbitrary vertices *vtx[i]* in 3D space for $i=0$ to $n-1$. Each vertex is an imaginary object with mass M.

2. Normalize the vertices so that the distance from each vertex to the origin is one. The vertices can be viewed as vectors. A normalized vector has unit length.

3. Establish a physical relation between each pair of vertices by connecting them with an imaginary spring. The spring is at rest when the distance between the vertices is two, which is the farthest distance on a sphere of unit radius. Otherwise, the spring will apply an attracting or repelling force on the two vertices. According to Hooke's law, the spring force on vertex i from all vertices j is:

```
f[i].x = f[i].y = f[i].z = 0;
```

```
for (j = 0; j < n; j++) if (i != j) {
  f[i].x = f[i].x + K*(direction.x*2 - vtx[i].x + vtx[j].x);
  f[i].y = f[i].y + K*(direction.y*2 - vtx[i].y + vtx[j].y);
  f[i].z = f[i].z + K*(direction.z*2 - vtx[i].z + vtx[j].z);
}
```

where K is the spring coefficient and *direction* is a unit vector along vertex i and j. Since x, y, and z components are basically the same and independent, in the rest of the discussion we only present the x component.

As we know, a spring will bounce back and forth forever if there is no damping force. Therefore, we add an air friction force proportional to the vertex's velocity. The vertices will eventually converge to stable coordinates after a number of iterations:

```
f[i].x = f[i].x - K1*dv[i].x;
// K1 is the velocity damping coefficient
```

4. Calculate the new coordinates of the vertices after a short period DT according to the physics relation: for each vertex,

```
ddv[i].x = f[i].x/M;
// the acceleration
```

```
dv[i].x = dv[i].x + ddv[i].x*DT;
// the new velocity and
```

```
vtx[i].x = vtx[i].x + dv[i].x*DT;
// the new position.
```

5. Repeat Steps 2 to 4 until a satisfactory condition is reached. Draw the current polyhedron. A satisfactory condition can be, for example, that each vertex velocity is smaller than some criterion.

The samples and source code for the above modeling method are at: http:// graphics.gmu.edu/polyhedra/

In the program, we can construct and display an equilateral triangle, a tetrahedron, an octahedron, or an icosahedron (Fig. 11.3) by simply specifying 3, 4,

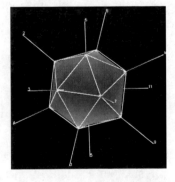

Fig. 11.3 An icosahedron

6, or 12 vertices respectively. We can also construct many specific irregular polyhedra. From the above example, we know that we can achieve many different shapes by specifying different physics relations among the vertices and the origin. This method is totally different from the traditional methods used to construct polyhedron models. Instead of using mathematical relations to find out the exact vertex coordinates, it relies on physics relations to dynamically construct the models. The construction process is a simulation of the designed physics relations. Many complex models could be constructed easily this way. Today, physics-based modeling is employed in some advanced graphics modeling tools for constructing certain 3D models.

11.5.2 Real-time Animation and Simulation: a Spider Web

The display refresh rate is the rate of reading from the frame buffer and sending the pixels to the display by the video controller. A refresh rate at 60 (frames per second) is smoother than one at 30, and 120 is marginally better than 60. However, if the image frame rate is much lower, the animation could be jittery. Sometimes, it is an easy-to-be-rendered model that takes time to be constructed. Sometimes, it is an easy-to-be-constructed model that takes time to be rendered. To achieve smooth animation, we need high performance algorithms as well as graphics hardware to efficiently carry out modeling, simulation, and graphics rendering. Graphical simulation, or simply simulation, animates certain processes or behaviors generated through scientific computation and modeling. A *simulation model* is a physics or math description of the simulated entity or system. Simulation can be used to achieve a static graphics model like a polyhedron, or dynamic behavior like a waving spider web. In the above example of modeling polyhedra, the simulation model describes the physical relationships among the vertices. The simulated results are used to generate the graphics models and control the animation behavior. That is, the simulation model describes the graphics model, and the graphics model is the simulation result.

A real-time simulation is a simulation where the time is the actual time in which the physical process (under simulation) occurs. Many real-time simulation systems are *event-driven*, in which the evolution of the simulation is determined by the complexity of both the computation and the graphics rendering. A real-time simulation can be synchronized with a wall clock, so that the simulation proceeds accurately on the physical time scale we perceive. The simulation will appear at the same speed on different computing platforms. The method is as follows. A variable (lastTime) is used to record the last time the simulation updated its state. Each time the simulation begins to update its state, it reads the computer's clock to get the current time (currentTime) and subtract lastTime from currentTime to determine the period between the current time and the last time when the state was updated. This period, the time slice passed — together with the simulation's old state — determines the simulation's new state. At the same time, lastTime will be updated to currentTime.

Real-time simulation often employs a wide range of physical laws that are functions of time. To retain numerical stability and to limit the numerical offset error, many activities cannot be calculated with a time slice bigger than a threshold. However, varying time slices between states can be so large that the numerical computation of the physics-based model diverges. Our solution to this problem is as follows. Let's assume that DT satisfies numerical stability and at simulation state m the time slice is DT_m. When DT_m is larger than DT, DT_m can be divided into a number of DTs and the physical phenomena can be simulated DT_m/DT times. The residue of the time division can be added to the next simulation period.

As an example, we simulate a spider walking on a web in real time synchronized with the wall clock. Again, we use springs to construct the simulation model. The data structure for the web is as in Fig. 11.4. The modeling method mainly includes the following steps:

1. Generate *4* vertex arrays *a[i], b[i], c[i], and d[i]* in 3D space for *i=0* to *n-1*. Each vertex is an imaginary object with mass *M*.

2. Fix the end points of the vertex arrays.

3. Rotate the web into an orientation of your choice. The vector *down* is a fixed direction pointing towards the ground after the rotation.

4. Establish a physical relationship between neighboring vertices by connecting them with a spring line, as in Fig. 11.4. The spring is at rest when the distance between the vertices is zero. Otherwise, the spring will apply an attracting force on the two neighboring

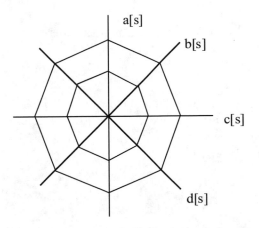

Fig. 11.4 A spiderweb data structure

vertices. According to Hooke's law, the spring force *Fa[i]* on vertex *a[i]* includes 4 components (in x, y, and z direction, respectively; here we only show the force in x direction):

```
Fa[i].x = K*(a[i+1].x - a[i].x) + K*(a[i-1].x - a[i].x);
// the force generated by
// the 2 springs along the diagonal line

Fa[i].x = Fa[i].x + K1*(b[i].x-a[i].x)+
        K1*(d[S-1-i].x-a[i].x);
// the force generated by
// the 2 springs along the circle line

Fa[i].x = Fa[i].x - K2*da[i].x;
// the air damping force according to
// the velocity of a[i]

Fa[i].x = Fa[i].x + gravity*down.x;
// the gravity force so the web will be
// drawn towards the ground

If (spider is at a[i])
    Fa[i].x = Fa[i].x + spiderWeight*down.x;
// the spider's weight. The spider is
// moving around on the web
```

5. Calculate the new coordinates of the vertices after a period

```
DTm = period() + (DTm % DT);
```

where *period()* returns the clock time passed since last time we updated the vertices, and *(DTm % DT)* is the remainder time from the last simulation. We repeat the following simulation *(DTm/DT)* times (except the acceleration, which only calculates once):

```
dda[i].x = fa[i].x/M;
// the acceleration

da[i].x = da[i].x + dda[i].x*DT;
// the new velocity and

a[i] = a[i]+da[i]*DT;
// the new position
```

6. Draw the current spider and web.

7. Move the spider. Repeat Steps 3 to 7.

Fig. 11.5 is a snapshot of the simulation result: a spider walking on the web. We may have multiple spiders in the environment as well. The samples and source code for the above modeling method are on line at: `http:// graphics.gmu.edu/spider/`

11.5.3 The Efficiency of Modeling and Simulation

Fortunately, in the above example the simulation and graphics rendering are both fast enough on an ordinary PC to achieve the web and spider behavior in

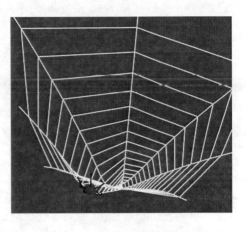

Fig. 11.5 A simulation of a spider web

real time. More often than not, the simulation efficiency and the physical and visual realism are contradictory to the point that we cannot achieve both. To achieve real time, we sacrifice the physical realism and/or the visual quality by simplifying the complex physics-based model and/or the graphics rendering method. The 3D graphics rendering speed is often the bottleneck of real-time simulation. The bottom line is that the associated processing loads must not reduce the system update rate below what we consider to be real time (24 frames per second). We can improve the simulation efficiency by changing the software or hardware, or both, to accommodate real time. A real-time graphics simulation pipeline is a loop that includes the following major processes:

1. Handle user input (keyboard, mouse, external sensors, VR trackers, etc.);

2. Calculate the new state of the simulation model;

3. Pre-process 3D objects (collision detection, clipping/culling, organization, etc.);

4. Render the virtual world. Repeat Steps 1 to 4.

Software Methods. For Step 2, we can simplify the simulation model to the point that it satisfies the minimum requirements, or use a simpler model that achieves the partial requirements. For Step 3, where there are different algorithms that provide collision detection and other graphics preprocessing functions, we can choose the most efficient algorithms. For Step 4, we have different rendering methods that will significantly change the efficiency. For example, we can use polygons instead of curved surfaces, shaded polygons instead of texture mapped polygons, flat polygons instead of shaded polygons, wire-frame objects instead of polygonal objects, etc. Choosing graphics rendering methods to improve efficiency often requires more understanding of the graphics system.

Hardware Methods. Many low-level graphics functions are implemented in the hardware on a graphics card. In fact, without a graphics card, no graphical simulation can be in real time. However, not all graphics cards are the same. Some functions are expensive to implement in hardware. The prices on the graphics cards are different. Therefore, it is important to know what graphics functions are necessary, and to purchase the card that comes with the necessary functions. For example, if a simulation application requires large-number polygon rendering, we may choose a specially configured intensive-polygon-rendering hardware. If a simulation requires frequent texture mapping, we will need texture mapping hardware. Texture mapping would be extremely slow if there were no hardware support. Some high performance graphics cards, such as Intense3D Wildcat 5110, have very large dedicated texture memory and frame buffers for hardware texture mapping. Hardware makes it possible to achieve advanced graphics effects such as lighting, texture mapping, volume rendering, antialiasing, and scene accumulation in real time.

11.6 Virtual Reality

Virtual Reality (VR) extends the 3D graphics world to include stereoscopic, acoustic, haptic, tactile, and other kinds of feedback to create a sense of immersion. A 3D image is like any ordinary picture we see, but a stereo image gives a strong sense of depth in 3D. It is generated by providing two slightly different views (images) of the same object to our two eyes separately.

The head-mounted device (HMD), the ImmersaDesk/CAVE, and the VREX stereo projectors are different kinds of display devices for stereo images. An HMD like VR8 has two separate display channels/screens to cover our two eyes. An ImmersaDesk or CAVE has only one channel, like an ordinary display screen, except that it displays two different images alternatively for our two eyes. Lightweight liquid crystal shutter glasses are worn by the viewer. These glasses activate each eye in succession. The glasses are kept synchronized with the two images through an infrared emitter. CAVE is the predecessor of ImmersaDesk, which is more expensive and has multiple display screens surrounding the viewer. Usually it has four walls (left, right, front, and ceiling walls). An ImmersaDesk can be considered to be a movable/flip-able one-wall CAVE. VREX's stereo projectors generate two images at the same time that can be viewed through lightweight, inexpensive polarized glasses.

The key hardware technologies for achieving VR are real-time graphics generators, stereo displays/views, tracking sensors, sound machines, and haptic devices. Real-time graphics (computer) and stereo displays (HMD, ImmersaDesk, CAVE, or VREX projectors) allow the user to view stereoscopic scenes and animation, and provide the user a sense of immersion. Tracking sensors, which get the position and orientation of the user's head, hands, body parts, or other inputs, enable the user to manipulate models and navigate in the virtual environment. Sound machines provide a sense of location and orientation of certain objects and activities in the environment. Like sound machines, haptic devices vibrate and touch the user's body, generating another feedback from the virtual environment in addition to stereoscopic view and 3D sound, enhancing the sense of immersion.

Some VR software tools are available that recognize well-defined commercial tracking sensors, sound machines, and haptic devices, in addition to functions for developing 3D virtual environments. SunMicrosystem's Java3D and Sense8's WorldToolKit are cross-platform software development systems for building real-time integrated 3D applications. MultiGen-Paradigm's Vega is a real-time visual and audio simulation software tool that includes stereo imaging. OpenInventor (based on SGI's Inventor standard) is a real-time programming system that sits on top of a graphics library. Lincom's VrTool is an OpenInventor-based toolkit used to provide a rapid prototyping capability that enables VR users to quickly get their application running with the minimum amount of effort. These VR tools are scene-graph based programming environments. *Scene-graph* is a data structure that describes 3D objects and environments.

Often non-immersive 3D graphics systems are also called VR systems. VRML (Virtual Reality Modeling Language) is a web-based 3D scene description language based on Inventor's 3D scene-graph structure. ActiveWorlds and DIVE (Distributed Interactive Virtual Environment) are internet-based multi-user VR systems where participants navigate in 3D space and see, meet and interact with other users and applications.

11.7 Graphics on the Internet: Web3D

The Internet has been the most dynamic new technology in the past decade. Many web-based 3D modeling, rendering, and animation tools have emerged. It is not difficult to foresee that Web3D will be the future of education, visualization, advertising, shopping, communication, and entertainment. Currently, most Web3D tools are individual plug-ins for a general web browser. Most of the tools are built on OpenGL or Direct3D, such as VRML browser and the Java3D programming environment.

11.7.1 Virtual Reality Modeling Language (VRML)

VRML is a scene description language that presents 3D objects and environments over the Internet. It is also a file format that defines the layout and content of a 3D world. VRML worlds usually have the file extension *.wrl* or *.wrl.gz* as opposed to *.html*. When a web browser sees a file with the *.wrl* file extension, it launches the VRML engine, which is usually a plug-in viewer. A VRML file containing complex interactive 3D worlds is similar to an ordinary HTML page in size.

11.7.2 Java3D

Java3D by Sun Microsystem, is a scene-graph based 3D API that runs on multiple platforms, which can be deployed over the Internet. 3D graphics can be easily integrated with Java applications and applets. VRML and other 3D files can be loaded into the Java3D environment, which are controlled and manipulated according to the program and user interactions.

On top of lower graphics libraries, many new web-based 3D API engines similar to Java3D have been developed by individuals and companies. VRML, HTML, Java, Java3D, Streaming Media, and dynamic database are evolving technologies, which will enable a new kind of 3D Hypermedia Web site.

12
Low-Level Graphics Libraries

Chapter Objectives:

- Introduce some basic graphics libraries
- Compile a reference list of low-level graphics libraries

12.1 Introduction

A low-level graphics library or package is a standard that defines the graphics functions. It is a software interface to graphics hardware, namely the application programmer's interface (API). It provides a set of graphics functions or output subroutines, which can specify primitive geometric models and their attributes to digitize and display. Some graphics subroutines or functions are integrated with special graphics hardware to improve the speed efficiency. Therefore, some graphics libraries are device dependent, which are implemented on specific platforms. Every graphics tool or application is built on top of a specific low-level graphics library.

12.2 OpenGL and Mesa

OpenGL is the most widely adopted device-independent 3D graphics API. It was first developed by SGI from its early device dependent GL (graphics library). Now the OpenGL Architecture Review Board (ARB) with leading computer companies controls the OpenGL technology standard (`http://www.opengl.org`). We have used OpenGL as an API to introduce the basic graphics principles of this book.

J.X. Chen, *Guide to Graphics Software Tools*, doi: 10.1007/978-1-84800-901-1_12,
© Springer-Verlag London Limited 2008

Mesa was developed by Brian Paul to simulate OpenGL functions on UNIX platforms that did not support OpenGL at the time (http://www.mesa3d.org/). Today, Mesa is the most convenient OpenGL API on Linux and an open software implementation for learners as well as developers to use and study.

12.3 Direct3D/DirectX

Microsoft's Direct3D is the de facto standard 3D graphics API for the Windows platform. It has an OpenGL-comparable feature set. Both Direct3D and OpenGL are widely supported by PC hardware graphics card vendors. Direct3D is part of DirectX, which is a set of APIs (DirectDraw, DirectSound, DirectPlay, Direct3D, DirectInput), available as COM (Component Object Model) objects. These APIs provide objects and functions for developing real-time, high-performance games and other applications on the Windows platform.

12.4 PHIGS and GKS-3D

PHIGS and GKS-3D are international standards that were defined in the 1980s. Some high-level graphics packages have been developed on PHIGS or GSK-3D. Many OpenGL and Direct3D functions have been evolved from the PHIGS or GKS-3D functions.

12.5 QuickDraw3D and XGL

QuickDraw3D is a relatively new graphics library that is implemented on top of QuickTime by Apple Computer. XGL is a graphics library developed by SUN Microsystems. An XGL application runs within a window environment managed by an X11 compatible server, such as the X11 server within Sun's OpenWindows environment. Both QuickDraw3D and XGL include drawing 3D primitives directly.

13
Visualization

Chapter Objectives:

- Introduce different visualization methods and tools
- Compile a reference list of visualization tools

13.1 Introduction

Visualization, the use of computer graphics to gain insight into complex phenomena, is a powerful instrument. Many visualization tools, built on top of a graphics library, are developed for certain applications, such as AVS for spatial and engineering data, Star-CD for CFD data, and 3DVIEWNIX for medical image data. Some of them are more general, while others are more specific to certain types of data. They provide insightful visualization solutions, but they more or less lose the flexibility of a low level graphics library as a general tool. We need either to find a good match of the visualization tool to our application, or to develop our own visualization application from a graphics library.

Visualization employs graphics to make pictures that give us insight into certain abstract data and symbols. The pictures may directly portray the description of the data, or completely present the content of the data in an innovative form. Many commercial and free visualization software packages exist in different application areas: medical imaging, computational fluid dynamics visualization, large-data-set visualization, information visualization, etc. It is difficult to categorize visualization tools since most of the tools contain a variety of functions covering many different applications. Many tools have overlapping visualization functions. Some tools include

J.X. Chen, *Guide to Graphics Software Tools*, doi: 10.1007/978-1-84800-901-1_13,
© Springer-Verlag London Limited 2008

the capabilities to do interactive modeling, animation, simulation, and graphical user interface construction. In the following, we briefly introduce several visualization tools as examples for different applications.

13.2 Multipurpose Visualization Tools

AVS/Express, IRIS Explorer, Data Explorer, MATLAB, PV-WAVE, Khoros, and VTK are multiple purpose visualization commercial products. AVS/Express has applications in many scientific areas, including engineering analysis, CFD, medical imaging, and GIS (Geographic Information Systems). It is built on top of OpenGL and runs on multiple platforms. IRIS Explorer includes visual programming environment for 3D data visualization, animation and manipulation. IRIS Explorer modules can be plugged together, which enable users to interactively analyze collections of data and visualize the results. IRIS Explorer is build on top of OpenInventor, an interactive 3D object scene management, manipulation, and animation tool. OpenInventor has been used as the basis for the emerging Virtual Reality Modeling Language (VRML). The rendering engine for IRIS Explorer and OpenInventor are OpenGL. IBM's Data Explorer (DX) is a general-purpose software package for data visualization and analysis. OpenDX is the open source software version of the DX Product. DX is build on top of OpenGL and runs on multiple platforms. MATLAB was originally developed to provide easy access to matrix software. Today, it is a powerful simulation and visualization tool used in a variety of application areas including signal and image processing, control system design, financial engineering, and medical research. PV-WAVE integrates charting, volume visualization, image processing, advanced numerical analysis, and many other functions. Khoros is a software integration, simulation, and visual programming environment that includes image processing and visualization. VTK is a graphics tool that supports a variety of visualization and modeling functions on multiple platforms. In VTK, applications can be written directly in C++ or in Tcl (an interpretive language).

13.3 Volume Rendering

Volume rendering or visualization is a method of extracting meaningful information from a set of volumetric data. It is also called imaging if the volumetric data are images. A sequence of 2D image slices of a body part can be reconstructed into a 3D volume model and visualized for diagnostic purposes or for planning treatment or surgery. For example, a set of volumetric data such as a deck of Magnetic Resonance Imaging (MRI) slices or Computed Tomography (CT) can be blended into a 2D X-ray image by firing rays through the volume and blending the voxels (volume pixels) along the rays. This is a rather costly operation and the blending methods vary.

The concept of volume rendering is also to extract the contours from given data slices. An isosurface is a 3D constant intensity surface represented by triangle strips or higher order surface patches within a volume. For example, the voxels on the surface of bones in a deck of MRI slices appear to be same intensity value. The Marching Cubes algorithm, which was introduced by Lorenson and Cline, examines each cubic element in the volume data and determines what the topology of an isosurface passing through this element would be.

3DVIEWNIX, Volumizer, ANALYZE, and VolVis are 3D imaging and volume rendering tools. The NIH's Visible Human Project (`http://www.nlm.nih.gov/research/visible/visible_human.html`) has created anatomically detailed 3D representations of the human body. The project has included the efforts of several universities and resulted in many imaging tools.

13.4 Vector Field and Fluid Flow

Tecplot, StarCD, FAST, pV3, FIELDVIEW, EnSight, and Visual3 are CFD (Computational Fluid Dynamics) visualization tools. Fluid flow is a rich area for visualization applications. Many CFD tools integrate interactive visualization with scientific computation of turbulence or plasmas for the design of new wings or jet nozzles, the prediction of atmospheric and oceanic activities, and the understanding of material behaviors.

13.5 Large Data Sets

The visualization of the large data sets from physical and natural sciences employ statistical analyses, cartography, Computer Aided Design (CAD), multiresolution analyses, and Geographic Information Systems (GIS) techniques. The integration of multidisciplinary data and information (e.g. atmospheric, oceanographic, and geographic) into visualization systems will help and support cross-disciplinary explorations and communications. The variety of data comes with different data geometries, sampling rates, and error characteristics.

NCAR, Vis5D, FERRET, GNUplot, and SciAn are software tools for visual presentation and examination of datasets from the physical and natural sciences, often requiring the integration of terabyte or gigabyte distributed scientific databases with visualization.

14
Modeling and Rendering

Chapter Objectives:

- Introduce different modeling, rendering, and animation tools
- Compile a reference list of modeling tools
- Compile a reference list of rendering tools

14.1 Modeling

Modeling is a process of constructing a 3D model from a real object or an imaginary entity. Modeling tools help create virtual objects and environments for CAD (computer-aided design), visualization, education, training, and entertainment. MultigenPro is a powerful modeling tool for 3D models and terrain generation/editing. AutoCAD and MicroStation are popular for 2D/3D mechanical designing and drawing. 3D Studio Viz is a multifunction tool for architectural and industrial designs. Rhino3D is for freeform curve surface models.

14.2 Rendering

Rendering is a process of creating images from graphics models. 3D graphics models are generated on the fly or loaded in computer memory from hard-disk files. The terms rasterization and scan-conversion are used to refer to low-level image generation. All modeling tools provide certain drawing capabilities to visualize the models generated. However, in addition to simply drawing (scan-converting) geometric objects, rendering tools often include lighting, shading, texture mapping,

J.X. Chen, *Guide to Graphics Software Tools*, doi: 10.1007/978-1-84800-901-1_14,
© Springer-Verlag London Limited 2008

color blending, raytracing, radiosity, and other advanced graphics capabilities. For example, RenderMan Toolkit includes photorealistic modeling and rendering of particle system, hair, and many other objects with advanced graphics functions such as raytracing, volume display, motion blur, depth-of-field, and so forth. Some successful rendering tools were free (originally developed by excellent researchers at their earlier career or school years), such as POVRay, LightScape, Rayshade, Radiance, and BMRT. POVRay is a popular raytracing package across multiple platforms that provides a set of geometric primitives and many surface and texture effects. LightScape employs radiosity and raytracing to produce realistic digital images and scenes. Rayshade is an extensible system for creating ray-traced images that includes a rich set of primitives, CSG (constructive solid geometry) functions, and texture tools. Radiance is a rendering package for the analysis and visualization of lighting in design. It is employed by architects and engineers to predict illumination, visual quality and appearance of design spaces, and by researchers to evaluate new lighting technologies. BMRT (Blue Moon Rendering Tools) is a RenderMan-compliant raytracing and radiosity rendering package. The package contains visual tools to help users create RenderMan Input Bytestream (RIB) input files.

14.3 Multipurpose Tools: Modeling, Rendering, and Animation

Many powerful graphics tools include modeling, rendering, animation, and other functions into one package, such as Alias|Wavefront's Studio series and Maya, SoftImage, 3DStudioMax, LightWave, and TrueSpace. It takes serious course training to use these tools. Alias|Wavefront's Studio series provide extensive tools for industrial design, automotive styling, and technical surfacing. Its Maya is a powerful and productive 3D software for character animation that has been used to create visual effects in some of the hottest recent film releases, including *A Bug's Life* and *Titanic*. SoftImage3D provides advanced modeling and animation features such as NURBS, skin, and particle systems that are excellent for special effects and have been employed in many computer games and films, including stunning animations in *Deep Impact* and *Air Force One*. 3DStudioMax is a popular 3D modeling, animation, and rendering package on the Windows platform for game development. Its open plug-in architecture makes it an idea platform for third party developer. LightWave is a powerful tool that has been successfully used in many TV feature movies, games, and

TV commercials. TrueSpace is another popular and powerful 3D modeling, animation, and rendering package for the Windows platform.

15
Animation and Simulation

Chapter Objectives:

- Introduce different animation and simulation tools
- Compile a reference list of animation tools
- Compile a reference list of simulation tools

15.1 Animation

Animation is an integral part of interactive computer graphics. Most visualization, modeling, rendering, and simulation tools, such as OpenInventor, Maya, Lightwave3D, and Activeworlds, include animation. In traditional storyboard animation, a high-level sequence of sketches are first developed, then keyframes and soundtrack are decided upon, the keyframes where sounds occur are correlated, and finally the inbetweenings are interpolated between keyframes. In computer graphics, animation is mostly interactive geometry or image transformations.

Computer animation is achieved by drawing frames of different images at more than 24 frames per second. To achieve smooth animation, we need high performance algorithms as well as graphics hardware to carry out scene modification and rendering efficiently. 3D Choreographer is an animation program designed for non-artists. Outlining your animation is as simple as casting "Actors", drawing "Paths", and issuing "Scripts". Poser 4 is a 3D-character animation and design tool for artists and animators. AnimationMaster is a spline based animation program that provides advanced features like inverse kinematics, raytracing, image mapping, and modeling of complex organic and mechanical objects. b3d Studio is an editing and production

J.X. Chen, *Guide to Graphics Software Tools*, doi: 10.1007/978-1-84800-901-1_15,
© Springer-Verlag London Limited 2008

package for 3D animated movies. Motivate 3D is primarily an animation tool for developing 3D games and interactive multimedia titles.

15.2 Simulation

A simulation is a process of constructing, executing, and visualizing a model to collect pertinent information about the behavior of a real-world or imaginary system. Here the model is a math, physics, or engineering representation of the system with its many characteristics. A graphical simulation emphasizes animation and visualization of the simulation process. A real-time simulation is one in which the time seems to be the actual time in which the physical process under simulation occurs. In graphics, it often means that the simulation is smoothly animated. Many real-time simulation systems are event-driven, in which the evolution of the simulation is determined by the complexity of both the computation and the graphics rendering.

Many animation tools, interactive game engines, and virtual environment enabling systems, such as Softimage, NetImmerse, Genesis3D, WorldUp, and ActiveWorlds, are also simulation tools, because they provide the means and environments to achieve significant simulations. IRIS Performer is a toolkit for real-time graphics simulation applications. It simplifies development of complex applications such as visual simulation, flight simulation, simulation-based design, virtual reality, interactive entertainment, broadcast video, CAD, and architectural walk-throughs. Vega is MultiGen-Paradigm's software environment for real-time visual and audio simulation, virtual reality, and general visualization applications. It provides the basis for building, editing, and running sophisticated applications quickly and easily. 20-sim is a modeling and simulation program for electrical, mechanical, and hydraulic systems or any combination of these systems. Mathematica is an integrated environment that provides technical computing, simulation, and communication. Its numeric and symbolic computation abilities, graphical simulation, and intuitive programming language are combined with a full-featured document processing system. MATLAB and Khoros contain modeling and simulation functions.

16
Virtual Reality

Chapter Objectives:

- Introduce different virtual reality methods and tools
- Compile a reference list of virtual reality tools

16.1 Virtual Reality

Virtual Reality (VR) can be divided into two categories: immersive VR and non-immersive VR. In an immersive VR system, users wear head-mounted devices (HMD) or special glasses to view stereoscopic images. The viewpoint usually follows the viewer's head movement in real time. In a non-immersive VR, which is usually a lot cheaper, users usually do not wear any device, and the viewpoint does not follow the user's head movement. But users navigate in the virtual world through input devices interactively and the image is usually a first-person view. In a VR system, navigation allows a user to move around and to view virtual objects and places, and interaction provides an active way for a user to control the appearance and behavior of objects.

A VR system is also a simulation system that describes and simulates certain real-world activities in various areas such as training, education, and entertainment. Therefore, many simulation tools like Vega and WorldUp are also VR tools. A VR system always repeats the following processing steps:

1. Handle user inputs from various devices — keyboard, mouse, VR trackers, sensors, voice recognition systems, etc.

J.X. Chen, *Guide to Graphics Software Tools,* doi: 10.1007/978-1-84800-901-1_16,
© Springer-Verlag London Limited 2008

2. Calculate the new state of the objects and the environment according to the simulation models.

3. Pre-process 3D objects including collision detection, levels of detail, clipping/culling, etc.

4. Render the virtual world.

In Step 2, different VR applications may use different simulation models. No matter what application a VR system implements, the software to handle the other three steps, a high-level graphics library called a VR tool (or VR toolkit), is always needed. Therefore, VR tools are usually independent of the applications. A VR system is usually a VR application implemented on top of a VR tool, which provides an API for the VR application to manipulate the objects according to the simulation models. VR tools are likely to be device dependent, built on low-level basic graphics libraries with interfaces to sensory devices.

Some VR tools, such as MR Toolkit, OpenInventor, and WorldToolkit, only provide APIs embedded in certain programming languages for VR developers. It requires more knowledge and programming skills to employ these toolkits, but they provide more flexibility in application implementations. Others, such as Alice and WorldUp (often called VR simulation tools), provide graphical user interfaces (GUIs) for the developers to build applications. Developers achieve virtual worlds and simulations by typing, clicking, and dragging through GUIs. Sometimes simple script languages are used to construct simulation processes. VR simulation tools allow developing a VR system quicker and easier, but the application developed is an independent fixed module that cannot be modified or integrated in a user-developed program. A VR simulation tool is generally developed on top of a VR toolkit, so it is one level higher than the VR toolkit in the VR software levels.

17
Web3D Tools and Networked Environment

Chapter Objectives:

- Introduce Web3D and distributed interactive simulation in a networked environment
- Compile a list of Web3D tools

17.1 Web3D

Web3D tools are graphics tools that deliver graphics through web browsers over the Internet. Many web-based 3D modeling, rendering, and animation tools emerged recently. It is not difficult to foresee that Web3D will be the future of education, visualization, advertising, shopping, communication, and entertainment. Currently, most Web3D tools are individual plug-ins for a general web browser. Most of the tools, such as VRML browser and the Java3D programming environment, are built on OpenGL or Direct3D. Individuals and companies have developed many new Web-based 3D API engines (similar to Java3D) on top of lower-level graphics libraries.

17.2 Distributed Interactive Simulation

In addition to Web3D tools, networked virtual environments have been developed to simulate highly interactive activities in critical mission training. Unlike Web3D tools, which develop applications for independent users without real-time constraints, distributed interactive simulation (DIS) systems immerse networked users in the same virtual environments across the network in real time.

J.X. Chen, *Guide to Graphics Software Tools,* doi: 10.1007/978-1-84800-901-1_17,
© Springer-Verlag London Limited 2008

In a distributed interactive virtual environment, multiple nodes (computer simulators) at different locations have the same entities (objects) and activities (behavior). NPSNET (www.npsnet.org/), MUVE (http://www.virtual.gmu.edu/muvees/), ExploreNet (http://www.cs.ucf.edu/ExploreNet/) are examples of such kind of environments. Today, most DIS environments call for a centralized infrastructure to control and manage information. The High Level Architecture (HLA) with a Run Time Infrastructure (RTI), which builds upon and generalizes the results in DIS, is advocated by the US government. HLA allows for nodes to coordinate the execution and exchange of information through the RTI.

There are two layers of communications in DIS/HLA: communicating between the multiple nodes at the network communication layer and synchronizing physical activities on top of the network communication. The low-level communication protocol determines the efficiency and reliability of the message transmission. The high-level time synchronization is vital for achieving fast DIS. Better solutions to these problems will improve the usability and speedup the simulation in DIS/HLA. For example, in Doom — a simple distributed multi-player game system — each node simply *broadcasts* the location of each entity that it maintains. Communication delay for time synchronization is ignored.

17.3 Synchronization in a DIS

When implementing a DIS/HLA, the commonly accepted approach to limit the rate of simultaneous updating of multiple nodes on a distributed simulation network is termed *Dead Reckoning*. Dead Reckoning is a method of position/orientation estimation that predicts and approximates the behavior of simulated entities among the networked nodes. Dead Reckoning's estimations eliminate the need for sending every change in position/orientation until a pre-specified threshold is exceeded; then, the behavior of the entities that changed is updated by new data sent across the network. In a DIS/HLA, an entity is either an *object* or a *ghost*. An object is the master entity running on its host node where the user controls its activities. Its copies running on other networked nodes are called its (Dead Reckoning) ghosts. The user has no control over the activities of ghosts, which proceed according to their object's original parameters (position, orientation, velocity, acceleration, etc). A ghost is running on the host node as well, so that Dead Reckoning algorithm can compare the parameters of the object and the ghost on the host node to estimate the errors in the networked ghosts, and update the ghosts with the object's parameters if necessary.

In a Dead Reckoning process, the logical time step used has to be synchronized (or uniform) across the network. The time management to synchronize the networked activities has been a major research issue. Centralized control and event-driven methods use time step ticks (heartbeats) to achieve the synchronization. In an event-driven system, the evolution of the simulation is determined both by the computational complexity of simulated objects and by the rapidity of network communication to update the behavior of those objects. Simulations involving close coordination of entities over long distances across multiple network nodes are not practical due to the introduction of unpredictable, but significant, latencies. The Clock Reckoning strategy uses system clocks to synchronize distributed entities across the network. Here, the physical time and simulation time are all unified under wall clock time.

17.3.1 The Clock Reckoning — Wall Clock Synchronization

The Clock Reckoning strategy uses a wall clock to synchronize distributed entities across the network. Each entity will have a local variable (lastTime) used to record the last time this entity updated its state. Each time an entity begins to update its state, it reads the host node's clock to get the current time (currentTime) and subtracts lastTime from currentTime to determine the period between the current time and the last time when the state was updated. This value is the time-step passed; its value together with the entity's old state uniquely determines its new state. At the same time, lastTime will be updated to currentTime. Overall, each entity proceeds at its own pace synchronized by a uniform time scale of the wall clock. No time step ticks are needed.

The next stage of the Clock Reckoning strategy involves synchronizing state-updates across multiple nodes, providing inter-entity synchronization across the network. When an entity receives a network update message, it must compute the network delay between the time when the message was sent and when it is received. The sending node can include a time stamp — the currentTime of the entity's state data. Assuming the system clocks have the same wall clock time, the receiving node can read its clock to get the local currentTime, and subtract the time stamp currentTime in the received data from the local currentTime to determine the network delay. Again, this value is the time step that determines the new state (together with the update state in the received data.)

Now, how are the node system clocks synchronized to the wall clock? A simple solution is as follows: a portable hardware called *wallClock* is designed that can be plugged into a node to synchronize the system clock time to its own time. Many wallClocks can be made, synchronized, and sent to multiple hosts. Fig. 17.1 shows that a wallClock is used to synchronize multiple hosts in a simplified DIS network.

The synchronization mechanism does not require transmitting event-driven heartbeat ticks, yet the time elapsed between events is accurately communicated. The time steps vary at different nodes yet the time order is guaranteed. All nodes can smoothly and accurately simulate a predictable physical activity despite unpredictable network latencies. So this time synchronization protocol is applicable to certain physics-based simulation.

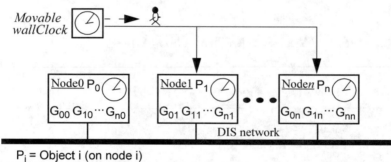

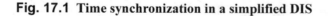

P_i = Object i (on node i)
G_{ij} = Ghost of Object i on node j

Fig. 17.1 Time synchronization in a simplified DIS

18
3D File Formats

Chapter Objectives:

- Introduce the relationships between 3D programming tool libraries and file formats
- Survey graphics file formats and format converting tools
- Compile a list of file format converting tools

18.1 Introduction

Today, people live not only in the real world, but also in 3D virtual worlds. We spend time on virtual reality systems, graphics games, films of imaginary worlds and characters, Web-based 3D environments, and distributed interactive simulations. People represented by 3D avatars can travel in virtual worlds and meet with one another over the Internet. Advances in graphics software and hardware have enabled many new applications, and many virtual worlds are constructed with different models and activities.

In order to reuse constructed models and to transmit virtual worlds across the Internet and on different platforms, 3D graphics files are created to save models, scenes, worlds, and animations. However, graphics developers have created many different 3D graphics file formats for different applications. Here, we survey and list some popular 3D graphics file formats, programming tool libraries that understand different formats, authoring tools that create virtual worlds and save them in graphics files, and format conversion tools that transform files from one format into another. We hope to provide a panoramic view of 3D virtual world technologies to facilitate 3D modeling, reuse, programming, and virtual world construction.

J.X. Chen, *Guide to Graphics Software Tools,* doi: 10.1007/978-1-84800-901-1_18,
© Springer-Verlag London Limited 2008

The relationships in an ordinary high-level 3D graphics tool are shown in Fig. 18.1. A 3D graphics tool is built on top of other 3D graphics tools or a low-level graphics library. Therefore, at the bottom of any graphics tool is a low-level graphics library. Low-level graphics libraries such as OpenGL or Direct3D are the rendering tools that actually draw 3D models into the display. 3D models can also be stored and transmitted as 3D graphics files. 3D authoring tools are modeling tools

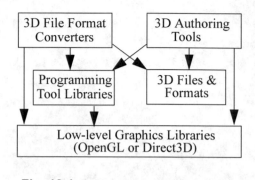

Fig. 18.1 **Relationships in 3D graphics tool**

that provide users with convenient methods to create, view, modify, and save models and virtual worlds. In general, a 3D authoring tool includes a 3D browser. 3D browsers or viewers are graphics tools that read, analyze, and convert 3D graphics files into the tools' internal formats, and then display the converted worlds to the user. 3D graphics viewers, authoring tools, and format converters may access 3D files directly, or go through programming tool library functions.

18.2 3D File Formats

There are different names for virtual worlds or environments. A virtual world is a scene database, which is composed of hierarchical 3D scenes, for example, as in OpenInventor. A 3D scene is an ordered collection of nodes that include 3D models, attributes, animations, and so forth. 3D graphics file formats are storage methods for virtual worlds. Due to the complexities of virtual worlds, 3D file formats include many specifications about how 3D models, scenes, and hierarchies are stored. In addition, different applications include different attributes and activities, and thus may require different file formats.

Over the years, many different 3D graphics file formats have been developed that are in use today. DFX, VRML, 3DS, MAX, RAW, LightWave, POV, and NFF are probably the most commonly used formats. Searching on the Internet, we found 80–90% of 3D models and scenes are in these formats.

18.3   3D Programming Tool Libraries

3D programming tool libraries provide powerful and easy-to-use functions for programs to handle 3D file imports and exports, model and scene constructions, and virtual world manipulations and display. They are also called high-level graphics libraries, built on top of low-level graphics libraries, but they are really primitive functions for higher-level graphics applications. They make sophisticated 3D file formats and virtual world hierarchies easy to handle, and thus reduce application developers' programming efforts. Many high-level graphics tools are built on top of certain programming tool libraries. Usually, a 3D programming tool library supports one 3D file format by providing a series of functions that an application program can call to store, import, parse, and manipulate 3D models or scenes. If we develop our own 3D applications, we save much time and effort by using a 3D programming tool library. In general, for the same file format, commercial products with customer service are much more reliable than freeware tools.

18.4   3D Authoring Tools

3D graphics authoring tools, which in general are modeling tools as discussed in Chapter 8, free us from constructing complicated objects, worlds, and dealing with complicated specifications of 3D graphics file format definitions and make our 3D world construction job much easier.

3D authoring tools usually have good user interfaces, which provide rich object editing tools (such as object extruding, splitting, and cutting, etc.) and flexible manipulation approaches. Using these tools, you can construct complicated 3D models conveniently even without knowing the 3D file formats.

18.5   3D File Format Converters

There are many 3D file formats in use. Every 3D file-format has its specific details. People have created and are still creating huge amounts of 3D models and 3D scenes with different 3D graphics file formats. Without knowing clearly the 3D file format specifications, is it possible — or is there a shortcut for us — to use these different formatted 3D resources and import (reuse) them into our own 3D worlds? Fortunately, the answer is: yes.

Some attributes and properties of the 3D models or scenes may be lost during the format converting. This is because some specifications of a 3D file format can't be translated into another 3D file format; the converters just throw these specifications away. So we should not anticipate that all the details of the 3D models or scenes will be fully translated from one 3D file format to another. Here we briefly introduce a couple of commonly used tools. A detailed list of the tools is provided later.

18.5.1 Built-In and Plug-In VRML Exporters

VRML is the standard 3D file format on the Web. Many 3D file converters can convert different file formats to VRML format. Many 3D authoring tools have the capability to import 3D models from some other file formats, and export 3D scenes to VRML file format. Here is a list of authoring tools that support VRML export: Alias/Wavefront's Maya, AutoCAD's Mechanical Desktop, Bentley MicroStation, CAD Studio, Kinetix's VRML Exporter (a free plug-in for 3D Studio MAX), Lightwave, Poser, and SolidWorks.

18.5.2 Independent 3D File Format Converters

Some independent 3D file format conversion tools, such as Crossroads 3D and 3DWinOGL, are free. Others are commercial products with reliable technique supports, such as Interchange and NuGraf.

Appendix A
Basic Mathematics for 3D Computer Graphics

A.1 Vector Operations

A vector v is a represented as (v_1, v_2, v_3), which has a length and direction. The location of a vector is actually undefined. We can consider it is parallel to the line from origin to a 3D point v. If we use two points (A_1, A_2, A_3) and (B_1, B_2, B_3) to represent a vector AB, then $AB = (B_1 - A_1, B_2 - A_2, B_3 - A_3)$, which is again parallel to the line from origin to $(B_1 - A_1, B_2 - A_2, B_3 - A_3)$. We can consider a vector as a ray from a starting point to an end point. However, the two points really specify a length and a direction. This vector is equivalent to any other vectors with the same length and direction.

A.1.1 The Length and Direction

The length of v is a scalar value as follows:

$$|v| = \sqrt{v_1^2 + v_2^2 + v_3^2}. \tag{EQ 1}$$

The direction of the vector, which can be represented with a unit vector with length equal to one, is:

$$normalize(v) = \left(\frac{v_1}{|v_1|}, \frac{v_2}{|v_2|}, \frac{v_3}{|v_3|} \right).$$

(EQ 2)

That is, when we normalize a vector, we find its corresponding unit vector. If we consider the vector as a point, then the vector direction is from the origin to that point.

A.1.2 Addition and Subtraction

If we have two points (A_1, A_2, A_3) and (B_1, B_2, B_3) to represent two vectors A and B, then you can consider they are vectors from the origin to the points. As we said, any parallel vectors with the same length and direction are equivalent. Therefore, we can move a vector in 3D space as long as it stays parallel. As shown in Fig. A.1, vector addition is just connecting the vectors. That is:

$$A+B = (A_1 + B_1, A_2 + B_2, A_3 + B_3).$$

(EQ 3)

A negative vector is just the original vector in reverse direction. Therefore, vector subtraction is just adding a negative vector.

$$A-B = (A_1 - B_1, A_2 - B_2, A_3 - B_3).$$

(EQ 4)

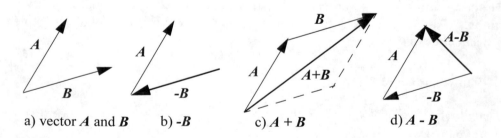

a) vector A and B b) $-B$ c) $A + B$ d) $A - B$

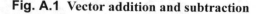

Fig. A.1 Vector addition and subtraction

A.1.3 Dot Product and Cross Product

The dot product of two vectors is a scalar value as follows:

$$A \bullet B = A_1 B_1 + A_2 B_2 + A_3 B_3. \tag{EQ 5}$$

The dot product is also equal to:

$$A \bullet B = |A||B|\cos\theta, \tag{EQ 6}$$

where θ is the angle between the two vectors. Therefore, given two vectors, we can easily find the angle between the two vectors according to Equation 5 and Equation 6. When the two vectors are unit vectors, their dot product is the cosine of their angle.

The cross product of two vectors **A** and **B** is a vector perpendicular to the two vectors and has a magnitude equal to the area of the parallelogram generated from the two vectors, as shown Fig. A.2.

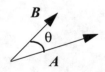
a) vector dot product

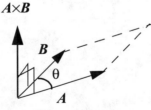
a) vector cross product

Fig. A.2 Vector dot product and cross product

The area of the parallelogram is:

$$|A \times B| = |A||B|\sin\theta. \tag{EQ 7}$$

The direction of the cross product is according to the right-hand rule, which is in the thumb's direction if our right-hand's four fingers go from vector A to B. Therefore, the order of the two vectors in the cross product equation matters. The cross product can be calculated by a determinant as follows:

$$A \times B = \begin{vmatrix} i & j & k \\ A_1 & A_2 & A_3 \\ B_1 & B_2 & B_3 \end{vmatrix},$$ (EQ 8)

where (i, j, k) represent (x, y, z) components. That is,

$$A \times B = (A_2 B_3 - A_3 B_2, A_3 B_1 - A_1 B_3, A_1 B_2 - A_2 B_1).$$ (EQ 9)

Cross products are often used to find a vector that is perpendicular to the two vectors. Also, according to Equation 7 and Equation 9, the cross products are often used to find sine of their angle.

A.1.4 Reflection

A reflection of vector A around vector N is a vector B as shown in Fig. A.3, which has the same length making the same angle around N.

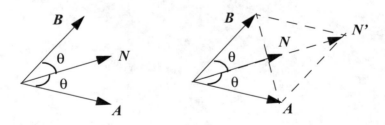

Fig. A.3 Vector reflection around a normal vector

As we can see,

$$B = N' - A;$$ (EQ 10)

$$N' = 2n|A|cos\theta.$$ (EQ 11)

where n is the unit vector along N:

$$n = N/|N|,$$

(EQ 12)

and

$$\cos\theta = n{\bullet}A/|A|.$$

(EQ 13)

Putting them all together,

$$B = 2N{\bullet}A/|N| - A.$$

(EQ 14)

Reflection is needed in ray tracing.

A.2 Matrix Operations

A matrix is represented as $A = (a_{i,j})$ for $i=1,...n$ rows; $j=1,...,m$ columns as follows:

$$A = \begin{bmatrix} a_{11} & \cdots & a_{1m} \\ \cdots & \cdots & \cdots \\ a_{n1} & \cdots & a_{nm} \end{bmatrix}.$$

(EQ 15)

A.2.1 Transpose

The transpose of $A = (a_{i,j})$ for $i=1,...n;$ $j=1,...,m$ is a matrix $A^T = (a_{j,i})$ for $i=1,...n;$ $j=1,...,m$, which swaps the rows with columns of the original matrix. That is:

$$A^T = \begin{bmatrix} a_{11} & \cdots & a_{n1} \\ \cdots & \cdots & \cdots \\ a_{1m} & \cdots & a_{nm} \end{bmatrix}.$$

(EQ 16)

A.2.2 Addition and Subtraction

For two matrices $A = (a_{i,j})$ and $B = (b_{i,j})$, $A + B = (a_{i,j} + b_{i,j})$ and $A - B = (a_{i,j} - b_{i,j})$ for $i=1,...n;\ j=1,...,m$. That is:

$$A + B = \begin{bmatrix} (a_{11} + b_{11}) & ... & (a_{1m} + b_{1m}) \\ ... & ... & ... \\ (a_{n1} + b_{n1}) & ... & (a_{nm} + b_{nm}) \end{bmatrix};$$

(EQ 17)

$$A - B = \begin{bmatrix} (a_{11} - b_{11}) & ... & (a_{1m} - b_{1m}) \\ ... & ... & ... \\ (a_{n1} - b_{n1}) & ... & (a_{nm} - b_{nm}) \end{bmatrix}.$$

(EQ 18)

For example,

$$\begin{bmatrix} 1 & 2 & 3 \\ 4 & 5 & 6 \\ 7 & 8 & 9 \end{bmatrix} + \begin{bmatrix} 3 & 2 & 1 \\ 7 & 8 & 9 \\ 4 & 5 & 6 \end{bmatrix} = \begin{bmatrix} (1+3) & (2+2) & (3+1) \\ (4+7) & (5+8) & (6+9) \\ (7+4) & (8+5) & (9+6) \end{bmatrix} = \begin{bmatrix} 4 & 4 & 4 \\ 11 & 13 & 15 \\ 11 & 13 & 15 \end{bmatrix}.$$

(EQ 19)

The transpose of two matrices added together is:

$$(A + B)^T = A^T + B^T.$$

(EQ 20)

A.2.3 Multiplications

If we multiply a matrix $A = (a_{i,j})$ for $i=1,...n;\ j=1,...,m$ with a scalar value c, the result is calculated by multiplying every element of A with c: $cA = (ca_{i,j})$ for $i=1,...n;\ j=1,...,m$. For example:

$$3 \begin{bmatrix} 3 & 2 & 1 \\ 7 & 8 & 9 \\ 4 & 5 & 6 \end{bmatrix} = \begin{bmatrix} 9 & 6 & 3 \\ 21 & 24 & 27 \\ 12 & 15 & 18 \end{bmatrix} \qquad \text{(EQ 21)}$$

$$\begin{bmatrix} 3 & 2 & 1 \\ 7 & 8 & 9 \\ 4 & 5 & 6 \end{bmatrix} / 3 = \begin{bmatrix} 1 & \dfrac{2}{3} & \dfrac{1}{3} \\ \dfrac{7}{3} & \dfrac{8}{3} & 3 \\ \dfrac{4}{3} & \dfrac{5}{3} & 2 \end{bmatrix} \qquad \text{(EQ 22)}$$

If we multiply two matrices together, it is required that the number of columns of the left matrix is the same as the number of rows of the right matrix. For example, if matrix $A = (a_{i,j})$ for $i=1,...n; j=1,...,m$, then matrix $B = (b_{i,j})$ has to be with $i=1,...m; j=1,...,n$ in order to have the matrix multiplication:

$$AB = \sum_{0 \le k \le n} (a_{i,k} b_{k,j}) \qquad \text{(EQ 23)}$$

That is:

$$AB = \begin{bmatrix} \displaystyle\sum_{1 \le k \le n} (a_{1,k} b_{k,1}) & \cdots & \displaystyle\sum_{1 \le k \le n} (a_{1,k} b_{k,m}) \\ \cdots & \cdots & \cdots \\ \displaystyle\sum_{1 \le k \le n} (a_{n,k} b_{k,1}) & \cdots & \displaystyle\sum_{1 \le k \le n} (a_{n,k} b_{k,m}) \end{bmatrix} \qquad \text{(EQ 24)}$$

For example,

$$\begin{bmatrix} 1 & 2 & 3 \\ 4 & 5 & 6 \end{bmatrix} \begin{bmatrix} 1 & 2 \\ 3 & 4 \\ 5 & 6 \end{bmatrix} = \begin{bmatrix} (1+6+15) & (2+8+18) \\ (4+15+30) & (8+20+36) \end{bmatrix} = \begin{bmatrix} 22 & 28 \\ 49 & 64 \end{bmatrix}. \qquad \text{(EQ 25)}$$

As we can see, matrix multiplication is not commutative. In general, $AB \neq BA$. The transpose of two matrices multiplied together is:

$$(AB)^T = B^T A^T. \qquad \text{(EQ 26)}$$

A.2.4 Square Matrix and Inverse

A square matrix is a matrix with the same number of rows and columns: $A = (a_{i,j})$ for $i=1,...n$ and $j=1,...n$. An identity matrix I, which is also called a unit matrix, is a square matrix with the main diagonal value equal to one ($a_{i,j} = 1$) and all other elements equal to zero. Any matrix multiply its identity matrix is the matrix itself: $AI = IA = I$. For example, for $n=3$,

$$I_3 = \begin{bmatrix} 1 & 0 & 0 \\ 0 & 1 & 0 \\ 0 & 0 & 1 \end{bmatrix}. \qquad \text{(EQ 27)}$$

If $AB = I$, then B is called the inverse or reciprocal matrix of A, denoted by A^{-1}. A has an inverse, which is called nonsingular or invertible, if and only if the determinant $|A| \neq 0$.

For a 2×2 matrix, $A = \begin{bmatrix} a_{11} & a_{12} \\ a_{21} & a_{22} \end{bmatrix}$,

$$A^{-1} = \frac{1}{|A|} \begin{bmatrix} a_{22} & -a_{12} \\ -a_{21} & a_{11} \end{bmatrix}. \qquad \text{(EQ 28)}$$

There are several methods to calculate the inverse, but they are numerically complex. The numerical complexity of matrix inversions is several orders of more calculations than matrix multiplications. In graphics, matrix inverse is implemented for transforming the normals and other applications.

Appendix B
Graphics Software Tools

Appendix Objectives:

- Provide a comprehensive list of graphics software tools.

- Categorize graphics tools according to their applications. Many tools come with multiple functions. We put a primary category name behind a tool name in the alphabetic index, and put a tool name into multiple categories in the categorized index according to its functions.

B.1   Graphics Tools Listed by Categories

We have no intention of rating any of the tools. Many tools in the same category are not necessarily of the same quality or at the same capacity level. For example, a software tool may be just a simple function of another powerful package, but it may be free.

Low-level Graphics Libraries

Visualization Tools

Modeling Tools

Rendering Tools

Animation Tools

Simulation Tools

Virtual Reality Tools

Web 3D Tools

3D File Format Converters

B.2   Alphabetical Listing and Description of Graphics Tools

Note: please contact the company or vendor for the actual prices. The prices listed are for reference and comparison only. When there is no available price for a tool, the number of "$" signs indicates the range of the price. For example, "$$$" indicates the price of the tool is in the range of $100–$999.

20-sim

1. PLATFORMS, PRICES, AND SUPPLIER/CREATOR

- Windows
- 20-sim 4.0 Professional
  - Corporate, Individual User: $8,400; Academic, Individual User: $1,400
- 20-sim 4.0 Standard
  - Corporate,Individual User: $4,200; Academic, Individual User: $700
- 20sim.com (CLP): http://www.20sim.com/index.html

2. APPLICATIONS

- 20-sim is a modeling and simulation program
- It is designed to be used to simulate the behavior of dynamic systems, such as electrical, mechanical and hydraulic systems or any combination of these

3. WEB RESOURCES

- Official website: http://www.20sim.com/index.html
- 20-sim Courses: http://www.20sim.com/courses/courses.html

3D CANVAS

1. PLATFORMS, PRICES, AND SUPPLIER/CREATOR

- Window
- 3D Canvas Plus-$34.95, 3D Canvas Pro-$69.95
- Amabilis, Inc.: http://www.amabilis.com

2. APPLICATIONS

- 3D Canvas is a 3D modeling and animation tool that can be used by graphic designers to make 3D games and animations

3. WEB RESOURCES

- Official website: http://www.amabilis.com/products.htm
- Wikipedia: http://en.wikipedia.org/wiki/3D_Canvas

3D Choreographer

1. PLATFORMS, PRICE, AND SUPPLIER/CREATOR

- Windows
- $$-$$$
- Animated Communications: http://www.3dchor.com

2. APPLICATIONS

- The 3D Choreographer family of products are three dimensional computer animation tools
- These tools are designed for non-artists, suitable for students, middle school and up to learn animation

3. WEB RESOURCES

- Official website: http://www.3dchor.com/

3D Grapher

1. PLATFORMS, PRICES, AND SUPPLIER/CREATOR

- Windows
- $24.95
- RomanLab Software: http://www.romanlab.com

2. APPLICATIONS

- 3D Grapher is graph plotting and data visualization software
- It can be used as a picture and animation creator to make 3D pictures and movies, suitable for students, engineers and anyone who needs to work with 2D and 3D graphs

3. WEB RESOURCES

- Official website: `http://www.romanlab.com/3dg/`
- Examples/Samples: `http://www.romanlab.com/3dg/graphs.htm`

3D INSTANT WEBSITE

1. PLATFORMS, PRICES, AND SUPPLIER/CREATOR

- Windows, Linux, Unix, Mac OS
- Freeware
- SolidWorks Corporation: `http://www.solidworks.com/`

2. APPLICATIONS

- 3D Instant Website is a web-publishing tool
- It enables designers to create and publish live web pages with 3D interactive content, and share 3D models with customers, co-workers, and suppliers

3. WEB RESOURCES

- Official website: `http://www.solidworks.com/pages/products/solutions/3dinstantwebsite.html`

3DSOM Pro

1. PLATFORM, PRICE, AND SUPPLIER/CREATOR

- Windows
- $1690
- Creative Dimension Software Ltd.: `http://www.3dsom.com/`

2. APPLICATIONS

- 3DSOM Pro is a image-based 3D modeling software for creating 3D content from still images
- A wide range of objects can be modeled including those with holes and difficult organic shapes, such as models of museums, toys, a gold ring, a sports training shoe, etc.

3. WEB RESOURCES

- Official website: `http://www.3dsom.com/`
- Examples/Samples: `http://www.3dsom.com/proexamples/index.html`

3D STUDIO MAX

1. PLATFORM, PRICE, AND SUPPLIER/CREATOR

- Windows
- $2,355 for regular price, $378.95 for student
- Autodesk: `http://www.autodesk.com`

2. APPLICATIONS

- A 3D modeling tool with rendering and animation functions
- It has been used for many modeling purposes, including special effects in films, virtual characters in games, and complex objects in virtual environments

3. WEB RESOURCES

- Official website: `http://www.autodesk.com/fo-products-3dsmax`
- Wikipedia: `http://en.wikipedia.org/wiki/3D_Studio_Max`
- Discussions: `http://www.3dlinks.com/forums_Display.cfm?id=6`

3D Studio VIZ

1. PLATFORM, PRICE, AND SUPPLIER/CREATOR

- Windows

- $1,995
- Autodesk Inc.: http://www.autodesk.com

2. APPLICATIONS

- 3D Studio VIZ is a 3D modeling, rendering, and animation program
- It can be used by architects, civil engineers and project planners for 3D visualizations of architectural and industrial products

3. WEB RESOURCES

- Official website: `http://www.3dv.com/3dsoftware/viz/viz.html`

3D Text Maker

1. PLATFORM, PRICE, AND SUPPLIER/CREATOR

- Windows
- Freeware
- MediaBuilder Network: `http://www.mediabuilder.com`

2. APPLICATIONS

- 3D Text Maker is an online 3D text banner creation tool used to enhance web pages, presentations and email

3. WEB RESOURCES

- Official website: `http://www.3dtextmaker.com/`

3D Win

1. PLATFORM, PRICES, AND SUPPLIER/CREATOR

- Windows
- $49.41
- TB Software: `http://www.tb-software.com`

2. APPLICATIONS

- 3DWin is a 3D file format converter for 3D industry professionals. It converts 3D file formats such as 3ds, obj, directx, vrml

3. WEB RESOURCES

- Official website: `http://www.tb-software.com/products_2.html`
- Examples/Samples: `http://www.tb-software.com/gallery.html`

3DField

1. PLATFORMS, PRICES, AND SUPPLIER/CREATOR

- Windows
- $99
- Vladimir Galouchko: `http://field.hypermart.net/`

2. APPLICATIONS

- 3DField is a contouring surface plotting program
- It can be used for the construction of 2D/3D maps of contours on the basis of numerical data

3. WEB RESOURCES

- Official website: `http://field.hypermart.net/`
- Manual: `http://field.hypermart.net/Help/index.htm`

3dom

1. PLATFORM, PRICE, AND SUPPLIER/CREATOR

- Unix, Linux
- Freeware
- KULeuven: `http://threedom.sourceforge.net/index.html`

2. APPLICATION

- 3dom is a 3D solid modeling tool
- It is capable of modeling reality with user-chosen accuracy, and user-chosen inclination for a particular global illumination purpose, and can be used for film, TV, games, web design, etc.

3. WEB RESOURCES

- Official website: `http://www.cs.kuleuven.ac.be/cwis/research/ graphics/graphics-E.shtml`
- Alternative 3dom Website: `http://www.dom.zip.com.au/3d/`

3DVIEWNIX

1. PLATFORM, PRICES, AND SUPPLIER/CREATOR

- Unix, Windows
- $1000
- Medical Image Processing Group(MIPG): `http://www.mipg.upenn.edu`

2. APPLICATIONS

- 3DVIEWNIX is a software for visualizing, manipulating, and analyzing multidimensional, multimodality image information

3. WEB RESOURCES

- Official website: `http://www.mipg.upenn.edu/~Vnews/index.html`
- User's manual: `http://mipgsun.mipg.upenn.edu/~Vnews/user_manual/ user_manual_contents.html`

3D World Studio

1. PLATFORM, PRICE, AND SUPPLIER/CREATOR

- Windows, Linux, Mac OS
- Builder Edition price: $119.95, Standard Edition price:$79.95

- Leadwerks Corporation: http://www.leadwerks.com/

2. APPLICATIONS

- 3D World Studio is a constructive solid geometry (CSG) modeler with support for object placement, terrain, and lighting
- This program can be used by architects, game developers, interior designers, and hobbyists to produce 3D walkthroughs, games, and simulations

3. WEB RESOURCES

- Official website: http://www.leadwerks.com/
- Wikipedia: http://en.wikipedia.org/wiki/3D_World_Studio

AC3D

1. PLATFORM, PRICE, AND SUPPLIER/CREATOR

- Windows, Mac OSX, Linux
- $79.95, http://www.inivis.com/buy.html
- Inivis Limited: http://www.inivis.com

2. APPLICATIONS

- AC3D is a 3D modeling program that is polygon and subdivision-surface based
- It can be used for a wide variety of purposes including game model creation, product prototypes, virtual reality simulations and data visualization

3. WEB RESOURCES

- Offical website: http://www.inivis.com/index.html
- Wikipedia: http://en.wikipedia.org/wiki/AC3D
- Manuals: http://ac3d.org/ac3d/tutorials

AccuRender

1. PLATFORM, PRICE, AND SUPPLIER/CREATOR

- Windows
- $495
- Robert McNeel & Associates: `http://www.accurender.com`

2. APPLICATIONS

- AccuRender is a rendering tool designed mainly for architects, delivering animation, virtual reality panoramas, lighting analysis, network rendering, lighting studies, and more

3. WEB RESOURCES

- Official website: `http://www.accurender.com`
- Examples/Samples: `http://gallery.mcneel.com/?g=43`

AccuTrans 3D

1. PLATFORMS, PRICES, AND SUPPLIER/CREATOR

- Windows
- $20
- MicroMouse Productions: `http://www.micromouse.ca/`

2. APPLICATIONS

- AccuTrans 3D is a file converter
- It translates 3D geometry information between different file formats used by many popular modeling programs

3. WEB RESOURCES

- Official website: `http://www.micromouse.ca/index.html`

ACIS 3D Toolkits

1. PLATFORM, PRICE, AND SUPPLIER/CREATOR

- Windows, Unix
- N/A
- Spatial Corp.: http://www.spatial.com/

2. APPLICATIONS

- ACIS 3D Toolkits are 3D geometric modeler and deformable modeling tools, including 3D ACIS Modeler (ACIS), 3D Deformable Modeling and Advanced Covering tool, etc.
- These software have been used by software developers for engineering applications including CAD/CAM/CAE, AEC, animation, visualization, and simulation

3. WEB RESOURCES

- Official website: http://www.spatial.com/products/index.html
- Tutorial: http://www.saxe-coburg.co.uk/pubs/descrip/acis.htm

ActiveWorlds

1. PLATFORMS, PRICES, AND SUPPLIER/CREATOR

- Windows, Linux
- $$
- The Activeworlds Corporation: http://www.activeworlds.com

2. APPLICATIONS

- Activeworlds is a collection of networked virtual environments
- It is capable of delivering real-time interactive 3D content over the web for some applications such as interactive shopping, gaming, chatting, corporate training, e-learning, etc.

3. WEB RESOURCES

- Official website: http://www.activeworlds.com/products/index.asp

- Wikipedia: http://en.wikipedia.org/wiki/Activeworlds
- Online Manual: http://www.activeworlds.com/help/aw36/

Active Dimensions 3

1. PLATFORM, PRICE, AND SUPPLIER/CREATOR

- Windows
- $24.95
- BMT Micro, Inc.: http://www.bmtmicro.com/

2. APPLICATIONS

- Active Dimensions 3 is a CAD and 3D modeling tool
- It can be used in industries such as graphics design, architecture and architectural engineering, civil engineering, factory layout, interior design, construction, electrical engineering, mechanical engineering, etc.

3. WEB RESOURCES

- Official website: http://www.bmtmicro.com/BMTCatalog/win/activedimensions.html

ADG Panorama Tools

1. PLATFORMS, PRICES, AND SUPPLIER/CREATOR

- Windows
- $39.99- $99.99 (Standard and Pro Editions Available)
- Albatross Design Group: http://www.albatrossdesign.com/

2. APPLICATIONS

- It is a panorama stitching software to create 360-degree web panoramas from series of photos for e-business needs such as enhanced interactive advertising and online marketing, or 3-D presentations on the Internet

3. WEB RESOURCES

- Official website: http://www.albatrossdesign.com/products/panorama/
- Examples/Samples: http://www.albatrossdesign.com/samples/

Adobe Illustrator CS

1. PLATFORMS, PRICES, AND SUPPLIER/CREATOR

- Windows, Mac OS
- $599
- Adobe: www.adobe.com

2. APPLICATIONS

- Adobe Illustrator CS is a vector-based drawing program with features such as 3D graphics effects, character and paragraph styles, and innovative text composition controls, etc.
- It can be used by anyone who needs to produce graphics for print, web, video, mobile, and motion designs

3. WEB RESOURCES

- Official website: http://www.adobe.com/products/illustrator/index.html
- Wikipedia: http://en.wikipedia.org/wiki/Adobe_Illustrator

AIR (Animation and Image Rendering)

1. PLATFORMS, PRICES, AND SUPPLIER/CREATOR

- Windows, Linux
- $375
- SiTex Graphics: http://www.sitexgraphics.com

2. APPLICATIONS

- AIR is a 3D graphics renderer combining scanline rendering, motion blur, and depth of field for accurate reflections, soft shadows, global illumination, and caustics
- It can be used by designers, architects, free-lance 3D artists, and production companies for the rapid production of high-quality images

3. WEB RESOURCES

- Official website: `http://www.novadesign.com/exoops/modules/freecontent/index.php?id=8`
- Tutorials: `http://www.novadesign.com/exoops/modules/mysections/`
- Wikipedia: `http://en.wikipedia.org/wiki/Aladdin4D`

Aladdin 4D

1. PLATFORMS, PRICES, AND SUPPLIER/CREATOR

- Windows, Linux, Mac OS, Amiga OS
- $99.95
- Nova Design, Inc.: `http://www.novadesign.com`

2. APPLICATIONS

- Aladdin4D is a software for modeling, rendering 3D graphics and animation
- It can be used for modeling purposes such as special effects in films, virtual objects in games or in virtual environments

3. WEB RESOURCES

- Official website: `http://www.novadesign.com/exoops/modules/freecontent/index.php?id=8`
- Tutorials: `http://www.novadesign.com/exoops/modules/mysections/`
- Wikipedia: `http://en.wikipedia.org/wiki/Aladdin4D`

AliasStudio

1. PLATFORMS, PRICES, AND SUPPLIER/CREATOR

- Windows, Mac OS, Linux
- N/A
- Autodesk, Inc.: `http://usa.autodesk.com`

2. APPLICATIONS

- The AliasStudio product family is design software with sketching, modeling, and visualization tools
- It can be used for design and styling in automotive, marine, aircraft, sporting equipment, electronic enclosure, children's toy, and fashion accessory markets

3. WEB RESOURCES

- Official website: `http://www.alias.com/studiotools`
- Documentation: `http://usa.autodesk.com/adsk/servlet/index?siteID=123112&id=9493464`

Alice

1. PLATFORMS, PRICES, AND SUPPLIER/CREATOR

- Windows, Linux, Mac OS
- Freeware
- Carnegie Mellon University: `http://www.alice.org`

2. APPLICATIONS

- Alice is a 3D programming environment for creating an animation for telling a story, playing an interactive game, or sharing a video on the web
- Alice can be used as a teaching tool to address problems in education for teaching and learning introductory programming concepts

3. WEB RESOURCES

- Official website: `http://www.alice.org`

- Wikipedia: http://en.wikipedia.org/wiki/Alice_%28software%29

Amapi 3D

1. PLATFORMS, PRICES, AND SUPPLIER/CREATOR

- Windows, Mac OS
- N/A
- Eovia Europe: http://www.eovia.fr/amapipro/amapi_pro.asp

2. APPLICATIONS

- Amapi 3D is a 3D modeler suited for working in conjunction with other 3D programs, such as Bryce, Poser and Carrara Studio, and it can be used by product designers, architects and advanced 3D modelers

3. WEB RESOURCES

- Official website: http://www.eovia.fr/amapipro/amapi_pro.asp
- Tutorial: http://www.thebest3d.com/amapi/tutorials/3Dtext

AMIRA

1. PLATFORMS, PRICES, AND SUPPLIER/CREATOR

- Windows, Linux, and Mac OS
- N/A
- Mercury Computer Systems, Inc.: http://www.tgs.com/default.asp

2. APPLICATIONS

- Amira is a tool for visualizing, manipulating, and understanding scientific data and bio-medical data
- Its application areas are related to health care including biology, medicine, medical research, bio-informatics, pharmaceuticals, etc.

3. WEB RESOURCES

- Official website: `http://www.amira.com/`
- Examples/Samples: `http://www.amira.com/gallery.html`

Amorphium

1. PLATFORMS, PRICES, AND SUPPLIER/CREATOR

- Windows, Mac OS
- $79-$99
- EI Technology Group: `http://www.eitechnologygroup.com/products/amorphium.html`

2. APPLICATIONS

- Amorphium is a 3D sculpting and painting tool
- It was designed for professional designers or graphics enthusiasts to create custom 3D graphics for websites, desktop publishing, business graphics, art education, personal creative projects, etc.

3. WEB RESOURCES

- Official website: `http://eitechnologygroup.com/products/amorphium`
- Manual: `http://www.eitechnologygroup.com/downloads/manuals/amorphium/a_pro_manual.pdf`

Analyze

1. PLATFORMS, PRICES, AND SUPPLIER/CREATOR

- Windows, Linux, Unix
- N/A
- Mayo Foundation: `http://mayoresearch.mayo.edu/mayo/research/robb_lab/`

2. APPLICATIONS

- Analyze is 3D biomedical image visualization and analysis software for multi-dimensional display, processing, and measurement of multi-modality biomedical images
- It can be used for medical tomographic scans from magnetic resonance imaging, computed tomography and positron emission tomography

3. WEB RESOURCES

- Official website: `http://mayoresearch.mayo.edu/mayo/research/robb_lab/analyze.cfm`
- Wikipedia: `http://en.wikipedia.org/wiki/Analyze`

Anark

1. PLATFORMS, PRICES, AND SUPPLIER/CREATOR

- Windows
- N/A
- Anark Corporation: `http://anark.com`

2. APPLICATIONS

- Anark provides a suite of 3D software for 3D modeling and simulation, including Anark Core, Anark Studio, Anark Client, etc.
- These tools can be used for product design, technical publications, virtual training, product visualization, immersive 3D based entertainment, etc.

3. WEB RESOURCES

- Official website: `http://anark.com/products_enterprise/overview.html`

Anfy 3D

1. PLATFORM, PRICES, AND SUPPLIER/CREATOR

- Windows

- $$-$$$
- Anfy Team: `http://anfyteam.com/indexen.html`

2. APPLICATIONS

- Anfy is web3D software designed for creating interactive 3D worlds, presentations, and rotating 3D letters with JAVA for graphic artists and web designers

3. WEB RESOURCES

- Official website: `http://anfyteam.com/indexen.html`

ANIM8OR

1. PLATFORMS, PRICES, AND SUPPLIER/CREATOR

- Windows
- Freeware
- R. Steven Glanville: `http://www.anim8or.com/main/index.html`

2. APPLICATIONS

- Anim8or is an OpenGL-based 3D modeling and animation program
- It can be used for games, films, architecture and architectural engineering, civil engineering, factory layout, interior design and architecture, construction, graphics design, mechanical engineering, etc.

3. WEB RESOURCES

- Official website: `http://www.anim8or.com/main/index.html`
- Wikipedia: `http://en.wikipedia.org/wiki/Anim8or`
- Tutorials: `http://members.lycos.nl/jonim8or/tutorials.html/`

Animation Master

1. PLATFORMS, PRICES, AND SUPPLIER/CREATOR

- Windows, Mac OS
- $299
- Hash, Inc.: `http://www.hash.com/2007web/`

2. APPLICATIONS

- It's a 3D character animation application that includes tools for modeling, animating, and rendering based on spline mesh technology
- Animation Master can be used for making movies, 3D story boards, building virtual reality, business presentations, etc.

3. WEB RESOURCES

- Official website: `http://www.hash.com/2007web/`
- Wikipedia: `http://en.wikipedia.org/wiki/Animation_Master`

ANIMATION STAND

1. PLATFORMS, PRICES, AND SUPPLIER/CREATOR

- Windows, Unix, Linux, Mac OS
- $595
- Linker Systems, Inc. `http://www.linkersystems.com`

2. APPLICATIONS

- Animation Stand is an animation system for computer-assisted 2 1/2D character animation, composition and film quality special effects
- It has been used by professional and industrial animation studios, postproduction, video facilities, etc.

3. WEB RESOURCES:

- Official website: `http://www.animationstand.com`

- Examples/samples: `http://www.animationstand.com/gallery/index.html`

Antics

1. PLATFORMS, PRICES, AND SUPPLIER/CREATOR

- Windows
- $595
- Antics Technologies Ltd.: `http://www.antics3d.com/index.php`

2. APPLICATIONS

- Antics is a 3D visualization software based upon gaming technology
- It has been used in the entertainment industry helping producers, directors, screenwriters, production designers and directors of photography to pitch their ideas and to pre-visualize scenes before committing money to shooting

3. WEB RESOURCES:

- Official website: `http://www.antics3d.com/index.php?action=content&content_id=116`

Art of Illusion

1. PLATFORMS, PRICES, AND SUPPLIER/CREATOR

- Windows, Unix, Linux, Mac OS
- Freeware
- Peter Eastman: `http://www.artofillusion.org/`

2. APPLICATIONS

- Art of Illusion is a 3D modeling and rendering studio
- It can be used for 3D modeling, texturing, ray tracing, and otherwise rendering computer generated imagery stills or animations (movies)

3. WEB RESOURCES

- Official website: `http://www.artofillusion.org/`
- Wikipedia: `http://en.wikipedia.org/wiki/Art_of_Illusion`
- Documentation: `http://www.artofillusion.org/documentation`

Astex Viewer

1. PLATFORMS, PRICES, AND SUPPLIER/CREATOR

- Windows, Unix, Linux, Mac OS
- Freeware
- Astex Therapeutics Ltd.: `http://www.astex-therapeutics.com/home.php`

2. APPLICATIONS

- AstexViewer is a molecular visualization tool
- It is designed to display coordinate and sequence information from macromolecules and small molecules, and it has been used in the structural biology community

3. WEB RESOURCES

- Official website: `http://www.ebi.ac.uk/msd-srv/apps/Viewer/ViewerServlet?id=1crn`
- Documentation: `http://www.ebi.ac.uk/msd-srv/apps/Viewer/index.html`

AutoCAD

1. PLATFORM, PRICE, COMPANY

- Windows
- AutoCAD 2008 is $3,995, AutoCAD LT 2008 is $899.
- Autodesk: `http://www.autodesk.com`

2. APPLICATIONS

- AutoCAD is a modeling tool for 2D and 3D design and drafting
- It can be used in industries such as architecture and architectural engineering, civil engineering, factory layout, interior design and architecture, construction, electrical engineering, graphics design, mechanical engineering and lighting design, etc.

3. WEB RESOURCES

- Official website: `http://www.autodesk.com/autocad`
- Wikipedia: `http://en.wikipedia.org/wiki/AutoCAD`
- Tutorials: `http://www.cadtutor.net/tutorials/autocad/index.php`

AVS5

1. PLATFORM, PRICE, COMPANY

- Unix, Linux, MAC OS
- N/A
- Advanced Visual Systems, Inc.: `http://www.avs.com/`

2. APPLICATIONS

- AVS5 is scientific and technical visualization software which consists of a suite of data visualization and analysis techniques that incorporates both traditional visualization tools (such as 2D plots and graphs and image processing) as well as advanced tools (such as 3D interactive rendering and volume visualization)
- It can be used in the fields of life science, medicine, oil&gas, earth science, drug discovery, engineering, scientific research, education, etc.

3. WEB RESOURCES

- Official website: `http://www.avs.com/avs5.html`
- Documentation: `http://help.avs.com/avs5/doc/doc.asp`

bCAD

1. PLATFORM, PRICE, AND SUPPLIER/CREATOR

- Windows
- $245 for Standard edition, $95 for Educational edition
- bCAD Team: http://www.propro.ru/eng/

2. APPLICATIONS

- bCAD is a 3D modeling tool to develop designs using sketches, drawings, illustrations, real-time visualization, animation, software rendering, 3D models and rapid prototypes
- It is designed for persons and organizations who need a graphical design, drafting and visualization environment, such as engineers, architects, designers and students

3. WEB RESOURCES

- Official website: http://www.propro.ru/eng/products/bcad.html
- Examples/Samples: http://www.propro.ru/eng/gallery/gallery.php

Behemot Graphics Editor

1. PLATFORM, PRICE, CREATOR/SUPPLIER

- Windows, Linux, Unix, Mac OS
- Freeware
- Behemot: http://www.behemot.com

2. APPLICATIONS

- Behemot Graphics Editor is a modeling program
- It can be used for modeling purposes, such as product prototypes, game model creation, and complex objects in virtual environments

3. WEB RESOURCES

- Official website: http://www.behemot.com/

Biturn

1. PLATFORM, PRICE, CREATOR/SUPPLIER

- Windows
- Freeware
- Mirex: `http://mirex.mypage.sk/`

2. APPLICATIONS

- Biturn is a converter among several game model formats

3. WEB RESOURCES

- Official website: `http://mirex.mypage.sk/`

Blaze 3D Studio

1. PLATFORMS, PRICES, AND SUPPLIER/CREATOR

- Windows
- $895
- Holomatix Ltd.: `http://www.holomatix.com/`

2. APPLICATIONS

- Blaze 3D Studio is an interactive web 3D rendering tool
- It can create photorealistic 3D contents to display on web pages for interactive 3D sales and marketing applications

3. WEB RESOURCES

- Official website: `http://www.holomatix.com/cat/about/`
- Tutorials: `http://www.holomatix.com/cat/blaze_tutorials/`

Blender

1. PLATFORMS, PRICES, AND SUPPLIER/CREATOR

- Windows, Linux, Irix, Solaris, Mac OS
- Freeware
- Blender Institute BV: http://www.blender3d.com

2. APPLICATIONS

- Blender is a 3D modeling, rendering, and animation package
- It can be used for modeling, UV unwrapping, texturing, rigging, skinning, animating, rendering, particle and other simulations, non-linear editing, composing, and creating interactive 3D applications in the media industry

3. WEB RESOURCES

- Official website: www.blender3d.org
- Tutorials: http://www.blender.org/education-help/tutorials/
- Wikipedia: http://en.wikipedia.org/wiki/Blender_(software)

Blueberry 3D

1. PLATFORMS, PRICES, AND SUPPLIER/CREATOR

- Windows
- N/A
- Bionatics: http://www.bionatics.com

2. APPLICATIONS

- Blueberry 3D is an interactive modeling tool for the creation, visualization and distribution of complex real-time 3D databases based on procedural technology
- It has been used for the application of training simulations, civil engineering, virtual reality, etc.

3. WEB RESOURCES

- Official website: `http://www.bionatics.com/Blueberry3D.php`
- Examples/Samples: `http://www.bionatics.com/Blueberry3D.php`

Body Paint 3D

1. PLATFORMS, PRICES, AND SUPPLIER/CREATOR

- Windows, Mac OS
- $895
- MAXON: `http://www.maxon.net/`

2. APPLICATIONS

- BodyPaint 3D is a modeling tool proving 3D painting, texturing, and UVW editing for professional 3D Applications
- It is created for 3D artists and offers direct translation plug-ins for Maya, Softimage XSI, 3ds Max, and LightWave 3D

3. WEB RESOURCES

- Official Website: `http://www.bodypaint3d.com/`
- Documentation: `http://www.maxon.net/pages/download/documentation_e.html`

Brand Worlds Tools

1. PLATFORMS, PRICES, AND SUPPLIER/CREATOR

- Windows
- $99
- Brand Worlds: `http://www.brandworlds.com/index.html`

2. APPLICATIONS

- Brand Worlds Tools are animation tools for the Web

- These tools are used by graphic artists, flash and web developers to make web and flash animations, and animated avatars from 3D models

3. WEB RESOURCES

- Official website: `http://www.brandworlds.com/products01.htm`
- Examples/Samples: `http://www.brandworlds.com/showroom01.htm`

Breeze Designer

1. PLATFORMS, PRICES, AND SUPPLIER/CREATOR

- Windows
- Freeware
- Neville Richards: `http://www.imagos.fl.net.au`

2. APPLICATIONS

- Breeze Designer is a 3D modeling and design tool
- This program has been written to interface with the Persistence of Vision raytracer (POV-Ray), and there is also support to export to a number of other renderers including Pixars's RenderMan, VRML viewers and Microsoft Silverlight

3. WEB RESOURCES

- Official website: `http://www.imagos.fl.net.au/`
- Examples/samples: `http://www.imagos.fl.net.au/gallery/photo.html`

BRL-CAD

1. PLATFORMS, PRICES, AND SUPPLIER/CREATOR

- Windows, Linux, Mac OS
- Freeware
- BRL-CAD developers: `http://brlcad.org/`

2. APPLICATIONS

- BRL-CAD is a system for constructive solid geometry (CSG), solid modeling and computer-aided design (CAD)
- It can be used in industries such as architecture and architectural engineering, civil engineering, factory layout, interior design and architecture, construction, electrical engineering, graphics design, mechanical engineering, etc.

3. WEB RESOURCES

- Official website: `http://brlcad.org/`
- Documentation: `http://brlcad.org/wiki/Documentation`
- Wikipedia: `http://en.wikipedia.org/wiki/BRL-CAD`

Bryce 3D

1. PLATFORMS, PRICE, AND SUPPLIER/CREATOR

- Windows, Mac OS
- $$$
- DAZ Productions, Inc. `http://www.daz3d.com/i.x/software/bryce/`

2. APPLICATIONS

- Bryce is a 3D modeling, rendering and animation program specializing in fractal landscapes
- It has been used by 3D graphics enthusiasts, professional designers, and artists of media such as print, video, multimedia or the web

3. WEB RESOURCES

- Official website: `http://www.daz3d.com/i.x/software/bryce/`
- Tutorials: `http://www.daz3d.com/i.x/software/bryce/-/tutorial`
- Wikipedia: `http://en.wikipedia.org/wiki/Bryce_(software)`

Calimax

1. PLATFORMS, PRICE, AND SUPPLIER/CREATOR

- Windows
- Freeware
- Andreas Koepke: `http://www.calimax.de/index.htm`

2. APPLICATIONS

- Calimax is a 3D modeling tool for making realistic pictures and animations with the two programs Calimax and Povray

3. WEB RESOURCES

- Official website: `http://www.calimax.de/software.htm`

Carrara

1. PLATFORMS, PRICES, AND SUPPLIER/CREATOR

- Windows, Mac OS
- $$$
- DAZ Productions, Inc.: `http://www.daz3d.com`

2. APPLICATIONS

- Carrara is a software package of 3D solutions for realistic figure posing, modeling, landscape design, physics, and animation
- It has been used by many digital content creators in many industries including magazines, comic books, newspapers, TV, games, film and more

3. WEB RESOURCES

- Official website: `http://www.daz3d.com/i.x/software/carrara`

Cheetah3D

1. PLATFORMS, PRICES, AND SUPPLIER/CREATOR

- Mac OS
- $129
- Martin Wengenmayer: http://www.cheetah3d.com/

2. APPLICATIONS

- Cheetah3D is 3D modeling, rendering and animation software
- This program is aimed at beginning and amateur 3D artists, but is also used by professionals

3. WEB RESOURCES

- Official website: http://www.cheetah3d.com/
- Wikipedia: http://en.wikipedia.org/wiki/Cheetah3D

CINEMA 4D

1. PLATFORM, PRICES, AND SUPPLIER/CREATOR

- Mac OS, Windows, Linux
- $895
- Maxon Computer Inc.: http://www.maxon.net

2. APPLICATIONS

- Cinema 4D is a 3D modeling, animation and rendering tool
- It is capable of procedural and polygonal/subdivision modeling, animating, lighting, texturing and rendering, and it has been used in the fields of film, television, architecture, the sciences and multimedia

3. WEB RESOURCES

- Official website: http://www.maxon.net/pages/products/cinema4d/cinema4d_e.html
- Wikipedia: http://en.wikipedia.org/wiki/Cinema_4D

ClayWorks

1. PLATFORMS, PRICE, AND SUPPLIER/CREATOR

- Windows, Mac OS
- Freeware
- Tim Lewis. `http://cs-svr1.swan.ac.uk/~cstim/clay/index.html`

2. APPLICATIONS

- A 3D modeling and rendering tool
- It allows users to model virtual objects and run computation-intensive deformation simulations for collaborative real-time modeling and high performance simulations

3. WEB RESOURCES

- Official website: `http://members.aol.com/luther2000/clay.htm`

Coin3D

1. PLATFORMS, PRICES, AND SUPPLIER/CREATOR

- Windows, Mac OS, Unix/Linux
- Freeware
- SIM (Systems in Motion): `http://www.km.kongsberg.com/sim`

2. APPLICATIONS

- Coin3D is a 3D graphics toolkit for 3D graphics development
- It allows the use of scene graph data structures to render 3D graphics in real-time for scientific and engineering visualization applications

3. WEB RESOURCES

- Official Website: `http://www.coin3d.org/`
- Documentation: `http://www.coin3d.org/doc/`

Cosmo Worlds

1. PLATFORMS, PRICES, AND SUPPLIER/CREATOR

- IRIX, Windows
- N/A
- SGI: http://www.sgi.com/

2. APPLICATIONS

- Cosmo Worlds is a Web3D authoring tool
- It can model complex objects and create animated worlds in VRML format for publishing on the World Wide Web

3. WEB RESOURCES

- Official website: http://techpubs.sgi.com/library/tpl/cgi-bin/ getdoc.cgi?coll=0650&db=relnotes&fname=/usr/relnotes/ cosmoworlds
- Manuals: http://oldsite.vislab.usyd.edu.au/users/manuals/ internet/cosmoworlds/index.html

Crystal 3D-Impact!Pro

1. PLATFORMS, PRICES, AND SUPPLIER/CREATOR

- Windows
- $79
- CrystalGraphics, Inc.: http://www.crystalgraphics.com

2. APPLICATIONS

- Crystal 3D-Impact!Pro is a 3D animation software
- It can enhance the user's web pages, presentations and videos with extraordinary 3D titles, logos, objects and buttons

3. WEB RESOURCES

- Official website: http://www.crystalgraphics.com/web/ 3dimpactpro.main.asp

- Examples/Samples: `http://www.crystalgraphics.com/web/3dimpactpro.features.asp`

CrystalGraphics PowerPlugs

1. PLATFORMS, PRICES, AND SUPPLIER/CREATOR

- Windows
- $$-$$$
- CrystalGraphics, Inc.: `http://www.crystalgraphics.com/`

2. APPLICATIONS

- CrystalGraphics PowerPlugs is a 3D graphics and animations tool
- The PowerPlugs series helps users add special effects such as 3D transition, flash animations, animated 3D titles, impressive charts, templates for web pages, videos, and presentations

3. WEB RESOURCES

- Official website: `http://www.crystalgraphics.com/`

Crystal Space

1. PLATFORMS, PRICES, AND SUPPLIER/CREATOR

- Windows, Linux, Mac OS
- Freeware
- Crystal Space Team: `http://www.crystalspace3d.org/main/Main_Page`

2. APPLICATIONS

- Crystal Space is a software development kit written in C++ based on OpenGL, with bindings for Python, Perl, and Java
- It can be used as a game engine but is more generally used for some kinds of 3D visualization

3. WEB RESOURCES

- Official website: `http://www.crystalspace3d.org/main/Features`
- Wikipedia: `http://en.wikipedia.org/wiki/Crystal_Space`

Cult3D

1. PLATFORMS, PRICES, AND SUPPLIER/CREATOR

- Windows, Mac OS
- Freeware
- Cycore: `http://www.cycore.com`

2. APPLICATIONS

- Cult3D is a real-time rendering engine which lets users interact with advanced 3D animations online
- It has been used for dynamic web marketing, product presentations, and interactive e-communication experiences

3. WEB RESOURCES

- Official website: `http://www.cult3d.com/`
- Examples/Samples: `http://www.oken3d.com/cult3d/html/cult3d.shtml`
- Cult 3D Community: `http://www.worldof3d.com/cgi-bin/Ultimate.cgi?action=intro`

CyberMotion 3D-Designer

1. PLATFORM, PRICE, SUPPLIER/CREATOR

- Windows
- $89
- Reinhard Epp Software: `http://www.3d-designer.com/index.html`

2. APPLICATIONS

- CyberMotion 3D-Designer is a 3D modeling, animation and rendering tool based on raytracing and global illumination algorithms
- It has been used for films, games, daily advertisements, personal creativities, and authors to illustrate their ideas

3. WEB RESOURCES

- Official website: `http://www.3d-designer.com/en/links/links.htm`
- Example/sample: `http://www.3d-designer.com/en/galery/galery.htm`

DAZ Studio

1. PLATFORMS, PRICE, AND SUPPLIER/CREATOR

- Windows, Mac OS
- Freeware
- DAZ Productions, Inc.: `http://www.daz3d.com/`

2. APPLICATIONS

- DAZ Studio is a 3D figure posing and animation tool for designing digital art and animation with virtual people, animals, props, vehicles, backgrounds and more
- It can be used for games, films, storyboarding, medical and technical illustrations, architectural and product design, education, etc.

3. WEB RESOURCES

- Official website: `http://www.daz3d.com/i.x/software/studio/-/?&_m=d`
- Wikipedia: `http://en.wikipedia.org/wiki/DAZ_Studio`

Deep Exploration Standard & CAD Edition

1. PLATFORMS, PRICE, AND SUPPLIER/CREATOR

- Windows

- The Standard Edition for $495, and the CAD Edition for $1,995
- Right Hemisphere Inc.: http://us.righthemisphere.com/

2. APPLICATIONS

- Deep Exploration Standard Edition&CAD Edition are modeling and visualization applications that delivers visual product communication and collaboration to enterprises
- Deep Exploration Standard Edition can increase 3D content across a variety of business and entertainment uses. Deep Exploration CAD Edition enables users to transform, author, and publish 2D and 3D product graphics and documents by using existing engineering CAD design data and other digital content

3. WEB RESOURCES

- Official website: http://us.righthemisphere.com/3dexploration/

Deep Creator

1. PLATFORMS, PRICES, AND SUPPLIER/CREATOR

- Windows
- N/A
- Right Hemisphere Inc.: http://us.righthemisphere.com/

2. APPLICATIONS

- Deep Creator is a 3D authoring application which includes a 3D modeler, a texture creator, and a scripting engine
- It can be used to create interactive 3D environments, assemblies and objects for training, simulations, as well as support, sales, and marketing applications

3. WEB RESOURCES

- Official website: http://www.righthemisphere.com/products/dcreator/index.html

Deep Paint 3D

1. PLATFORMS, PRICES, AND SUPPLIER/CREATOR

- Windows
- $$$-$$$$
- Right Hemisphere: http://www.righthemisphere.com/

2. APPLICATIONS

- Deep Paint 3D is a 3D texturing and painting tool for creative artists or graphics designers
- It can be used by film studios, broadcast, and interactive entertainment companies

3. WEB RESOURCES

- Official website: http://www.righthemisphere.com/products/dp3d/ Deep3D_UV/index.html
- Examples/Samples: http://www.righthemisphere.com/gallery/ deep_paint_3d_gallery.php3

DeleD 3D Editor

1. PLATFORMS, PRICES, AND SUPPLIER/CREATOR

- Windows
- $74.95
- Delgine Website: http://www.delgine.com/

2. APPLICATIONS

- DeleD 3D Editor is a 3D modeling tool which is mainly focused on 3D game development
- It is capable of creating contents for game development, educational services, web design, prototyping and image creation

3. WEB RESOURCES

- Official website: `http://www.delgine.com/index.php?filename=product_deled`
- Tutorials: `http://www.delgine.com/index.php?filename=deled_tutorials`

DesignCAD 3000

1. PLATFORMS, PRICE, AND SUPPLIER/CREATOR

- Windows
- $99.95
- Upperspace Corporation: `http://www.upperspace.com/`

2. APPLICATIONS

- DesignCAD is a suite of computer-aided design software
- These software are designed for creating drafting, modeling and animation for modeling furniture, floor plans, engineering layouts and architectural drawings

3. WEB RESOURCES

- Official website: `http://www.upperspace.com/products/designcad.asp`
- DesignCAD Wiki: `http://www3.designcadcommunity.com/tiki-index.php`

DESIGN WORKSHOP PRO

1. PLATFORMS, PRICE, AND SUPPLIER/CREATOR

- Windows, Mac OS
- $$$
- Artifice, Inc.: `http://www.artifice.com/index.htmlApplications`

2. APPLICATIONS

- Design Workshop Pro is a design-oriented 3D modeling tool

- It can be used by interior designers, landscape architects, and exhibit and production designers for creating built-environment projects, models, and images

3. WEB RESOURCES

- Official website: http://www.artifice.com/index.html
- Tutorial: http://www.artifice.com/tutorial.html

DICE

1. PLATFORMS, PRICE, AND SUPPLIER/CREATOR

- Windows
- N/A
- DynArray Corporation: http://www.dynarray.com

2. APPLICATIONS

- Dice Application System is a facility for running prepackaged algorithms (called personalities) as a dynamic link library
- It provides an industrial array-oriented base on which a variety of visualization applications can be built by creating personalities

3. WEB RESOURCES

- Official website: http://www.dynarray.com/Dyndice1.htm

DigiCad 3D

1. PLATFORMS, PRICE, AND SUPPLIER/CREATOR

- Windows, Mac OS
- Regular price is $585; Educational price is $175
- DigiCad 3D: http://www.interstudio.net/index.html

2. APPLICATIONS

- DigiCad 3D is modeling software for creating 3D models from photographs

- It is capable of dealing with images, drawings, photographs of buildings, regular or irregular surfaces and maps, and can be used in photogrammetry, cartography, and architectural photogrammetry

3. WEB RESOURCES

- Official website: `http://www.interstudio.net/DigicadE.html`

Director 8.5 Shockwave Studio

1. PLATFORMS, PRICES, AND SUPPLIER/CREATOR

- Windows, Mac OS
- $1,199
- Macromedia, Inc.: `http://www.macromedia.com/`

2. APPLICATION

- The Shockwave Studio 8.5 studio is a multimedia-authoring suite including Director, Fireworks, Shockwave Multiuser Server and some freebie software
- These software are designed for professional web developers and 3D content developers to combine graphics, sound, animation, text and video to create streaming, interactive, multi-user contents

3. WEB RESOURCES

- Official website: `http://www.macromedia.com/software/director/`

DirectX (Dirct3D)

1. PLATFORMS, PRICE, AND SUPPLIER/CREATOR

- Windows
- Freeware
- Microsoft Corporation: `http://www.microsoft.com/`

2. APPLICATIONS

- DirectX is a collection of application programming interfaces for multimedia, especially game programming and video

3. WEB RESOURCES

- Official website: `http://www.gamesforwindows.com/en-US/AboutGFW/Pages/directx10-a.aspx`
- Wikipedia: `http://en.wikipedia.org/wiki/DirectX`

DIVE (Distributed Interactive Virtual Environment)

1. PLATFORMS, PRICES, AND SUPPLIER/CREATOR

- Windows, Unix, Irix, Solaris
- Freeware
- Swedish Institute of Computer Science: `http://www.sics.se/`

2. APPLICATIONS

- DIVE is an internet-based multi-user VR system, which supports the development of virtual environments, user interfaces and applications based on shared 3D synthetic environments, also is especially tuned to multi-user applications, where several networked participants interact over a network
- DIVE applications and activities include virtual battlefields, spatial models of interaction, virtual agents, real-world robot control and multi-modal interaction

3. WEB RESOURCES:

- Official website: `http://www.sics.se/dive/dive.html`

DIVERSE

Device Independent Virtual Environments — Reconfigurable, Scalable, Extensible

1. PLATFORMS, PRICES, AND SUPPLIER/CREATOR

- Linux, Irix, Windows, mac OS

- Free (GNU LGPL and GPL) software
- Open Tech, Inc.: `http://www.opentechinc.com/`

2. APPLICATIONS

- DIVERSE is an API for developing virtual reality applications
- It is designed to enable developers to build applications that can run on the desktop as well as with various immersive systems

3. WEB RESOURCES

- Official website: `http://diverse-vr.org/index.php`
- Documentation: `http://diverse-vr.org/index.php?page=documentation`

DMesh

1. PLATFORMS, PRICES, AND SUPPLIER

- Windows
- N/A
- Bruce D Lamming: `http://www.geocities.com/SoHo/Studios/4500/index.htm`

2. APPLICATIONS

- DMesh is a mesh creation and deformation tool for use with 3D modeling, rendering and animation software
- It can be used to create smooth-surfaced and texture-aware organic objects such as heads, arms and torso's, or for other more inanimate objects such as hanging ropes, flowing curtains, wrought iron fences, or twisted and distorted objects

3. WEB RESOURCES

- Official website: `http://www.geocities.com/SoHo/Studios/4500/index.htm`

Draw3D

1. PLATFORMS, PRICES, AND SUPPLIER

- Windows
- Freeware
- Shervin Emamit: `http://www.geocities.com/SunsetStrip/Stage/8513/Draw3D.html`

2. APPLICATIONS

- Draw3D is a modeler for creating and modifying 3D objects
- It can be used for modeling purposes, such as virtual objects in games, complex objects in virtual environments

3. WEB RESOURCES

- Official website: `http://www.geocities.com/SunsetStrip/Stage/8513/Draw3D.html`
- Tutorials: `http://www.geocities.com/SunsetStrip/Stage/8513/Draw3D.html`

Effect3D

1. PLATFORMS, PRICES, AND SUPPLIER/CREATOR

- Windows
- $99.95
- Reallusion: `http://www.reallusion.com`

2. APPLICATIONS

- Effect3D is an editing tool to create professional 3D animated graphics
- It is capable of creating 3D objects, adding animation, and using a variety of effects including backgrounds, rendering effects, material settings, lighting, and animation effects for presentations

3. WEB RESOURCES

- Official website: `http://www.reallusion.com/e3dstudio/`

- Tutorial: `http://www.reallusion.com/e3dstudio/e3ds_tutorial.asp`
- Examples/Samples: `http://www.reallusion.com/e3dstudio/e3ds_gallery.asp`

EIAS

1. PLATFORMS, PRICES, AND SUPPLIER/CREATOR

- Windows, Mac OS
- $795
- EI Technology Group LLC.: `http://www.eitechnologygroup.com/`

2. APPLICATIONS

- EIAS is a suite of 3D rendering and animation software including Animator, Camera, Renderama, and Radiosity
- These software are capable of creating character animations, building worlds with 3D painting, and designing sophisticated products; they can be used in film and television productions

3. WEB RESOURCES

- Official website: `http://www.eitechnologygroup.com/products/electric_image_animation_system`
- Wikipedia: `http://en.wikipedia.org/wiki/Electric_Image_Animation_System`

ElectricImage Animation System

1. PLATFORMS, PRICES, AND SUPPLIER/CREATOR

- Windows, Mac OS
- $795
- EI Technology Group, LLC: `http://www.eitechnologygroup.com`

2. APPLICATIONS

- ElectricImage Animation System is a 3D modeling, rendering, and animation suite including Animator, Camera, Renderama, Radiosity, etc.

- This suite of applications is capable of creating character animations, building worlds with 3D painting, and designing sophisticated products, and can be used by architects and engineers, as well as product designers and illustrators

3. WEB RESOURCES

- Official website: `http://www.eitechnologygroup.com/`

- Examples/Samples: `http://eitechnologygroup.com/gallery`

Endorphin

1. PLATFORMS, PRICES, AND SUPPLIER/CREATOR

- Windows

- N/A

- NaturalMotion Ltd.: `http://www.naturalmotion.com/company.htm`

2. APPLICATIONS

- Endorphin is 3D character animation software based on dynamic motion synthesis that combines artificial intelligence, biomechanics, and dynamics simulation

- It is in use at visual effects studios, game studios and simulation companies

3. WEB RESOURCES

- Official website: `http://www.naturalmotion.com/products.htm`

- Tutorials: `http://download.naturalmotion.com/filesfrom/Tutorials.pdf`

EnLiten

1. PLATFORMS, PRICE, AND SUPPLIER/CREATOR

- Windows, Unix, Linux, Mac OS

- Freeware
- Computational Engineering International (CEI): http://www.ceintl.com/

2. APPLICATIONS

- EnLiten is a 3D geometry viewer to display, manipulate and analyze complex visualization scenarios
- It can be used for computational fluid dynamics (CFD), finite element analysis (FEA), crash analysis, aerodynamics, scientific visualization, etc.

3. WEB RESOURCES

- Official website: http://www.ceintl.com/enliten.html
- Tutorials: http://www.ensight.com/ensight-tutorials-12.html

Ensight

1. PLATFORM, PRICES, AND SUPPLIER/CREATOR

- Windows, Mac OS, Unix
- $625 for academic; $2500 up
- Computational Engineering International: http://www.ensight.com

2. APPLICATIONS

- Ensight is a visualization tool with VR and parallel post-processing capabilities designed for presenting and analyzing large datasets resulting from computer simulations and testing
- It can be used for computational fluid dynamics (CFD), structural analysis, combustion modeling, thermodynamics, electromagnetics, crashworthiness, atmospherics, particle physics, and injection molding

3. WEB RESOURCES

- Official website: http://www.ensight.com/
- Examples/Samples: http://www.ensight.com/gallery/index.php

EON STUDIO

1. PLATFORMS, PRICES, AND SUPPLIER/CREATOR

- Windows
- $3,795
- EON Reality Inc.: http://www.eonreality.com

2. APPLICATIONS

- EON Studio is software for creating and deploying interactive real-time 3D simulations
- Its popular application areas include marketing and sales, product development, simulation based training, architectural studies, and community planning

3. WEB RESOURCES

- Official website: http://www.eonreality.com/
  index.php?ref=products/software/studio

Equinox-3D

1. PLATFORMS, PRICES, AND SUPPLIER/CREATOR

- Linux, Irix, Mac OS
- Freeware
- Gabor Nagy: http://www.equinox3d.com/

2. APPLICATIONS

- Equinox-3D is a 3D modeler with a multi-threaded ray-tracer
- It can be used for modeling purposes such as product prototypes, game model creation, and complex objects in virtual environments

3. WEB RESOURCES

- Official website: http://www.equinox3d.com/
- Examples/Samples: http://www.equinox3d.com/Gallery.html

Evolver

1. PLATFORMS, PRICES, AND SUPPLIER/CREATOR

- Linux, Mac OS, Windows, Solaris
- Freeware
- Morgan McGuire: `http://www.cs.brown.edu/~morgan/aa/index.html`

2. APPLICATIONS

- Evolver is an animation program, which contains effects such as Gaussian blur, particle system, zoom, rotation, distortion, environment mapping, and edge filter, as well as an entire interpreted programming language framework and genetic algorithm implementation
- This program is used by graphics developers for researching computer-generated artwork

3. WEB RESOURCES

- Official website: `http://www.cs.brown.edu/~morgan/aa/index.html`
- Examples/Samples: `http://www.cs.brown.edu/~morgan/aa/gallery/index.html`

eZ-Motion

1. PLATFORMS, PRICES, AND SUPPLIER/CREATOR

- Windows, Mac OS
- $64.99
- Beatware Inc.: http://testou.free.fr/www.beatware.com/index-2.html

2. APPLICATIONS

- eZ-Motion is a tool for web animation and graphics
- It is capable of importing and animating 3D models, generating 3D text and animation from some modifiable templates or an animation editor for an electronic presence over the web

3. WEB RESOURCES

- Official website: `http://testou.free.fr/www.digitalriver.com/dr/`
  `v2/ec_MAINa0ce.html?CID=0&PN=5&SP=10007&SID=22016&PID=283760`

Facial Studio

1. PLATFORMS, PRICES, AND SUPPLIER/CREATOR

- Windows
- $899
- Di-O-Matic, Inc.: `http://www.di-o-matic.com/`

2. APPLICATIONS

- Facial Studio is a software for creating 3D heads
- It can be used for games, films, storyboarding, medical and technical illustration, education, etc.

3. WEB RESOURCES

- Official website: `http://www.di-o-matic.com/products/Software/`
  `FacialStudio/`
- Examples/Samples: `http://www.di-o-matic.com/products/Software/`
  `FacialStudio/gallery.html`

FAST (Flow Analysis Software Toolkit)

1. PLATFORMS, PRICE, AND SUPPLIER/CREATOR

- IRIX
- N/A
- NAS, a division of NASA: `http://www.nas.nasa.gov/`

2. APPLICATIONS

- FAST is a software environment for analyzing data from numerical simulations

- This package can be used to visualize scalar and vector data that can be mapped to a PLOT3D or unstructured grid

3. WEB RESOURCES

- Official website: http://www.nas.nasa.gov/Resources/Software/swdescriptions.html#FAST
- Examples/Samples: http://www.nas.nasa.gov/News/Images/images.html

FERRET

1. PLATFORMS, PRICES, AND SUPPLIER/CREATOR

- Unix, Windows using X windows for display
- Freeware
- PMEL, NOAA: http://www.pmel.noaa.gov/

2. APPLICATIONS

- Ferret is an interactive computer visualization and analysis package
- It can be used in the oceanographic community to analyze data and create publication-quality graphics

3. WEB RESOURCES

- Official website: http://ferret.pmel.noaa.gov/Ferret/
- Documentation: http://ferret.pmel.noaa.gov/Ferret/documentation

Fieldview

1. PLATFORMS, PRICE, AND SUPPLIER/CREATOR

- HP-UX, IBM, LINUX, MAC OS,SGI, SUN, WINDOWS, COMPAQ
- $$$$$
- Intelligent Light Company: http://www.ilight.com/index.php

2. APPLICATIONS

- FieldView is post-processing software for computational fluid dynamics
- It allows interactive exploration to examine and compare cases, extract critical values, and make compelling presentations

3. WEB RESOURCES

- Official website: `http://www.ilight.com/nparc.htm`
- Reference manual: `http://www.erc.wisc.edu/~hessel/research/manuals/FVReference_Manual8win.pdf`

Finalrender

1. PLATFORMS, PRICE, AND SUPPLIER/CREATOR

- Windows
- N/A
- Cebas Computer GmbH: `http://www.cebas.com/`

2. APPLICATIONS

- FinalRender is a raytracing graphics rendering engine
- It can be used with Autodesk media and entertainment's 3D Studio Max, Maya, and Maxon's Cinema 4D software for modeling or animation

3. WEB RESOURCES

- Official website: `http://www.finalrender.com/products/overview.php?UD=10-7888-35-788&PAID=1`
- Wikipedia: `http://en.wikipedia.org/wiki/FinalRender`

FORM-Z

1. PLATFORMS, PRICES, AND SUPPLIER/CREATOR

- Windows, MAC OS
- $1,495

- AutoDesSys, Inc.: `http://www.formz.com/`

2. APPLICATIONS

- FORM-Z is a general purpose solid and surface modeler
- It can be used by architects, landscape architects, urban designers, engineers, animators and illustrators, and industrial and interior designers in design fields that deal with the articulation of 3D spaces and forms

3. WEB RESOURCES

- Official website: `http://www.formz.com/products/formz/formz.html`
- Examples/Samples: `http://www.formz.com/gallery/gallery.html`

Freeworld3D

1. PLATFORMS, PRICES, AND SUPPLIER/CREATOR

- Windows
- $30
- Soconne Inc.: `http://freeworld3d.org/`

2. APPLICATIONS

- Freeworld3D is an interactive real-time 3D terrain editor and world editor specifically designed for game development

3. WEB RESOURCES

- Official website: `http://freeworld3d.org/`
- Examples/Samples: `http://freeworld3d.org/gallery.html`

Gamebryo

1. PLATFORMS, PRICES, AND SUPPLIER/CREATOR

- Windows, Xbox, Playstation, GameCube
- N/A

- Emergent Game Technologies (EGT): http://www.emergent.net/

2. APPLICATIONS

- Emergent's Gamebryo is a 3D computer graphics engine targeted to game development
- It provides the rendering, animation and special effects features necessary to create a genre of games, and can be used by game developers and artists

3. WEB RESOURCES

- Official website: http://www.ndl.com/en/Products/Gamebryo/
- Wikipedia: http://en.wikipedia.org/wiki/NetImmerse

GameSpace

1. PLATFORMS, PRICES, AND SUPPLIER/CREATOR

- Windows
- N/A
- Caligari: http://www.caligari.com

2. APPLICATIONS

- GameSpace is a 3D graphics authoring environment designed for game developers
- It is capable of creating characters, worlds, weapons and more, with import and export for major games and game development formats

3. WEB RESOURCES

- Official website: http://www.caligari.com/gamespace/
- Tutorial: http://www.caligari.com/gamespace/tutorial/video.asp

Genesis3D

1. PLATFORMS, PRICE, AND SUPPLIER/CREATOR

- Windows

- Freeware
- Eclipse Entertainment: `http://www.genesis3d.com/`

2. APPLICATIONS

- Genesis3D is real-time 3D rendering software for game developing
- It allows game creators to use 3D moving characters that are supported by an inner frame (bone system), allowing for animation to create complex movement and the game world

3. WEB RESOURCES

- Official website: `http://www.genesis3d.com/`
- Wikipedia: `http://en.wikipedia.org/wiki/Genesis3D`
- Tutorials: `http://welcome.to/genesis3d-university/`

GenTools

1. PLATFORMS, PRICE, AND SUPPLIER/CREATOR

- Windows
- $299 for GenHead, and $399 for GenCrowd 3D
- Genemation: `http://www.genemation.com/New_Pages/company_main.cfm`

2. APPLICATIONS

- The GenTools product consists of GenHead and GenCrowd 3D, designed for both professional and amateur digital content artists
- GenHead is software to create 3D heads from 2D digital photographs, and GenCrowd 3D is a tool to generate hundreds of realistic, copyright-free, 3D heads by age, gender and ethnicity

3. WEB RESOURCES

- Official website: `http://www.genemation.com/New_Pages/gentools.cfm`
- Tutorials: `http://www.genemation.com/new_pages/genhead_tutorials.cfm`

Geomagic Studio

1. PLATFORMS, PRICE, AND SUPPLIER/CREATOR

- Windows
- N/A
- Geomagic, Inc.: http://www.geomagic.com/

2. APPLICATIONS

- Geomagic Studio is a 3D modeling tool for product design, re-engineering of parts and customization to engineering analysis, prototyping and digital archiving
- It can be used by professionals in industries such as automotives, aerospace, medical devices and consumer products

3. WEB RESOURCES

- Official website: http://www.geomagic.com/en/products/studio/
- Examples/Samples: http://www.geomagic.com/en/products/studio/demos/index.php

Geomview

1. PLATFORMS, PRICES, AND SUPPLIER/CREATOR

- Unix, Mac OS, Windows using Cygwin
- Free software available under the terms of the GNU Lesser General Public License (GPL)
- Geomview team: http://www.geomview.org/

2. APPLICATIONS

- Geomview is a 3D interactive geometry program focusing on mathematical visualization with options to allow hyperbolic space to be visualized
- It can be used as a viewer to see and manipulate objects, or a display engine for other programs which produce dynamically changing geometry

3. WEB RESOURCES

- Official website: http://www.geomview.org/overview/

- Wikipedia: http://en.wikipedia.org/wiki/Geomview
- Documentation: http://www.geomview.org/docs/

GKS-3D

1. PLATFORM, PRICE, AND SUPPLIER/CREATOR
- Windows, Unix, Linux, Irix
- Around $13,000
- CERN: cern.web.cern.ch/CERN/

2. APPLICATIONS
- GKS-3D is a 3D extension to the graphical kernel system
- It provides both GKS compatibility and the additional functionality necessary for 3D capability, which allows the production of 3-D objects

3. WEB RESOURCES
- Official website: http://wwwasdoc.web.cern.ch/wwwasdoc/WWW/gks/gksguide.html
- Documentation: http://wwwasdoc.web.cern.ch/wwwasdoc/gks_html3/node151.html

GL Studio

1. PLATFORMS, PRICE, AND SUPPLIER/CREATOR
- Windows, IRIX, Linux
- N/A
- DIST (Distributed Simulation Technology), Inc.: http://www.simulation.com/index.html

2. APPLICATIONS

- GL Studio is a prototyping and design tool, which can export code for use applications, for use in reusable simulation objects, for use in Java applications, and for use in Active-X controls
- It can be used for prototype instruments, maintenance and part task trainers, computer based training, virtual simulators, etc.

3. WEB RESOURCES

- Official website: `http://www.simulation.com/products/glstudio/glstudio.html`
- Examples/Samples: `http://www.simulation.com/products/glstudio/content/demos/executable.html`

Glu3D

1. PLATFORMS, PRICE, AND SUPPLIER/CREATOR

- Windows, Linux
- $295
- 3daliens inc.: `http://3daliens.com/glu3D/index.htm`

2. APPLICATIONS

- Glu3d is fluid simulations software that uses particles to simulate liquid behavior, and generates a multi-resolution polygonal surface to display the liquid surface

3. WEB RESOURCES

- Official website: `http://3daliens.com/glu3D/index.htm`
- Wikipedia: `http://en.wikipedia.org/wiki/Glu3d`

GL4Java (OPENGL FOR JAVA)

1. PLATFORMS, PRICES, AND SUPPLIER/CREATOR

- Windows, Linux, Irix, Mac, Solaris

- Freeware
- Jausoft: http://www.jausoft.com/

2. APPLICATIONS

- GL4Java is an OpenGL language and Java language combined solution which maps the complete OpenGL API and the complete GLU API to Java
- It is developed for using 3D in serious applications, as well as in games and web pages

3. WEB RESOURCES

- Official website: http://www.jausoft.com/gl4java/
- Tutorial: http://www.softwareburner.de/tutorial.htm
- Documentation: http://gl4java.sourceforge.net/docs/

GNUPlot

1. PLATFORMS, PRICES, AND SUPPLIER

- Windows, Linux, Unix, Mac OS
- Freeware
- Thomas Williams, Colin Kelley: http://www.gnuplot.info

2. APPLICATIONS

- GNUPlot is a plotting tool that can generate 2D and 3D plots of functions and data
- It can be used as a plotting engine with various scripting languages, such as Python (via Gnuplot-py and SAGE), Ruby (via rgnuplot) and Smalltalk (Squeak and GNU Smalltalk)

3. WEB RESOURCES

- Official website: http://www.gnuplot.info/
- Wikipedia: http://en.wikipedia.org/wiki/GNUPlot
- Tutorial: http://www.eng.hawaii.edu/Tutor/Gnuplot/

GRAFITTI

1. PLATFORMS, PRICES, AND SUPPLIER/CREATOR

- Windows, Mac OS
- $299
- Boris FX: http://www.borisfx.com/products/GRAFFITI/

2. APPLICATION

- Graffiti is an integrated 2D and 3D vector title animation tool
- It is capable of creating sophisticated title animation including type on text, text on a path, 3D text with bump maps reflections and more, for the innovative and user friendly titling for in the industry or business

3. WEB RESOURCES

- Official Site: http://www.borisfx.com/product/graffiti/
- Tutorials: http://www.borisfx.com/tutorials/

Grome Modeler

1. PLATFORMS, PRICES, AND SUPPLIER/CREATOR

- Windows, Mac OS
- EUR299 for Grome Professional Edition, and EUR89 for Grome Standard Edition
- Quad Software: http://www.quadsoftware.com/

2. APPLICATION

- Grome Modeler is a terrain and game scene modeling application
- It is used by professional game developers and companies in the 3D simulation industry, also used by several universities for graphics courses and multimedia projects

3. WEB RESOURCES

- Official website: http://www.quadsoftware.com/ index.php?m=section&sec=product&subsec=editor

- Tutorial: `http://www.quadsoftware.com/ index.php?m=section&sec=product&subsec=editor&target=editor_ tutorials`

GURU 3D-CONVERTER

1. PLATFORM, PRICE, AND SUPPLIER

- Windows
- $10
- Morgan Gunnarsson: `http://hem3.passagen.se/sardonyx`

2. APPLICATIONS

- It is a 3D-Converter, which converts 3D Studio files (.3ds) to the DirectX file (.x) format

3. WEB RESOURCES

- Official website: `http://hem.passagen.se/sardonyx/`

Hexagon

1. PLATFORM, PRICE, AND SUPPLIER

- Windows, Mac OS
- $$$
- DAZ Productions, Inc.: `http://www.daz3d.com`

2. APPLICATIONS

- Hexagon is a 3D polygonal modeler for three-dimensional computer art
- It delivers 3D modeling tools for illustrators, graphic artists and expert modelers and animators

3. WEB RESOURCES

- Official website: `http://www.daz3d.com/i.x/software/hexagon/-/ ?&_m=d`

- Examples/Samples: `http://www.daz3d.com/i.x/software/hexagon/-/gallery?&_m=d`

HOUDINI

1. PLATFORMS, PRICES, AND SUPPLIER/CREATOR

- Windows, Linux, Irix
- Houdini Escape: $1,995, Houdini Master: $7,995, and Houdini Batch: $1495
- Side Effects Software Inc.: `http://www.sidefx.com/`

2. APPLICATIONS

- Houdini software is a family of animation tools for visual effects artists and technical directors
- Houdini Escape can be used to model, animate, render and composite, and is suitable for character animation
- Houdini Master is mainly used for 3D animation and visual effects with node-based procedural workflow Houdini Batch is capable of generating render scene description files, geometry archive files, batch process dynamic simulation or constructing large numbers of scene files using shared assets

3. WEB RESOURCES

- Official website: `http://www.sidefx.com/community/learn/index.html`
- Examples/Samples: `http://www.sidefx.com/index.php?option=com_content&task=blogsection&id=22&Itemid=279`

HyperFun

1. PLATFORMS, PRICE, AND CONTRIBUTORS

- Windows
- N/A
- HyperFun Team: `http://www.hyperfun.org/`

2. APPLICATIONS

- HyperFun is a programming language and software based on a mathematical framework for geometry and function representation (FRep)
- It has been used to create, visualize, and fabricate volumetric 3D and higher dimensional models

3. WEB RESOURCES

- Official website: http://www.hyperfun.org/
- Wikipedia: http://en.wikipedia.org/wiki/HyperFun
- Tutorial: http://www.itn.liu.se/~andhe/TNM079-2004/hyperfun/HF_Tut_e.html

iClone

1. PLATFORMS, PRICES, AND SUPPLIER/CREATOR

- Windows
- $$-$$$
- Reallusion Inc.: http://www.reallusion.com

2. APPLICATIONS

- iClone is a 3D filmmaking tool to create talking animated custom characters, clothing, 3D scenes and special effects for animated movies

3. WEB RESOURCES

- Official website: http://www.reallusion.com/products.asp

ICA (Internet Character Animator)

1. PLATFORM, PRICE, AND SUPPLIER/CREATOR

- Widows
- $179.95
- ParallelGraphics: http://www.parallelgraphics.com

2. APPLICATIONS

- ICA is a character animator allowing the user to add a variety of expressions, gestures and movements
- Animated characters can be published on the web or placed into Internet scene assembler worlds

3. WEB RESOURCES

- Related information: `http://www.download.com/Internet-Character-Animator/3000-6677_4-10041161.html?tag=pub`

IDL

1. PLATFORM, PRICES, AND SUPPLIER/CREATOR

- Windows, Unix, Mac OS
- N/A
- ITT Corporation: `http://www.rsinc.com/idl/`

2. APPLICATIONS

- IDL is software for data analysis, visualization, and cross-platform application development
- It can be used for technical professionals to develop algorithms, interfaces, and visualizations, as well as crunch through large numerical problems

3. WEB RESOURCES

- Official website: `http://www.ittvis.com/idl/idl7.asp`
- Manual: `http://translate.google.com/translate?hl=en&sl=de&u=http://www.uni-giessen.de/hrz/software/idl/&prev=/search%3Fq%3DIDL%26start%3D60%26hl%3Den%26lr%3D%26sa%3DN`

Igor Pro

1. PLATFORM, PRICES, AND SUPPLIER/CREATOR

- Windows, Mac OS
- $550 for Standard, $395 for Academic, and $85 for Student
- Wavemetrics Inc.: http://www.wavemetrics.com

2. APPLICATIONS

- Igor Pro is scientific data analysis software aimed at time series analysis, curve fitting and image processing
- It can be used for experimentation with scientific and engineering data and for the production of publication-quality graphs and page layouts

3. WEB RESOURCES

- Official website: http://www.wavemetrics.com/products/igorpro/igorpro.htm
- Wikipedia: http://en.wikipedia.org/wiki/IGOR_Pro

Image Modeler

1. PLATFORMS, PRICE, AND SUPPLIER/CREATOR

- Windows, Mac OS
- $$$
- ImageModeler: http://imagemodeler.realviz.com/photomodeling-software-products/imagemodeler/modeling-software.php

2. APPLICATIONS

- ImageModeler is a 2D to 3D modeling software suite
- It is capable of measuring and creating photo-textured 3D objects from multiple photographs taken around an object, and can be used for 3D Web content, movies, games, etc.

3. WEB RESOURCES

- Official website: `http://imagemodeler.realviz.com/photomodeling-software-products/imagemodeler/modeling-software.php`
- Tutorials: `http://imagemodeler.realviz.com/photomodeling-software-tutorials/imagemodeler`

iModeller 3D

1. PLATFORMS, PRICE, AND SUPPLIER/CREATOR

- Windows, Mac OS
- iModeller 3D Professional is EUR 719,00, and iModeller 3D Web is EUR 189,00
- iModeller.com: `http://www.imodeller.com/en/`

2. APPLICATIONS

- The iModeller 3D series are modeling tools which can create 3D objects with textures from photographs
- These software are suitable for further 3D rendering, animation or sophisticated web and graphics design

3. WEB RESOURCES

- Official website: `http://www.imodeller.com/en/`
- Tutorials: `http://www.imodeller.com/en/tutorials/`

Indigo (Renderer)

1. PLATFORMS, PRICES, AND SUPPLIER/CREATOR

- Windows
- Freeware
- The Indigo Community: `http://www.indigorenderer.com`

2. APPLICATIONS

- Indigo is a physically-based rendering tool capable of achieving realistic rendering results through features such as metropolis light transport, spectral light calculus, virtual camera model, and physical sky

- It can be used as a renderer for many different modeling programs, such as Blender, 3D Studio MAX, Maya, Rhinoceros 3D, Cinema4D, Sketchup, etc.

3. WEB RESOURCES

- Official webSite: `http://www.indigorenderer.com`

- Manuals & Tutorials: `http://www.indigorenderer.com/joomla/index.php?option=com_docman&task=cat_view&gid=31&Itemid=62`

INSPIRE

1. PLATFORMS, PRICE, AND SUPPLIER/CREATOR

- Windows

- N/A

- Integra Inc.: `http://www.integra.jp/en/inspirer/index.html`

2. APPLICATIONS

- Inspire is a rendering and modeling tool for realistic light simulation

- It allows the user to virtually reproduce spaces and objects and to simulate various lighting effects for analysis of illumination characteristics, and can be used by lighting, automobile and aerospace manufacturers as well as in architectural offices

3. WEB RESOURCES

- Official website: `http://www.integra.jp/en/inspirer/index.html`

- Examples: `http://www.mpi-inf.mpg.de/resources/atrium/atrium_old/welcome.html`

Insta3D Pro

1. PLATFORM, PRICES, AND SUPPLIER/CREATOR

- Windows
- Freeware
- UtahSoft, Inc.: `http://www.utah3d.com`

2. APPLICATIONS

- Insta3D Pro is 3D scene authoring and animation software for broadcast graphics
- It provides powerful features for creating 3D on air graphics, including 3D scene composition, fast animation and rendering, and template generation, for various broadcast applications such as news, sports, and elections

3. WEB RESOURCES

- Official website: `http://www.utah3d.com`

ISA (INTERNET SCENE ASSEMBLER)

1. PLATFORMS, PRICES, AND SUPPLIER/CREATOR

- Windows
- Price $749.95
- ParallelGraphics: `http://www.parallelgraphics.com`

2. APPLICATIONS

- Internet Scene Assembler Pro is a 3D and VRML authoring tool
- It facilitates the creation of interactive and dynamic applications such as distance training manuals, maintenance and support guides and interactive product presentations, among others

3. WEB RESOURCES

- Official website: `http://www.parallelgraphics.com/products/isa/`
- Examples/Samples: `http://www.parallelgraphics.com/products/isa/examples`

ISB (INTERNET SPACE BUILDER)

1. PLATFORMS, PRICES, AND SUPPLIER/CREATOR

- Windows
- $78.95
- Parallel Graphics: http://www.parallelgraphics.com

2. APPLICATIONS

- ISB is a Web 3D authoring tool suitable for designers of all levels
- Its possible uses include revamping websites, establishing virtual exhibitions and galleries, architecture and design, and creating virtual worlds

3. WEB RESOURCES

- Official website: http://www.parallelgraphics.com/products/isb/
- Examples/Samples: http://www.parallelgraphics.com/products/isb/examples

IRIS Explorer

1. PLATFORMS, PRICE, AND SUPPLIER/CREATOR

- Windows, Unix, Linux
- N/A
- Numerical Algorithms Group (NAG): http://www.nag.com

2. APPLICATIONS

- IRIS Explorer is a visual programming environment for 3D visualization, animation and manipulation
- It has been used by industry, universities, and research institutions in a wide variety of areas such as life sciences, mechanical engineering, chemistry, aerospace engineering, automotive engineering, multimedia, medical imaging and research, electrical engineering, etc.

3. WEB RESOURCES

- Official website: http://www.nag.com/Welcome_IEC.asp

• Documentation: `http://www.nag.com/visual/IE/iecbb/DOC/Index.asp`

iSpace

1. PLATFORM, PRICE, AND SUPPLIER/CREATOR

• Windows
• $99
• Caligari Corporation: `http://www.caligari.com/`

2. APPLICATIONS

• iSpace is a web 3D tool that uses advanced 3D rendering techniques (such as transparency, shadows, reflections, textures, true lighting and high quality anti-aliasing) to create photo-realistic pages
• It has been used by web designers and developers who want to design different looks for their websites

3. WEB RESOURCES

• Official website: `http://www.caligari.com/products/iSpace/is1/ Brochure/Realism.asp?Cate=BRealism%20`
• Tutorials: `http://www.caligari.com/products/iSpace/is1/ Tutorials/TUTORIALS1.asp?Cate=Tutorials`

JAVA 3D

1. PLATFORMS, PRICES, COMPANY

• PC, Mac OS, IRIX
• Freeware
• Sun Microsystems: `http://java.sun.com/`

2. APPLICATIONS

• Java 3D is a scene graph-based 3D application programming interface (API) for the Java platform

- It provides a set of object-oriented interfaces which enables users to incorporate high quality, scalable, platform-independent 3D graphics into applications and applets based on Java technology

3. WEB RESOURCES

- Official website: `http://java.sun.com/products/java-media/3D/`
- Tutorials: `http://java.sun.com/developer/onlineTraining/java3d/index.html`
- Wikipedia: `http://en.wikipedia.org/wiki/Java_3D`
- Java 3D wiki: `http://wiki.java.net/bin/view/Javadesktop/Java3D`

Jet 3D

1. PLATFORMS, PRICES, AND SUPPLIER/CREATOR

- Windows
- Free Open Source License
- Jet3D TEAMS: `http://www.jet3d.com/`

2. APPLICATIONS

- Jet3D is a 3D graphics engine built for high performance real-time rendering
- It offers advanced lighting features, 3D modeling support, seamless soft-skin polygonal characters and many other innovations for creating complex virtual environments, games, etc.

3. WEB RESOURCES:

- Official website: `http://www.jet3d.com/`
- Jet3D Wiki: `http://www.jet3d.com/joomla/index.php?option=com_mambowiki&Itemid=49/`
- Wikipedia: `http://gpwiki.org/index.php/Jet3D`

JIG

1. PLATFORMS, PRICES, AND SUPPLIER/CREATOR

- Linux, Irix, Windows
- $$$-$$$$
- Steamboat Software, Inc.: `http://www.steamboat-software.com`

2. APPLICATIONS

- Jig is a production-oriented 3D renderer
- It provides a solution for rendering traditional geometry, photorealistic hair, volumes, particles and more, and can be used by special effects companies and post production facilities

3. WEB RESOURCES

- Official website: `http://www.steamboat-software.com/jigwhat.html`
- Examples/Samples: `http://www.steamboat-software.com/gallerymain.htmlhttp://www.highend3d.com/jig/`

Jmol

1. PLATFORMS, PRICES, AND SUPPLIER/CREATOR

- Windows, Mac OS, Linux, Unix
- Freeware
- Jmol development team: `http://www.jmol.org/`

2. APPLICATIONS

- Jmol is a Java molecular modeling and visualization tool for chemical structures in 3D with features for chemicals, crystals, materials and biomolecules
- It has been used by students, educators, and researchers in chemistry and biochemistry

3. WEB RESOURCES

- Official website: `http://jmol.sourceforge.net/`

- Wikipedia: `http://en.wikipedia.org/wiki/Jmol`
- Jmol Wiki: `http://wiki.jmol.org:81/index.php/Main_Page`

Jogl (Java OpenGL)

1. PLATFORMS, PRICES, AND SUPPLIER/CREATOR

- Windows, Linux, Unix, Solaris, Mac OS
- Freeware
- Game Technology Group at Sun Microsystems Inc.: `http://www.sun.com/`

2. APPLICATIONS

- JOGL is a library which provides access to the APIs in the OpenGL specification and integrates with the AWT and Swing widget sets of Java

3. WEB RESOURCES

- Official website: `https://jogl.dev.java.net/`
- User's guide: `https://jogl.dev.java.net/nonav/source/browse/ *checkout*/jogl/doc/userguide/index.html?rev=HEAD&content- type=text/html`
- Wikipedia: `http://en.wikipedia.org/wiki/Java_OpenGL`

Jsprited

1. PLATFORMS, PRICES, AND SUPPLIER/CREATOR

- Windows, Linux
- Freeware
- Mainreactor: `http://www.mainreactor.net/`

2. APPLICATIONS

- JSprited is a tool which supports tile and multiple-image-based animation and is mainly used to create sprites for the game *Holotz's Castle*

3. WEB RESOURCES

- Official website: `http://www.mainreactor.net/jsprited/en/index_en.html`

JustCad

1. PLATFORMS, PRICES, AND SUPPLIER/CREATOR

- Windows
- Freeware
- Jon Hoke: `http://justcad.com/`

2. APPLICATIONS

- JustCad is a program designed for beginners to make CAD drawings
- It can be used for drafting, modeling and animation for engineering layouts, architectural drawings, furniture, etc.

3. WEB RESOURCES

- Official website: `http://justcad.com/`

K-3D

1. PLATFORMS, PRICES, AND SUPPLIER/CREATOR

- Windows, UNIX/Linux, Mac OS
- Freeware
- K-3D: `http://www.k-3d.org/wiki/Main_Page`

2. APPLICATIONS

- K-3D is a 3D modeling, animation, and rendering system capable of generating motion picture and animation for the needs of professional artists

3. WEB RESOURCES

- Official website: `http://www.k-3d.org/wiki/Main_Page`

- Examples/Samples: `http://www.k-3d.org/wiki/Animation_Gallery`

Khoros

1. PLATFORMS, PRICES, AND SUPPLIER/CREATOR

- Linux, Irix, Solaris, Windows
- $$$
- Khoral Research, Inc.: `http://www.khoral.com/`

2. APPLICATIONS

- KhorosPro is a scientific visualization program for information processing, data exploration and data visualization
- It has a wide variety of applications in science, education, engineering (e.g., product visualization), interactive multimedia, medicine, etc.

3. WEB RESOURCES

- Official website: `http://www.khoral.com/`
- Examples/Samples: `http://www.khoral.com/khoros/khoros2/ toolboxes/sampledata.html`

KiNG

1. PLATFORMS, PRICES, AND SUPPLIER/CREATOR

- Window, Unix, Linux, Mac OS
- Freeware
- Duke Biochemistry: `http://kinemage.biochem.duke.edu/`

2. APPLICATIONS

- KiNG is an interactive system for three-dimensional vector graphics
- It supports a set of graphics primitives that make it suitable for many types of graphs, plots, and other illustrations; it can also display macromolecular structures for biophysical research

3. WEB RESOURCES

- Official website: `http://kinemage.biochem.duke.edu/software/king.php`
- Manual: `http://kinemage.biochem.duke.edu/kinemage/king-manual.html`

Kyra Sprite Engine

1. PLATFORMS, PRICES, AND SUPPLIER/CREATOR

- Window, Mac OS, Unix, Linux
- Freeware
- Lee Thomason: `http://www.grinninglizard.com/`

2. APPLICATIONS

- Kyra is a Sprite engine which is the drawing and rendering component of 2D and quasi-3D games

3. WEB RESOURCES

- Official website: `http://www.grinninglizard.com/kyra/`
- Tutorial: `http://www.grinninglizard.com/kyra/tutorial.htm`

LandForm

1. PLATFORM, PRICE COMPANY

- Windows
- $$$
- Rapid Imaging Software, Inc.: `http://www.landform.com`

2. APPLICATIONS

- LandForm C3 is flight and terrain visualization software which features simultaneous 3-D views and map views

- It allows realistic flight and terrain visualization with 6 degrees of freedom of motion, and can save flights as movies for presentations, or as VRML files for virtual reality applications

3. WEB RESOURCES

- Official website: `http://www.landform.com/pages/landformc3.htm`

Lattice Technology Products

1. PLATFORMS, PRICES, AND SUPPLIER/CREATOR

- Windows
- N/A
- Lattice Technology, Inc.: `http://www.lattice.co.jp/`

2. APPLICATIONS

- Lattice Technology Products are 3D modeling programs including XVL Studio, XVL Web Master, XVL Converters, and XVL Player Pro, for the creation, management and integration of 3D content
- These software are capable of creating interactive 3D documents for uses ranging from technical illustrations and electronic training manuals (IETM) to 3D sales presentations and assembly instructions

3. WEB RESOURCES

- Official website: `http://www.lattice3d.com/`
- Examples/Samples: `http://www.lattice3d.com/solutions_view_3d_software.html`

LIFESTUDIO:HEAD

1. PLATFORMS, PRICES, AND SUPPLIER/CREATOR

- Windows
- N/A

- Lifemode Interactive: `http://www.lifemi.com/`

2. APPLICATIONS

- LifeStudio:HEAD is a 3D facial animation package
- It is designed for game developers, distance training, e-learning, and web bloggers, or for someone with a need for a live cyber assistant

3. WEB RESOURCES

- Official website: `http://www.lifemi.com/`
- Examples/Samples: `http://www.lifemi.com/products/gallery/`

LightRay3D

1. PLATFORMS, PRICES, AND SUPPLIER/CREATOR

- Windows
- EUR 68.90
- SXcreations.com: `http://www.sxcreations.com`

2. APPLICATIONS

- Lightray3D is modeling, rendering, animation and game creation software
- It has been used for creating game models, game engine contents, and general visualization data

3. WEB RESOURCES

- Official website: `http://www.sxcreations.com/lr3d/lightray3d.php`
- Examples/Samples: `http://www.sxcreations.com/lr3d/lightray3d.php?page=6`

Lightscape

1. PLATFORMS, PRICES, AND SUPPLIER/CREATOR

- Windows

- $$$
- Lightscape Systems: http://www.lightscapesystems.com/

2. APPLICATIONS

- Lightscape is a tool for lighting design and rendering
- It has been used by digital content creators to illuminate and render real-time environments for film, broadcast, web and interactive gaming applications

3. WEB RESOURCES

- Official website: http://www.lightscapesystems.com/page.php?pi=33
- Examples/Samples: http://www.lightscape.org.uk/gallery.html

LightWave 3D

1. PLATFORMS, PRICES, AND SUPPLIER/CREATOR

- Windows, Mac OS, Amiga
- $$$
- NewTek, Inc.: http://www.newtek.com/

2. APPLICATIONS

- LightWave 3D is a computer graphics program with a built-in radiosity render engine
- It offers features such as ray tracing, motion blur, depth of field, variable lens settings, and other special effects that allow users to create images and animations for business, art forms, film, games, etc.

3. WEB RESOURCES

- Official website: http://www.newtek.com/lightwave/index.php
- Wikipedia: http://en.wikipedia.org/wiki/Lightwave

Lightworks

1. PLATFORMS, PRICES, AND SUPPLIER/CREATOR

- Unix, Windows, Mac OS
- $$-$$$
- LightWork Design: `http://www.lightworkdesign.com/`

2. APPLICATIONS

- LightWorks is a suite of products focusing on a specific area of rendering functionality for market and 3D design applications

3. WEB RESOURCES

- Official website: `http://www.lightworkdesign.com/`
- Examples/Samples: `http://www.lightworkdesign.com/gallery.php?name=New`

Lipservice

1. PLATFORMS, PRICES, AND SUPPLIER/CREATOR

- Window, Linux, OSX
- $$-$$$
- Joe Alter, Inc.: `http://www.joealter.com/`

2. APPLICATIONS

- Lipservice is a 3D facial sculpting and animation program with two distinct components including the Lipservice program and the Lightwave displacement plug-in
- It is capable of controlling the character's morph targets to create a live performance, and it has been used to make a 3D animation movie

3. WEB RESOURCES

- Official website: `http://www.lbrush.com/`
- Tutorials: `http://www.robpowers.com/Tutorials/lipservicedoc.htm`

LithTech Development System

1. PLATFORM, PRICES, AND SUPPLIER/CREATOR

- Windows, Linux, Unix, Mac OS
- N/A
- Monolith Corporation: http://www.monolith.com/

2. APPLICATIONS

- The LithTech Development System (LTDS) is comprised of platform-independent game engines
- It can be used by 3D programmers and game programmers to make 3D based applications

3. WEB RESOURCES

- Official website: http://www.touchdownentertainment.com/
- Wikipedia: http://en.wikipedia.org/wiki/Lithtech

LS-DYNA

1. PLATFORMS, PRICE, AND SUPPLIER/CREATOR

- Unix, Linux, Widows
- $$$
- Livermore Software Technology Corp: http://www.dyna3d.com

2. APPLICATIONS

- LS-DYNA is a general purpose transient dynamic finite element program capable of simulating complex real world problems
- It has been used by automobile, aerospace, military, manufacturing, and bioengineering companies, etc.

3. WEB RESOURCES

- Official website: http://www2.lstc.com/lsdyna.htm
- Wikipedia: http://en.wikipedia.org/wiki/LS-DYNA

- Manuals: `http://www2.lstc.com/manuals.htm`

LSS Vista

1. PLATFORMS, PRICES, AND SUPPLIER/CREATOR

- Windows
- $$$-$$$$
- Company: McCarthy Taylor Systems Ltd.: `http://www.mccarthytaylor.com/`

2. APPLICATIONS

- LSS is a digital terrain modeling (DTM) system capable of importing a wide range of 3D data, including raw land survey information from EDM or GPS instruments, CAD systems and user-definable coordinate formatted data
- It can be used in the fields of archaeology, civil engineering industry, police accident survey, hydrographic survey, geomatics/land survey, mining & quarry, visual & environmental impact, etc.

3. WEB RESOURCES

- Official website: `http://www.mccarthytaylor.com/`

LumeTools

1. PLATFORMS, PRICES, AND SUPPLIER/CREATOR

- Windows, Mac OS, Irix
- $$$-$$$$
- Lume, Inc.: `http://www.lume.com/company.html`

2. APPLICATIONS

- The LumeTools Collection is a series of shaders which mainly consists of five individual sets including LumeLandscape, LumeWater, LumeLight, LumeMatter, and LumeWorkbench

- These tools are designed to meet the needs of professional artists and animators

3. WEB RESOURCES

- Official website: http://www.lume.com/description.html
- Manuals: http://www.lume.com/manual/Contents.html

MapRender3D

1. PLATFORMS, PRICES, AND SUPPLIER/CREATOR

- Windows
- $295 for MapRender3D Pro
- Digital Wisdom Inc.: http://www.digiwis.com

2. APPLICATIONS

- MapRender3D is a terrain modeling, rendering, and visualization software package using either a supplied world-wide elevation database or widely available public domain DEM files
- It can be used by designers, technicians and artists who wish to generate realistic relief shaded landscape perspectives of local, regional, national and worldwide areas for use in a wide range of media, including print, multimedia, animations, web, presentations, publications and in other software applications

3. WEB RESOURCES

- Official website: http://www.maprender3d.com
- Examples/Samples: http://www.maprender3d.com/gallery.htm

Massive

1. PLATFORMS, PRICES, AND SUPPLIER/CREATOR

- Windows, Linux
- $17,999 for Massive Prime, and $5,999 for Massive Jet
- Massive Software: http://www.massivesoftware.com

2. APPLICATIONS

- Massive is a computer animation and artificial intelligence software package used for generating crowd-related visual effects for film and television

3. WEB RESOURCES

- Official website: `http://www.massivesoftware.com/products/`
- Wikipedia: `http://en.wikipedia.org/wiki/Massive_%28software%29`

Materialize 3D!

1. PLATFORM, PRICE, COMPANY

- Windows
- $29.95
- Indotek.com.: `http://www.indotek.com`

2. APPLICATIONS

- Materialize 3D! is a 3D model converter, material and texture editor, and polygon processor
- It is capable of rendering 3D models in a real-time 3D environment with textures and lighting, and can be used for 3D Studio Max, AutoCAD, Direct3D and Persistence of Vision files

3. WEB RESOURCES

- Official website: `http://www.indotek.com/material.php?ad=special_offer_tdxl`

Mathematica

1. PLATFORMS, PRICES, AND SUPPLIER/CREATOR

- Windows, Linux, Unix, Mac OS
- $$$$
- Wolfram Research, Inc.: `http://www.wri.com/`

2. APPLICATIONS

- Mathematica is a specialized computer program used mainly in scientific and mathematical fields

- It provides support for tasks such as symbolic or numerical calculations, arbitrary precision arithmetic, data processing, visualization and simulation, etc.

3. WEB RESOURCES

- Official website: http://www.wolfram.com/products/mathematica/index.html

- Wikipedia: http://en.wikipedia.org/wiki/Mathematica

MATLAB

1. PLATFORMS, PRICES, AND SUPPLIER/CREATOR

- Windows, Linux, Solaris, Mac OS

- $500

- The MathWorks, Inc.: http://www.mathworks.com/

2. APPLICATIONS

- Matlab is a numerical computing environment and programming language offering some functions such as modeling, simulation, visualization, etc.

- It supports a wide range of applications, including signal and image processing, numeric and symbolic computation, engineering and scientific graphics, communications, control design, test and measurement, financial modeling and analysis, computational biology, etc.

3. WEB RESOURCES

- Official website: http://www.mathworks.com/products/matlab/

- Wikipedia: http://en.wikipedia.org/wiki/Matlab

- Documentation: http://www.mathworks.com/access/helpdesk/help/techdoc/matlab.shtml

- Tutorial: http://www.glue.umd.edu/~nsw/ench250/matlab.htm

Maxwell Render

1. PLATFORMS, PRICES, AND SUPPLIER/CREATOR

- Windows, Mac OS, Linux
- N/A
- Next Limit Team: http://www.maxwellrender.com/

2. APPLICATIONS

- Maxwell Render is a rendering engine capable of simulating light as in the real world
- It can be used in areas such as architectural visualization, industrial and product design, prototyping and 3D production

3. WEB RESOURCES

- Official website: http://www.maxwellrender.com/
- Wikipedia: http://en.wikipedia.org/wiki/Maxwell_Render

Maya

1. PLATFORMS, PRICES, AND SUPPLIER/CREATOR

- Windows, Irix, Linux, Mac OS
- $1,995
- Autodesk, Inc.: http://usa.autodesk.com/

2. APPLICATIONS

- Maya software is an integrated 3D modeling, animation and rendering software
- It delivers efficient tools and workflows for creating high-resolution characters, environments, and performances in film, TV, computer and video games, etc.

3. WEB RESOURCES

- Official website: http://usa.autodesk.com/adsk/servlet/index?siteID=123112&id=7635018
- Wikipedia: http://en.wikipedia.org/wiki/Maya_(software)

- Documentation: `http://usa.autodesk.com/adsk/servlet/index?siteID=123112&id=8782084`

MentalRay

1. PLATFORMS, PRICES, AND SUPPLIER/CREATOR

- Unix, Linux, Windows
- $1,000 - $2,500
- Mental Images: `http://www.mentalimages.com/index.html`

2. APPLICATIONS

- MentalRay is a rendering software using advanced acceleration and recursive sampling techniques for faster rendering
- It has been used by special effects and digital film studios, game developer companies, and in the automotive and aerospace industries

3. WEB RESOURCES

- Official website: `http://www.mentalimages.com/2_1_0_mentalray/index.html`
- Wikipedia: `http://en.wikipedia.org/wiki/Mental_Ray`
- Documentation: `http://www.mentalimages.com/2_1_8_documents/index.html`

Merlin 3D

1. PLATFORMS, PRICES, AND SUPPLIER/CREATOR

- Windows
- $595.95
- Merlin3D: `http://www.merlin3d.com`

2. APPLICATIONS

- Merlin 3D is a modeling, rendering, and animation package supporting features such as subdivision surfaces, radiosity rendering and more
- It can be used by creative professionals for a variety of applications such as CAD, digital video, game development, design, architecture, etc.

3. WEB RESOURCES

- Official website: `http://www.merlin3d.com`

Mesa

1. PLATFORM, PRICE, AND DEVELOPERS

- Windows, Linux, Unix, Mac OS
- Freeware
- Tungsten Graphics, Inc.: `http://www.mesa3d.org/`

2. APPLICATIONS

- Mesa 3D is a system for rendering interactive 3D graphics used in many different environments ranging from software emulation to complete hardware acceleration for modern GPUs

3. WEB RESOURCES

- Official website: `http://www.mesa3d.org/`
- Wikipedia: `http://en.wikipedia.org/wiki/Mesa_3D`

Meshwork

1. PLATFORMS, PRICES, AND SUPPLIER/CREATOR

- Mac OS
- $30
- Codenautics: `http://codenautics.com`

2. APPLICATIONS

- Meshwork is a 3D triangle-mesh modeling program
- It was designed especially for making compact, efficient models of the sort needed for games, VRML, POV-Ray, and other OpenGL applications

3. WEB RESOURCES

- Official website: `http://codenautics.com/meshwork/index.html`

Messiah Studio

1. PLATFORMS, PRICES, AND SUPPLIER/CREATOR

- Windows
- $399
- pmG Worldwide, LLC: `http://www.projectmessiah.com/`

2. APPLICATIONS

- Messiah Studio is an animation and rendering software package specifically designed to handle the most demanding character animation and rendering needs
- It has been used in feature films, commercials, games, music videos and print ads

3. WEB RESOURCES

- Official website: `http://www.projectmessiah.com/`

Metris Systems

1. PLATFORMS, PRICES, AND SUPPLIER/CREATOR

- Windows
- N/A
- Metris, Inc.: `http://www.metris.com/`

2. APPLICATIONS

- Metris Systems offer a complete range of metrology solutions including coordinate measuring machines (CMMs), optical CMMs, 3D laser scanners, laser radar, iGPS systems and metrology software for 3D inspection and reverse engineering

- These systems are employed in the aerospace, automotive and other engineering industries where dimensions and tolerances are of crucial importance to guarantee the manufacturing of quality products

3. WEB RESOURCES

- Official website: `http://www.metris.com/`

MicroStation TriForma

1. PLATFORMS, PRICES, AND SUPPLIER/CREATOR

- Windows
- N/A
- Bentley Systems, Inc.: `http://www.bentley.com`

2. APPLICATIONS

- MicroStation TriForma is a modeling tool for architectural and engineering design
- It provides a set of capabilities for object management, geometric modeling, drafting, information and standards management, visualization, drawing and report extraction, integration with analytical tools, interference review, etc.

3. WEB RESOURCES

- Official website: `http://www.bentley.com/products/triforma/`
- Wikipedia: `http://en.wikipedia.org/wiki/MicroStation`
- Examples/Samples: `http://www.bentley.com/en-US/Products/MicroStation/Gallery/`

MilkShape 3D

1. PLATFORMS, PRICES, AND SUPPLIER/CREATOR

- Windows
- $35
- chUmbaLum sOft: http://chumbalum.swissquake.ch

2. APPLICATIONS

- MilkShape 3D is a low-polygon modeler which allows low-level editing on vertices and surfaces and exporting the results to morph target animations or skeletal animations
- It is used mainly by people compiling models for games and other applications

3. WEB RESOURCES

- Official website: http://chumbalum.swissquake.ch/
- Wikipedia: http://en.wikipedia.org/wiki/MilkShape_3D
- Tutorials: http://chumbalum.swissquake.ch/ms3d/tutorials.html

MindsEye

1. PLATFORMS, PRICES, AND SUPPLIER/CREATOR

- Linux, Unix
- Free - GNU General Public License (GPL)
- Mindseye: http://mindseye.sourceforge.net

2. APPLICATIONS

- MindsEye is a 3D modeling and animation package which allows multiple scenes and provides extensive network support

3. WEB RESOURCES

- Official website: http://mindseye.sourceforge.net/
- Documentation: ftp://ftp.freeengineer.org/pub/misc/obsolete-mindseye-doc.tar.gz

Mirai

1. PLATFORMS, PRICES, AND SUPPLIER/CREATOR

- Windows
- $6,495
- IZware LLC: http://www.izware.com/

2. APPLICATIONS

- Mirai is a suite of real-time content creation tools
- It has been used primarily by game developers and companies that need a character animator, biomechanical motion editing, or inverse kinematics (IK) tools

3. WEB RESOURCES

- Official website: http://www.izware.com/mirai/index.htm
- Tutorials: http://www.izware.com/support/mirai-tips.htm
- Wikipedia: http://en.wikipedia.org/wiki/Mirai_%28software%29

Misfit Model 3D

1. PLATFORMS, PRICES, AND SUPPLIER/CREATOR

- Windows, Linux, Mac OS
- Freeware
- Kevin Worcester: http://www.misfitcode.com

2. APPLICATIONS

- Misfit Model 3D is an OpenGL-based 3D model editor that works with triangle-based models
- It supports skeletal animations, texturing, scripting, command-line batch processing, and a plug-in system for adding new model and image filters

3. WEB RESOURCES

- Official website: http://www.misfitcode.com/misfitmodel3d/

Model Magic 3D

1. PLATFORMS, PRICES, AND SUPPLIER/CREATOR

- Windows
- $129
- Imageware Development: http://www.imagewaredev.com/

2. APPLICATIONS

- ModelMagic3D is a modeling tool to create OpenGL rendered 3D Scenes
- It can build 2D and 3D objects from pre-defined primitives adding texture, lighting, shadows, audio effects, and particle simulation and animation for web graphics, screen savers and other graphic applications

3. WEB RESOURCES

- Official website: http://www.imagewaredev.com/modelmagic3d.htm
- Examples/Samples: http://www.imagewaredev.com/gallery_frame.htm

Modo

1. PLATFORMS, PRICES, AND SUPPLIER/CREATOR

- Windows, Mac OS
- $895
- Luxology, LLC: http://www.luxology.com/whatismodo/

2. APPLICATIONS

- Modo is a polygon, subdivision surface, modeling, sculpting, 3D painting, animation, and rendering package
- It is used by designers and artists working in the areas of industrial design, architectural visualization, package design, game development, film and broadcast, education and scientific studies

3. WEB RESOURCES

- Official website: http://www.luxology.com/whatismodo/

- Wikipedia: http://en.wikipedia.org/wiki/Modo_%28software%29

Mojoworld

1. PLATFORMS, PRICES, AND SUPPLIER/CREATOR

- Windows, Mac OS
- $$$
- Pandromeda Inc.: http://www.pandromeda.com/

2. APPLICATIONS

- MojoWorld is a fractal-based modeling program for the creation of digital landscapes
- It can be used by 3D artists, graphic designers, game developers, animators, video production pros and enthusiasts alike

3. WEB RESOURCES

- Official website: http://www.pandromeda.com/products/
- Examples/Samples: http://www.pandromeda.com/gallery/still_thumbnails.php
- Wikipedia: http://en.wikipedia.org/wiki/Mojoworld_Generator

Moray

1. PLATFORMS, PRICES, AND SUPPLIER/CREATOR

- Windows
- $101
- SoftTronics: http://www.stmuc.com/moray/index.html

2. APPLICATIONS

- Moray is an interactive wire-frame modeler designed to create 3D models and scenes to be used with the POV-Ray raytracer

3. WEB RESOURCES

- Official website: `http://www.stmuc.com/moray/`
- Documentation: `http://www.stmuc.com/moray/medocs.html`

MotionBuilder

1. PLATFORMS, PRICES, AND SUPPLIER/CREATOR

- Windows, Mac OS
- N/A
- Autodesk, Inc.: `http://usa.autodesk.com/`

2. APPLICATIONS

- MotionBuilder is a 3D character animation productivity suite for game, film, broadcast, and multimedia production

3. WEB RESOURCES

- Official website: `http://usa.autodesk.com/adsk/servlet/index?siteID=123112&id=6861400`
- Documentation: `http://usa.autodesk.com/adsk/servlet/index?siteID=123112&id=9693656`

Mova Contour

1. PLATFORMS, PRICES, AND SUPPLIER/CREATOR

- Windows, Mac OS
- N/A
- Mova LLC: `http://www.mova.com/`

2. APPLICATIONS

- Mova Contour is a detailed face motion capture tool
- It can be used for games, films, storyboarding, medical and technical illustration, education, etc.

3. WEB RESOURCES

- Official website: `http://www.mova.com/`
- Examples/Samples: `http://www.mova.com/gallery.php`

MultiGen Creator PRO

1. PLATFORMS, PRICES, AND SUPPLIER/CREATOR

- Windows, Irix
- N/A
- MultiGen-Paradigm: `http://www.multigen-paradigm.com`

2. APPLICATIONS

- MultiGen Creator PRO is software for creating real-time 3D content
- It brings together a polygon modeler, vector modeler, and terrain creation into one integrated package for use in visual simulations, interactive games, urban simulations, and other applications

3. WEB RESOURCES

- Official website: `http://www.multigen.com/products/database/creator/modules/mod_creator_pro.shtml`
- Examples/Samples: `http://www.multigen-paradigm.com/news/gallery/index.shtml`

Mvox

1. PLATFORMS, PRICES, AND SUPPLIER/CREATOR

- Unix, Linux, Irix
- Mvox for Linux: $1,465, Mvox for SGI: $2,945
- Anamedic: `http://www.mortenbronielsen.net/anamedic/index.sht`

2. APPLICATIONS

- Mvox is a medical visualization and modeling software which uses advanced OpenGL rendering algorithms and computer graphics hardware to produce 3D visualizations
- It has been used by medical researchers for analyzing medical images

3. WEB RESOURCES

- Official website: http://www.mortenbronielsen.net/anamedic/news/publications.sht
- Examples/Samples: http://www.mortenbronielsen.net/anamedic/customers/index.sht

Natural Motion

1. PLATFORMS, PRICES, AND SUPPLIER/CREATOR

- PlayStation, Xbox 360, Nintendo Wii and PC platforms
- N/A
- NaturalMotion Ltd.: http://www.naturalmotion.com/company.htm

2. APPLICATIONS

- THe Natural Motion family is a 3D character animation system that combine artificial intelligence, biomechanics, and dynamics simulation, including endorphin, euphoria, and morpheme
- These software are in use in games, film, post production and broadcast markets

3. WEB RESOURCES

- Official website: http://www.naturalmotion.com/products.htm
- Tutorial: http://www.naturalmotion.com/education.htm
- Wikipedia: http://en.wikipedia.org/wiki/NaturalMotion

NATURAL SCENE DESIGNER

1. PLATFORMS, PRICES, AND SUPPLIER/CREATOR

- Windows, Mac OS
- $139
- Natural Graphics: http://www.naturalgfx.com/index.htm

2. APPLICATIONS

- Natural Scene Designer is a 3D program
- It is capable of creating realistic natural outdoor scenes with trees, clouds, rocks, bushes, lakes, atmospheric effects, imported 3D objects, and snow in creating realistic pictures, animations, maps, and interactive virtual reality panoramas

3. WEB RESOURCES

- Official website: http://www.naturalgfx.com/products.htm
- Examples/Samples: http://www.naturalgfx.com/examples.htm

Navigram Planner

1. PLATFORMS, PRICES, AND SUPPLIER/CREATOR

- Windows
- $87.50/month
- Navigram: http://www.navigram.com/

2. APPLICATIONS

- Navigram Planner is software for online 3D interior planning, design and configuration
- It aims at those who want to present 3D sketches involved in the furniture business or interior design, such as interior products retailers, furniture manufacturers, and interior designers

3. WEB RESOURCES

- Official website: http://www.navigram.com/index.php?page=planner&lang=en

NCAR Command Language and NCAR Graphics

1. PLATFORMS, PRICES, AND SUPPLIER/CREATOR

- Unix, Linux
- N/A
- The National Center for Atmospheric Research: `http://www.ncar.ucar.edu`

2. APPLICATIONS

- The NCAR Command Language is a free interpreted language designed specifically for scientific data processing and visualization
- NCAR Graphics is a Fortran and C based software package for drawing contours, maps, vectors, streamlines, weather maps, surfaces, histograms, X/Y plots, annotations, and more for scientific visualization

3. WEB RESOURCES

- Official website: `http://www.ncl.ucar.edu/overview.shtml`, `http://www.ncarg.ucar.edu/`
- NCL documentation: `http://ngwww.ucar.edu/ncl/documentation.html`
- NCAR Graphics documentation: `http://ngwww.ucar.edu/ng/documentation.html`

NetImmerse

1. PLATFORMS, PRICES, AND SUPPLIER/CREATOR

- PC, Xbox, SDKs, PS2, Gamecube
- N/A
- Emergent Game Technologies (EGT): `http://www.ndl.com/`

2. APPLICATIONS

- NetImmerse is a 3D gaming engine used by game developers, including developers of PlayStation 2, Xbox, and Gamecube games.
- In addition to providing a programming environment, artists can use it without programming to develop content

3. WEB RESOURCES

- Official website: http://www.ndl.com/
- Wikipedia: http://en.wikipedia.org/wiki/NetImmerse

Now3D

1. PLATFORMS, PRICES, AND SUPPLIER/CREATOR

- Windows
- Freeware
- Giuliano Cornacchiola: http://www.now3d.it/Eng/

2. APPLICATIONS

- Now3D is a 3D modeling tool intended for creating 3D computer graphics and ray-tracing applications for visualizing the planets and stars

3. WEB RESOURCES

- Official website: http://www.now3d.it/Eng/
- Tutorials: http://www.now3d.it/Eng/
- Manual: http://www.now3d.it/Eng/

NuGraf

1. PLATFORMS, PRICES, AND SUPPLIER/CREATOR

- Windows
- $495
- Okino Computer Graphics: http://www.okino.com/default.htm

2. APPLICATIONS

- NuGraf is a 3D rendering and scene composition program
- It can be used by engineers, mechanical designers, industrial designers, architects and CAD/CAM

3. WEB RESOURCES

- Official website: `http://www.okino.com/nrs/nrs.htm`
- Examples/Samples: `http://www.okino.com/mainpic.htm?0`

OpenDX (Open Data Explorer)

1. PLATFORM, PRICES, AND SUPPLIER/CREATOR

- Windows, Unix, Linux
- Freeware
- IBM, the original developer of DX: `http://www.research.ibm.com`

2. APPLICATIONS

- OpenDX is an application and development software package for visualizing data
- It is capable of manipulating, transforming, processing, realizing, rendering and animating data, which can be applied to gain new insights into data from applications in the fields of science, engineering, medicine, and business

3. WEB RESOURCES

- Official website: `http://www.research.ibm.com/dx/`
- Documentation: `http://www.research.ibm.com/dx/docs/legacyhtml/refguide.htm`

OpenFX

1. PLATFORM, PRICES, AND SUPPLIER/CREATOR

- Windows
- Freeware
- Stuart Ferguson: `http://www.openfx.org/index.html`

2. APPLICATIONS

- OpenFX is a 3D modeling, animation and rendering suite

- It can be used in the areas of digital animation, digital post-production, game development, film and broadcast, etc.

3. WEB RESOURCES

- Official website: `http://www.openfx.org/index.html`
- Wikipedia: `http://en.wikipedia.org/wiki/OpenFX`

OpenGL

1. PLATFORM, PRICE, AND SUPPLIER/CREATOR

- Windows, Unix, Linux, Mac OS
- Freeware
- OpenGL.org organization: `http://www.opengl.org`, Silicon Graphics, Inc.: `http://www.sgi.com/company_info/`

2. APPLICATIONS

- OpenGL (Open Graphics Library) is a standard specification defining a cross-platform API for writing applications that produce 2D and 3D computer graphics
- It can be widely used to develop application for CAD, virtual reality, scientific visualization, information visualization, flight simulation, video games, etc.

3. WEB RESOURCES

- Official website: `http://www.opengl.org/`
- Red book: `http://www.glprogramming.com/red/`
- Wikipedia: `http://en.wikipedia.org/wiki/Opengl`

OPENGL FOR JAVA (GL4Java)

1. PLATFORM, PRICE, AND SUPPLIER/CREATOR

- Windows, Linux, Irix, Mac OS, Solaris
- Freeware
- Jausoft: `http://www.jausoft.com/`

2. APPLICATIONS

- GL4Java is an OpenGL language and Java language combined solution for using 3D in serious applications, as well as in games and web pages

3. WEB RESOURCES

- Official website: http://www.jausoft.com/gl4java/
- Tutorial: http://www.softwareburner.de/tutorial.htm
- Documentation: http://gl4java.sourceforge.net/docs/

OpenGL VoLumizer

1. PLATFORM, PRICES, AND SUPPLIER/CREATOR

- Irix, Windows, Linux
- Freeware
- SGI: http://www.sgi.com

2. APPLICATIONS

- OpenGL Volumizer is a graphics API designed for the visualization of large volumetric data sets
- It provides radiologists, physicians, geologists and researchers with visualization and exploration capabilities, so can be used in the fields of energy, manufacturing, medicine, and the sciences

3. WEB RESOURCES

- Official website: http://www.sgi.com/products/software/volumizer/
- Documentation: http://www.sgi.com/products/software/volumizer/documents.html

OpenGVS

1. PLATFORM, PRICES, AND SUPPLIER/CREATOR

- Windows, Linux

- N/A
- Quantum3D, Inc.: `http://www.quantum3d.com`

2. APPLICATIONS

- OpenGVS is scene manager software with object-oriented programming interface (API) for 3D application developers

3. WEB RESOURCES

- Official website: `http://www.quantum3d.com/products/opengvs/about.htm`
- Tutorial: `http://www.quantum3d.com/products/opengvs/tutorial1.htm`
- Examples/Samples: `http://www.quantum3d.com/products/opengvs/gallery.htm`

Open Inventor

1. PLATFORMS, PRICES, AND SUPPLIER/CREATOR

- IRIX, Linux, Solaris, Windows
- Freeware
- SGI: `http://www.sgi.com`

2. APPLICATION

- Open Inventor is an object-oriented 3D toolkit offering a comprehensive solution to interactive graphics programming problems
- It presents a programming model based on a 3D scene database that simplifies graphics programming, and can be used for a wide range of scientific and engineering visualization systems

3. WEB RESOURCES

- Official website: `http://oss.sgi.com/projects/inventor/`
- Wikipedia: `http://en.wikipedia.org/wiki/Open_Inventor`

OpenWorlds

1. PLATFORM, PRICES, AND SUPPLIER/CREATOR

- Windows, Irix, Linux
- OpenWorlds Merchant: $495, OpenWorlds Horizon: free
- OpenWorlds Inc.: `http://www.openworlds.com/index.html`

2. APPLICATIONS

- OpenWorlds is an open X3D-compatible system which extends applications with immersive Web 3D graphics, multimedia, animation and VR capabilities, including OpenWorlds Merchant, OpenWorlds Horizon and OpenWorlds AppKit
- OpenWorlds Merchant is a suite of import libraries for reading in VRML 97 and X3D into various rendering libraries
- OpenWorlds Horizon is Web 3D and multimedia browsers (supporting VRML and X3D) with extensible node Software Development Kit (SDK)
- OpenWorlds AppKit are C++ libraries that bring 3D graphics, animation, sound, and Web graphics support to new or legacy application

3. WEB RESOURCES

- Official website: `http://www.openworlds.com/index.html`

ParticleIllusion

1. PLATFORM, PRICES, AND SUPPLIER/CREATOR

- Windows, Mac OS
- $399
- Wondertouch: `http://www.wondertouch.com/`

2. APPLICATIONS

- ParticleIllusion is a particle effects application system
- It can create effects such as explosions, smoke, fire, sparkles, motion graphics backgrounds, space effects, creatures and abstract artistic effects, which can be used in TV shows, commercials, feature films, game titles, and music videos

3. WEB RESOURCES

- Official website: `http://www.wondertouch.com/`
- Wikipedia: `http://en.wikipedia.org/wiki/ParticleIllusion`

PeoplePutty

1. PLATFORM, PRICES, AND SUPPLIER/CREATOR

- Windows
- $49.95
- Haptek Inc.: `http://www.haptek.com/`

2. APPLICATIONS

- PeoplePutty is a tool to create realistic, emoting, 3-D artificial human characters using photographs and the user's voice, built for virtual reality applications and gaming

3. WEB RESOURCES

- Official website: `http://www.haptek.com/`

PerfKit

1. PLATFORM, PRICES, AND SUPPLIER/CREATOR

- Windows
- Freeware
- NVIDIA: `http://developer.nvidia.com/`

2. APPLICATIONS

- PerfKit is a suite of performance tools to help debug and profile OpenGL and Direct3D applications

- It gives user access to low-level performance counters inside the driver and hardware counters inside the GPU itself. The counters can be used to determine exactly how the user's application is using the GPU and identify performance issues

3. WEB RESOURCES

- Official website: `http://developer.nvidia.com/object/nvperfkit_home.html`
- User guide: `http://developer.download.nvidia.com/tools/NVPerfKit/2.1/User_Guide_NVPerfKit.pdf`
- Documentation: `http://developer.nvidia.com/page/documentation.html`

PhotoModeler

1. PLATFORMS, PRICES, AND SUPPLIER/CREATOR

- Windows
- $$$
- Eos Systems Inc.: `http://www.photomodeler.com/index.htm`

2. APPLICATIONS

- PhotoModeler is a software program for creating 3D models and measurements from photographs
- It can be used by professionals in the fields of accident reconstruction, architecture, archaeology, engineering, forensics, web page design, and 3D graphics

3. WEB RESOURCES

- Official website: `http://www.photomodeler.com/products/photomodeler.htm`
- Examples/Samples: `http://www.photomodeler.com/producttour.htm`

Pixel 3D

1. PLATFORMS, PRICES, AND SUPPLIER/CREATOR
- Windows
- $29.95
- Forward Designs: http://www.forwarddesiqn.com/

2. APPLICATIONS
- Pixel 3D is a design tool for creating and converting 3D logos and objects
- It can be used to create high quality 3D graphics for web site construction or imaging work

3. WEB RESOURCES
- Official website: http://www.forwarddesign.com

PLOT3D

1. PLATFORMS, PRICES, AND SUPPLIER/CREATOR
- Windows
- Freeware
- HyperScope Software: http://www.plot3d.net/gallery.html

2. APPLICATIONS
- PLOT3D is a program for the mathematical visualization of graphs from equations
- It is designed for students, teachers and all persons who enjoy mathematical ideas and computer art

3. WEB RESOURCES
- Official website: http://www.plot3d.net/
- Examples/Samples: http://www.plot3d.net/gallery.html

Pointstream 3DImageSuite

1. PLATFORMS, PRICES, AND SUPPLIER/CREATOR

- Windows
- N/A
- Arius3D Inc.: `http://www.arius3d.com`

2. APPLICATIONS

- Pointstream 3DImageSuite is a specialized application for processing point cloud data captured using three dimensional imaging systems
- It enables the to research, present, and share unique physical objects in digital form, and supports wide ranging applications in culture and heritage, research, education, entertainment, etc.

3. WEB RESOURCES

- Official website: `http://www.arius3d.com/main.html?contentId=6#`

PolyTrans

1. PLATFORM, PRICES, AND SUPPLIER/CREATOR

- Windows
- $395
- Okino Computer Graphics, Inc.: `http://www.okino.com`

2. APPLICATIONS

- PolyTrans is a 3D conversion tool which converts major CAD file formats to non-CAD file format
- It is in use by some production companies who regularly use 3DS Max, Maya, XSI, Lightwave, Cinema-4D, trueSpace and related common file formats such as DirectX, OpenFlight, VRML and others

3. WEB RESOURCES

- Official website: `http://www.okino.com/conv/conv.htm`
- Examples/Samples: `http://www.okino.com/mainpic.htm`

Poser

1. PLATFORM, PRICES, AND SUPPLIER/CREATOR

- Windows, Mac OS
- $249
- Smith Micro Software (NASDAQ: SMSI): `http://graphics.smithmicro.com`

2. APPLICATIONS

- Poser is 3D rendering and animation software optimized for models that depict the human figure in 3D form
- It can be used for graphic and web design, fine art, comics, pre-viz/storyboarding, medical and technical illustration, architectural and product design, and education

3. WEB RESOURCES

- Official website: `http://graphics.smithmicro.com/go/poser`
- Wikipedia: `http://en.wikipedia.org/wiki/Poser`
- Tutorial: `http://www.e-frontier.com/article/articleview/1680/1/290?sbss=290`

POVLAB

1. PLATFORM, PRICE, AND VENDOR/SUPPLIER

- Windows, Mac OS, Unix, Linux
- Freeware
- Povlab: `http://pdelagrange.free.fr/povlab/index.html`

2. APPLICATION

- POVLAB is a 3D graphic modeler, which models 3D objects for the photo-realistic povteam Persistence Of Vision Raytracer (POV-Ray)

3. WEB RESOURCES

- Official website: `http://pdelagrange.free.fr/povlab/download.html`

- Tutorial: `http://pdelagrange.free.fr/povlab/tutorial/tut_main.htm`

POV-Ray (Persistence of Vision Raytracer)

1. PLATFORMS, PRICES, AND SUPPLIER/CREATOR

- Windows, Mac OS, Unix, Linux
- Freeware
- Persistence of Vision Raytracer Pty. Ltd.: `http://www.povray.org/`

2. APPLICATIONS

- POV-Ray is a program using a rendering technique called ray-tracing
- It can produce high quality images with realistic reflections, shading, perspective and other effects for artistic applications, computer graphics education, etc.

3. WEB RESOURCES

- Official website: `http://www.povray.org/resources/`
- Wikipedia: `http://en.wikipedia.org/wiki/POV-Ray`
- POV-Wiki: `http://wiki.povray.org/content/Main_Page`

Pro-Engineer (PRO/E)

1. PLATFORMS, PRICES, AND SUPPLIER/CREATOR

- Windows, Unix
- N/A
- ProENGINEER.com: `http://www.proengineer.com/`

2. APPLICATIONS

- Pro-Engineer (commonly referred to as Pro/E or ProE) is an integrated 3D CAD/CAM/CAE software which introduces the concept of parametric, feature-based solid modeling

- It has been used by engineers, architects, manufacturers, and draftsmen for design, development and manufacturing

3. WEB RESOURCES

- Official website: http://www.proengineer.com/proengineer.php
- Wikipedia: http://en.wikipedia.org/wiki/Pro/E

ProPak 3D

1. PLATFORMS, PRICES, AND SUPPLIER/CREATOR

- Windows, Mac OS
- $49.99-$74.99
- Webpromotion, Inc.: http://www.webpromotion.com/

2. APPLICATIONS

- ProPak3D is a series of website concept, design and development tools, which contains an array of web-based 3D animations to satisfy the Webmaster

3. WEB RESOURCES

- Official website: http://www.webpromotion.com/propak3.html

Punch! Software

1. PLATFORMS, PRICES, AND SUPPLIER/CREATOR

- Mac OS, Windows
- $$-$$$
- Punch! Software: http://www.punchsoftware.com/index.htm

2. APPLICATIONS

- Punch! Software is a suite of home and landscape design software, including Punch! Home Design Architectural Series, Punch! Landscape, Deck and Patio Designer, and Punch! Home Design Studio

- It can be used in industries such as architecture and architectural engineering, civil engineering, factory layout, interior design and architecture, construction, graphics design, etc.

3. WEB RESOURCES

- Official website: `http://www.punchsoftware.com/index.htm`

pV3 (PARALLEL VISUAL3)

1. PLATFORMS, PRICES, AND SUPPLIER/CREATOR

- Compaq ALPHA, HP, IBM RS/6000, Silicon Graphics, Linux, Sun, Windows machines
- Freeware
- MIT, Department of Aeronautics and Astronautics: `http://raphael.mit.edu/`

2. APPLICATIONS

- pV3 is a three dimensional, distributed, unsteady, unstructured, CFD visualization software for supercomputers, parallel machines and clusters of workstations
- This software is used for co-processing multi-dimensional visualizations of scalar, vector, and tensor data generated in a distributed and parallel computing environment during runtime

3. WEB RESOURCES

- Official website: `http://raphael.mit.edu/pv3/pv3.html`
- Manual: `http://raphael.mit.edu/pv3/pV3users2.pdf`

PV-WAVE

1. PLATFORMS, PRICES, AND SUPPLIER/CREATOR

- Unix, Linux, Windows
- $$$$

- Visual Numerics, Inc.: `http://www.vni.com/`

2. APPLICATIONS

- The PV-WAVE family of products, which includes PV-WAVE, TS-WAVE, and JWAVE, provides software developers with the tools needed to meet data analysis requirements
- It can import, manipulate, analyze and visualize data to detect and display patterns, trends, anomalies and other vital information for technical or business applications

3. WEB RESOURCES:

- Official website: `http://www.vni.com/products/wave/`
- Documentation: `http://www.vni.com/products/wave/documentation.php`

Quartz Composer

1. PLATFORMS, PRICES, AND SUPPLIER/CREATOR

- Mac OS
- Freeware
- Apple: `http://www.apple.com`

2. APPLICATIONS

- Quartz Composer is a development tool for processing and rendering graphical data
- It is capable of making sophisticated animations for keynote or presentations, and creating animated screensavers

3. WEB RESOURCES:

- Official website: `http://developer.apple.com/documentation/GraphicsImaging/Conceptual/QuartzComposerUserGuide`
- Wikipedia: `http://en.wikipedia.org/wiki/Quartz_Composer`
- Wiki: `http://www.quartzcompositions.com/phpBB2/mediawiki/index.php/Main_Page`

Quick3D

1. PLATFORMS, PRICES, AND SUPPLIER/CREATOR

- Windows
- Quick3D Professional: $199.00, Quick3D Geometry: $129.00, and Quick3D Viewer: $59.00
- Quick3D: `http://www.quick3d.org/index.html`

2. APPLICATIONS

- Quick3D software products are a 3D file converter, translator and viewer for 3D industry professionals and artists

3. WEB RESOURCES

- Official website: `http://www.quick3d.org/index.html`
- User's Guide: `http://www.quick3d.org/guide/index.html`

QuickDraw3D

1. PLATFORM, PRICE, AND SUPPLIER/CREATOR

- Mac OS
- Freeware
- Apple Inc.: `http://www.apple.com`

2. APPLICATIONS

- QuickDraw 3D (QD3D for short) is a graphics API for developing 3D applications for CAD, virtual reality, scientific visualization, information visualization, flight simulation, video games, etc.

3. WEB RESOURCES

- Official website: `http://developer.apple.com/documentation/QuickTime/QD3D/qd3dintroduction.htm`
- Wikipedia: `http://en.wikipedia.org/wiki/QuickDraw_3D`

RADIANCE

1. PLATFORMS, PRICE, AND SUPPLIER/CREATOR

- Unix
- Freeware
- Building Technologies Department: http://eetd.lbl.gov/btp

2. APPLICATIONS

- Radiance is a suite of programs for the analysis and visualization of lighting in design
- It is used by architects and engineers to predict illumination, and visual quality and appearance of innovative design spaces, and by researchers to evaluate new lighting and daylighting technologies

3. WEB RESOURCES

- Official Website: http://radsite.lbl.gov/radiance/HOME.html
- Examples/Samples: http://radsite.lbl.gov/radiance/frameg.html

Rasmol

1. PLATFORMS, PRICE, AND SUPPLIER/CREATOR

- Windows, Unix, Linux, Mac OS
- Freeware
- Originally developed by Roger Sayle, now maintenance is done at ARCiB laboratory of Dowling College: http://www.rasmol.org/

2. APPLICATIONS

- RasMol is a molecular graphics program
- It is designed for the visualization of proteins, nuclear acids and small molecules, and has been used for education as well as research in structural biology

3. WEB RESOURCES

- Official website: http://www.rasmol.org/

- Wikipedia: `http://en.wikipedia.org/wiki/Rasmol`

Rayshade

1. PLATFORMS, PRICE, AND DISTRIBUTOR

- Unix, Windows, Mac OS, Amiga
- Freeware
- Craig E. Kolb and Rod Bogart: `http://graphics.stanford.edu/~cek/rayshade`

2. APPLICATIONS

- Rayshade is a 3D rendering tool whose main function is to read a multi-line ASCII file describing a scene to be rendered and produce a file containing the ray-traced image
- It is used by universities for teaching ray tracing, and used for research on rendering and object generation

3. WEB RESOURCES

- Official website: `http://www-graphics.stanford.edu/~cek/rayshade`
- User's guide and manual: `http://www-graphics.stanford.edu/~cek/rayshade/doc/guide/guide.html`

Realflow

1. PLATFORMS, PRICES, AND SUPPLIER/CREATOR

- Linux, Mac OS, Windows
- $2000-$6700 (in 2 CPU, 4 CPU, 8 CPU, and 16 CPU options for use on one machine)
- Next Limit: `http://www.nextlimit.com/`

2. APPLICATIONS

- RealFlow is 3D modeling and simulation software for the simulation of fluids, water surfaces, rigid bodies, soft bodies, fibers, and meshes
- It has been used for the production of spectacular effects in movies, as well as used to produce effects for commercials and television products

3. WEB RESOURCES

- Official website: http://www.nextlimit.com/realflow/
- Tutorials: http://www.nextlimit.com/realflow/te_resources.htm
- Wikipedia: http://en.wikipedia.org/wiki/RealFlow

Realimation

1. PLATFORMS, PRICES, AND SUPPLIER/CREATOR

- Windows, Unix
- A development package costs $5,000; a run-time application costs $100
- US Army Corps of Engineers: http://www.tec.army.mil

2. APPLICATIONS

- RealiMation is a software toolset designed for developing real time 3D interactive applications
- Four components comprise the suite: a Software Development Kit (SDK); a Space Time Editor (STE) for creating and maintaining interactive scenes; RealiStorm plug-ins for 3D Studio MAX, AutoCAD, MicroStation and Softimage (for interactive previews inside the modeler of choice); and a RealiView and Internet plug-in (allowing data to be sent to other users)

3. WEB RESOURCES

- Official website: http://www.tec.army.mil/research/products/TD/tvd/survey/RealiMation.html

Realsoft 3D

1. PLATFORMS, PRICES, AND SUPPLIER/CREATOR

- Windows, Mac OS, Unix, Linux, Irix
- $100-$700
- Realsoft Graphics: http://www.realsoft.com/

2. APPLICATIONS

- Realsoft is a 3D modeling, rendering and animation software package for producing high quality photorealistic images and animation
- It is used in different applications, such as by artists working in the advertising industry, architects, product designers, educational institutions, game industry and hobby users

3. WEB RESOURCES

- Official website: http://www.realsoft.com/

RenderDrive

1. PLATFORMS, PRICES, AND SUPPLIER/CREATOR

- Window, Linux, Unix, Mac OS
- $$$$$
- Advanced Rendering Technology: http://www.art-render.com/

2. APPLICATIONS

- RenderDrive is a 3D rendering appliance developed for 3D artists capable of generating high quality images with details that can also be used for engineering applications

3. WEB RESOURCES

- Official website: http://www.art-render.com/

RenderMan

1. PLATFORMS, PRICE, COMPANY

- Mac OS, Linux, Windows
- RenderMan Studio is $3500 ($875 for student), and RenderMan ProServer is $3,500 ($875 for student)
- Pixar: `http://www.pixar.com`

2. APPLICATIONS

- RenderMan is a tool suite that includes rendering and animation functionality to create digital photorealistic images
- These tools are in use at visual effects studios, movie studios, game studios, simulation companies, etc.

3. WEB RESOURCES

- Official website: `http://renderman.pixar.com`
- Wikipedia: `http://en.wikipedia.org/wiki/PhotoRealistic_RenderMan`
- Discussions: `http://www.renderman.org/`

RenderPark

1. PLATFORMS, PRICE, COMPANY

- Unix
- Freeware
- Computer Graphics Research Group, Katholieke University Leuven: `http://www.cs.kuleuven.ac.be/cwis/research/graphics/RENDERPARK/index.shtml`

2. APPLICATIONS

- RenderPark is a system for physically based photo-realistic image synthesis
- It has been used for research and teaching, also used by engineers, architects, designers and artists for physics-based global illumination rendering

3. WEB RESOURCES:

- Official website: http://www.cs.kuleuven.ac.be/cwis/research/
graphics/RENDERPARK/index.shtml

Rhino

1. PLATFORMS, PRICES, AND SUPPLIER/CREATOR

- Windows
- Commercial price: $995, Educational price: $195
- McNeel: http://www.rhino3d.com/

2. APPLICATIONS

- Rhino is a modeling and rendering tool for animation, drafting, engineering, analysis, and manufacturing or construction
- Its common fields of use include industrial design, aerodynamics, marine design, apparel design, architecture, mechanical design, aircraft design, spacecrafts, entertainment & multimedia, educational purposes, health & medical studies, advertising, etc.

3. WEB RESOURCES

- Official website: http://www.rhino3d.com/index.htm
- Example/Sample: http://gallery.mcneel.com/?language=&g=1

RXscene

1. PLATFORMS, PRICES, AND SUPPLIER/CREATOR

- Windows, Irix
- N/A
- Awaron AG: http://www.realax.com/, http://www.realax.com/docs/
html/products/urxsc.htm

2. APPLICATIONS

- RXscene is a polygon and spline based modeler for the design of complex virtual worlds
- It can be used for modeling purposes, such as complex objects in virtual environments, product prototypes, game model creation, etc.

3. WEB RESOURCES

- Official website: `http://www.awaron.com/en/products/rx-software/rxscene.asp`

Satellite Tool Kit (STK)

1. PLATFORMS, PRICES, AND SUPPLIER/CREATOR

- Windows, Linux, Unix
- N/A
- Analytical Graphics, Inc. (AGI): `http://www.stk.com`

2. APPLICATIONS

- Satellite Tool Kit (STK) is a suite of software that allows engineers and scientists to design and develop complex dynamic simulations of real-world problems
- Its common fields of use include space exploration, geospacial intelligence, spacecraft mission design, missile defense, spacecraft operations, etc.

3. WEB RESOURCES

- Official website: `http://www.stk.com/products/desktopApp/stkFamily/`
- Wikipedia: `http://en.wikipedia.org/wiki/Satellite_Tool_Kit`

SCED (Constraint Based Scene Design)

1. PLATFORMS, PRICES, AND SUPPLIER/CREATOR

- Unix

- Freeware
- Stephen Chenny: `http://www.cs.wisc.edu/~schenney`

2. APPLICATIONS

- SCED is a modeling program that makes use of geometric constraints to edit objects in a virtual world
- The scenes created by this program can be exported to other programs such as POVray, Radiance, Rayshade, RenderMan, and VRML browsers

3. WEB RESOURCES

- Official website: `http://gd.tuwien.ac.at/graphics/sced/sced.html`
- Tutorial: `http://gd.tuwien.ac.at/graphics/sced/tutorials/starting.html`, `http://gd.tuwien.ac.at/graphics/sced/tutorials/tute-2.html`

Shade

1. PLATFORM, PRICE, AND SUPPLIER/CREATOR

- Mac OS, Windows
- $900 for Professional Edition, and $200 for Standard Edition
- Smith Micro Software: `http://graphics.smithmicro.com/`

2. APPLICATIONS

- Shade is a 3D modeling tool with rendering and animation functions for designers, illustrators and architects

3. WEB RESOURCES

- Official website: `http://graphics.smithmicro.com/go/products`
- Tutorials: `http://www.e-frontier.com/go/shade/tutorials`

ShapeCapture

1. PLATFORM, PRICE, AND SUPPLIER/CREATOR

- Windows
- $$$$
- ShapeQuest Inc.: `http://www.shapecapture.com/index.html`

2. APPLICATIONS

- ShapeCapture is a software package for 3D measurement and modeling
- Its areas of application include aerospace, defense, forensics, industrial processes, control and measurement, architecture, archaeology, 3D modeling, 3D animation, non-contact measurement, etc.

3. WEB RESOURCES

- Official website: `http://www.shapecapture.com/shapecape_2002.htm`
- Examples/Samples: `http://www.shapecapture.com/SQ_SMEX.htm`

Shave and a Haircut

1. PLATFORM, PRICE, AND SUPPLIER/CREATOR

- Mac OS, Windows
- $899.99 for Professional Edition, and $199.99 for Standard Edition
- Smith Micro Software: `http://graphics.smithmicro.com/`

2. APPLICATIONS

- Shade is a 3D modeling tool with rendering and animation functions
- It can be used for graphic and web design, fine art, comics, pre-viz/storyboarding, medical and technical illustration, architectural and product design, and education

3. WEB RESOURCES

- Official website: `http://graphics.smithmicro.com/article/articleview/1784/1/652?sbss=652`
- Tutorials: `http://graphics.smithmicro.com/go/shade/tutorials`

Shout3D

1. PLATFORMS, PRICES, AND SUPPLIER/CREATOR

- Java-based platform
- N/A
- Shout3D used to be available from Eyematic, and now is maintained by one of the original founders Paul Isaacs: `http://www.shout3dllc.com/`

2. APPLICATIONS

- Shout3D is a web3D toolset based on Java applet
- It provides a way to display interactive 3D graphics and animation over the Internet for games, visualizations, and e-commerce

3. WEB RESOURCES

- Official website: `http://www.shout3dllc.com/`
- Tutorials: `http://webreference.com/3d/lesson75/index.html`

Silo

1. PLATFORMS, PRICES, AND SUPPLIER/CREATOR

- MacOS, Windows
- $159
- Nevercenter Ltd. Co.: `http://nevercenter.com`

2. APPLICATIONS

- Silo is tool for organic, architectural and mechanical modeling
- It can be used to create 3D characters for video games and movies or explore 3D architectural ideas for artist, architects and character modelers

3. WEB RESOURCES

- Official website: `http://nevercenter.com/about/`
- Wikipedia: `http://en.wikipedia.org/wiki/Silo_%28software%29`
- Manual: `http://nevercenter.com/support/help/`

Simi MotionCapture3D

1. PLATFORMS, PRICES, AND SUPPLIER/CREATOR

- Windows
- N/A
- SIMI Reality Motion Systems: http://www.simi.com/

2. APPLICATIONS

- Simi MotionCapture3D is a 3D motion tracking system for acquiring the movements of objects such as humans, animals or machines in three-dimensional space
- Its common fields of application include computer animation sequences for television and cinema, computer and video games, cartoons, simulations

3. WEB RESOURCES

- Official website: http://www.simi.com/en/markets/entertainment/mocap/index.html
- Examples/Samples: http://www.simi.com/en/examples/index.html

SIMUL8

1. PLATFORMS, PRICES, AND SUPPLIER/CREATOR

- Windows
- SIMUL8 Standard is $1,495, SIMUL8 Professional is $4,995, and SIMUL8 for Education is $1,995
- SIMUL8 Corporation: http://www.simul8.com

2. APPLICATIONS

- Simul8 is a simulation package that provides planning, modeling, validation, animation, and other functions
- It is capable of creating a visual model of the system under investigation in a realistic 3D environment, and so is used by engineers in enterprises to make important decisions

3. WEB RESOURCES

- Official website: `http://www.simul8.com`

SketchUp

1. PLATFORMS, PRICES, AND SUPPLIER/CREATOR

- Windows, Mac OS
- Google Sketchup 6: Free, and Google Sketchup 6 Pro: $495
- Google, Inc.: `http://www.sketchup.com`

2. APPLICATIONS

- SketchUp is a 3D modeling program designed for professional architects, civil engineers, filmmakers, game developers, and those in related professions
- It can be used in industries such as architecture, interior design, landscape architecture, stage set design, urban planning, and game development; it has also been used to design buildings to be displayed on Google Earth

3. WEB RESOURCES

- Official website: `http://www.sketchup.com/`
- Wikipedia: `http://en.wikipedia.org/wiki/Sketchup`

Softimage 3D

1. PLATFORMS, PRICES, AND SUPPLIER/CREATOR

- Windows, Linux
- $495 for Foundation version, $4,995 for Advanced version, and $295 for students
- Softimage Inc.: `http://www.softimage.com`, a subsidiary of Avid Technologies Inc.: `http://www.avid.com`

2. APPLICATIONS

- SOFTIMAGE|XSI is 3D animation software capable of handling detailed models with millions of polygons, while subdivision surfaces are integrated into it

- It is intended for use in games, film and television, and so is mainly used by entertainment companies

3. WEB RESOURCES

- Official website: http://www.softimage.com/products/
- Wikipedia: http://en.wikipedia.org/wiki/Softimage

SOLIDS++

1. PLATFORMS, PRICES, AND SUPPLIER/CREATOR

- Windows, Unix/Linux
- N/A
- IntegrityWare, Inc.: www.integrityware.com

2. APPLICATIONS

- Solids++ is an object-oriented non-manifold modeling kernel related to solids modeling, surface modeling, curve modeling, polygonal modeling and non-manifold modeling, etc.
- It can be used in industrial and graphical design

3. WEB RESOURCES

- Official website: http://www.integrityware.com/products/SOLIDS++/ solids++.html

SolidThinking

1. PLATFORMS, PRICES, AND SUPPLIER/CREATOR

- Mac OS, Windows
- N/A
- SolidThinking: http://www.solidthinking.com

2. APPLICATIONS

- SolidThinking is 3D modeling and rendering software which combines NURBS curve, surface, and solid modeling, as well as polygonal and pointcloud creation and manipulation

- It is mainly used by manufacturing industries, professional designers and architects for industrial design

3. WEB RESOURCES

- Official website: http://www.solidthinking.com

- Wikipedia: http://en.wikipedia.org/wiki/SolidThinking

SolidWorks

1. PLATFORMS, PRICES, AND SUPPLIER/CREATOR

- Windows

- N/A

- SolidWorks Corporation: http://www.solidworks.com

2. APPLICATIONS

- SolidWorks is a 3D mechanical CAD program for 3D modeling, assembly, drawing, sheetmetal, weldments, and freeform surfacing

- It includes a suite of products such as Mechanical Design, Design Validation, Data Management, Collaboration, and Productivity Enhancement. These tools can be used by mechanical engineers and designers

3. WEB RESOURCES

- Official website: http://www.solidworks.com/pages/products/ products.html

- Wikipedia: http://en.wikipedia.org/wiki/SolidWorks

SPECTER

1. PLATFORMS, PRICES, AND SUPPLIER/CREATOR

- Windows
- N/A
- Integra Inc.: http://www.integra.jp/en/index.html

2. APPLICATIONS

- Specter is simulation software for optical analysis and design
- It can be used by optical designers, engineers and researchers working in the lighting, automobile and aerospace industries

3. WEB RESOURCES

- Official website: http://www.integra.jp/en/specter/index.html
- Example/Samples: http://www.integra.jp/en/specter/gallery/index.html

STAR-CD

1. PLATFORMS, PRICES, AND SUPPLIER/CREATOR

- Unix, Windows, Linux
- N/A
- CD-adapco: http://www.cd-adapco.com/about/index.html

2. APPLICATIONS

- STAR-CD is a computational fluid dynamics (CFD) program for performing multi-physics simulations
- It gives solutions for engineering problems for industrial users in automotive, power generation, turbomachinery, aerospace, civil and offshore structures and safety, environment, marine and more

3. WEB RESOURCES

- Official website: http://www.cd-adapco.com/products/STAR-CD/index.html

- Wiki: http://www.cfd-online.com/Wiki/STAR-CD

StereoPOV

1. PLATFORMS, PRICES, AND SUPPLIER/CREATOR

- Windows, Mac OS, Unix, Linux
- Freeware
- Ichthyostega: http://stereopov.ichthyostega.de/

2. APPLICATIONS

- StereoPOV is a raytracer, which enables some of the camera types built into POV-Ray to generate real 3D output by generating stereoscopic pairs of images

3. WEB RESOURCES

- Official website: http://stereopov.ichthyostega.de/

Strata Live 3D

1. PLATFORMS, PRICES, AND SUPPLIER/CREATOR

- Windows, Mac OS
- $495
- Strata: http://www.strata.com/

2. APPLICATIONS

- Strata Live 3D is a real-time 3D application for creating content for the web, Flash and PDF documents
- It is capable of creating real-time 3D models that contain animation, full textures, reflective surfaces, interactivity and more. It is mainly used by some corporations to communicate, teach, market and sell

3. WEB RESOURCES

- Official website: http://www.strata.com/

- Examples/Samples: `http://www.strata.com/showcase.asp`

Summit 3D

1. PLATFORMS, PRICES, AND SUPPLIER/CREATOR

- Windows
- N/A
- Summit Graphics, Inc.: `http://www.summit3d.com/`

2. APPLICATIONS

- Summit 3D is a 3D program for developing virtual reality simulations and 3D animations
- Summit worlds including animation, lighting, and sounds can be used as part of web pages for industrial and business applications

3. WEB RESOURCES

- Official website: `http://www.summit3d.com/summit.htm`

Superficie

1. PLATFORMS, PRICE, AND SUPPLIER/CREATOR

- Linux, Unix
- Freeware
- Juan Pablo Romero: `http://superficie.sourceforge.net/`

2. APPLICATIONS

- Superficie (surface) is a small program that allows the user to visualize 3D surfaces, and to have certain interaction with them
- It can be used by designers, architects, free-lance 3D artists, and production companies for the rapid production of 3D surfaces

3. WEB RESOURCES

- Official website: http://superficie.sourceforge.net/

Swift 3D — 3D Vector Graphics Tool

1. PLATFORMS, PRICE, AND SUPPLIER/CREATOR

- Windows, Mac OS
- $249
- Electric Rain, Inc.: http://www.swift3d.com

2. APPLICATIONS

- Swift 3D is Web3D software for creating 3D animations
- It enables multimedia designers to create 3D content for Adobe Flash, video, print, Papervision3D projects, etc.

3. WEB RESOURCES

- Official website: http://www.swift3d.com/
- Wikipedia: http://en.wikipedia.org/wiki/Swift_3D
- Tutorials: http://www.erain.com/support/Tutorials

SyFlex

1. PLATFORMS, PRICE, AND SUPPLIER/CREATOR

- Windows, Linux
- N/A
- Syflex LLC.: http://syflex.biz/

2. APPLICATIONS

- SyFlex is a simulator which can simulate cloth, hair, flesh, skin, ropes, sails, ghosts and water

- It can be used in animated TV shows, commercials, game cinematics and short films

3. WEB RESOURCES

- Official website: `http://syflex.biz/`
- Tutorial: `http://syflex.biz/tut.html`

Tao Framework

1. PLATFORMS, PRICE, AND SUPPLIER/CREATOR

- Windows, Mac OS, Linux, Solaris
- Freeware
- The Tao Framework: `http://www.taoframework.com/`

2. APPLICATIONS

- The Tao Framework is a library which gives .NET and Mono developers access to popular graphics and gaming libraries such as OpenGL and SDL

3. WEB RESOURCES

- Official website: `http://www.taoframework.com/`
- Wikipedia: `http://en.wikipedia.org/wiki/Tao_(software)`
- Tutorial: `http://members.hellug.gr/nkour/Tao.OpenGL_Builder/SimpleIntro_Borland.html`

Tecplot

1. PLATFORMS, PRICES, AND SUPPLIER/CREATOR

- Windows, Linux, Unix, Mac OS
- $6,000 for Windows, $1,600 for Linux, and $12,000 for Multi-Platform
- Tecplot, Inc.: `http://www.tecplot.com`

2. APPLICATIONS

- Tecplot is a Computational Fluid Dynamics (CFD) and numerical simulation software package for scientific and engineering data visualization
- It can be used by engineers and scientists to analyze, explore and understand complex data and relationships, and its applications include visualization of 3D surfaces and volumes, metal cutting simulation, streamlines and vector, and animation

3. WEB RESOURCES

- Official website: `http://www.tecplot.com/products/index.aspx`
- Wikipedia: `http://en.wikipedia.org/wiki/Tecplot`

T.Ed

1. PLATFORMS, PRICES, AND SUPPLIER/CREATOR

- Windows
- $27.99
- The Game Creators Ltd.: `http://www.thegamecreators.com/?f=company_info`

2. APPLICATIONS

- T.Ed is a terrain and environment modeling tool
- It is designed primarily for game programmers and 3D artists to make virtual landscape

3. WEB RESOURCES

- Official website: `http://www.thegamecreators.com/?f=ted`

Terragen

1. PLATFORMS, PRICE, AND SUPPLIER/CREATOR

- Windows, Mac OS

- Freeware
- Planetside Software: `http://www.planetside.co.uk/`

2. APPLICATIONS

- Terragen is a scenery generator, created with the goal of generating photorealistic landscape images and animations
- It has been used in a variety of commercial applications including film, television and music videos, games and multimedia, books, magazines and print advertisements

3. WEB RESOURCES

- Official website: `http://www.planetside.co.uk/terragen/productmain.shtml`
- Wikipedia: `http://en.wikipedia.org/wiki/Terragen`
- Tutorial: `http://www.terrasource.net/`

TerraTools

1. PLATFORMS, PRICE, AND SUPPLIER/CREATOR

- Windows
- $23,000
- TerraSim, Inc.: `http://www.terrasim.com/`

2. APPLICATIONS

- TerraTools is 3D geospatial modeling software for generating 3D simulation databases from cartographic source materials
- Its customers are from diverse markets, including defense modeling and simulation, site modeling for intelligence preparation, and civil applications for 3D visualization

3. WEB RESOURCES

- Official website: `http://www.terrasim.com/products/terratools/`

Texture Lab: Tiling Tools

1. PLATFORM, PRICE, AND SUPPLIER/CREATOR

- Windows
- $245
- Digimation: http://www.digimation.com

2. APPLICATIONS

- Texture Lab is a collection of nine procedural maps including fire, water, fog, electrics, strata, noise, tiling geometry, tiling lattices, and tiling tesselations
- These procedural maps perform in much the same way as the ones that ship with 3DS Max to produce some special effects

3. WEB RESOURCES

- Official website: http://www.digimation.com/home/

The 3D Gamemaker

1. PLATFORM, PRICE, AND SUPPLIER/CREATOR

- Windows
- $34.99
- The Game Creators Ltd.: http://t3dgm.thegamecreators.com/

2. APPLICATIONS

- The 3D Gamemaker is a game engine that allows users to create a variety of exciting game scenarios

3. WEB RESOURCES

- Official website: http://t3dgm.thegamecreators.com/
- Wikipedia: http://en.wikipedia.org/wiki/The_3D_Gamemaker

Tile Studio

1. PLATFORMS, PRICES, AND SUPPLIER/CREATOR

- Windows
- Freeware
- Wiering Software: http://www.wieringsoftware.nl/

2. APPLICATIONS

- Tile Studio is a development utility for graphics in tile-based games, and contains a bitmap editor for creating tiles and sprites and a map editor for designing level maps
- The output format is programmable, so it can be used together with most programming languages

3. WEB RESOURCES

- Official website: http://tilestudio.sourceforge.net/
- Tutorial: http://tilestudio.sourceforge.net/drawing.html
- Wikipedia: http://en.wikipedia.org/wiki/Tile_Studio

TopSolid

1. PLATFORMS, PRICES, AND SUPPLIER/CREATOR

- Windows
- N/A
- Missler Software: http://www.topsolid.com/

2. APPLICATIONS

- TopSolid is integrated CAD and CAM software
- It can be used in industries such as architecture and architectural engineering, civil engineering, factory layout, interior design and architecture, construction, electrical engineering, graphics design, mechanical engineering and lighting design, etc.

3. WEB RESOURCES

- Official website: http://www.topsolid.com/products/2008/?menu=10
- Wikipedia: http://en.wikipedia.org/wiki/TopSolid

TrueSpace

1. PLATFORMS, PRICES, AND SUPPLIER/CREATOR

- Windows
- $595 is the listed price, and $273 is the educational price
- Caligari Corporation: http://www.caligari.com/

2. APPLICATION

- TrueSpace is a tool for 3D presentation, design, animation, games and art
- It has been used in advertisements, games, art work, and animated virtual environments

3. WEB RESOURCES

- Official website: http://www.caligari.com/Products/trueSpace/tS75/brochure/intro.asp?Cate=BIntro
- Wikipedia: http://en.wikipedia.org/wiki/TrueSpace

Tucan Series

1. PLATFORMS, PRICES, AND SUPPLIER/CREATOR

- Windows
- Tucan professional is EUR 9,980, Tucan studio is EUR 4,980
- Awaron AG: http://www.awaron.com/

2. APPLICATION

- Tucan Series is a toolset for real-time visualization and virtual reality, which includes Tucan Design xt, Tucan Radiosity, Tucan Animate, Tucan Predesign

- These tools can be used for different branches and areas such as 3D real-time presentations, stereo-able multi-screen projections and virtual reality

3. WEB RESOURCES

- Official website: `http://www.awaron.com/en/products/tucan/ tucan_update72.asp`

TurboCAD

1. PLATFORM, PRICES, AND SUPPLIER/CREATOR

- Windows, Mac OS
- $$$-$$$$
- International Microcomputer Software Inc. (IMSI): `http:// www.imsisoft.com`

2. APPLICATIONS

- TurboCAD is CAD software for 2D and 3D design and drafting
- It is designed for both the mechanical and the AEC (Architecture, Engineering and Construction) markets

3. WEB RESOURCES

- Official website: `http://www.turbocad.com/`
- Manual: `http://download.imsisoft.com/turbocad/ TC10_UserGuidePDF.zip`
- Wikipedia: `http://en.wikipedia.org/wiki/TurboCAD`

Ulead COOL 3D

1. PLATFORM, PRICES, AND SUPPLIER/CREATOR

- Windows
- $49.99
- Corel Corporation.: `http://www.ulead.com/cool3d/runme.htm`

2. APPLICATION

- Unlead COOL 3D is 3D animation software to create 3D titles and animated motion graphics for web pages, video productions, presentation and documents

3. WEB RESOURCES

- Official website: `http://www.ulead.com/cool3d/runme.htm`
- Tutorials: `http://www.ulead.com/learning/cool3d.htm`

Ultimate Unwrap 3D

1. PLATFORM, PRICES, AND SUPPLIER/CREATOR

- Windows
- Ultimate Unwrap 3D Pro is $59.95, and Ultimate Unwrap 3D (SE) is $49.95
- Ultimate Unwrap 3D Developer: `http://www.unwrap3d.com/index.aspx`

2. APPLICATIONS

- Ultimate Unwrap 3D is a tool for unwrapping 3D models
- It can be used by gamers, artists, modelers, and hobbyists, and by all levels of computer users

3. WEB RESOURCES

- Official website: `http://www.unwrap3d.com/downloads.aspx`
- Tutorial: `http://www.unwrap3d.com/tutorials.aspx`

Unity

1. PLATFORM, PRICES, AND SUPPLIER/CREATOR

- Windows, Mac OS
- Unity Indie is $199, Unity Pro is $1,499, and the Unity Asset Server is $499
- Unity Technologies: `http://unity3d.com/`

2. APPLICATIONS

- Unity is a multi-platform game development tool and 3D engine
- Unity is generally used for creating 3D video games or other interactive content such as architectural visualizations or real-time 3D animations

3. WEB RESOURCES

- Official website: `http://unity3d.com/unity/`
- Wikipedia: `http://en.wikipedia.org/wiki/Unity_%28game_engine%29`
- Discussions: `http://unity3d.com/support/community`

Unreal Engine

1. PLATFORM, PRICES, AND SUPPLIER/CREATOR

- Windows, Linux, Unix, Mac OS
- Freeware
- Epic Games: `http://www.unrealtechnology.com/`

2. APPLICATION

- Unreal Engine is a game engine which provides various tools to assist with content creation for game designers and artists

3. WEB RESOURCES

- Official website: `http://www.unrealtechnology.com/html/homefold/home.shtml`
- Wikipedia: `http://en.wikipedia.org/wiki/Unreal_Engine`
- Discussions: `http://wiki.beyondunreal.com/wiki/`

UVMapper Professional

1. PLATFORMS, PRICES, AND SUPPLIER/CREATOR

- Windows, Mac OS
- $59.95

- Stephen L Cox: http://www.uvmapper.com/

2. APPLICATION

- UVMapper Professional is a texture mapping utility for the creation and modification of UV coordinates for n-sided polygonal 3D models
- It is capable of providing a beginner, intermediate or professional 3D artist with what they need to texture map the most demanding models

3. WEB RESOURCES

- Official website: http://www.uvmapper.com/
- Tutorial: http://www.uvmapper.com/tutorials.html

VARKON

1. PLATFORMS, PRICES, AND SUPPLIER/CREATOR

- Windows, Unix, Linux
- Free for Unix (shareware) and $875 for other platforms
- Originally developed by Microform AB in Sweden, http://www.microform.se/index.htm. Now maintained and further developed by the CAD group at the Department of Technology at Orebro University in Sweden, http://varkon.sourceforge.net/

2. APPLICATIONS

- VARKON is a CAD system and development tool which does 2D drafting, 2D and 3D modeling, sculptured surface modeling, and animations
- Its common applications include engineering, Computer Aided Design, product modeling, etc.

3. WEB RESOURCES

- Official website: http://varkon.sourceforge.net/
- Documentation: http://varkon.sourceforge.net/man.htm

Vecta 3D MAX

1. PLATFORM, PRICES, AND SUPPLIER/CREATOR

- Windows
- $$-$$$
- Ideaworks3D Limited: http://www.vecta3d.com/

2. APPLICATIONS

- Vecta3D-Max is a 3ds max plug-in that converts 3-D models into vector images and animated Flash movies

3. WEB RESOURCES

- Official website: http://www.vecta3d.com/

VectorWorks

1. PLATFORM, PRICE, AND SUPPLIER/CREATOR

- Windows, Mac OS
- N/A
- Nemetschek: http://www.nemetschek.net

2. APPLICATIONS

- VectorWorks including VectorWorks Fundamentals, VectorWorks Architect, VectorWorks Landmark, VectorWorks Spotlight and VectorWorks Designer, offers 2D, 3D production management and presentation capabilities for the design process
- These software have been used by architecture professionals, designers (such as machine designers, site and landscape designers, lighting designers), as well as by machine shops, fabricators, etc.

3. WEB RESOURCES

- Official website: http://www.nemetschek.net/
- Wikipedia: http://en.wikipedia.org/wiki/Vectorworks

VEGA

1. PLATFORMS, PRICES, AND SUPPLIER/CREATOR

- Windows, Linux, Solaris
- N/A
- Presagis Inc.: http://www.presagis.com/

2. APPLICATIONS

- Vega Prime is 3D simulation software for real-time 3D application
- It is intended for the creation and deployment of visual simulation, urban simulation, and general visualization applications

3. WEB RESOURCES

- Official website: http://www.presagis.com/products/visualization/details/vegaprime/

VFleet

1. PLATFORM, PRICE, AND SUPPLIER/CREATOR

- Unix
- Freeware
- Pittsburgh SuperComputer Center: http://www.psc.edu/Packages/VFleet_Home/

2. APPLICATIONS

- VFleet is a volume renderer that produces color images from 3D volumes of data
- It is designed for use in computational science, in that it can handle large datasets representing multiple variables within the same physical system

3. WEB RESOURCES

- Official website: http://www.psc.edu/Packages/VFleet_Home/
- Documentation: http://www.psc.edu/general/software/packages/vfleet/package_docs/development/vfleet1.1.html

View3D

1. PLATFORMS, PRICE, AND SUPPLIER/CREATOR

- Linux, Solaris, Unix
- N/A
- Interactive Network Technologies (INT), Inc.: http://www.int.com/

2. APPLICATIONS

- View3D is 3D visualization software for the X/Motif environment that offers the application developer a way of creating 3D data displays
- It can be used in industries as diverse as oil and gas, telecommunications, environmental, Geographic Information Systems (GIS), aerospace, medical imaging, and other businesses requiring sophisticated presentations and interaction with complex data

3. WEB RESOURCES

- Official website: http://www.int.com/products/widget_info/view3d/view3d.htm

Virtools Dev

1. PLATFORMS, PRICE, AND SUPPLIER/CREATOR

- Windows, Mac OS
- N/A
- Virtools SA, Inc.: http://www.virtools.com

2. APPLICATIONS

- Virtools Dev is software to develop and deploy interactive, game-quality applications for the web, CD ROM and Virtual Reality
- It has been used in the video game market as well as for other interactive 3D experiences in web marketing and virtual product maintenance

3. WEB RESOURCES

- Official website: `http://www.virtools.com/solutions/products/virtools_dev.asp`
- Wikipedia: `http://en.wikipedia.org/wiki/Virtools`
- Tutorial: `http://www.tinkering.net/tutorials.html`

Vis5D+

1. PLATFORMS, PRICE, SUPPLIER

- Linux, Unix, Irix, Solories, Windows
- Freeware
- SourceForge: `http://vis5d.sourceforge.net/Free`

2. APPLICATIONS

- Vis5D+ is an OpenGL based volumetric visualization program for scientific datasets in 3+ dimensions
- It is intended for interactive visualization of large 5D gridded data sets (three space dimensions, one time dimension, and a dimension for enumerating multiple physical variables) such as those produced by numerical models in the atmospheric sciences

3. WEB RESOURCES

- Official website: `http://vis5d.sourceforge.net/`
- Documentation: `http://vis5d.sourceforge.net/#documentation`

VisAD

1. PLATFORMS, PRICE, AND SUPPLIER/CREATOR

- Java-based platform
- Freeware

- (1) SSEC Visualization Project at the University of Wisconsin-Madison Space Science and Engineering Center: `http://www.ssec.wisc.edu/~billh/vis.html` (2)Unidata Program Center: `http://www.unidata.ucar.edu/` (3)National Center for Supercomputer Applications: `http://www.ncsa.edu/` (4)Australian Bureau of Meteorology: `http://www.ncsa.edu/`

2. APPLICATIONS

- VisAD (Visualization for Algorithm Development) is a Java component library for interactive and collaborative visualization and analysis of numerical data
- It can be used for data in 3-D and 2-D displays, statistics visualization, GIS, collaborative geographic visualization, rainfall estimation, interactive globe display of earth topography and bathymetry, interactive curve and surface fitting, etc.

3. WEB RESOURCES

- Official website: `http://www.ssec.wisc.edu/~billh/visad.html`
- Tutorial: `http://www.ssec.wisc.edu/~billh/tutorial/index.html`

VisiQuest

1. PLATFORMS, PRICE, AND SUPPLIER/CREATOR

- Linux, Irix, Solaris, Windows
- Commercial & Govt. Price is $995, Academic Research Use price is $495, and Academic Classroom Price is $595
- AccuSoft: `http://www.accusoft.com/company/`

2. APPLICATIONS

- VisiQuest is a scientific visualization program for image display and manipulation, animation, 2-D and 3-D plotting, and volumetric and geometric rendering
- Its applications can be found in science, medicine, engineering (e.g., product visualization), interactive multimedia, education, etc.

3. WEB RESOURCES

- Official website: http://www.accusoft.com/products/visiquest/overview.asp
- Tutorials: http://www.accusoft.com/resourcecenter/tutorials.asp

VISVIVA AUTHORING STUDIO

1. PLATFORMS, PRICE, AND SUPPLIER/CREATOR

- Windows, Mac OS
- $$$
- Visviva Software Inc.: http://www.visviva.com

2. APPLICATIONS

- Visviva includes Object Design Workbench Tool, 3D Object Modeler Tool, Animation Composition Tool, Illustration Tool, Image Painting Tool, Hypertext Documentation Tool, and Scripting Tool
- These tools are designed for object design, animation composition, 3D modeling, image painting, vector drawing, and hypertext editing, and can be used in the design of 3D multimedia software applications, digital visualizations, interactive video, business presentations, and games

3. WEB RESOURCES

- Official website: http://www.visviva.com

Visual3

1. PLATFORMS, PRICE, AND SUPPLIER/CREATOR

- DEC/ UNIX, HP/UX, IBM/AIX, SGI/IRIX, SUN/ Solaris
- Freeware
- Bob Haimes, MIT: http://raphael.mit.edu/visual3/visual3.html

2. APPLICATIONS

- Visual3 is an interactive graphics environment for the visualization of 3D, structured and unstructured data
- It can handle a wide variety of grids, and deal with generic scalar and vector data, making it suitable for a wide range of physical applications

3. WEB RESOURCES

- Official website: `http://raphael.mit.edu/visual3/visual3.html`

Visual Nature Studio

1. PLATFORMS, PRICE, AND SUPPLIER/CREATOR

- Windows
- $2,475.00
- 3D Nature, LLC: `http://3dnature.com/`

2. APPLICATIONS

- Visual Nature Studio is a 3D visualization program, which produces photorealistic still images or animations of real or fictional landscapes by using digital elevation model (DEM) and geographic information system (GIS) data as input
- This software has been used by some universities and press agencies to generate images of 3D terrain

3. WEB RESOURCES

- Official website: `http://3dnature.com/`
- Wikipedia: `http://en.wikipedia.org/wiki/Visual_Nature_Studio`

VMD

1. PLATFORMS, PRICES, AND SUPPLIER/CREATOR

- Windows, Unix, Mac OS
- Freeware

- University of Illinois at Urbana-Champaign: `http://www.ks.uiuc.edu/Research/vmd/`

2. APPLICATIONS

- VMD is a molecular visualization program for displaying, animating, and analyzing large biomolecular systems using 3-D graphics and built-in scripting
- It is primarily developed for viewing and analyzing the results of molecular dynamics simulations, but also for working with volumetric data, sequence data, and arbitrary graphics objects

3. WEB RESOURCES

- Official website: `http://www.ks.uiuc.edu/Research/vmd/`

VolVis

1. PLATFORMS, PRICE, AND SUPPLIER/CREATOR

- Unix
- Freeware
- Visualization Laboratory of the Department of Computer Science at the State University of New York at Stony Brook: `http://www.cs.sunysb.edu/~vislab/volvis_home.html`

2. APPLICATIONS

- VolVis is a volume visualization system that unites numerous visualization methods within a comprehensive visualization system
- It has been used by scientists and engineers as well as visualization developers and researchers in some scientific disciplines ranging from geophysics to the biomedical sciences

3. WEB RESOURCES

- Official website: `http://www.cs.sunysb.edu/~vislab/volvis_home.html`
- Examples/Samples: `http://www.cs.sunysb.edu/~vislab/gallery_list.html`

VoxBlast

1. PLATFORMS, PRICES, AND SUPPLIER/CREATOR

- Windows, Mac OS, Unix
- N/A
- VayTek Inc.: http://www.vaytek.com/

2. APPLICATIONS

- VoxBlast is a 3-D digital imaging application for science, engineering and medicine, providing 3-D measurement, 3-D reconstruction, 3-D volume visualization, and 3-D rendering

3. WEB RESOURCES

- Official website: http://www.vaytek.com/VoxBlast.html
- Reference Guide: http://www.vaytek.com/VBquikref.html

VP-Sculpt

1. PLATFORMS, PRICE, AND SUPPLIER/CREATOR

- Windows
- $995 per seat (20% educational discount for universities: $796)
- Visible Productions: http://www.engr.colostate.edu/~dga/vpsculpt.html

2. APPLICATIONS

- VP-Sculpt is software used for interactive computer-assisted editing and free-form sculpting of 3D polygonal mesh surface models

3. WEB RESOURCES

- Official website: http://www.engr.colostate.edu/~dga/vpsculpt.html

VPYTHON

1. PLATFORMS, PRICES, AND SUPPLIER/CREATOR
- Windows, Linux, Unix, Mac OS
- Freeware
- VPYTHON: http://www.vpython.org

2. APPLICATIONS
- VPYTHON is a real-time 3D modeling addition for Python, providing a toolkit for the creation of basic 3D objects
- VPYTHON has been used for the illustration of simple physics, especially in the educational environment

3. WEB RESOURCES
- Official website: http://www.vpython.org/index.html
- Wikipedia: http://en.wikipedia.org/wiki/VPython
- Tutorials: http://vpython.erikthompson.com/

Vray

1. PLATFORMS, PRICES, AND SUPPLIER/CREATOR
- Windows
- $998.95
- Chaos Group: http://www.chaosgroup.com/

2. APPLICATIONS
- V-Ray is a rendering engine as an extension of certain 3D computer graphics software
- V-Ray has been used in the development of film productions and game productions, also used in making realistic 3D renderings for architecture

3. WEB RESOURCES
- Official website: http://www.chaosgroup.com/software/vray/

- Wikipedia: `http://en.wikipedia.org/wiki/Vray`

VREK (MindRender Virtual Reality Explore Kit)

1. PLATFORM, PRICE, AND SUPPLIER/CREATOR

- Windows
- Regular price: $425, Education price: $336.65
- Themekit Systems Limited: `http://www.themekit.com`

2. APPLICATIONS

- MindRender VREK is software that combines realtime 3D modeling and interactive scene design
- This package is suitable for creating functional, interactive and immersive environments for education, 3D design, VR art, game development, training and simulation, etc.

3. WEB RESOURCES

- Official website: `http://www.themekit.com`
- Examples/Samples: `http://www.themekit.com/f_demo.htm`

VRML

1. PLATFORM, PRICE, AND SUPPLIER/CREATOR

- Windows, Linux, Unix, Mac OS
- Freeware
- Web3D Consortium: `http://www.web3d.org/index.html`

2. APPLICATIONS

- VRML (Virtual Reality Modeling Language) is a standard file format for representing 3D interactive vector graphics
- VRML has been used for education and research where an open specification is most valued, and used as a file format for the interchange of 3D models

3. WEB RESOURCES

- Official website: http://www.web3d.org/x3d/specifications/vrml/
- Wikipedia: http://en.wikipedia.org/wiki/Vrml

VTK — the Visualization ToolKit

1. PLATFORMS, PRICES, AND SUPPLIER/CREATOR

- Unix, Windows, Mac OS
- Freeware
- Kitware Inc.: http://www.kitware.com/

2. APPLICATIONS

- The Visualiztion ToolKit (VTK) is a software system for 3D computer graphics, image processing, and visualization

3. WEB RESOURCES

- Official website: http://www.vtk.org/
- Wikipedia: http://en.wikipedia.org/wiki/VTK

Vue

1. PLATFORMS, PRICES, AND SUPPLIER/CREATOR

- Windows, Mac OS
- $$$
- e-on software: http://www.e-onsoftware.com/

2. APPLICATIONS

- Vue product line is a suite of 3D studio software that allows the user to create, render, and animate realistic 3D natural scenery
- These software are designed for civil engineering, land planning, environmental or geographical research, etc.

3. WEB RESOURCES

- Official website: `http://www.e-onsoftware.com/products/`
- Tutorial: http://www.e-onsoftware.com/support/tutorials/

WebMol

1. PLATFORMS, PRICE, AND SUPPLIER/CREATOR

- Windows, Unix, Linux, Mac OS
- Freeware
- Dirk Walther: `http://www.cmpharm.ucsf.edu/~walther/`

2. APPLICATIONS

- WebMol is Java PDB visualization software designed to display and analyze structural information contained in the Brookhaven Protein Data Bank (PDB)
- It has been used by students, educators, and researchers in chemistry and biochemistry

3. WEB RESOURCES

- Official website: `http://www.cmpharm.ucsf.edu/cgi-bin/webmol.pl`
- WebMol API: `http://www.cmpharm.ucsf.edu/~walther/webmol`

WebSphere Studio

1. PLATFORMS, PRICE, AND SUPPLIER/CREATOR

- Windows, Linux
- N/A
- IBM: `http://www.ibm.com/`

2. APPLICATIONS

- WebSphere is an integrated tool to set up, operate and integrate e-business applications across multiple computing platforms using web technologies

3. WEB RESOURCES

- Official website: `http://www-306.ibm.com/software/info1/websphere/index.jsp?tab=products/studio`
- Wikipedia: `http://en.wikipedia.org/wiki/IBM_WebSphere`

Wings 3D

1. PLATFORMS, PRICE, AND SUPPLIER/CREATOR

- MacOS, Windows, Linux
- Freeware
- Wings 3D: `http://www.wings3d.com/`

2. APPLICATIONS

- Wings 3D is a 3D modeling tool for polygon mesh subdivision modeling based on the winged edge data structure
- It is suited for modeling and texturing low to medium density polygon meshes, and can be combined with raytracing programs such as POV-Ray, YafRay, or Art of Illusion to produce high-quality images

3. WEB RESOURCES

- Official website: `http://www.wings3d.com/`
- Wikipedia: `http://en.wikipedia.org/wiki/Wings3d`

WorldBuilder

1. PLATFORMS, PRICES, AND SUPPLIER/CREATOR

- Windows
- Professional Version is $999; Educational Version is $399
- Digital Element, Inc.: `http://www.digi-element.com/wb/index.htm`

2. APPLICATIONS

- WorldBuilder is a scene builder and renderer for rendering 3D outdoor environments which can work as a plug-in for 3D Studio MAX, 3D Studio VIZ, LightWave 3D or Maya
- It has been used for architecture, game development, movie production, and computer graphics, etc.

3. WEB RESOURCES

- Official website: `http://www.digi-element.com/wb/index.htm`
- Tutorials: `http://www.digi-element.com/wb/tutorials.htm`
- Wikipedia: `http://en.wikipedia.org/wiki/WorldBuilder`

World Construction Set

1. PLATFORMS, PRICES, AND SUPPLIER/CREATOR

- Windows
- $500
- 3D Nature, LLC: `http://3dnature.com/`

2. APPLICATIONS

- World Construction Set is a landscape generation package for a wide variety of visualization and artistic needs
- Its common fields of use include land planning, landscape architecture, civil engineering, cartography, forestry and resource management, historical and archaeological recreation, etc.

3. WEB RESOURCES

- Official website: `http://3dnature.com/wcs6info.html`
- Examples/Samples: `http://www.3dnworld.com/galapp.php`

WorldToolKit

1. PLATFORMS, PRICES, AND SUPPLIER/CREATOR

- Windows, Linux, Unix
- N/A
- SENSE8: http://www.sense8.com/

2. APPLICATIONS

- WorldToolKit (WTK) is a 3D and virtual reality development tool with an object-oriented C/C++ library for configuring, interacting with, and controlling real-time simulations
- It is designed for developing and deploying 3D and virtual reality applications for scientific and commercial use

3. WEB RESOURCES

- Official website: http://www.bubu.com/baskara/wtk.htm
- Online course: http://www.cs.uic.edu/~jbell/Courses/Eng591_F1999/Sense8Course/

World Up

1. PLATFORMS, PRICE, AND SUPPLIER/CREATOR

- Windows
- N/A
- SENDSE8: http://www.sense8.com/

2. APPLICATIONS

- World Up is a 3D modeling, rendering, and simulation tool that provides real-time functionality in an interactive, object-oriented environment for building 3D and VR applications

3. WEB RESOURCES

- Official website: http://www.sense8.com/products/wup.html

Xara3D

1. PLATFORMS, PRICES, AND SUPPLIER/CREATOR

- Windows
- $$
- Xara: `http://www.xara.com/`

2. APPLICATIONS

- Xara3D is a tool to create 3D titles and logos for use on web pages
- Both professional web designers and home users can use Xara3D to make still and animated 3D text and graphics

3. WEB RESOURCES

- Official website: `http://www.xara.com/downloads/xara3d`
- Examples/Samples: `http://www.xara.com/products/xara3d/examples/`

XGL

1. PLATFORMS, PRICES, AND SUPPLIER/CREATOR

- Solaris, Unix
- Freeware
- Sun Microsystems, Inc.: `http://www.sun.com`

2. APPLICATIONS

- XGL is a 2D and 3D library designed to support a wide variety of graphics-based applications, layered on top of OpenGL via glitz
- It provides the applications programmer with the graphics capabilities such as immediate-mode rendering, loadable device pipelines, separate 2D and 3D graphics pipelines, broad primitive and coordinate type support, NURBS surfaces, multi-primitive operators, etc.

3. WEB RESOURCES

- Official website: `http://docs.sun.com/app/docs/doc/801-6670/6i11gqgs7?a=view`

XNA

1. PLATFORMS, PRICES, AND SUPPLIER/CREATOR

- Windows
- Freeware
- Microsoft: http://www.xna.com

2. APPLICATIONS

- XNA is a game development library and IDE that facilitates computer game design, development, and management for professional game developers

3. WEB RESOURCES

- Official website: http://www.xna.com/
- Wikipedia: http://en.wikipedia.org/wiki/Microsoft_XNA

YafRay

1. PLATFORMS, PRICES, AND SUPPLIER/CREATOR

- Windows, Linux, Irix, Mac OS
- Freeware
- YafRay Team: http://www.yafray.org/

2. APPLICATIONS

- YafRay is a ray tracing program
- It can be used as a render engine, using its own scene description format

3. WEB RESOURCES

- Official website: http://www.yafray.org/index.php?s=1
- Wikipedia: http://en.wikipedia.org/wiki/YafRay

ZBrush

1. PLATFORMS, PRICE, AND SUPPLIER/CREATOR

- Mac OS, Windows
- $595
- Pixologic: Http://www.pixologic.com

2. APPLICATION

- ZBrush is a digital sculpting tool that combines 3D/2.5D modeling, texturing and painting using "pixol" technology which stores lighting, color, material, and depth information for all objects on the screen
- ZBrush can be used to create high-resolution models for movies, games, and animations, etc.

3. WEB RESOURCES

- Official website: http://www.pixologic.com/zbrush/
- Documentation: http://www.pixologic.com/docs/index.php/ Main_Page
- Wikipedia: http://en.wikipedia.org/wiki/ZBrush

Index

Printed by Publishers' Graphics LLC